~~Leaving~~ SURVIVING MEGALOPOLIS™

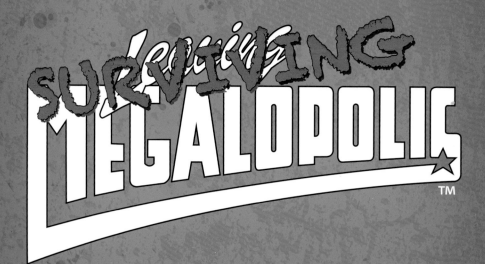

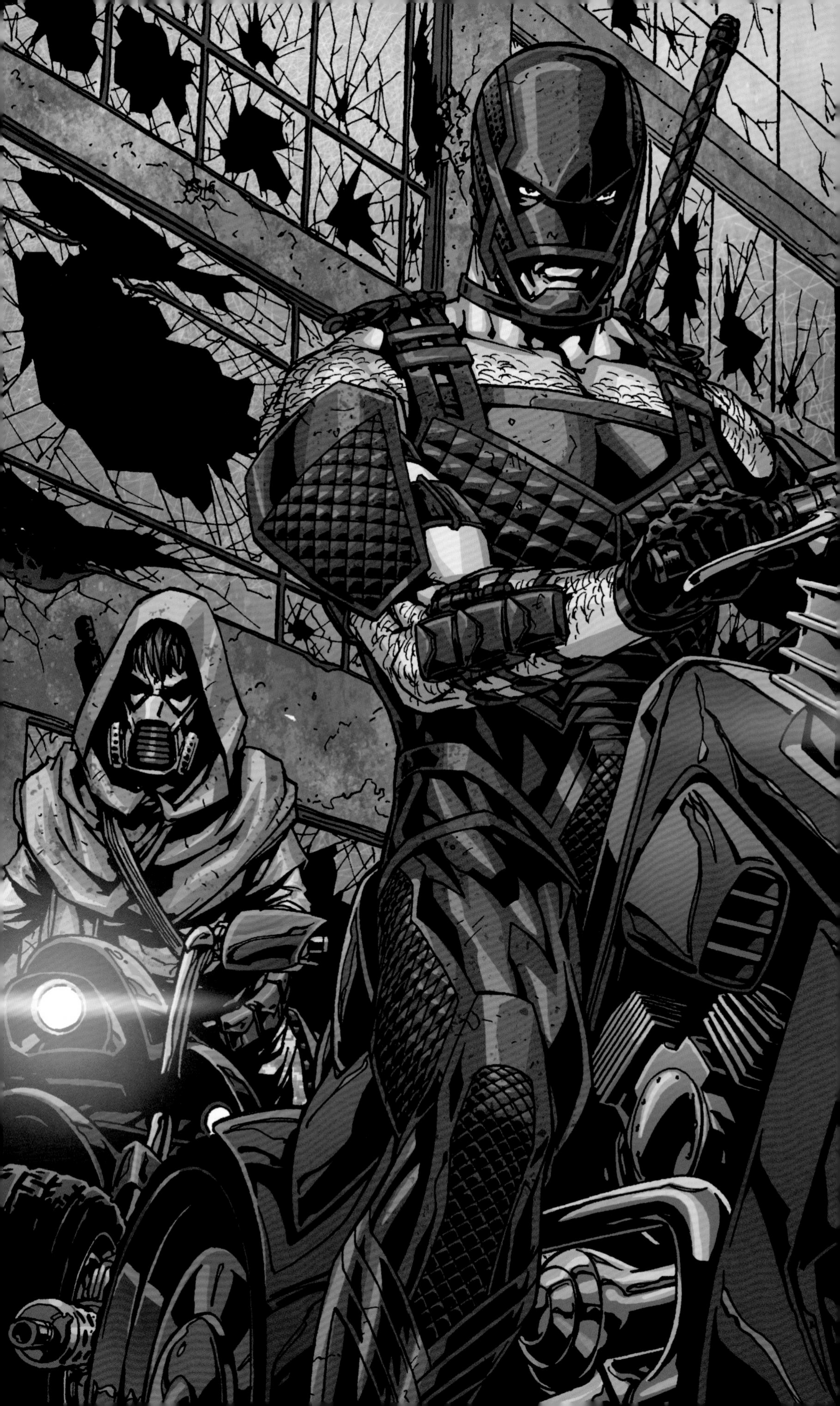

SURVIVING MEGALOPOLIS™

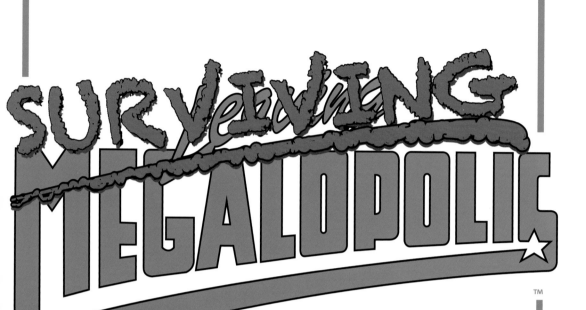

VOLUME 2

by
GAIL SIMONE
&
J. CALAFIORE

colorist
JASON WRIGHT

letterer
DAVE SHARPE

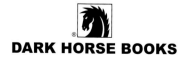

®
DARK HORSE BOOKS

president & publisher
MIKE RICHARDSON
editor
PATRICK THORPE
assistant editors
EVERETT PATTERSON & CARDNER CLARK
designer
HUNTER SHARP
digital art technician
CHRISTINA McKENZIE

This volume collects issues #1–#6 of the Dark Horse Comics series *Leaving Megalopolis: Surviving Megalopolis*.

Published by
Dark Horse Books
A division of Dark Horse Comics, Inc.
10956 SE Main Street
Milwaukie, OR 97222
DarkHorse.com
To find a comics shop in your area,
call the Comic Shop Locator Service
toll-free at 1-888-266-4226.

International Licensing: (503) 905-2377

First edition: January 2017
ISBN 978-1-50670-049-6

Custom edition: January 2017
ISBN 978-1-50670-371-8

1 3 5 7 9 10 8 6 4 2
Printed in China

Library of Congress Cataloging-in-Publication Data

Names: Simone, Gail. | Calafiore, Jim, illustrator. | Wright, Jason (Jason St. John) illustrator. | Sharpe, Dave (Letterer) illustrator.
Title: Leaving megalopolis : surviving megalopolis / by Gail Simone & J. Calafiore ; colorist, Jason Wright ; letterer, Dave Sharpe.
Description: First edition. | Milwaukie, OR : Dark Horse Books, 2016.
Identifiers: LCCN 2016015901 | ISBN 9781506700496 (hardback)
Subjects: LCSH: Supervillains--Comic books, strips, etc. | Graphic novels. | BISAC: COMICS & GRAPHIC NOVELS / Superheroes.
Classification: LCC PN6727.S51579 L44 2016 | DDC 741.5/973--dc23
LC record available at https://lccn.loc.gov/2016015901

Leaving Megalopolis Volume 2: Surviving Megalopolis

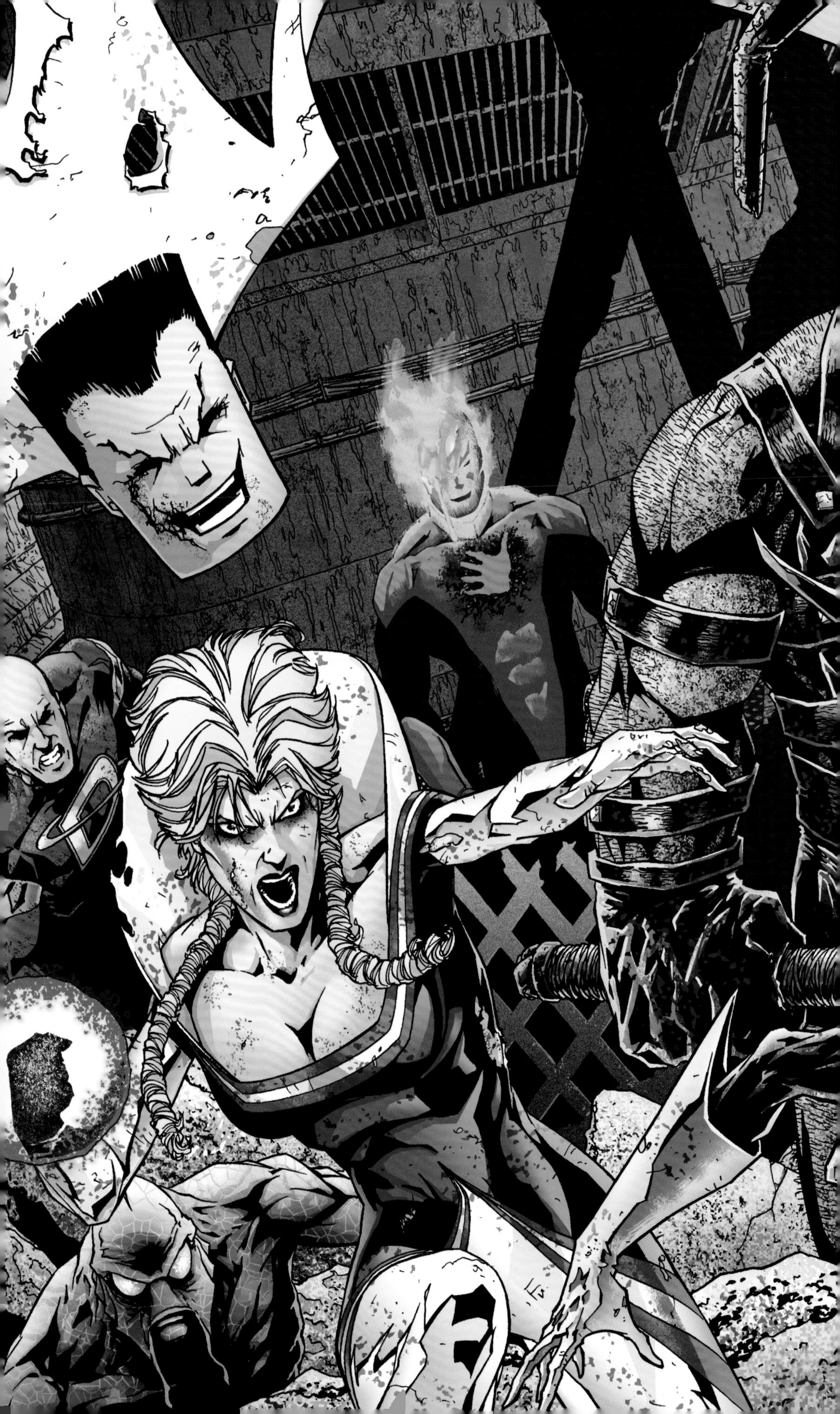

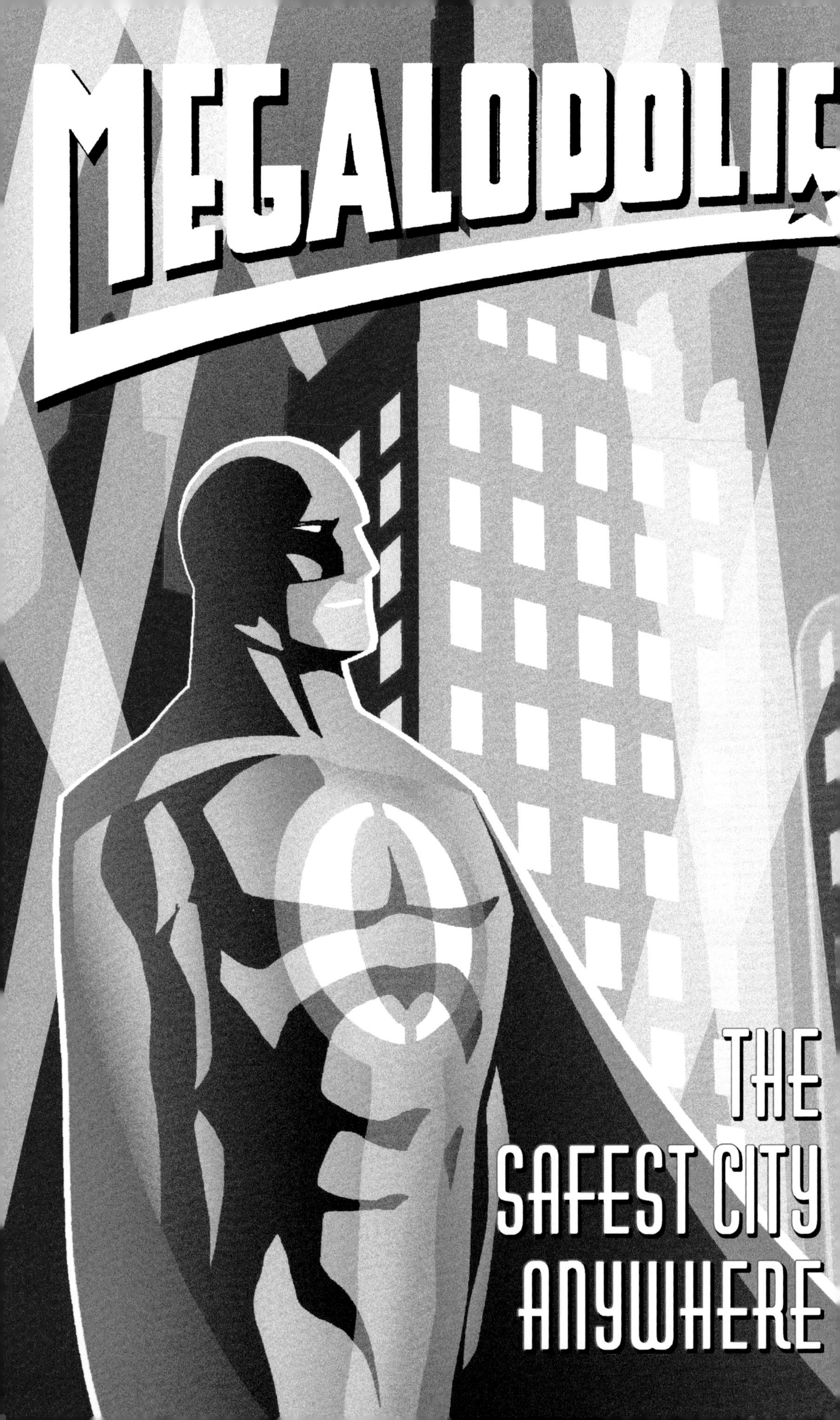
MEGALOPOLIS
THE
SAFEST CITY
ANYWHERE

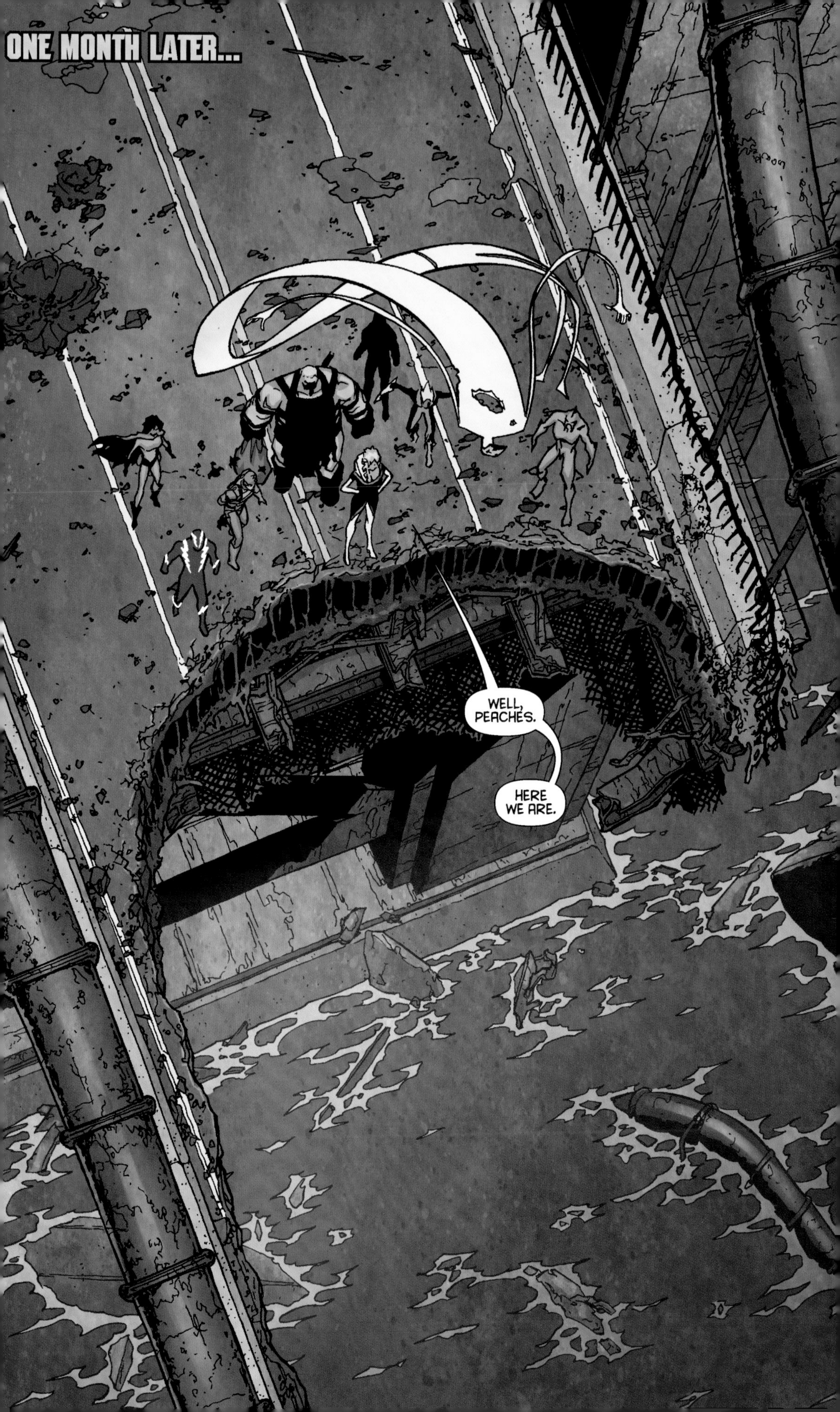
ONE MONTH LATER...
WELL, PEACHES.
HERE WE ARE.

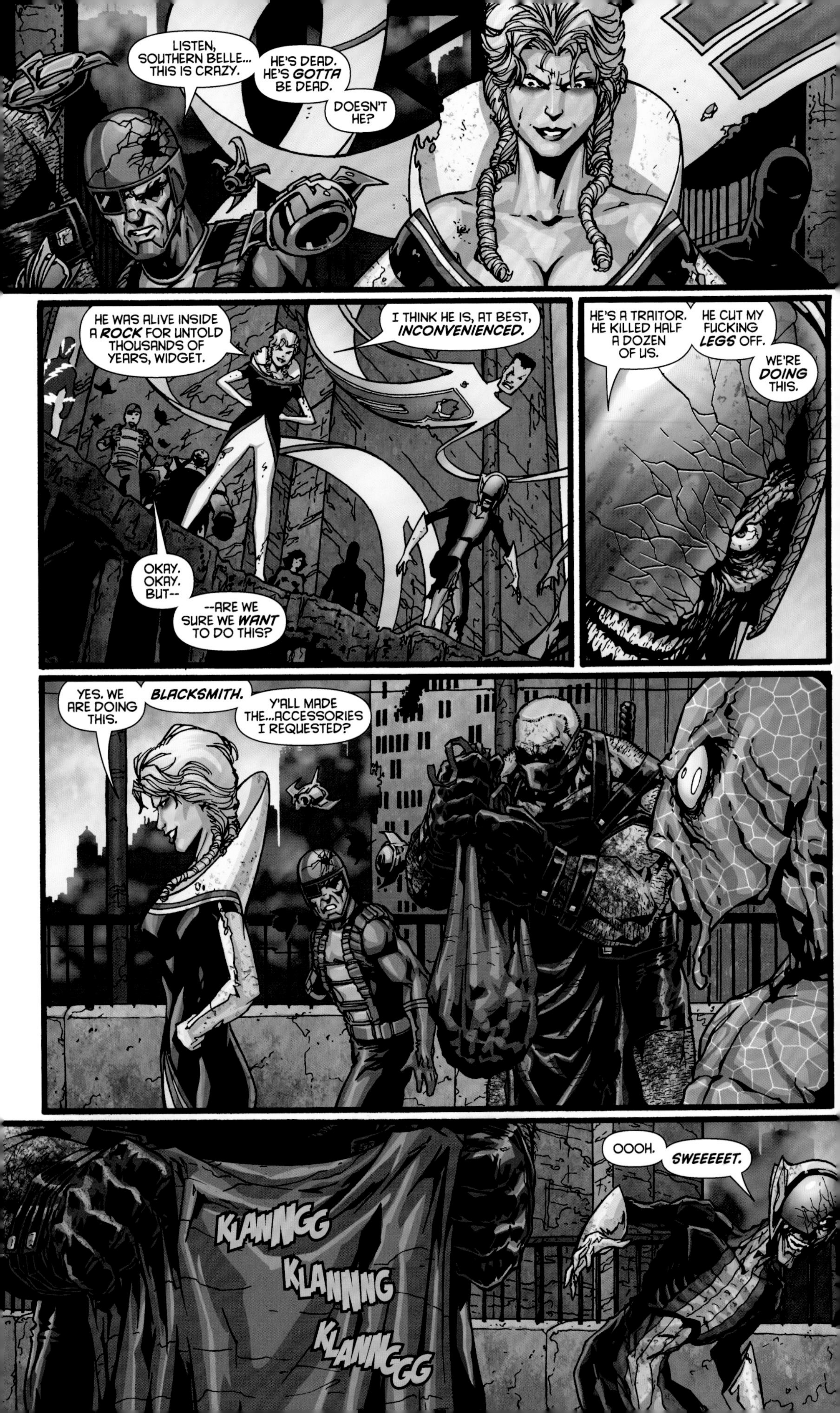

LISTEN, SOUTHERN BELLE... THIS IS CRAZY.
HE'S DEAD. HE'S GOTTA BE DEAD.
DOESN'T HE?
HE WAS ALIVE INSIDE A ROCK FOR UNTOLD THOUSANDS OF YEARS, WIDGET.
I THINK HE IS, AT BEST, INCONVENIENCED.
OKAY. OKAY. BUT--
--ARE WE SURE WE WANT TO DO THIS?
HE'S A TRAITOR. HE KILLED HALF A DOZEN OF US.
HE CUT MY FUCKING LEGS OFF.
WE'RE DOING THIS.
YES. WE ARE DOING THIS.
BLACKSMITH.
Y'ALL MADE THE...ACCESSORIES I REQUESTED?
KLANNGG
KLANNNG
KLANNGGG
OOOH.
SWEEEEET.

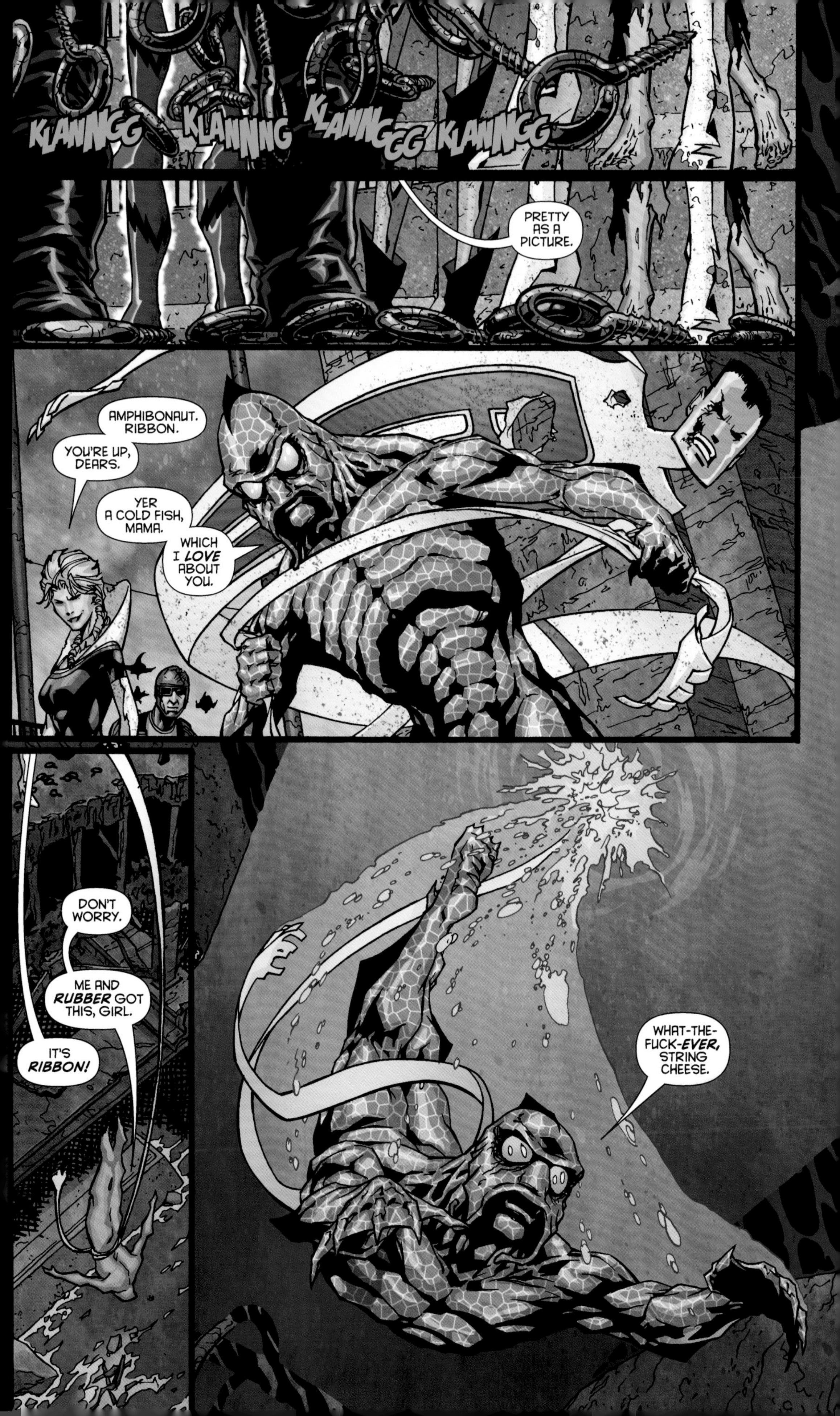
KLANNGG KLANNNG KLANNGGG KLANNGG
PRETTY AS A PICTURE.
AMPHIBONAUT. RIBBON.
YOU'RE UP, DEARS.
YER A COLD FISH, MAMA.
WHICH I LOVE ABOUT YOU.
DON'T WORRY.
ME AND RUBBER GOT THIS, GIRL.
IT'S RIBBON!
WHAT-THE-FUCK-EVER, STRING CHEESE.

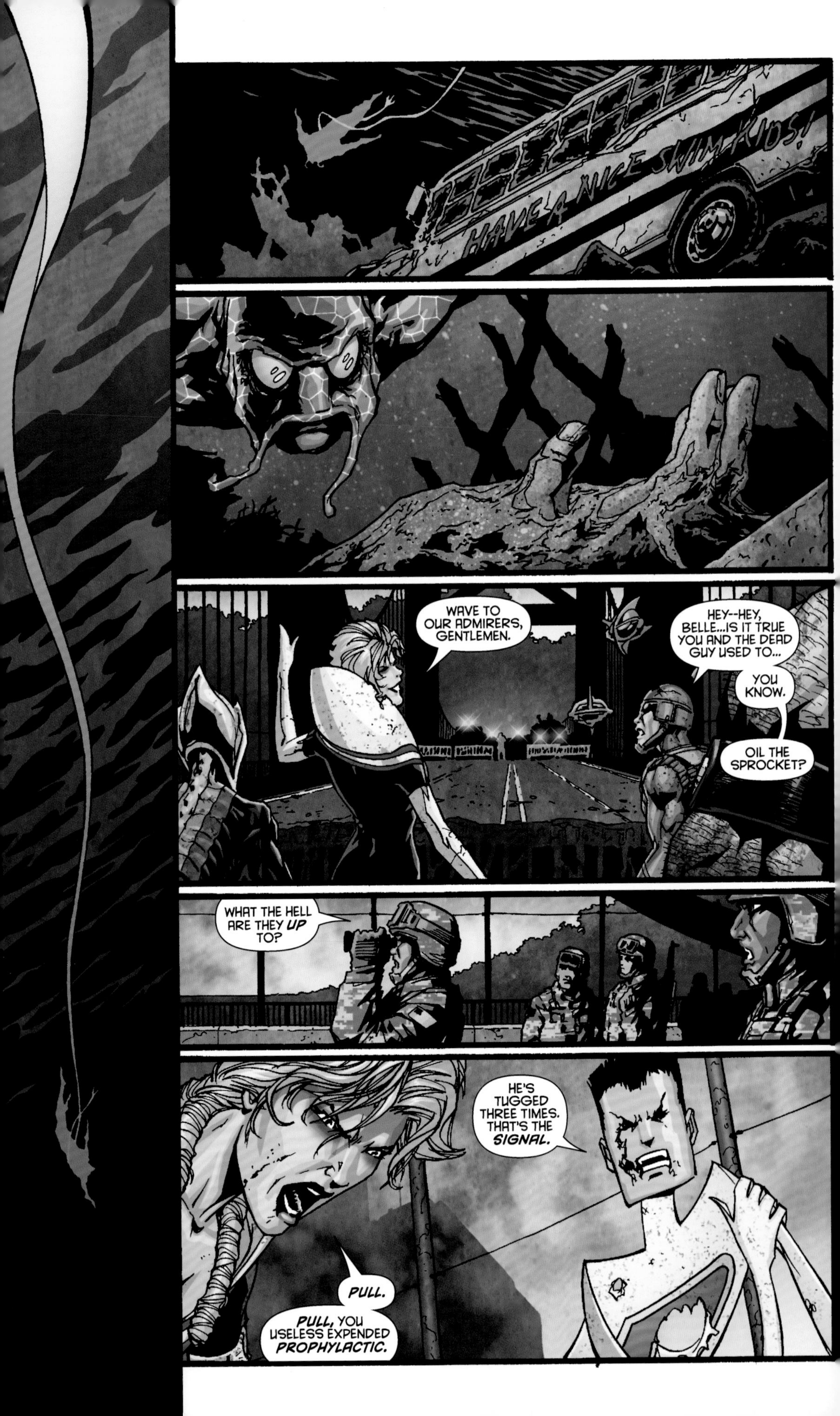
HAVE A NICE SWIM KIDS!
WAVE TO OUR ADMIRERS, GENTLEMEN.
HEY--HEY, BELLE...IS IT TRUE YOU AND THE DEAD GUY USED TO...
YOU KNOW.
OIL THE SPROCKET?
WHAT THE HELL ARE THEY UP TO?
HE'S TUGGED THREE TIMES. THAT'S THE SIGNAL.
PULL.
PULL, YOU USELESS EXPENDED PROPHYLACTIC.

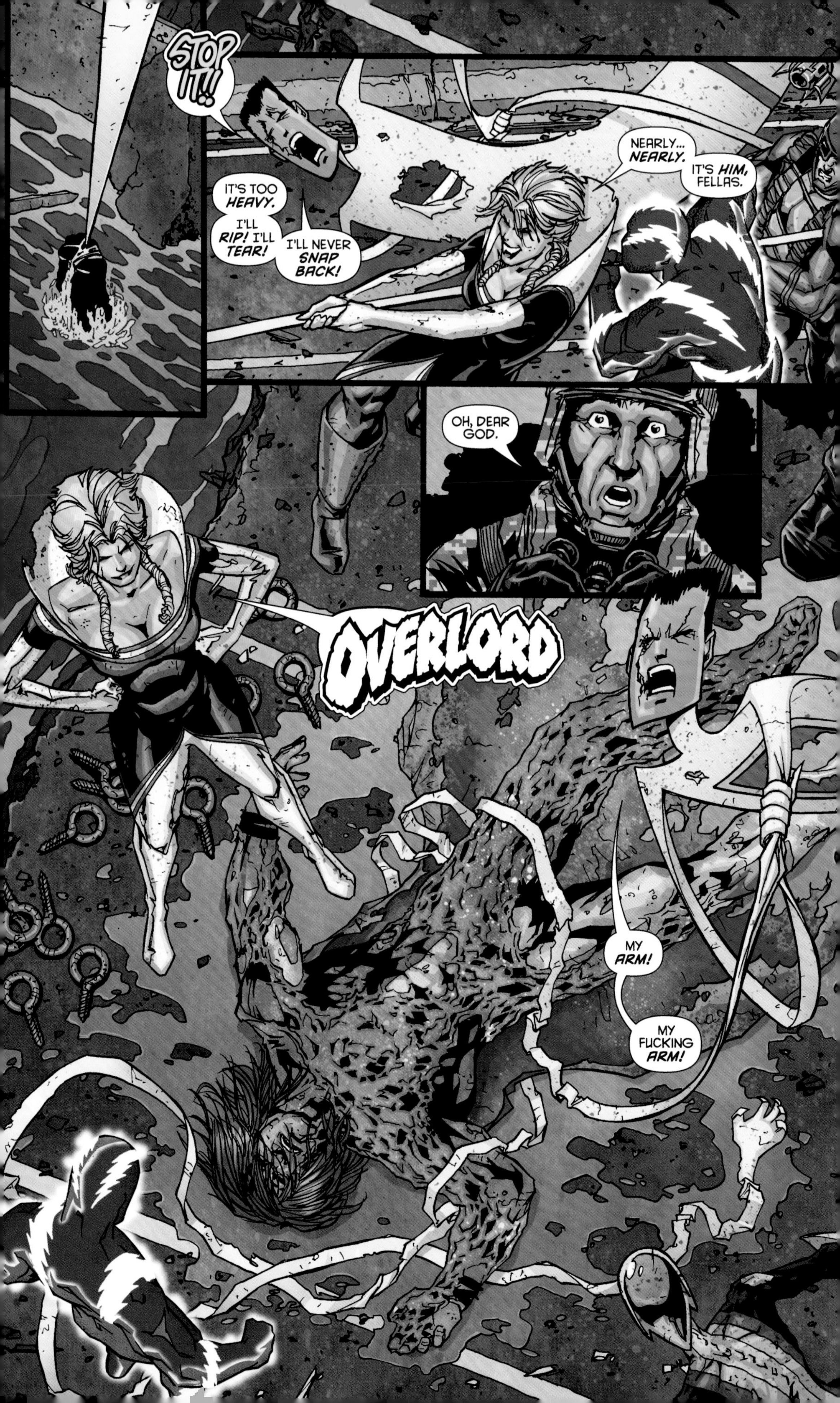

STOP IT!!
IT'S TOO HEAVY.
I'LL RIP! I'LL TEAR!
I'LL NEVER SNAP BACK!
NEARLY... NEARLY.
IT'S HIM, FELLAS.
OH, DEAR GOD.
OVERLORD
MY ARM!
MY FUCKING ARM!

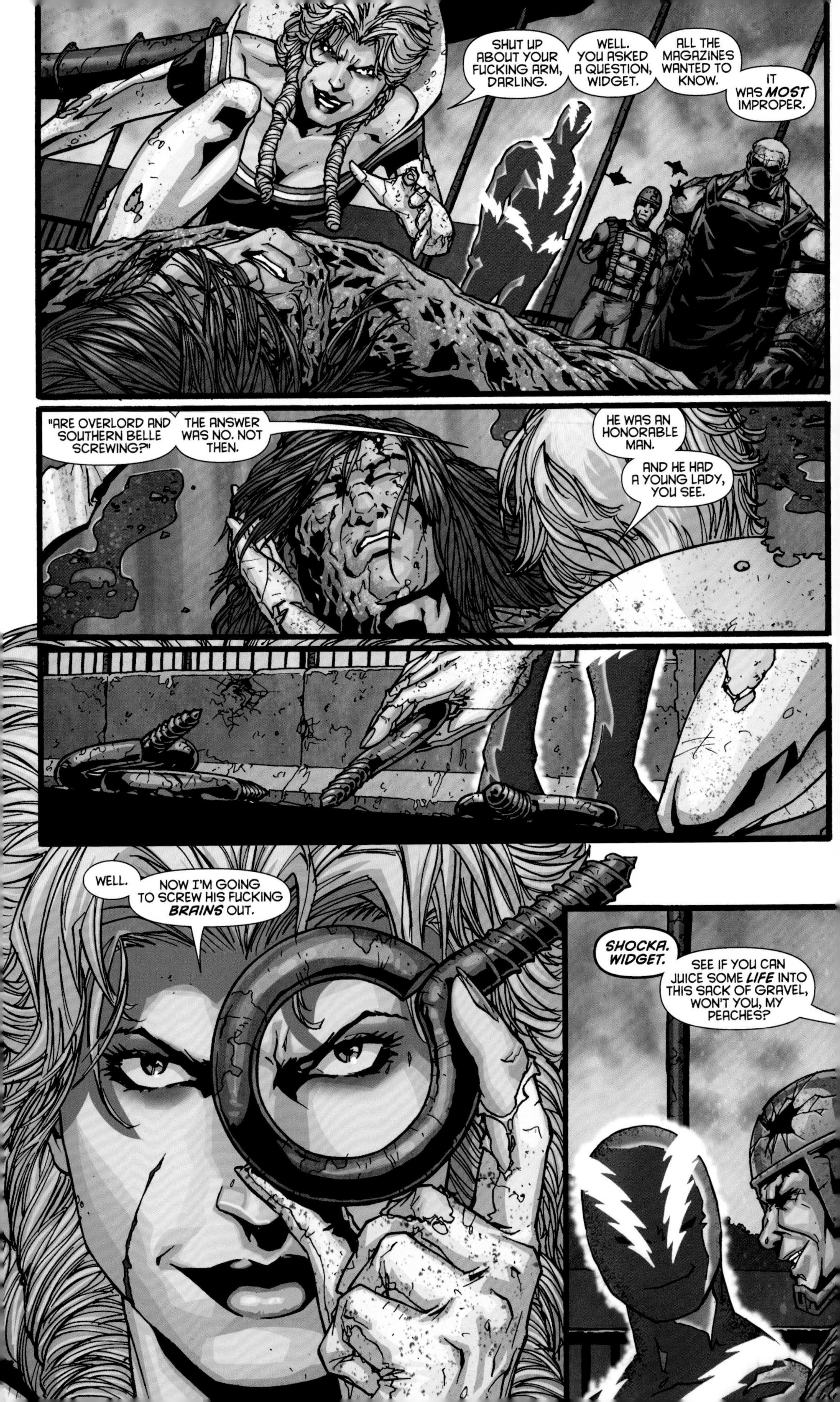
SHUT UP ABOUT YOUR FUCKING ARM, DARLING.
WELL. YOU ASKED A QUESTION, WIDGET.
ALL THE MAGAZINES WANTED TO KNOW.
IT WAS *MOST* IMPROPER.
"ARE OVERLORD AND SOUTHERN BELLE SCREWING?"
THE ANSWER WAS NO. NOT THEN.
HE WAS AN HONORABLE MAN.
AND HE HAD A YOUNG LADY, YOU SEE.
WELL.
NOW I'M GOING TO SCREW HIS FUCKING ***BRAINS*** OUT.
SHOCKA. WIDGET.
SEE IF YOU CAN JUICE SOME ***LIFE*** INTO THIS SACK OF GRAVEL, WON'T YOU, MY PEACHES?

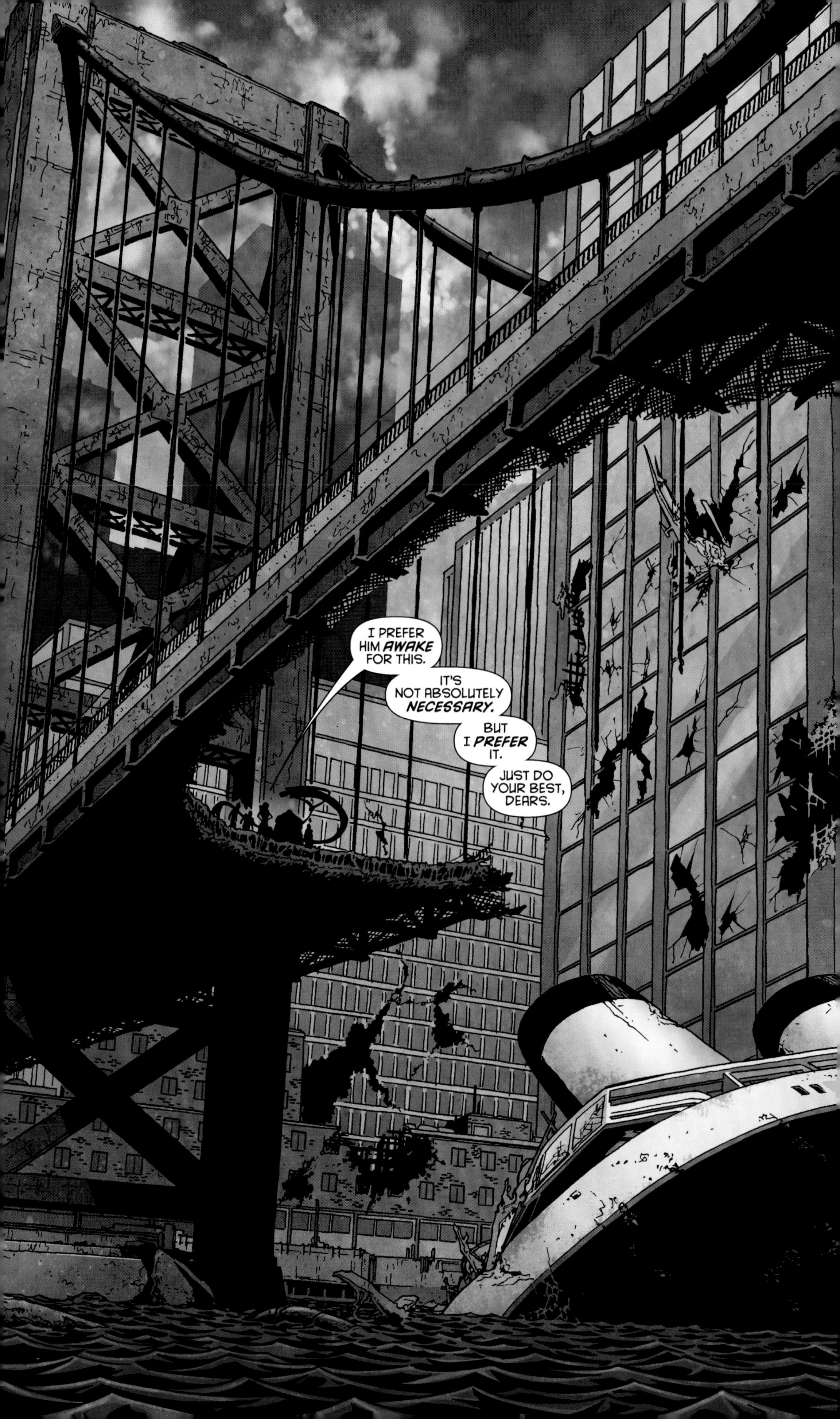
I PREFER HIM AWAKE FOR THIS.
IT'S NOT ABSOLUTELY NECESSARY.
BUT I PREFER IT.
JUST DO YOUR BEST, DEARS.

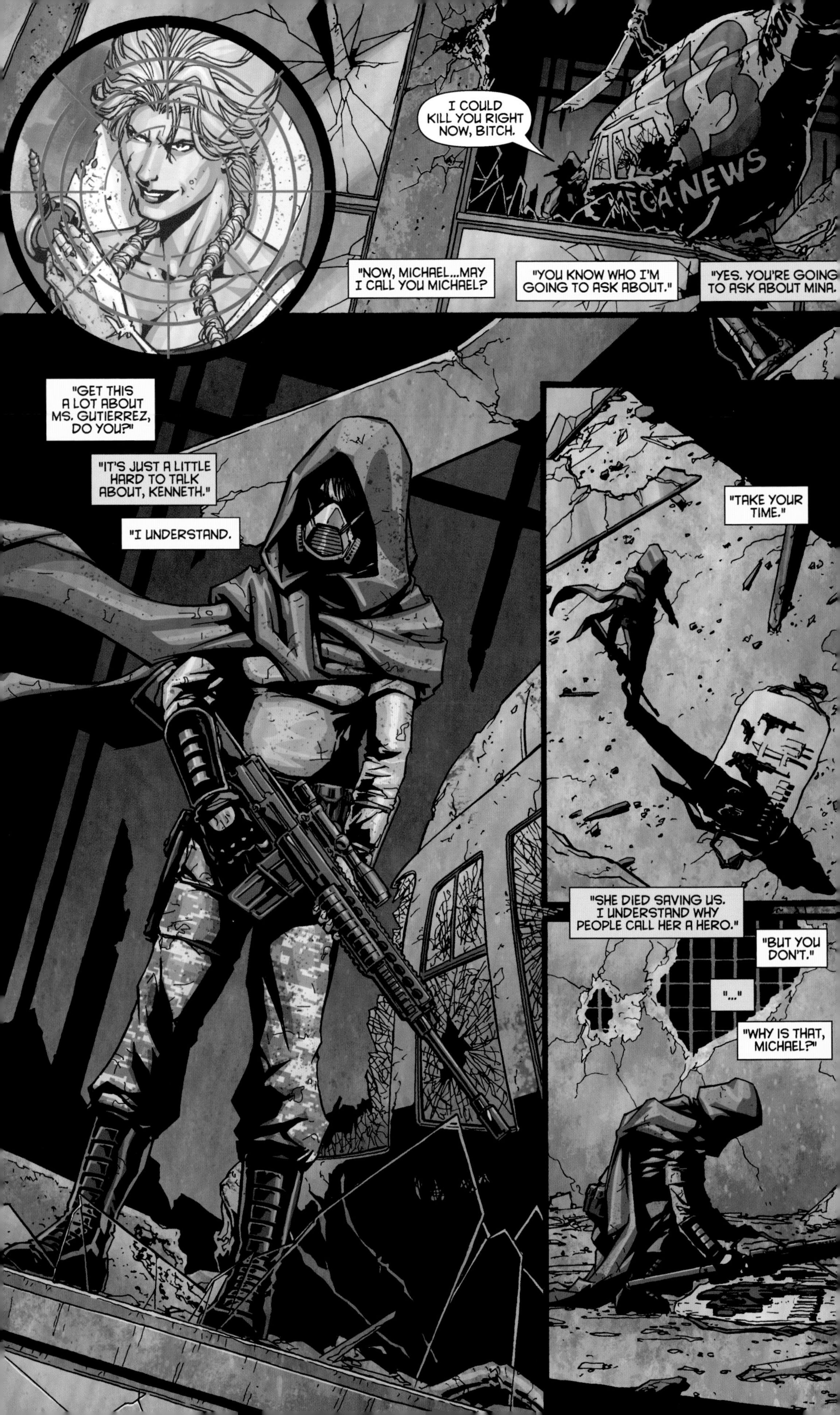
I COULD KILL YOU RIGHT NOW, BITCH.
"NOW, MICHAEL...MAY I CALL YOU MICHAEL?
"YOU KNOW WHO I'M GOING TO ASK ABOUT."
"YES. YOU'RE GOING TO ASK ABOUT MINA.
MEGA-NEWS
"GET THIS A LOT ABOUT MS. GUTIERREZ, DO YOU?"
"IT'S JUST A LITTLE HARD TO TALK ABOUT, KENNETH."
"I UNDERSTAND.
"TAKE YOUR TIME."
"SHE DIED SAVING US. I UNDERSTAND WHY PEOPLE CALL HER A HERO."
"BUT YOU DON'T."
"..."
"WHY IS THAT, MICHAEL?"

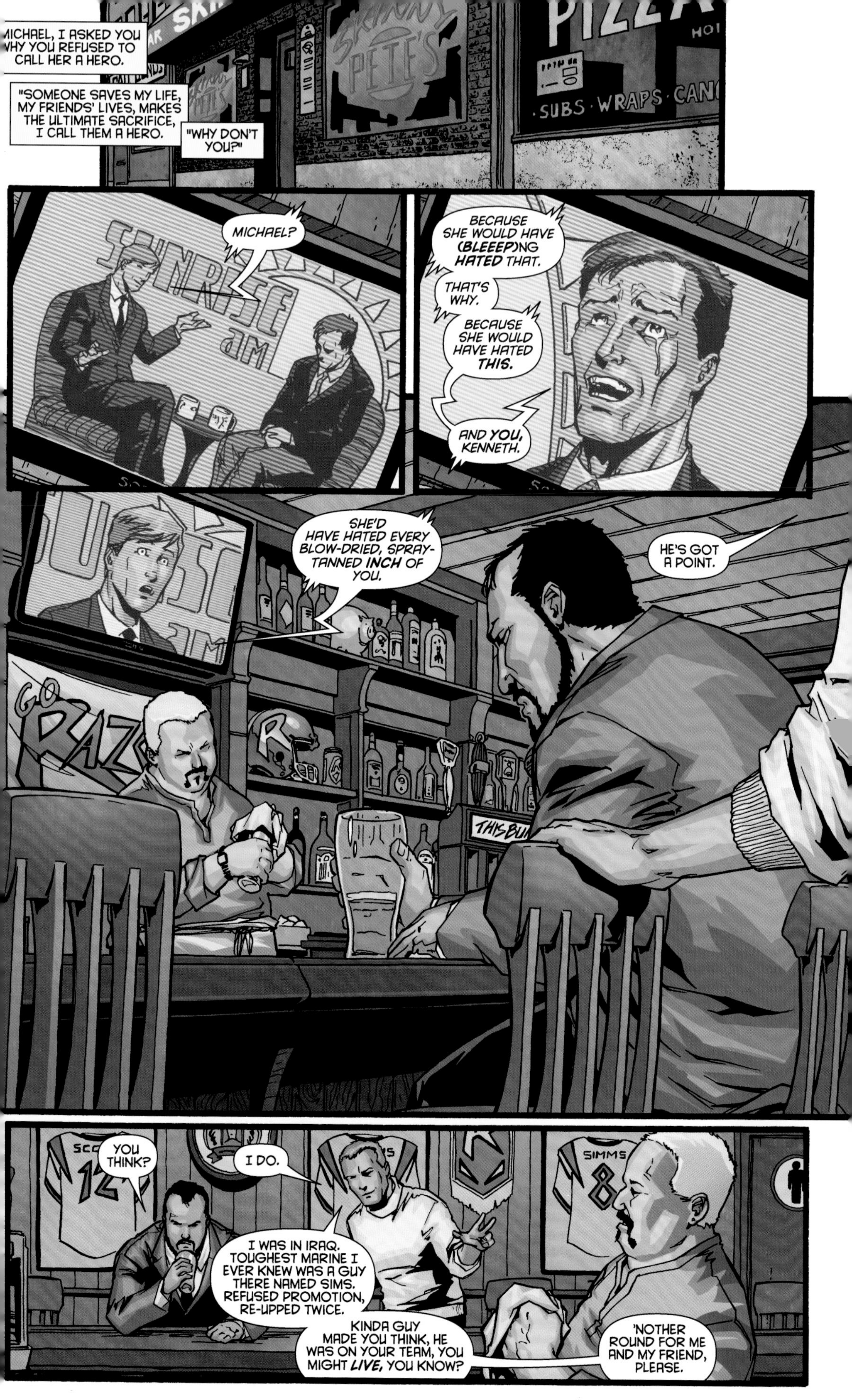

MICHAEL, I ASKED YOU WHY YOU REFUSED TO CALL HER A HERO.
"SOMEONE SAVES MY LIFE, MY FRIENDS' LIVES, MAKES THE ULTIMATE SACRIFICE, I CALL THEM A HERO.
"WHY DON'T YOU?"
SKINNY PETE'S
PIZZA
SUBS · WRAPS · CAN
MICHAEL?
BECAUSE SHE WOULD HAVE (BLEEEP)NG HATED THAT.
THAT'S WHY.
BECAUSE SHE WOULD HAVE HATED THIS.
AND YOU, KENNETH.
SHE'D HAVE HATED EVERY BLOW-DRIED, SPRAY-TANNED INCH OF YOU.
HE'S GOT A POINT.
GO
THIS BU
YOU THINK?
I DO.
SIMMS
8
I WAS IN IRAQ. TOUGHEST MARINE I EVER KNEW WAS A GUY THERE NAMED SIMS. REFUSED PROMOTION, RE-UPPED TWICE.
KINDA GUY MADE YOU THINK, HE WAS ON YOUR TEAM, YOU MIGHT LIVE, YOU KNOW?
'NOTHER ROUND FOR ME AND MY FRIEND, PLEASE.

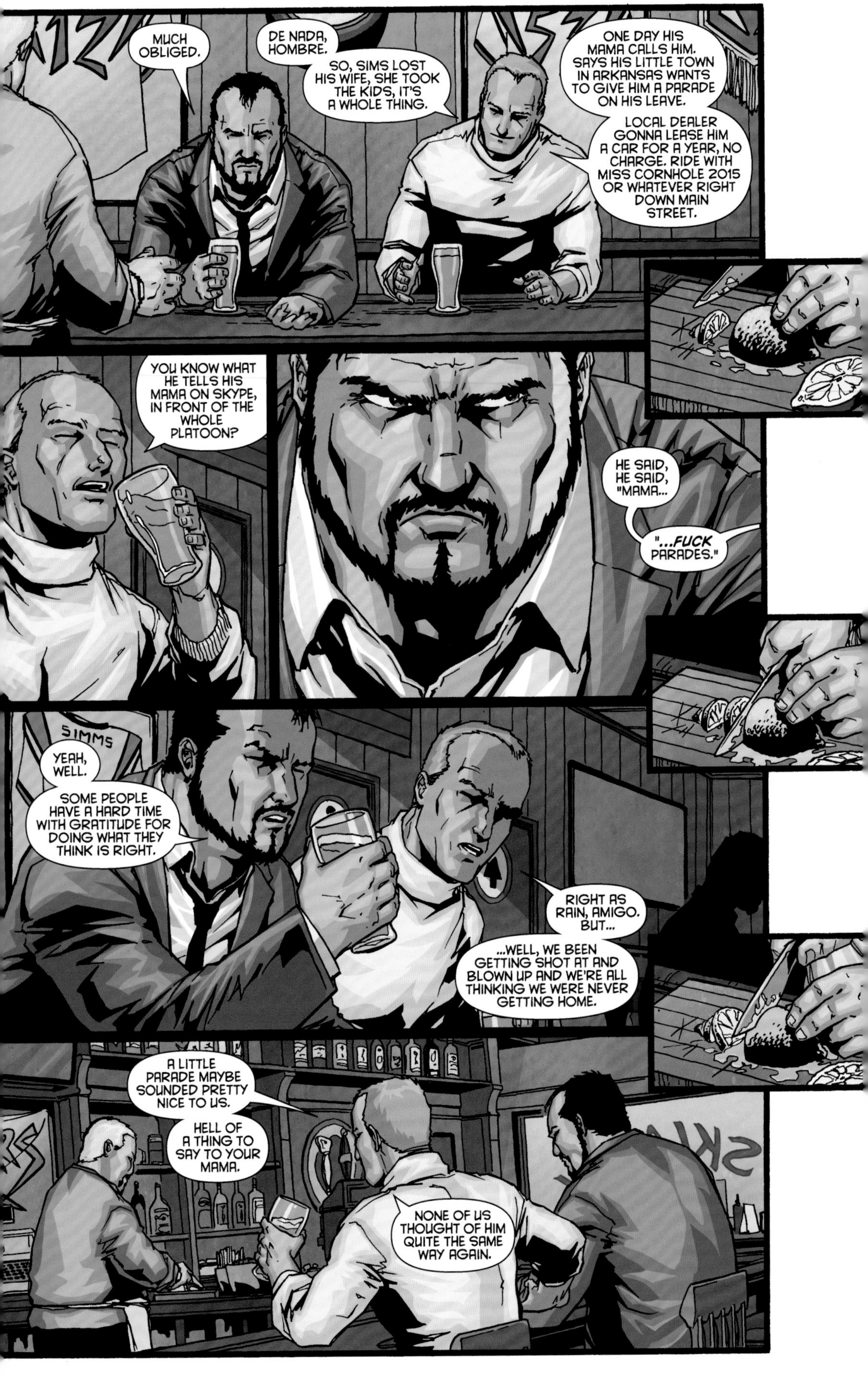
MUCH OBLIGED.
DE NADA, HOMBRE.
SO, SIMS LOST HIS WIFE, SHE TOOK THE KIDS, IT'S A WHOLE THING.
ONE DAY HIS MAMA CALLS HIM. SAYS HIS LITTLE TOWN IN ARKANSAS WANTS TO GIVE HIM A PARADE ON HIS LEAVE.
LOCAL DEALER GONNA LEASE HIM A CAR FOR A YEAR, NO CHARGE. RIDE WITH MISS CORNHOLE 2015 OR WHATEVER RIGHT DOWN MAIN STREET.
YOU KNOW WHAT HE TELLS HIS MAMA ON SKYPE, IN FRONT OF THE WHOLE PLATOON?
HE SAID, HE SAID, "MAMA...
"...FUCK PARADES."
SIMMS
YEAH, WELL.
SOME PEOPLE HAVE A HARD TIME WITH GRATITUDE FOR DOING WHAT THEY THINK IS RIGHT.
RIGHT AS RAIN, AMIGO. BUT...
...WELL, WE BEEN GETTING SHOT AT AND BLOWN UP AND WE'RE ALL THINKING WE WERE NEVER GETTING HOME.
A LITTLE PARADE MAYBE SOUNDED PRETTY NICE TO US.
HELL OF A THING TO SAY TO YOUR MAMA.
NONE OF US THOUGHT OF HIM QUITE THE SAME WAY AGAIN.

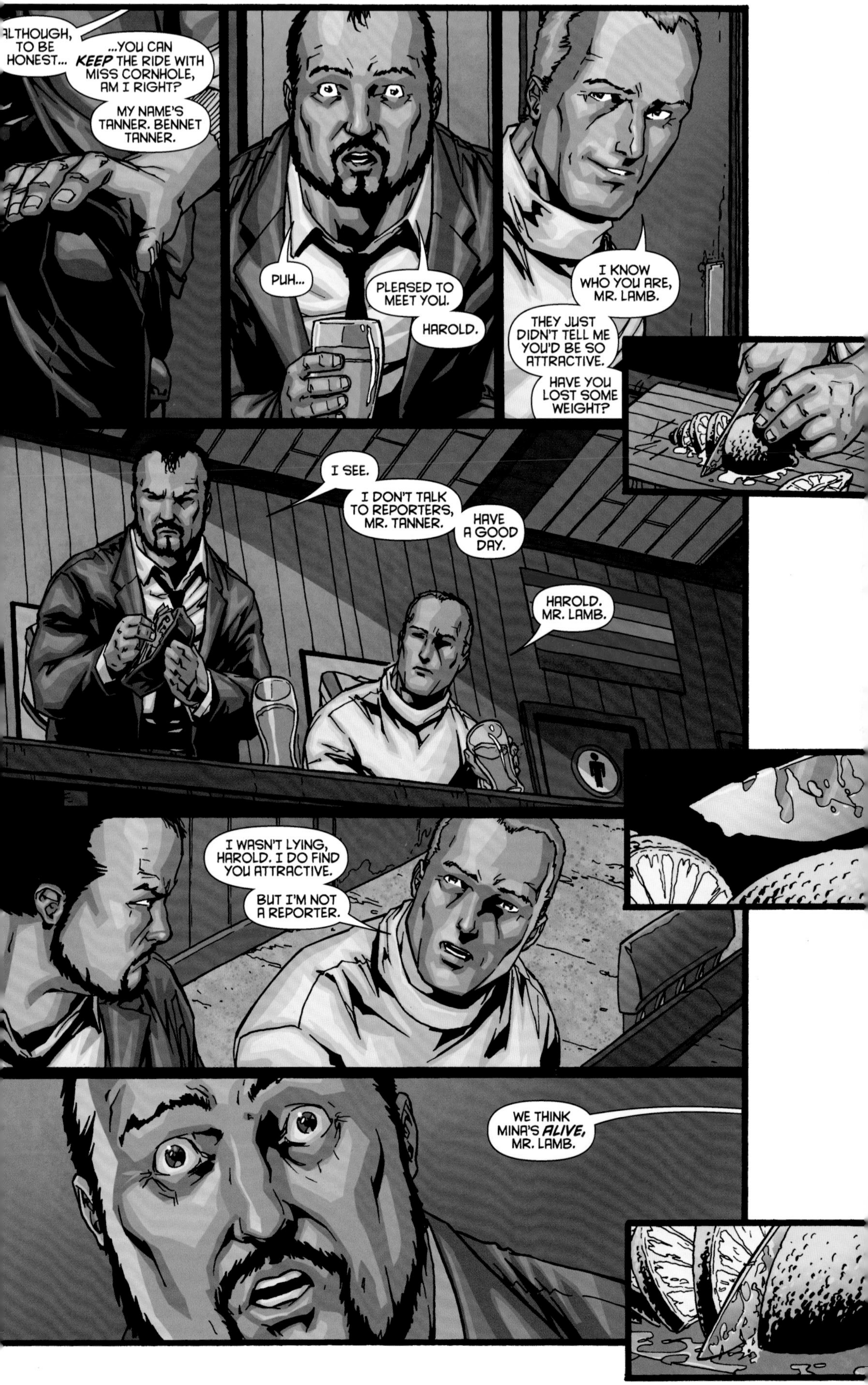

ALTHOUGH, TO BE HONEST...
...YOU CAN KEEP THE RIDE WITH MISS CORNHOLE, AM I RIGHT?
MY NAME'S TANNER. BENNET TANNER.
PUH...
PLEASED TO MEET YOU.
HAROLD.
I KNOW WHO YOU ARE, MR. LAMB.
THEY JUST DIDN'T TELL ME YOU'D BE SO ATTRACTIVE.
HAVE YOU LOST SOME WEIGHT?
I SEE.
I DON'T TALK TO REPORTERS, MR. TANNER.
HAVE A GOOD DAY.
HAROLD. MR. LAMB.
I WASN'T LYING, HAROLD. I DO FIND YOU ATTRACTIVE.
BUT I'M NOT A REPORTER.
WE THINK MINA'S ALIVE, MR. LAMB.

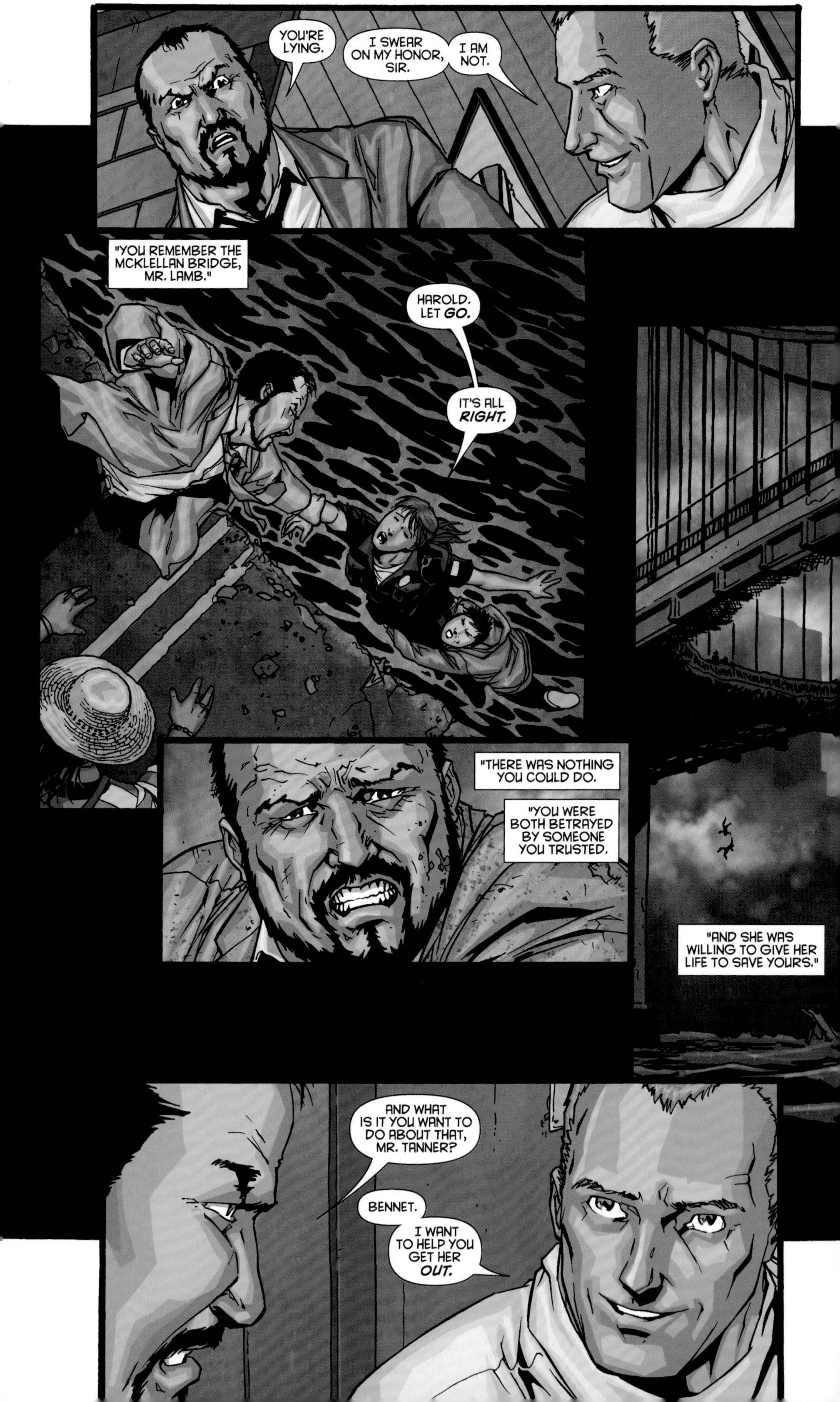
YOU'RE LYING.
I SWEAR ON MY HONOR, SIR.
I AM NOT.
"YOU REMEMBER THE MCKLELLAN BRIDGE, MR. LAMB."
HAROLD. LET GO.
IT'S ALL RIGHT.
"THERE WAS NOTHING YOU COULD DO.
"YOU WERE BOTH BETRAYED BY SOMEONE YOU TRUSTED.
"AND SHE WAS WILLING TO GIVE HER LIFE TO SAVE YOURS."
AND WHAT IS IT YOU WANT TO DO ABOUT THAT, MR. TANNER?
BENNET.
I WANT TO HELP YOU GET HER OUT.

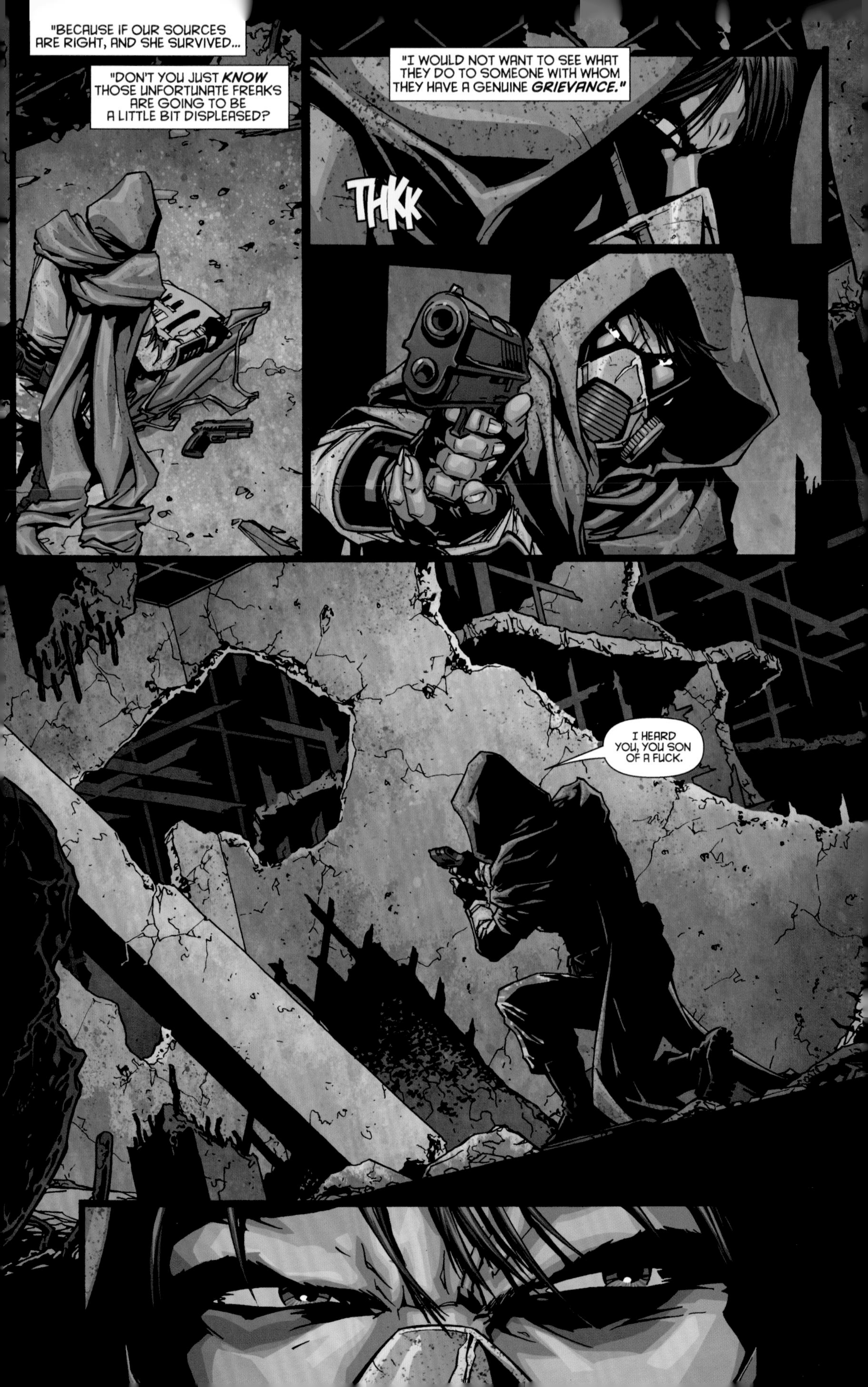
"BECAUSE IF OUR SOURCES ARE RIGHT, AND SHE SURVIVED...
"DON'T YOU JUST KNOW THOSE UNFORTUNATE FREAKS ARE GOING TO BE A LITTLE BIT DISPLEASED?
"I WOULD NOT WANT TO SEE WHAT THEY DO TO SOMEONE WITH WHOM THEY HAVE A GENUINE GRIEVANCE."
THKK
I HEARD YOU, YOU SON OF A FUCK.

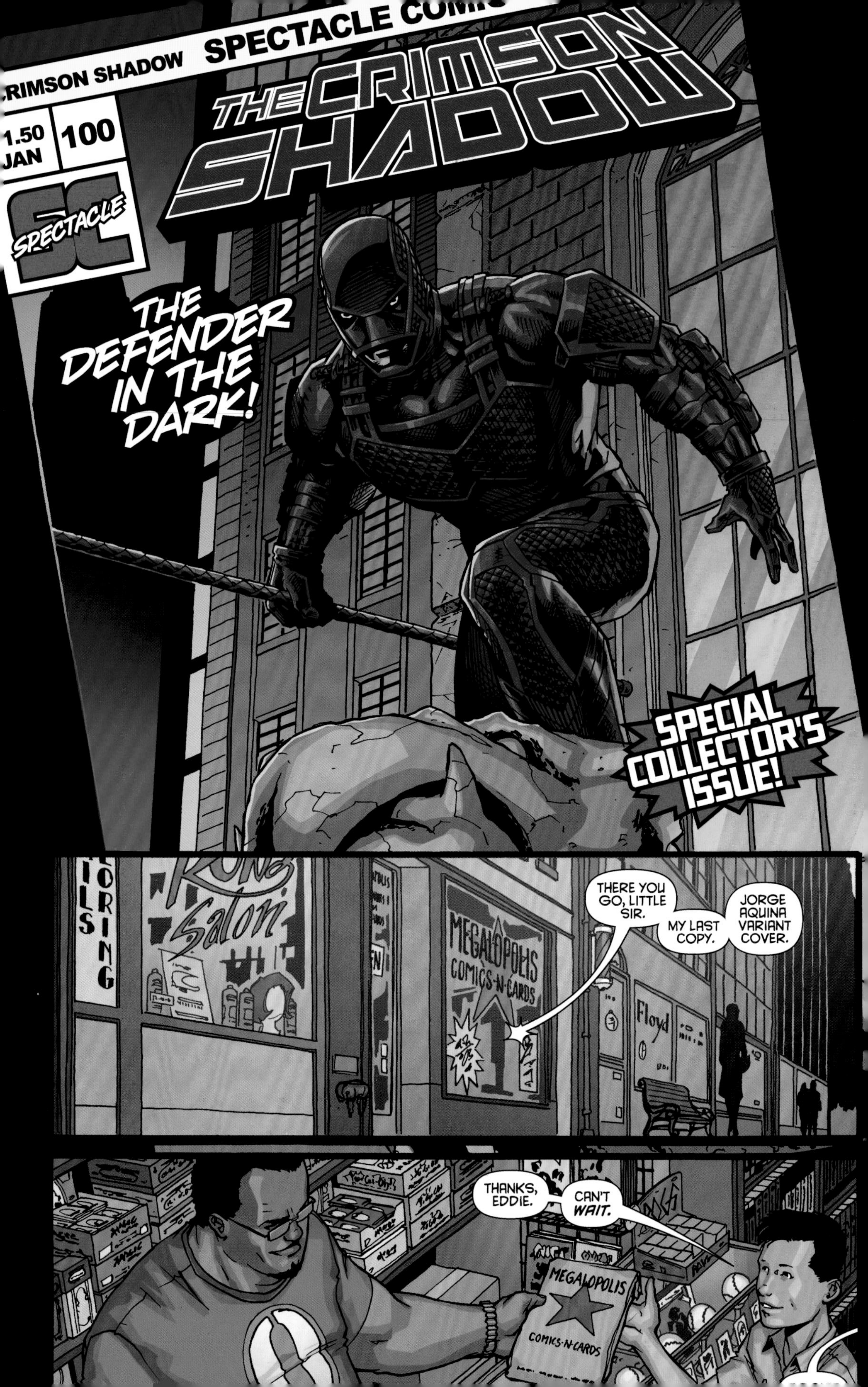
SPECTACLE COMIC
CRIMSON SHADOW
1.50
JAN
100
SPECTACLE
THE CRIMSON SHADOW
THE DEFENDER IN THE DARK!
SPECIAL COLLECTOR'S ISSUE!
Salon
MEGALOPOLIS COMICS-N-CARDS
Floyd
THERE YOU GO, LITTLE SIR.
MY LAST COPY.
JORGE AQUINA VARIANT COVER.
THANKS, EDDIE.
CAN'T *WAIT*.
MEGALOPOLIS
COMICS-N-CARDS

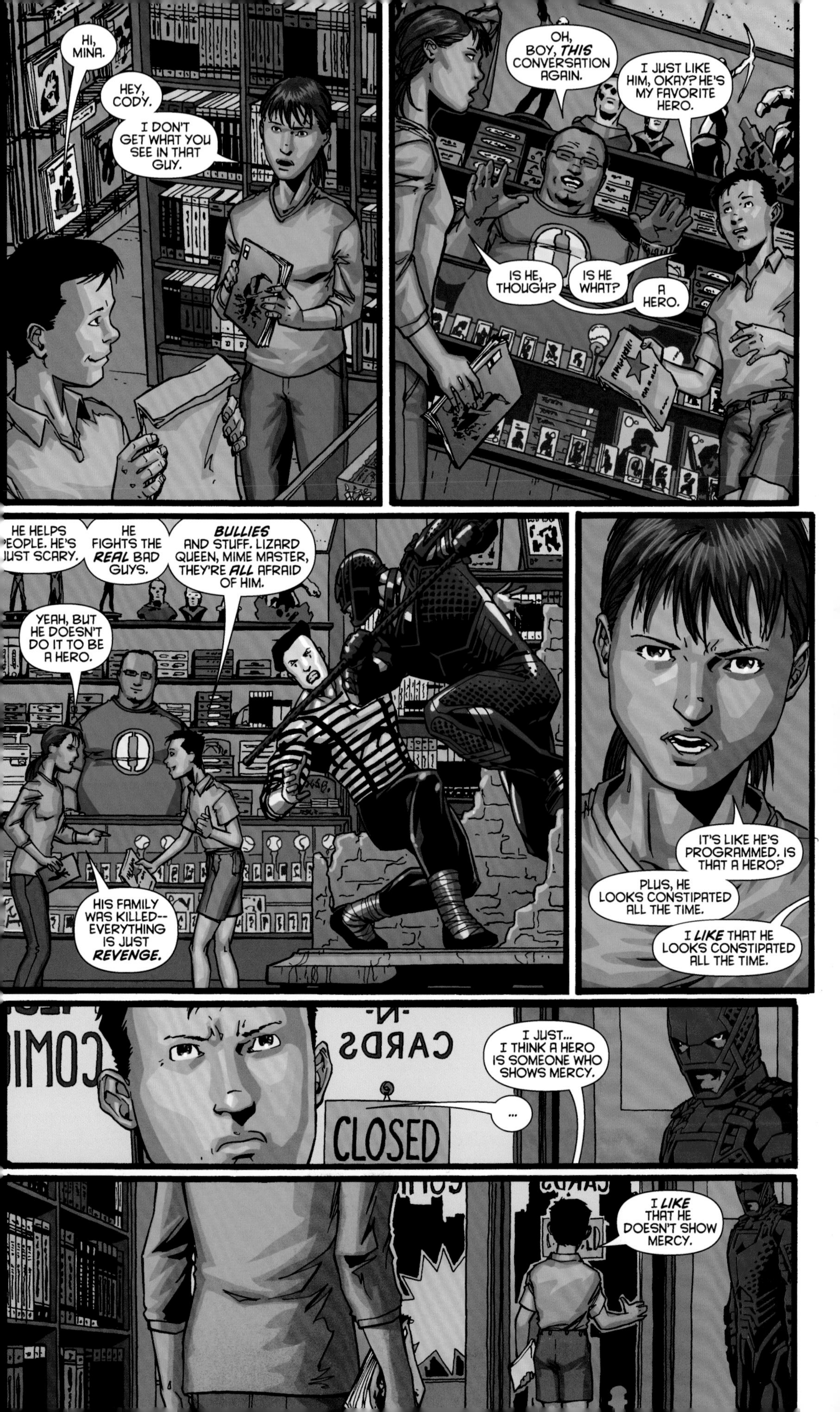
HI, MINA.
HEY, CODY.
I DON'T GET WHAT YOU SEE IN THAT GUY.
OH, BOY, THIS CONVERSATION AGAIN.
I JUST LIKE HIM, OKAY? HE'S MY FAVORITE HERO.
IS HE, THOUGH?
IS HE WHAT?
A HERO.
HE HELPS PEOPLE. HE'S JUST SCARY.
HE FIGHTS THE REAL BAD GUYS.
BULLIES AND STUFF. LIZARD QUEEN, MIME MASTER, THEY'RE ALL AFRAID OF HIM.
YEAH, BUT HE DOESN'T DO IT TO BE A HERO.
HIS FAMILY WAS KILLED-- EVERYTHING IS JUST REVENGE.
IT'S LIKE HE'S PROGRAMMED. IS THAT A HERO?
PLUS, HE LOOKS CONSTIPATED ALL THE TIME.
I LIKE THAT HE LOOKS CONSTIPATED ALL THE TIME.
-N-
CARDS
CLOSED
I JUST... I THINK A HERO IS SOMEONE WHO SHOWS MERCY.
...
I LIKE THAT HE DOESN'T SHOW MERCY.

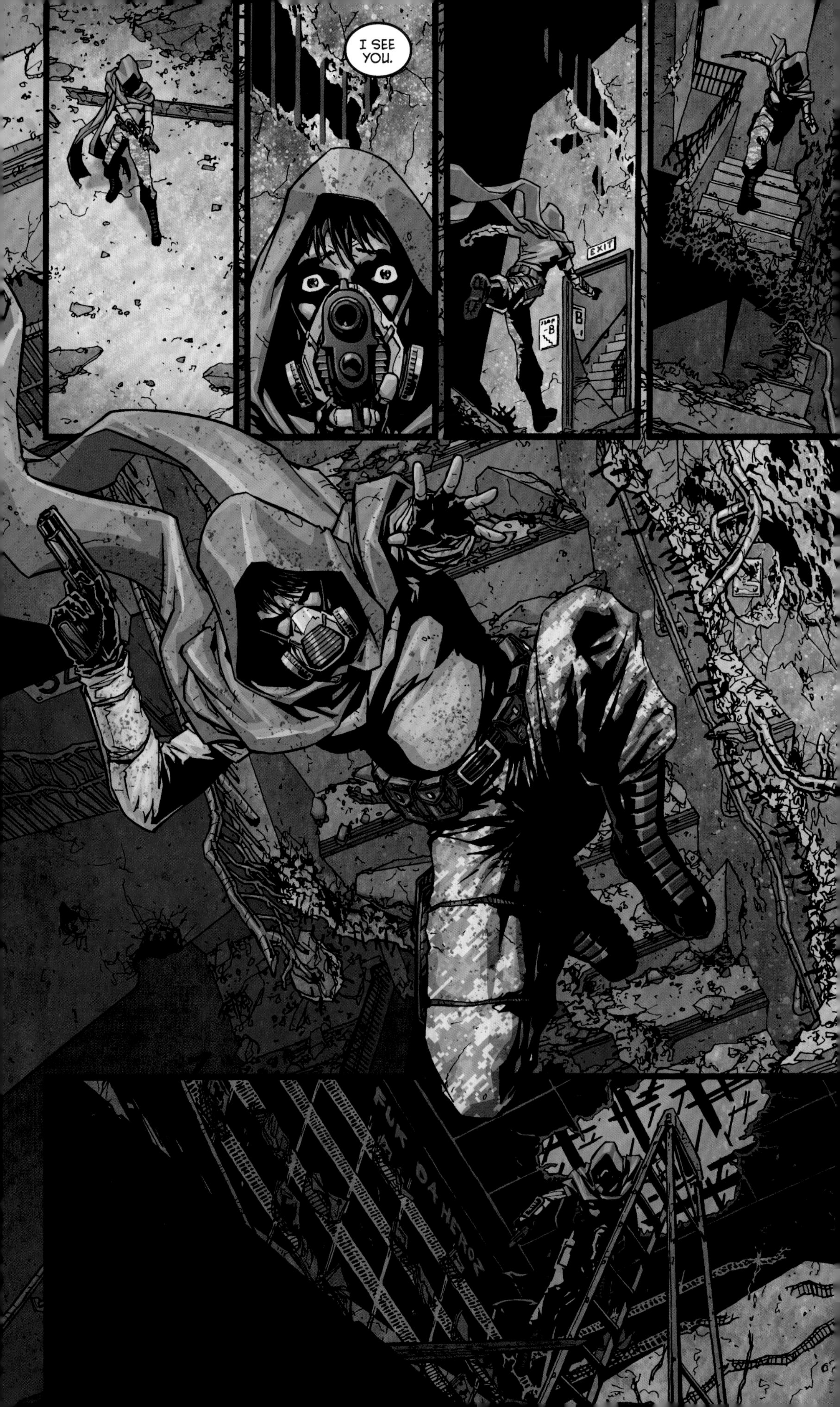
I SEE YOU.
EXIT
B
FUK DA HEROZ

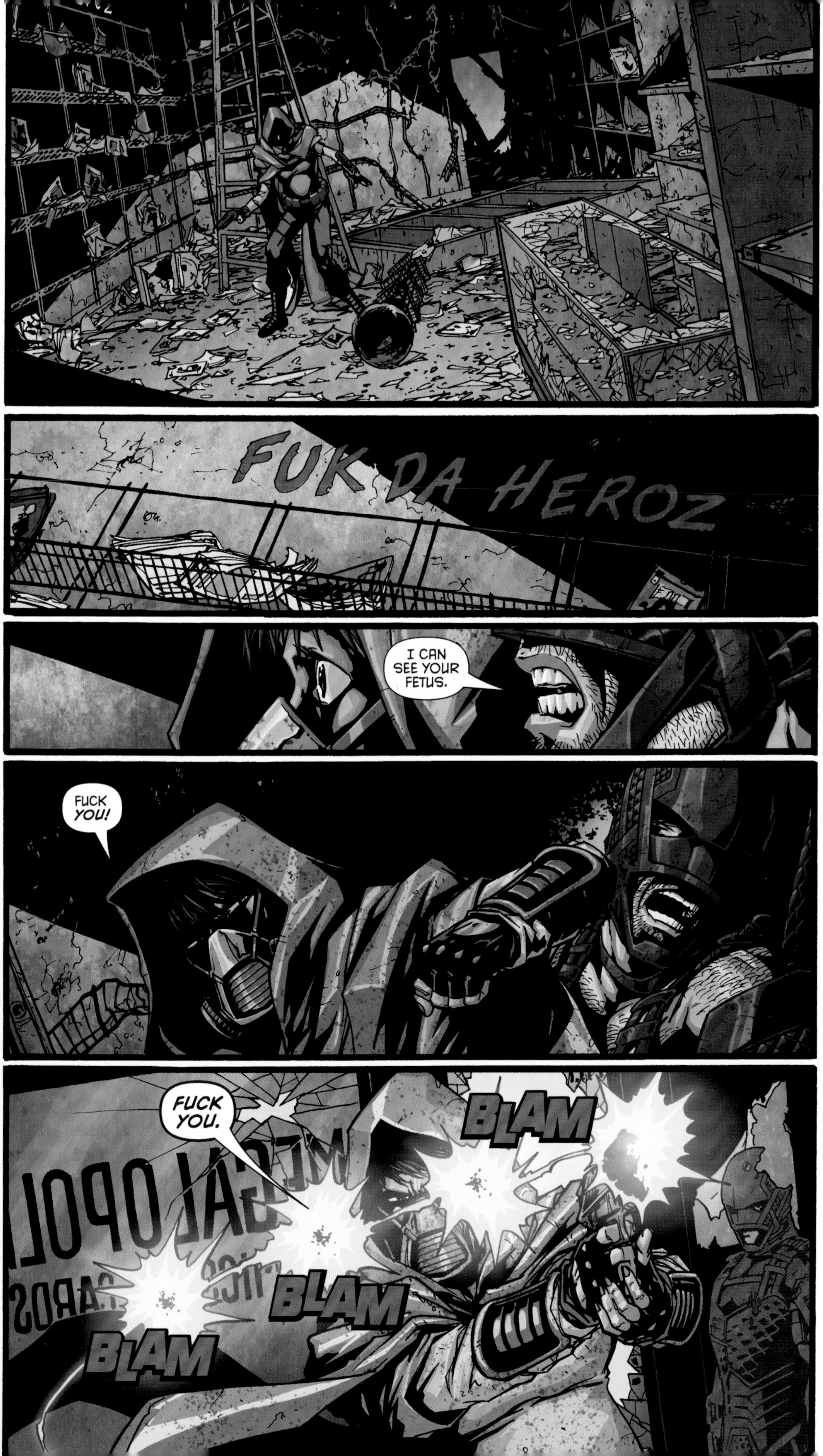
FUK DA HEROZ
I CAN SEE YOUR FETUS.
FUCK YOU!
FUCK YOU.
BLAM
BLAM
BLAM

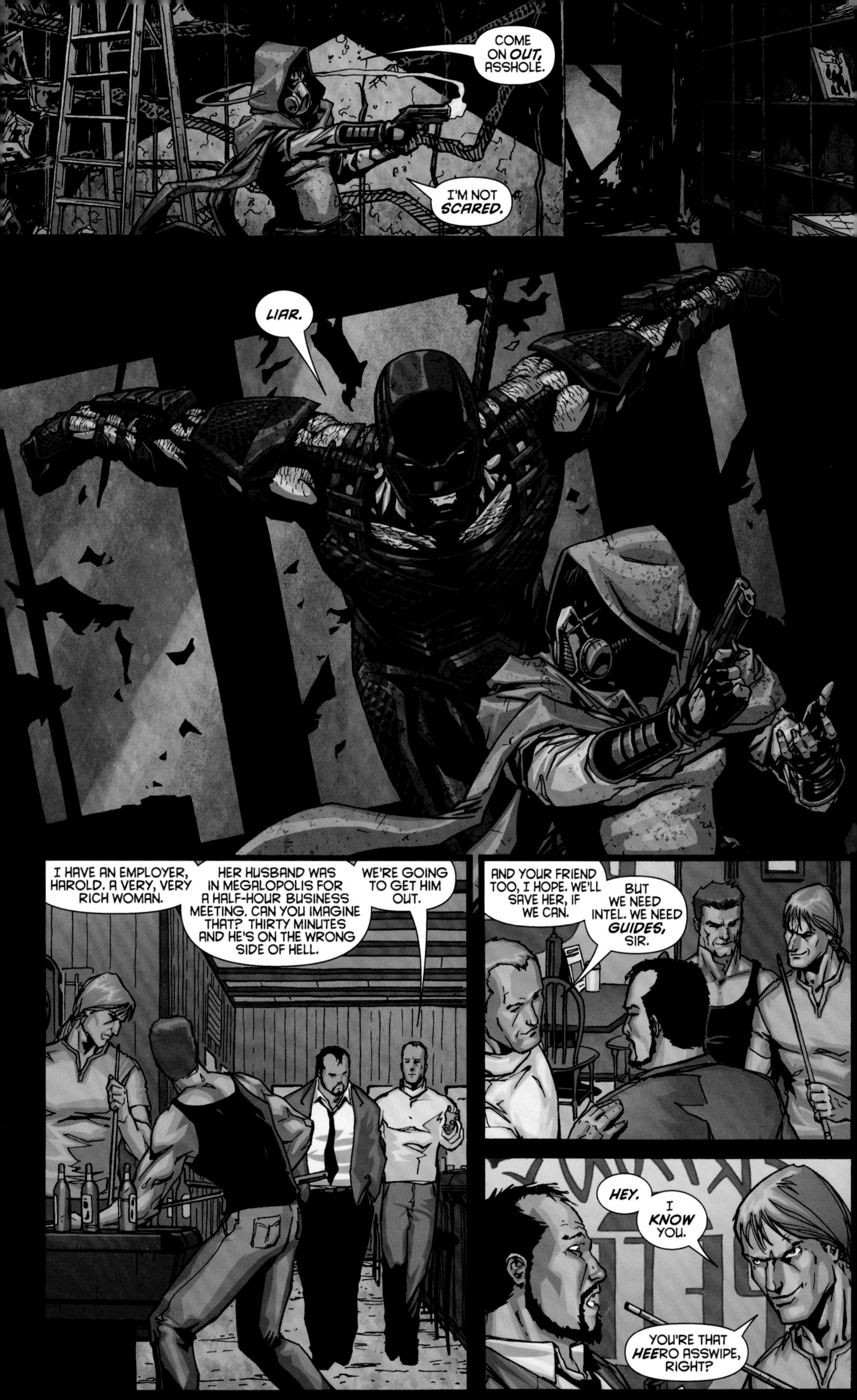
COME ON OUT, ASSHOLE.
I'M NOT SCARED.
LIAR.
I HAVE AN EMPLOYER, HAROLD. A VERY, VERY RICH WOMAN.
HER HUSBAND WAS IN MEGALOPOLIS FOR A HALF-HOUR BUSINESS MEETING. CAN YOU IMAGINE THAT? THIRTY MINUTES AND HE'S ON THE WRONG SIDE OF HELL.
WE'RE GOING TO GET HIM OUT.
AND YOUR FRIEND TOO, I HOPE. WE'LL SAVE HER, IF WE CAN.
BUT WE NEED INTEL. WE NEED GUIDES, SIR.
HEY.
I KNOW YOU.
YOU'RE THAT HEERO ASSWIPE, RIGHT?

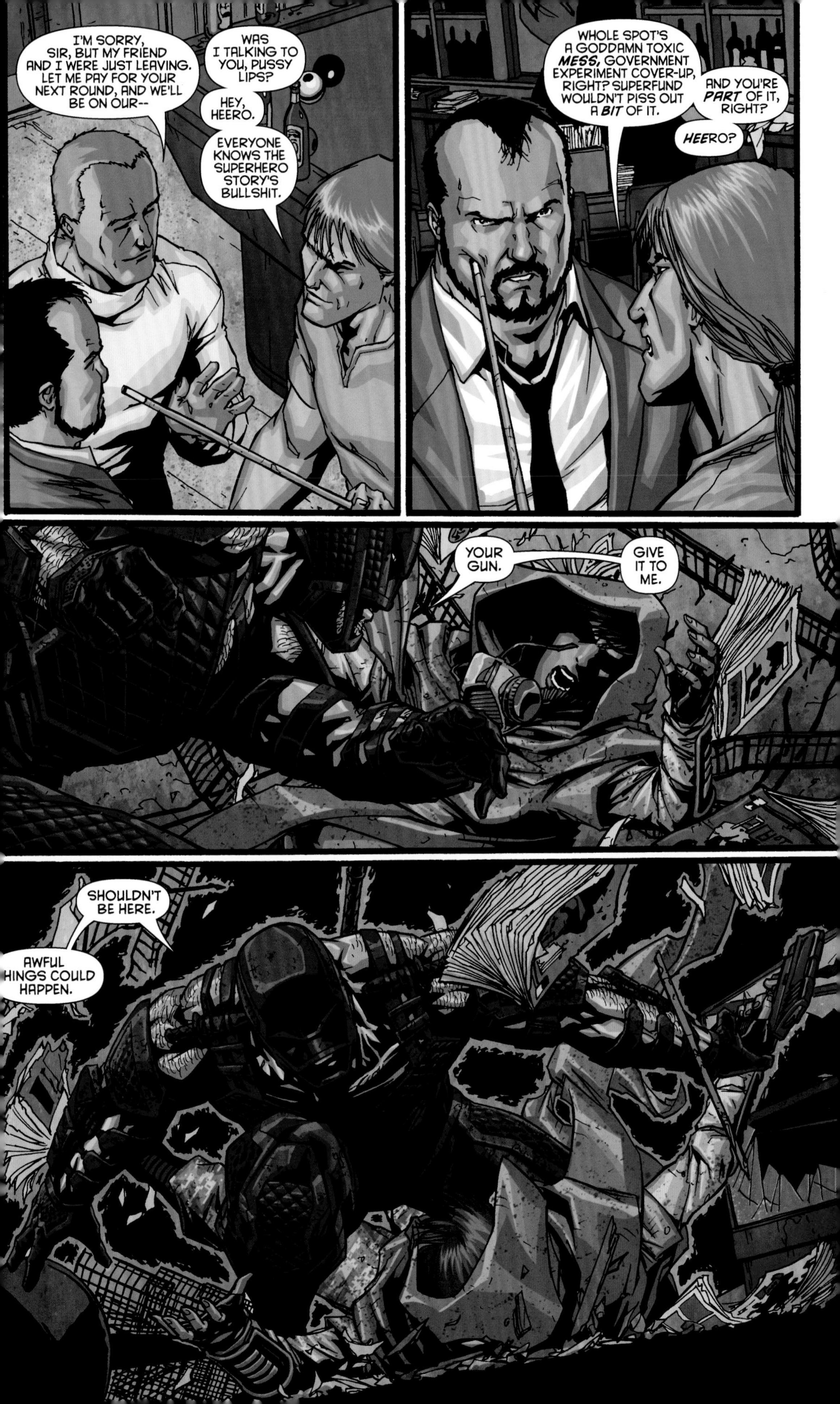

I'M SORRY, SIR, BUT MY FRIEND AND I WERE JUST LEAVING. LET ME PAY FOR YOUR NEXT ROUND, AND WE'LL BE ON OUR--
WAS I TALKING TO YOU, PUSSY LIPS?
HEY, HEERO.
EVERYONE KNOWS THE SUPERHERO STORY'S BULLSHIT.
WHOLE SPOT'S A GODDAMN TOXIC MESS, GOVERNMENT EXPERIMENT COVER-UP, RIGHT? SUPERFUND WOULDN'T PISS OUT A BIT OF IT.
AND YOU'RE PART OF IT, RIGHT?
HEERO?
YOUR GUN.
GIVE IT TO ME.
SHOULDN'T BE HERE.
AWFUL HINGS COULD HAPPEN.

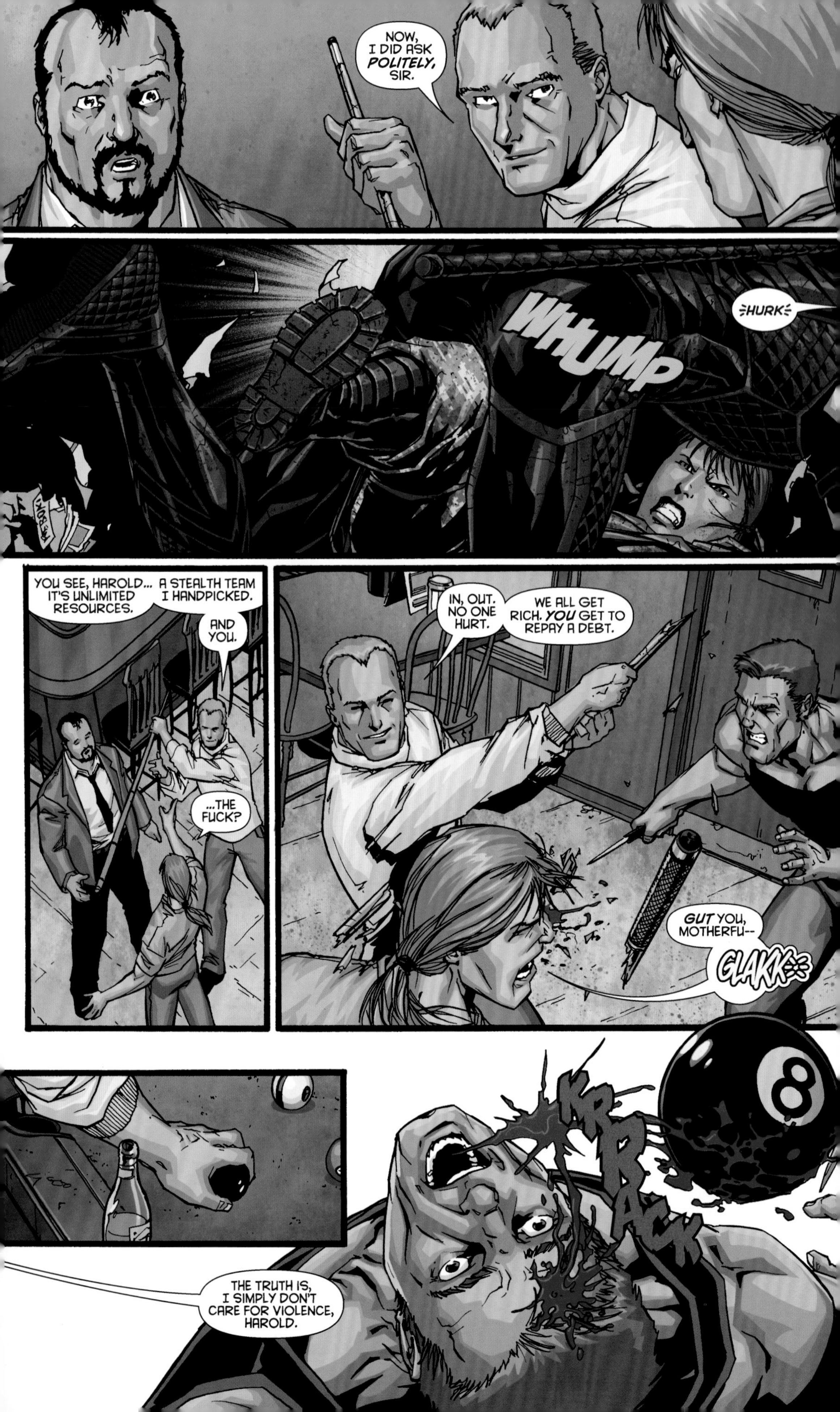

NOW, I DID ASK *POLITELY,* SIR.
WHUMP
HURK
YOU SEE, HAROLD... IT'S UNLIMITED RESOURCES.
A STEALTH TEAM I HANDPICKED.
AND YOU.
...THE FUCK?
IN, OUT. NO ONE HURT.
WE ALL GET RICH. *YOU* GET TO REPAY A DEBT.
GUT YOU, MOTHERFU--
GLAKK
8
KRRACK
THE TRUTH IS, I SIMPLY DON'T CARE FOR VIOLENCE, HAROLD.

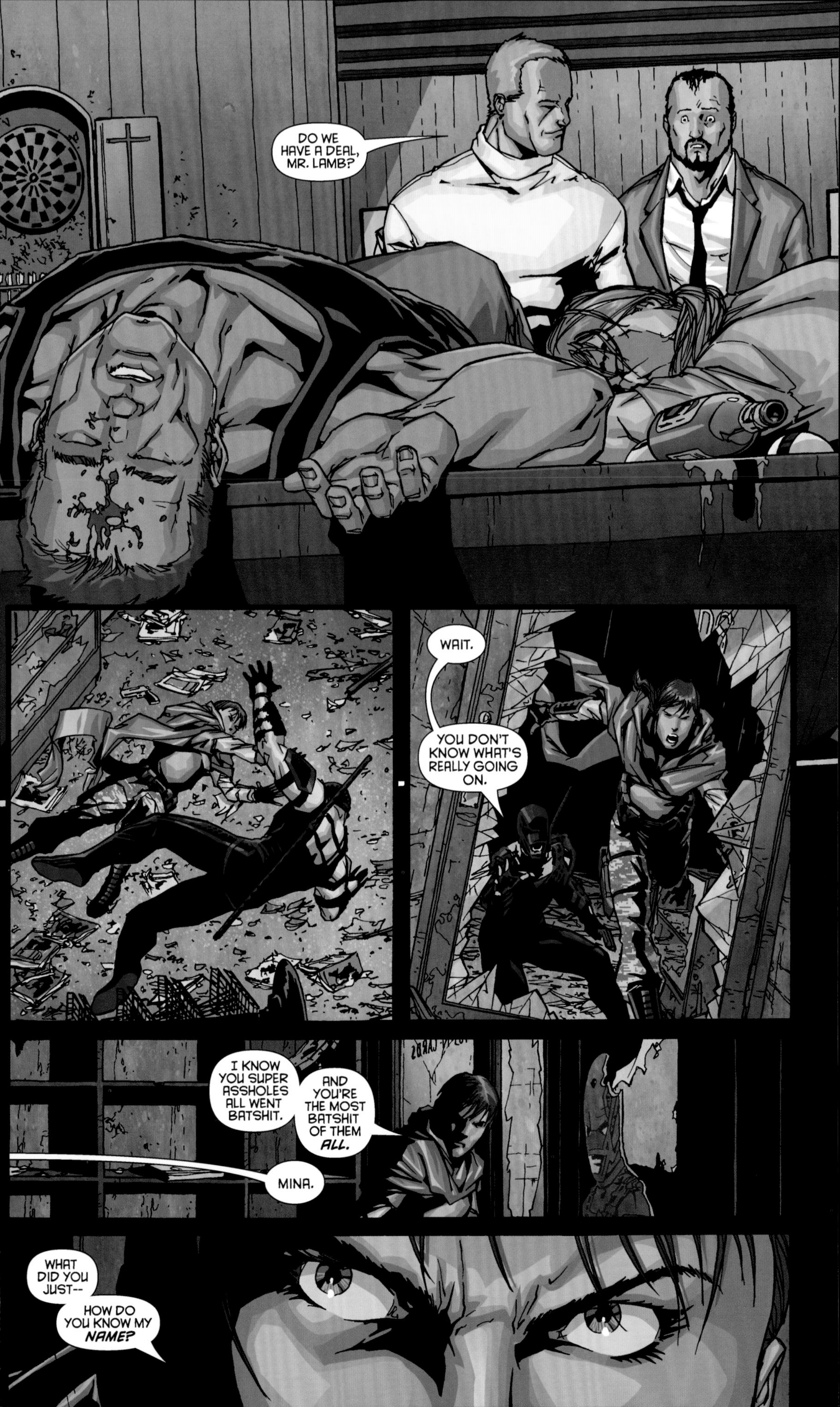

DO WE HAVE A DEAL, MR. LAMB?
WAIT.
YOU DON'T KNOW WHAT'S REALLY GOING ON.
I KNOW YOU SUPER ASSHOLES ALL WENT BATSHIT.
AND YOU'RE THE MOST BATSHIT OF THEM ALL.
MINA.
WHAT DID YOU JUST--
HOW DO YOU KNOW MY NAME?

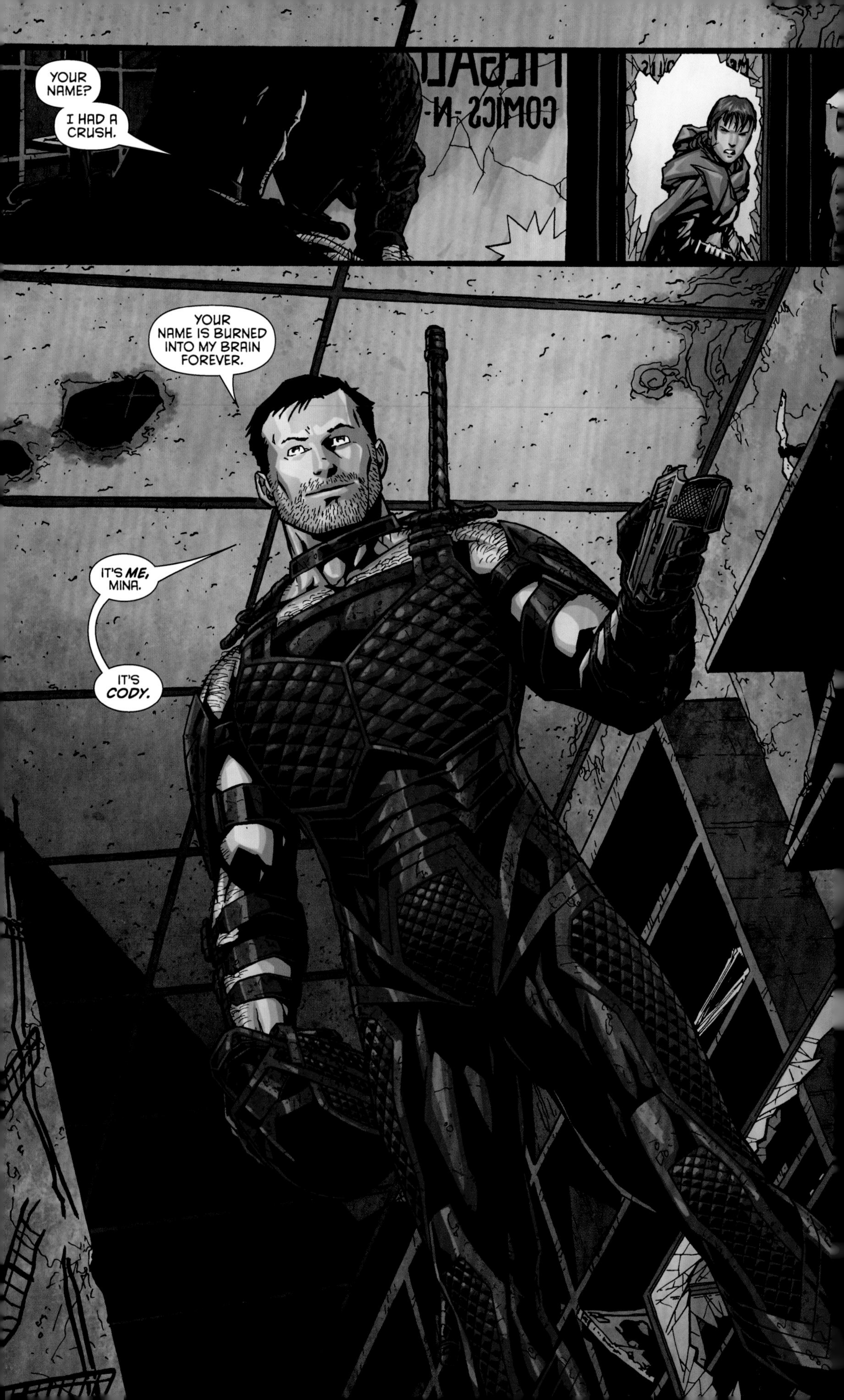

YOUR NAME?
I HAD A CRUSH.
YOUR NAME IS BURNED INTO MY BRAIN FOREVER.
IT'S ME, MINA.
IT'S CODY.

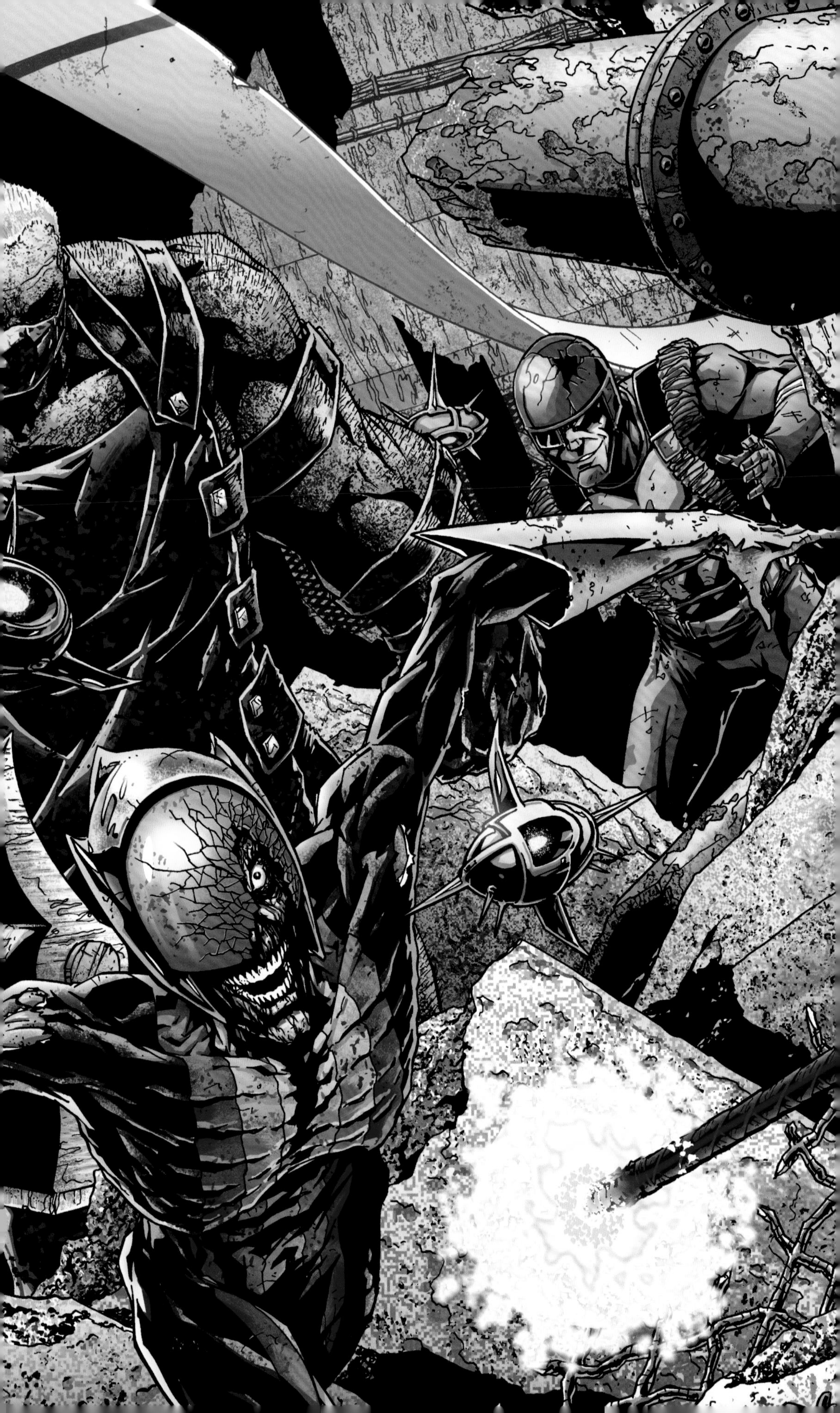

BENNY'S FOR EATS

Open 24 Hours ★ *All Day* ★ *Every Day*

★ MEGALOPOLIS' BEST EATS ★

For Starters

WIDGET SLIDERS
5 Hi-Tech Mini-Burgers...............**5.95**

SHOCKA SPICY NACHOS
With Electric Guacamole Dip..........**6.95**

RED FLAME 5-ALARM CHILI
Guaranteed to Burn..........**7.95**

LADY FLAME 2-ALARM CHILI
Guaranteed Not to Burn.......**6.95**

Main Eats

OVERLORD GRANITE BURGER
12 Ounces of Real Man Beef...**8.95**
American Cheese .... add **.95**
Bacon Strips .... add **1.75**

BLACKSMITH CAJUN BURGER
Spicy Blackened Beef...... **9.95**

RIBBON PULLED PORK
Pork Shoulder Yanked Good........ **8.95**

BIG GUY TRIPLE DECKER
Ham, Turkey, Lettuce & Tomato Really High....**9.95**

GEO ROCKIN' FLAPJACKS
3 Buttermilk Pancakes............**5.95**

JUNIOR GEO SHORT STACK
2 Buttermilk Pancakes..........**4.95**

AMPHIBONAUT'S CATCH
Fishy Fish Sticks..........**7.95**

SOUTHERN BELLE GUMBO
Louisiana Bitchin' Spice.......**6.95**

On The Side

TOM-O-HAWK TATERS
Red Potato Chunks...............**3.95**

FLEET FRIES
Speedy Fried..........**4.95**

CUPID CURLY FRIES
Spiced So They're Flamin' **5.95**

Mite Brigadiers

MAXI-GIRL MAC-N-CHEESE

ATOMIC PYTHON MINI-DOGS

VISUA'S MYSTERY SURPRISE

BO-ROBO STEEL-CUT OATMEAL

SEVENTH WONDER PBJ

SCOUT CHICKEN NUGGETS

Drinkables

PURPLE HAZE GRAPE SLUSHY
Brain Freeze..............**3.95**

CRIMSON SHADOW SHAKE
Strawberry with Brown Chunks..........**5.95**

THE NAMELESS COFFEE
Best Mud This Side of Hell **4.95**

Eat In   Eat Out   Eat Me

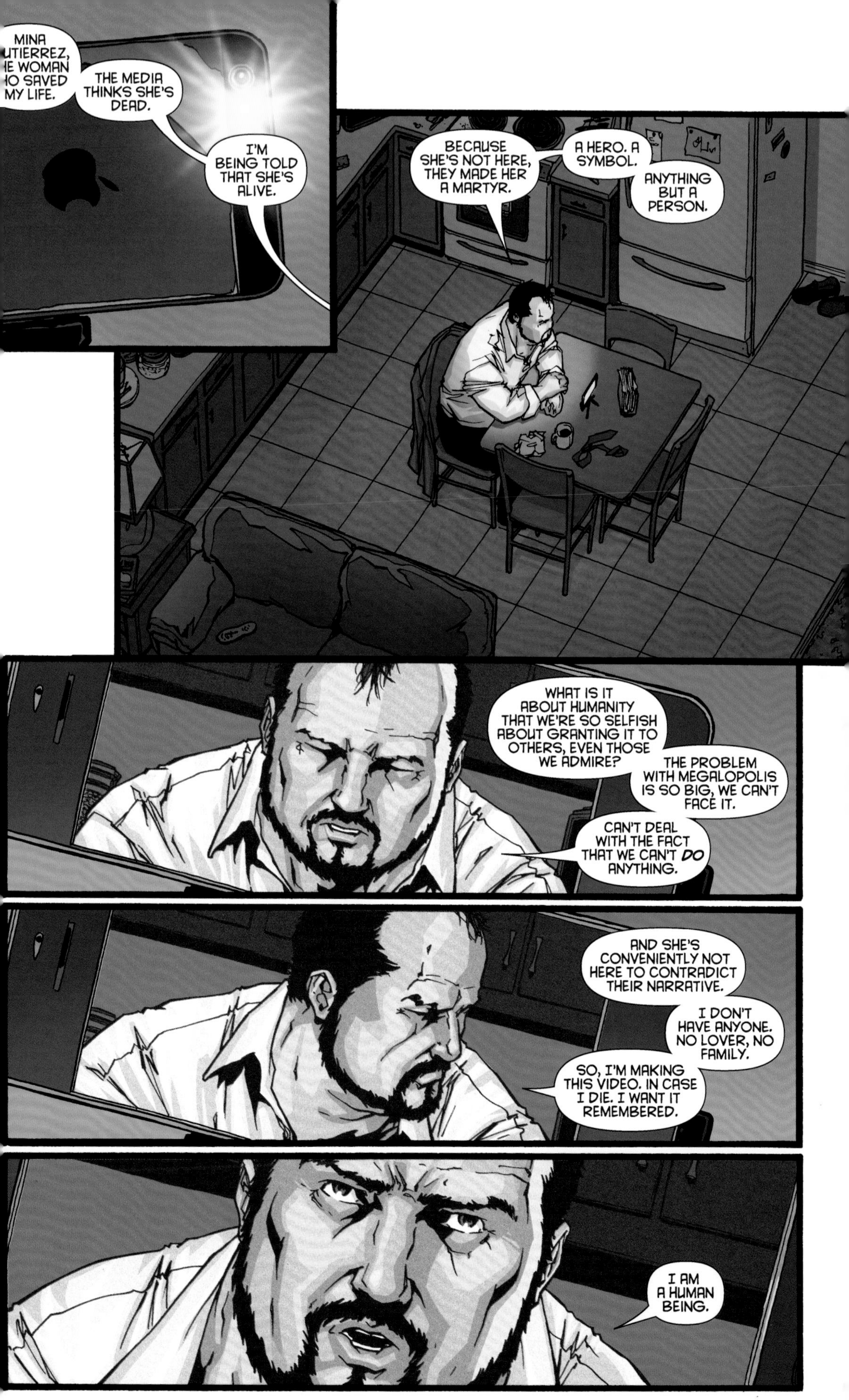
MINA
UTIERREZ,
HE WOMAN
HO SAVED
MY LIFE.
THE MEDIA THINKS SHE'S DEAD.
I'M BEING TOLD THAT SHE'S ALIVE.
BECAUSE SHE'S NOT HERE, THEY MADE HER A MARTYR.
A HERO. A SYMBOL.
ANYTHING BUT A PERSON.
WHAT IS IT ABOUT HUMANITY THAT WE'RE SO SELFISH ABOUT GRANTING IT TO OTHERS, EVEN THOSE WE ADMIRE?
THE PROBLEM WITH MEGALOPOLIS IS SO BIG, WE CAN'T FACE IT.
CAN'T DEAL WITH THE FACT THAT WE CAN'T *DO* ANYTHING.
AND SHE'S CONVENIENTLY NOT HERE TO CONTRADICT THEIR NARRATIVE.
I DON'T HAVE ANYONE. NO LOVER, NO FAMILY.
SO, I'M MAKING THIS VIDEO. IN CASE I DIE. I WANT IT REMEMBERED.
I AM A HUMAN BEING.

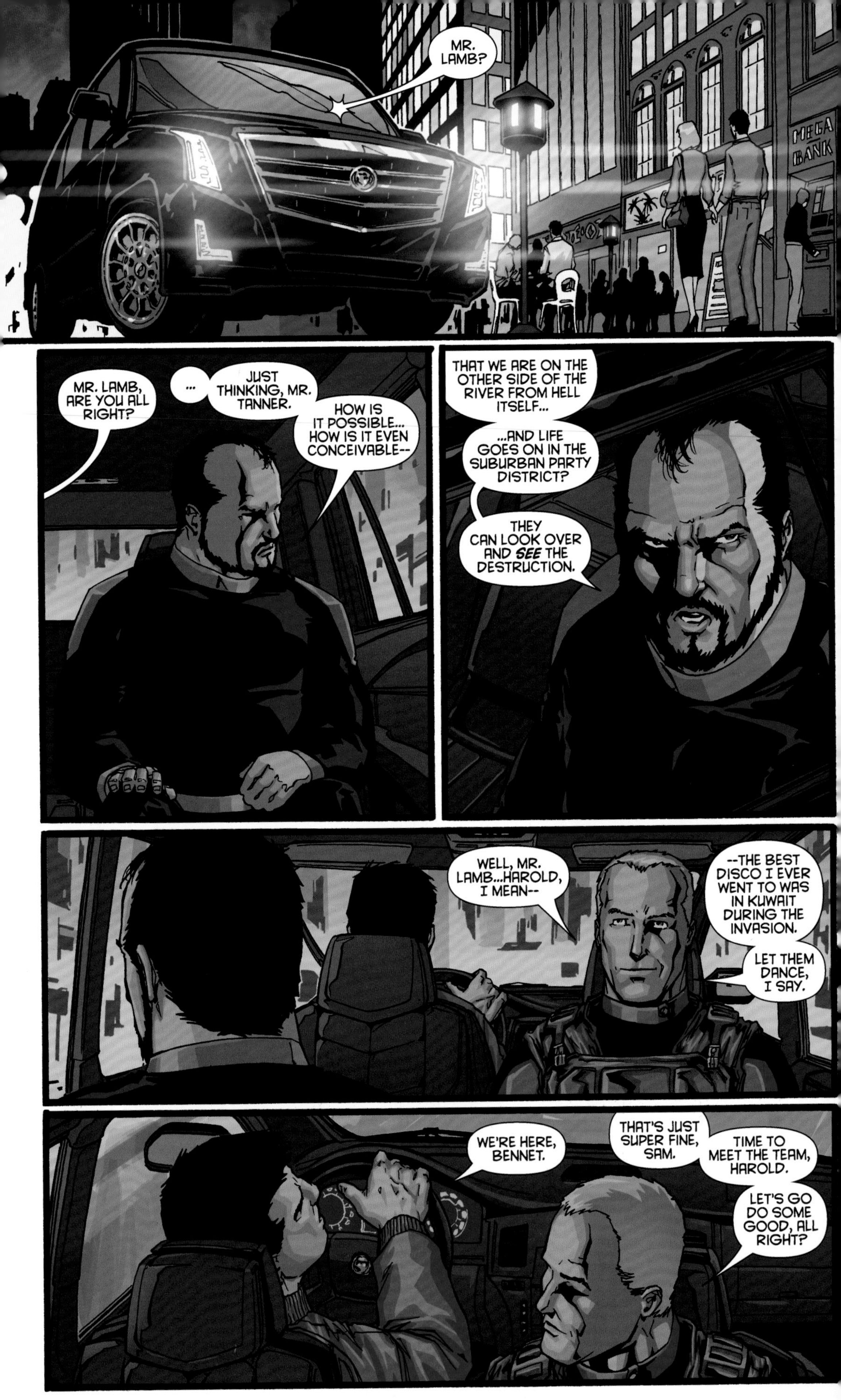
MR. LAMB?
MEGA BANK
MR. LAMB, ARE YOU ALL RIGHT?
...
JUST THINKING, MR. TANNER.
HOW IS IT POSSIBLE... HOW IS IT EVEN CONCEIVABLE--
THAT WE ARE ON THE OTHER SIDE OF THE RIVER FROM HELL ITSELF...
...AND LIFE GOES ON IN THE SUBURBAN PARTY DISTRICT?
THEY CAN LOOK OVER AND ***SEE*** THE DESTRUCTION.
WELL, MR. LAMB...HAROLD, I MEAN--
--THE BEST DISCO I EVER WENT TO WAS IN KUWAIT DURING THE INVASION.
LET THEM DANCE, I SAY.
WE'RE HERE, BENNET.
THAT'S JUST SUPER FINE, SAM.
TIME TO MEET THE TEAM, HAROLD.
LET'S GO DO SOME GOOD, ALL RIGHT?

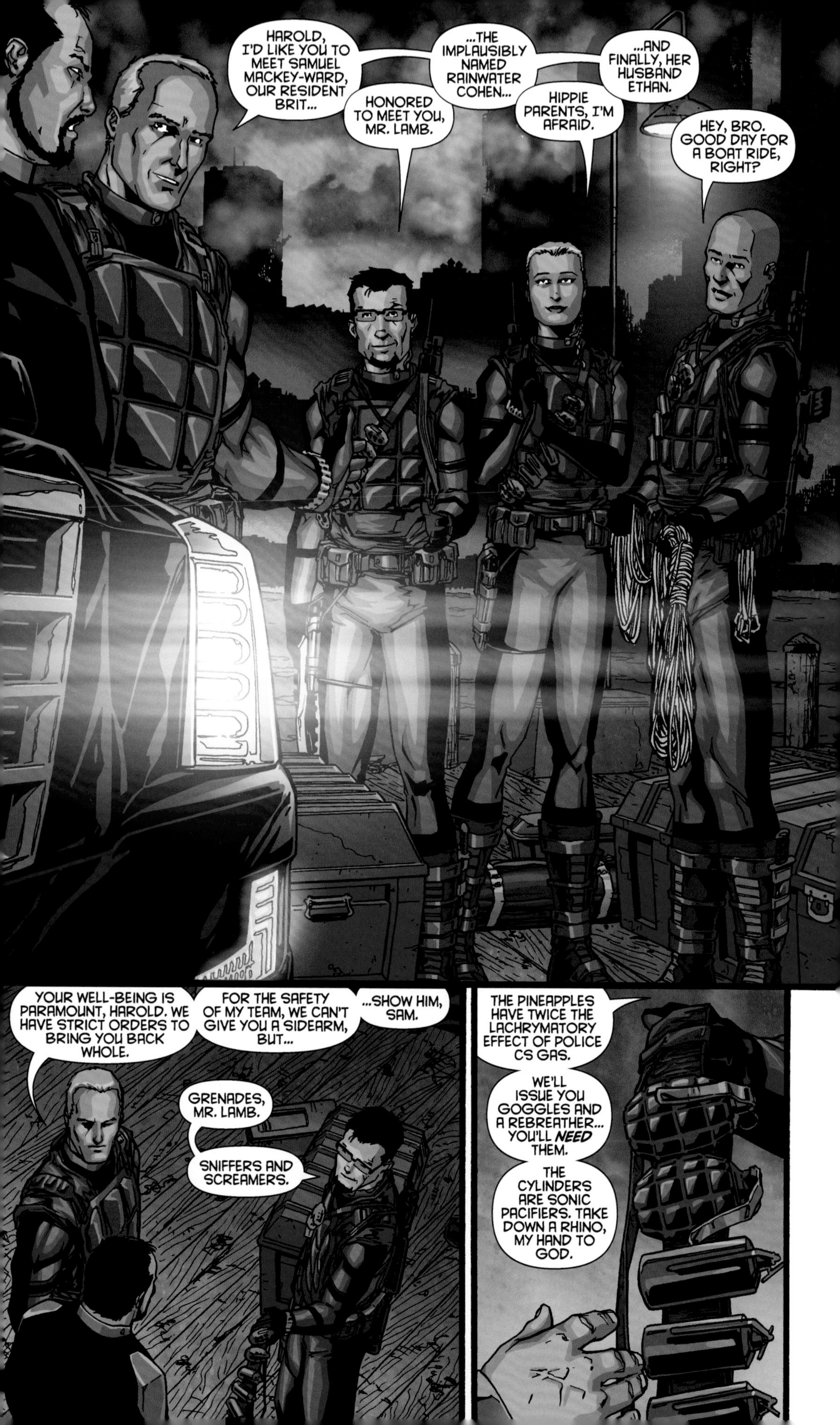
HAROLD, I'D LIKE YOU TO MEET SAMUEL MACKEY-WARD, OUR RESIDENT BRIT...
HONORED TO MEET YOU, MR. LAMB.
...THE IMPLAUSIBLY NAMED RAINWATER COHEN...
HIPPIE PARENTS, I'M AFRAID.
...AND FINALLY, HER HUSBAND ETHAN.
HEY, BRO. GOOD DAY FOR A BOAT RIDE, RIGHT?
YOUR WELL-BEING IS PARAMOUNT, HAROLD. WE HAVE STRICT ORDERS TO BRING YOU BACK WHOLE.
FOR THE SAFETY OF MY TEAM, WE CAN'T GIVE YOU A SIDEARM, BUT...
...SHOW HIM, SAM.
GRENADES, MR. LAMB.
SNIFFERS AND SCREAMERS.
THE PINEAPPLES HAVE TWICE THE LACHRYMATORY EFFECT OF POLICE CS GAS.
WE'LL ISSUE YOU GOGGLES AND A REBREATHER... YOU'LL *NEED* THEM.
THE CYLINDERS ARE SONIC PACIFIERS. TAKE DOWN A RHINO, MY HAND TO GOD.

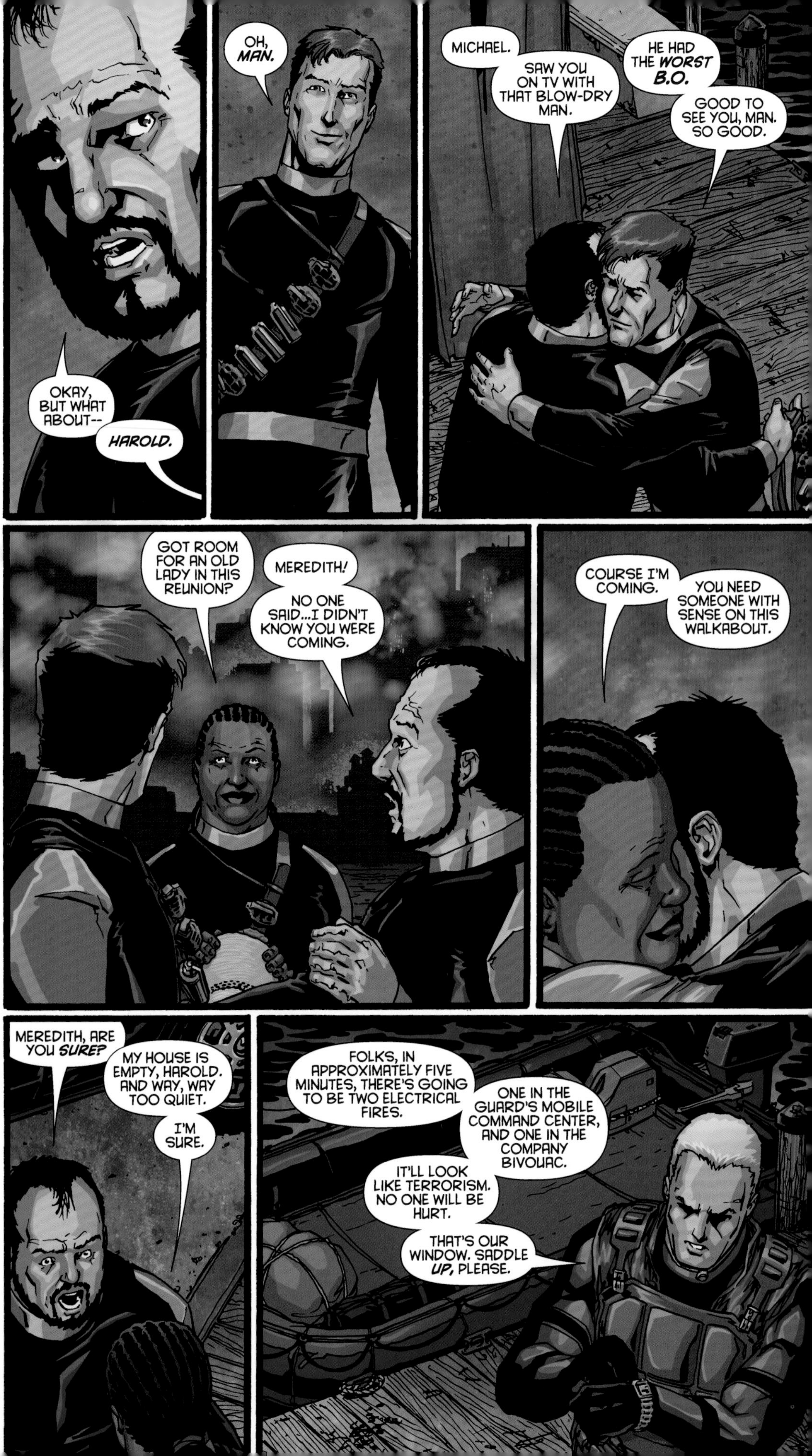

OKAY, BUT WHAT ABOUT--
HAROLD.
OH, MAN.
MICHAEL.
SAW YOU ON TV WITH THAT BLOW-DRY MAN.
HE HAD THE WORST B.O.
GOOD TO SEE YOU, MAN. SO GOOD.
GOT ROOM FOR AN OLD LADY IN THIS REUNION?
MEREDITH!
NO ONE SAID...I DIDN'T KNOW YOU WERE COMING.
COURSE I'M COMING.
YOU NEED SOMEONE WITH SENSE ON THIS WALKABOUT.
MEREDITH, ARE YOU SURE?
MY HOUSE IS EMPTY, HAROLD. AND WAY, WAY TOO QUIET.
I'M SURE.
FOLKS, IN APPROXIMATELY FIVE MINUTES, THERE'S GOING TO BE TWO ELECTRICAL FIRES.
ONE IN THE GUARD'S MOBILE COMMAND CENTER, AND ONE IN THE COMPANY BIVOUAC.
IT'LL LOOK LIKE TERRORISM. NO ONE WILL BE HURT.
THAT'S OUR WINDOW. SADDLE UP, PLEASE.

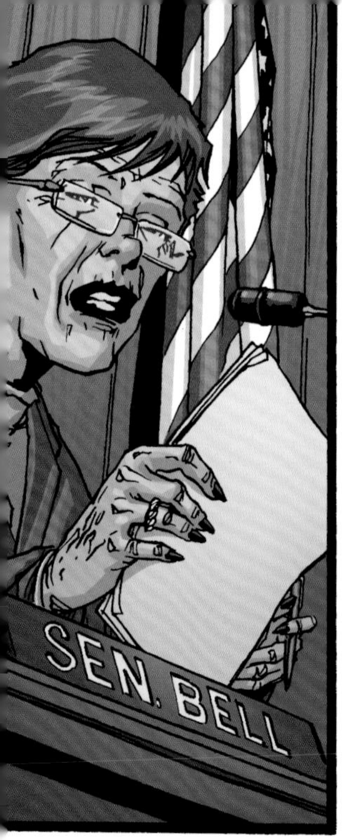
SEN. BELL

SENATOR BELL: Now, Colonel Culver, I'd like to speak about the evolving focus of humanitarian aid for a moment, if I could.

CULVER: Absolutely, Senator.

SENATOR BELL: In the days immediately following the event, was there any attempt to provide relief for the civilians in the quarantine zone?

CULVER: Yes, Senator. We attempted food drops by airlift, but those planes were attacked by the infected--

SENATOR BELL: Afflicted.

CULVER: Excuse me, ma'am?

SENATOR BELL: Protocol is asking that we use the word "afflicted" when discussing the megahumans in question, Colonel, rather than "infected."

CULVER: I was not made aware of this change in vernacular, ma'am.

SENATOR BELL: We don't need a panic, Colonel. We are trying to avoid inflammatory language.

CULVER: Understood, Senator.

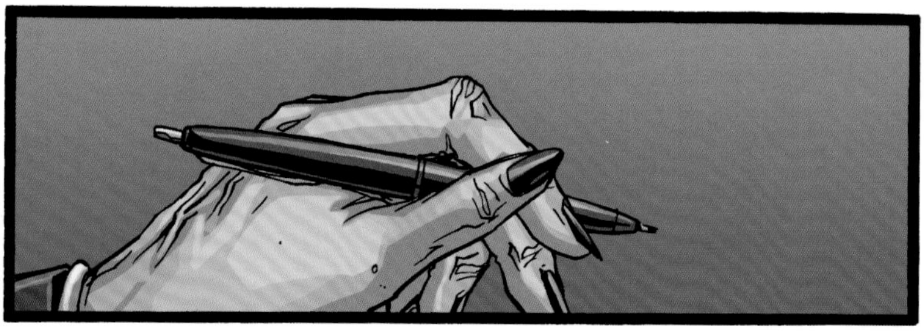

SENATOR BELL: Please continue. You were saying--

CULVER: So we switched to unmanned water delivery. In the early days, it was primarily military MREs from the National Guard's own supply, but--

SENATOR BELL: "MREs?"

CULVER: Meals Ready to Eat, Senator. 1,300 calories each, shelf life of ten years or thereabouts.

CULVER: Wartime rations for troops unable to make mess hall.

SENATOR BELL: I see. And these are, I'm assuming, not exactly fine dining?

CULVER: They are not, ma'am. My first tour of duty, we called the spaghetti pouch "opening a can of worms."

CULVER: A flameless ration heater was included in each early crate.

CULVER: There were vegan, halal, and kosher meals in each shipment, sporadically. But an attempt ***WAS*** made.

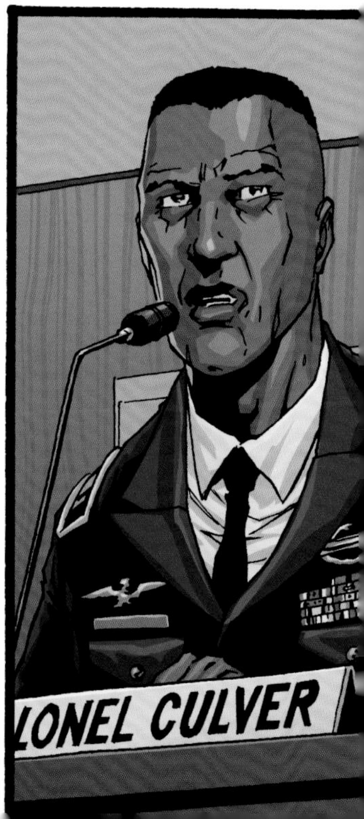
LONEL CULVER

SENATOR BELL: Admirable. And how long was this operation in effect?

CULVER: Well, a few days. Our supply was limited, and eventually, aid agencies like the Red Cross were able to move a wider range of food staples. It was felt that if we provided basics after the initial shock wore off, the trapped citizens--

SENATOR BELL: --The quarantined, if you please, Colonel.

CULVER: Right, the quarantined . . . They would be able to gain independence more quickly without the MREs, if they had to make their OWN meals from the basic foodstuffs we provided.

CULVER: With the hope of a surcease of all external food aid at some future date.

CULVER: We coordinated with local food banks, restaurants, and farmers.

CULVER: Basically, if it was about to go bad . . . across the river it went.

SENATOR BELL: And was food the only provision we sent over?

CULVER: No, ma'am.

CULVER: We sent over seeds and basic hydroponic equipment, some surplus e-tools, as well as some rudimentary medical supplies.

SENATOR BELL: And this is where--

CULVER: We ran into problems, yes, ma'am.

CULVER: You see, the inf--the AFFLICTED would destroy any shipment containing what might be considered nonsubsistence items.

CULVER: If we sent blankets, shoes, jackets, or generators, the entire shipment was destroyed.

CULVER: They would allow the quarantined to live.

CULVER: They would not allow them to be COMFORTABLE.

CULVER: December, we took a chance. We sent a shipment of donated holiday items: toys, decorations, et cetera.

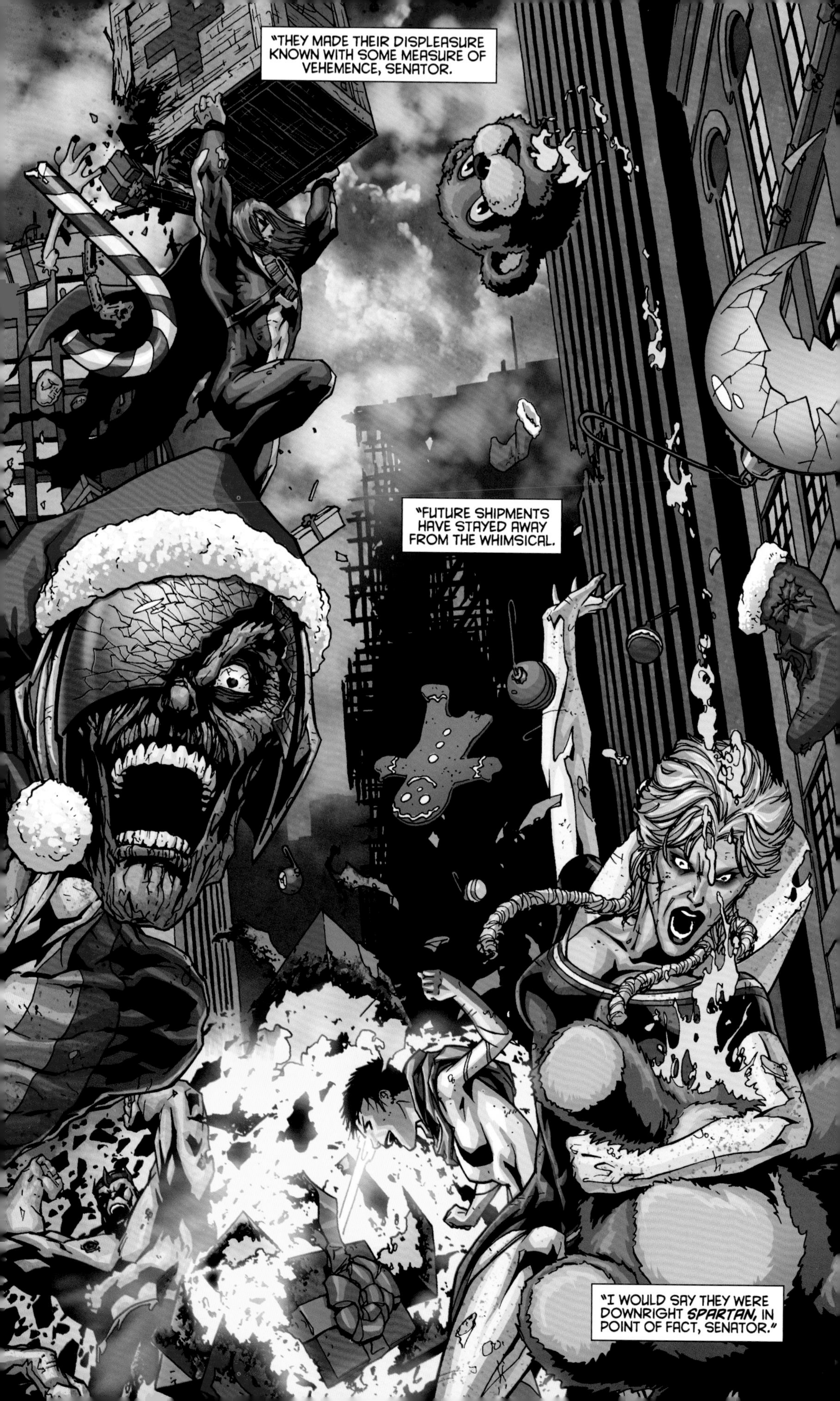
"THEY MADE THEIR DISPLEASURE KNOWN WITH SOME MEASURE OF VEHEMENCE, SENATOR.
"FUTURE SHIPMENTS HAVE STAYED AWAY FROM THE WHIMSICAL.
"I WOULD SAY THEY WERE DOWNRIGHT SPARTAN, IN POINT OF FACT, SENATOR."

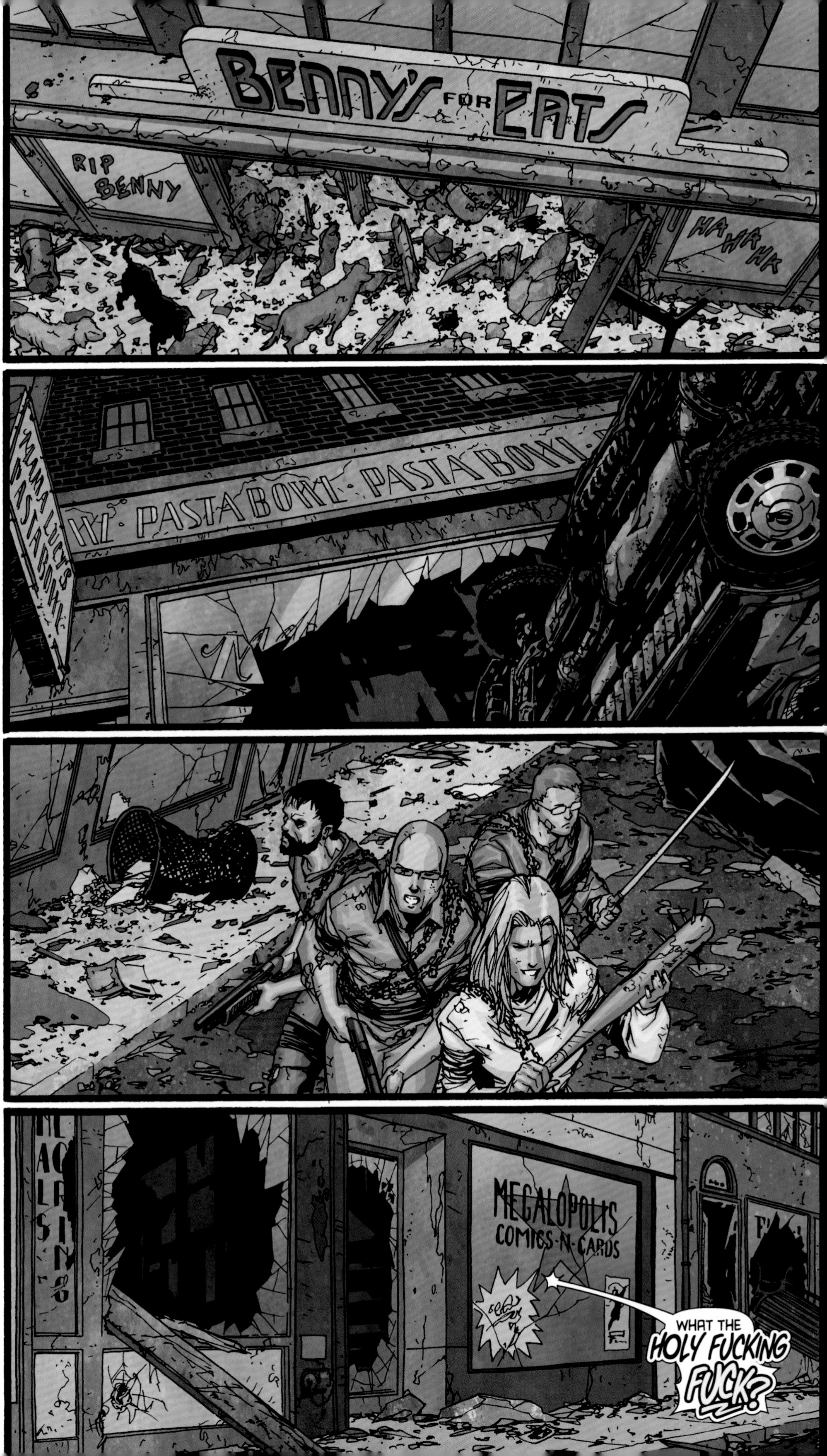
BENNY'S FOR EATS
RIP BENNY
HA HA HA HK
MAMA LUCY'S PASTA BOWL
PASTA BOWL · PASTA BOWL
MEGALOPOLIS
COMICS-N-CARDS
WHAT THE
HOLY FUCKING
FUCK?

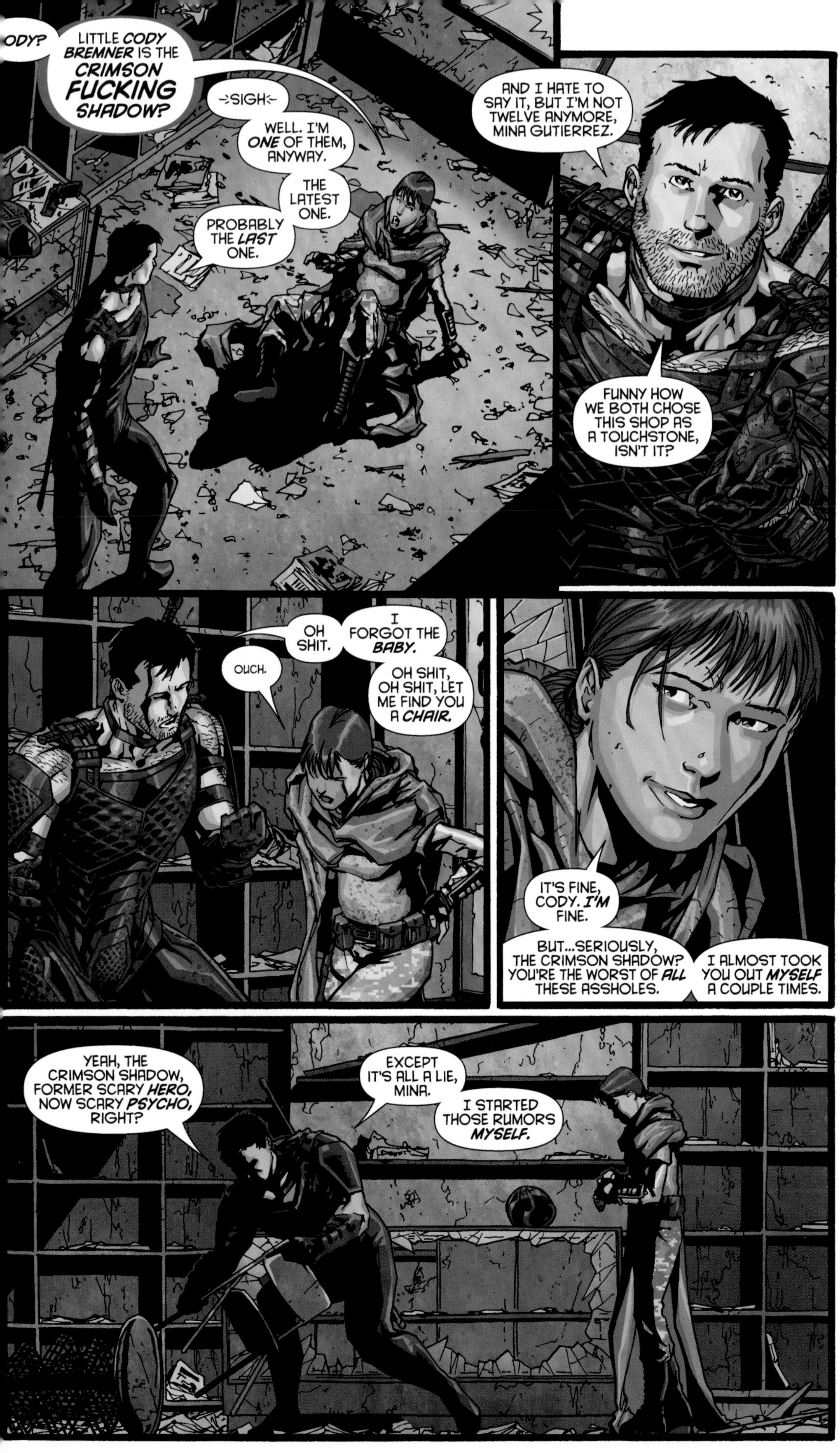
ODY?
LITTLE CODY BREMNER IS THE CRIMSON FUCKING SHADOW?
-SIGH-
WELL. I'M ONE OF THEM, ANYWAY.
THE LATEST ONE.
PROBABLY THE LAST ONE.
AND I HATE TO SAY IT, BUT I'M NOT TWELVE ANYMORE, MINA GUTIERREZ.
FUNNY HOW WE BOTH CHOSE THIS SHOP AS A TOUCHSTONE, ISN'T IT?
OH SHIT.
I FORGOT THE BABY.
OUCH.
OH SHIT, OH SHIT, LET ME FIND YOU A CHAIR.
IT'S FINE, CODY. I'M FINE.
BUT...SERIOUSLY, THE CRIMSON SHADOW? YOU'RE THE WORST OF ALL THESE ASSHOLES.
I ALMOST TOOK YOU OUT MYSELF A COUPLE TIMES.
YEAH, THE CRIMSON SHADOW, FORMER SCARY HERO, NOW SCARY PSYCHO, RIGHT?
EXCEPT IT'S ALL A LIE, MINA.
I STARTED THOSE RUMORS MYSELF.

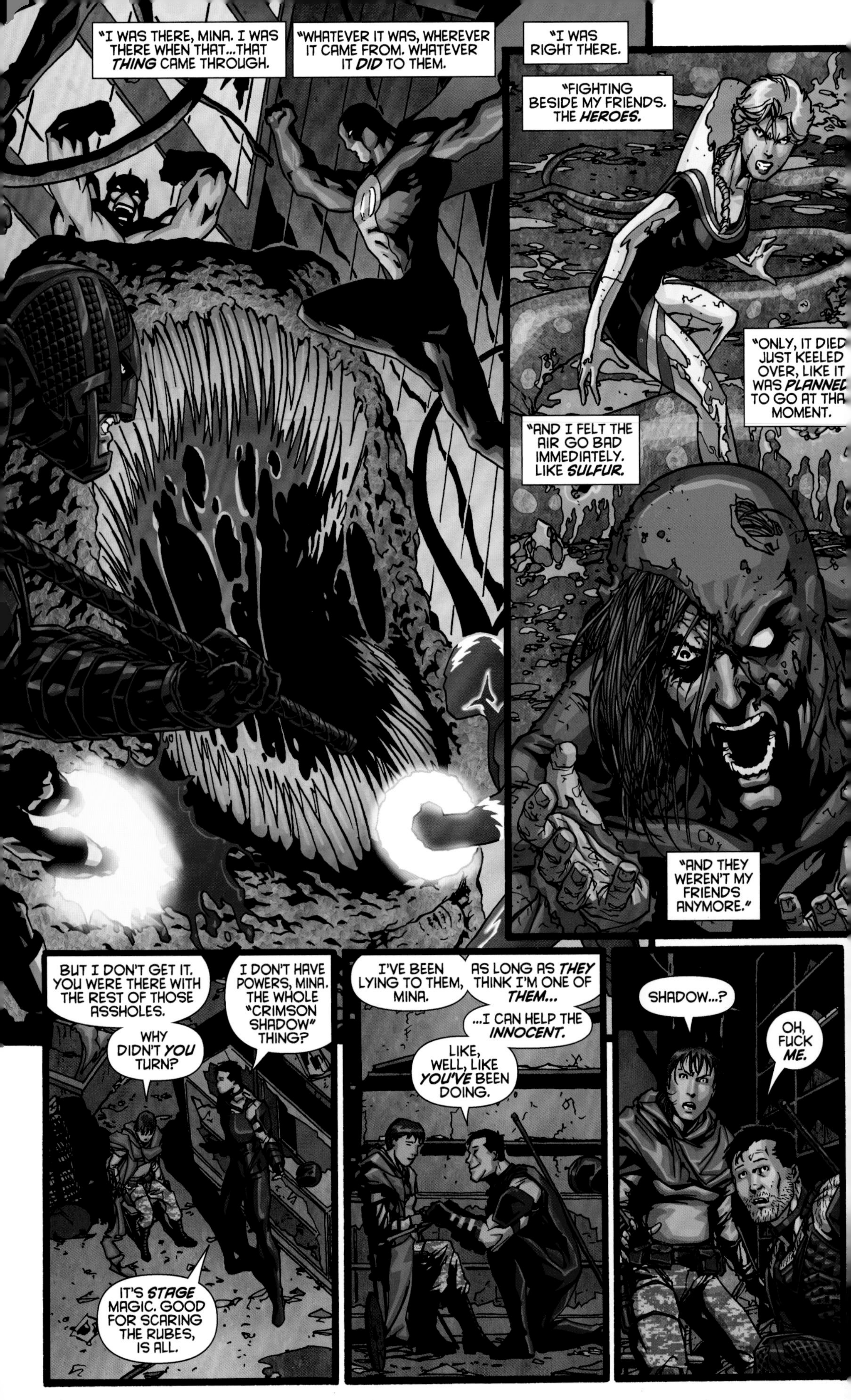
"I WAS THERE, MINA. I WAS THERE WHEN THAT...THAT THING CAME THROUGH.
"WHATEVER IT WAS, WHEREVER IT CAME FROM. WHATEVER IT DID TO THEM.
"I WAS RIGHT THERE.
"FIGHTING BESIDE MY FRIENDS. THE HEROES.
"AND I FELT THE AIR GO BAD IMMEDIATELY. LIKE SULFUR.
"ONLY, IT DIED JUST KEELED OVER, LIKE IT WAS PLANNED TO GO AT THA MOMENT.
"AND THEY WEREN'T MY FRIENDS ANYMORE."
BUT I DON'T GET IT. YOU WERE THERE WITH THE REST OF THOSE ASSHOLES.
WHY DIDN'T YOU TURN?
I DON'T HAVE POWERS, MINA. THE WHOLE "CRIMSON SHADOW" THING?
IT'S STAGE MAGIC. GOOD FOR SCARING THE RUBES, IS ALL.
I'VE BEEN LYING TO THEM, MINA.
AS LONG AS THEY THINK I'M ONE OF THEM...
...I CAN HELP THE INNOCENT.
LIKE, WELL, LIKE YOU'VE BEEN DOING.
SHADOW...?
OH, FUCK ME.

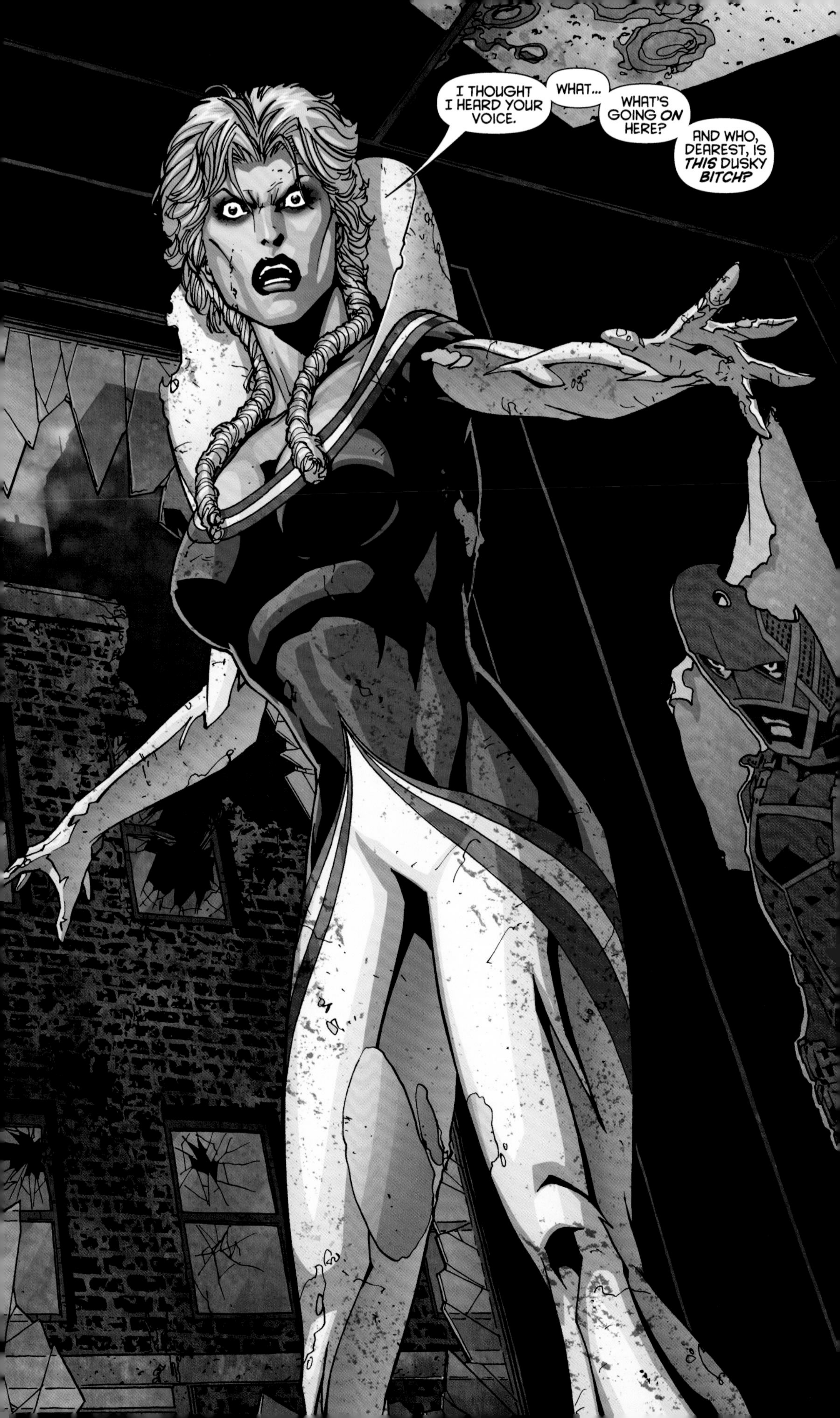
I THOUGHT I HEARD YOUR VOICE.
WHAT...
WHAT'S GOING ON HERE?
AND WHO, DEAREST, IS THIS DUSKY BITCH?

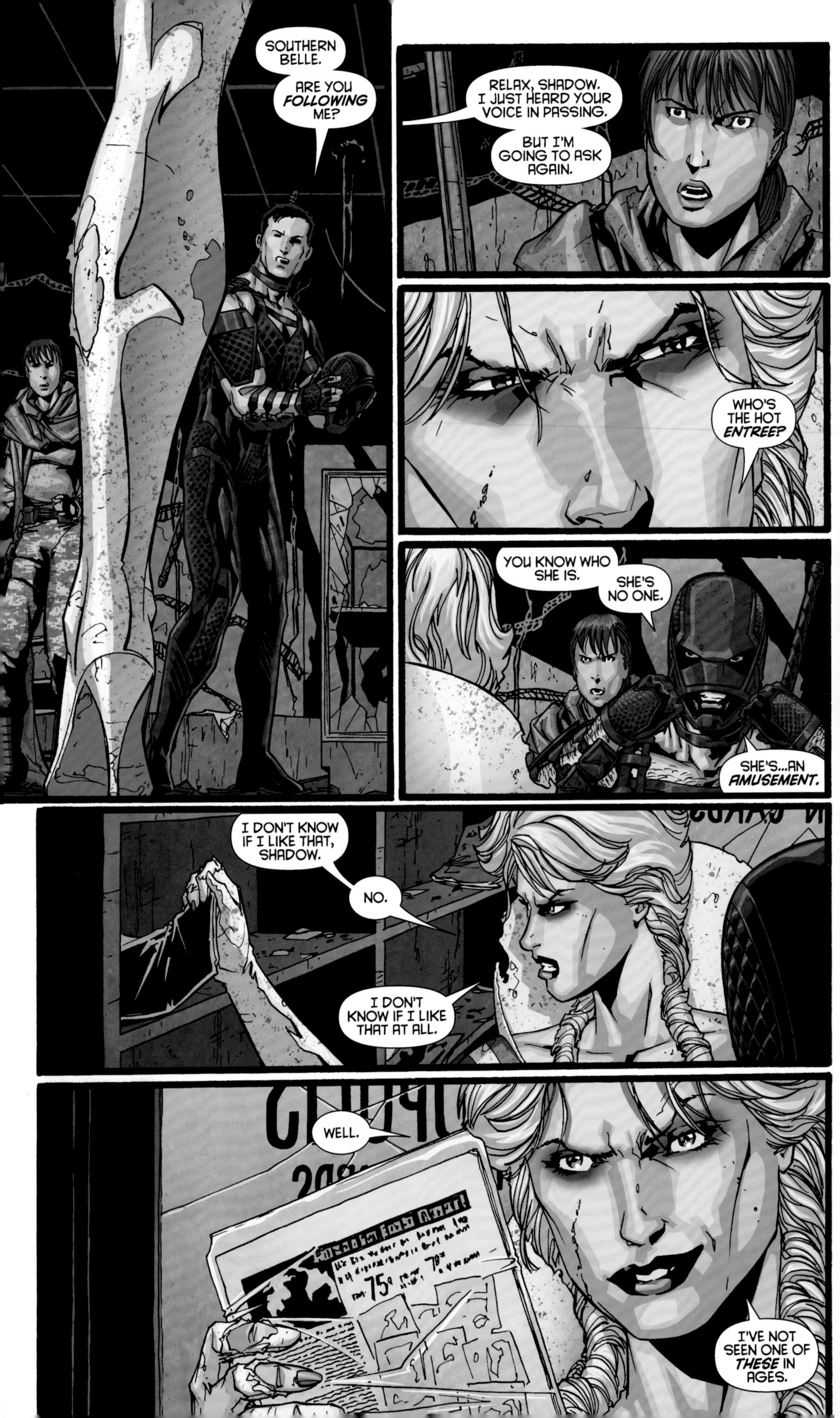
SOUTHERN BELLE.
ARE YOU *FOLLOWING* ME?
RELAX, SHADOW. I JUST HEARD YOUR VOICE IN PASSING.
BUT I'M GOING TO ASK AGAIN.
WHO'S THE HOT *ENTREE?*
YOU KNOW WHO SHE IS.
SHE'S NO ONE.
SHE'S...AN *AMUSEMENT.*
I DON'T KNOW IF I LIKE THAT, SHADOW.
NO.
I DON'T KNOW IF I LIKE THAT AT ALL.
WELL.
I'VE NOT SEEN ONE OF *THESE* IN AGES.

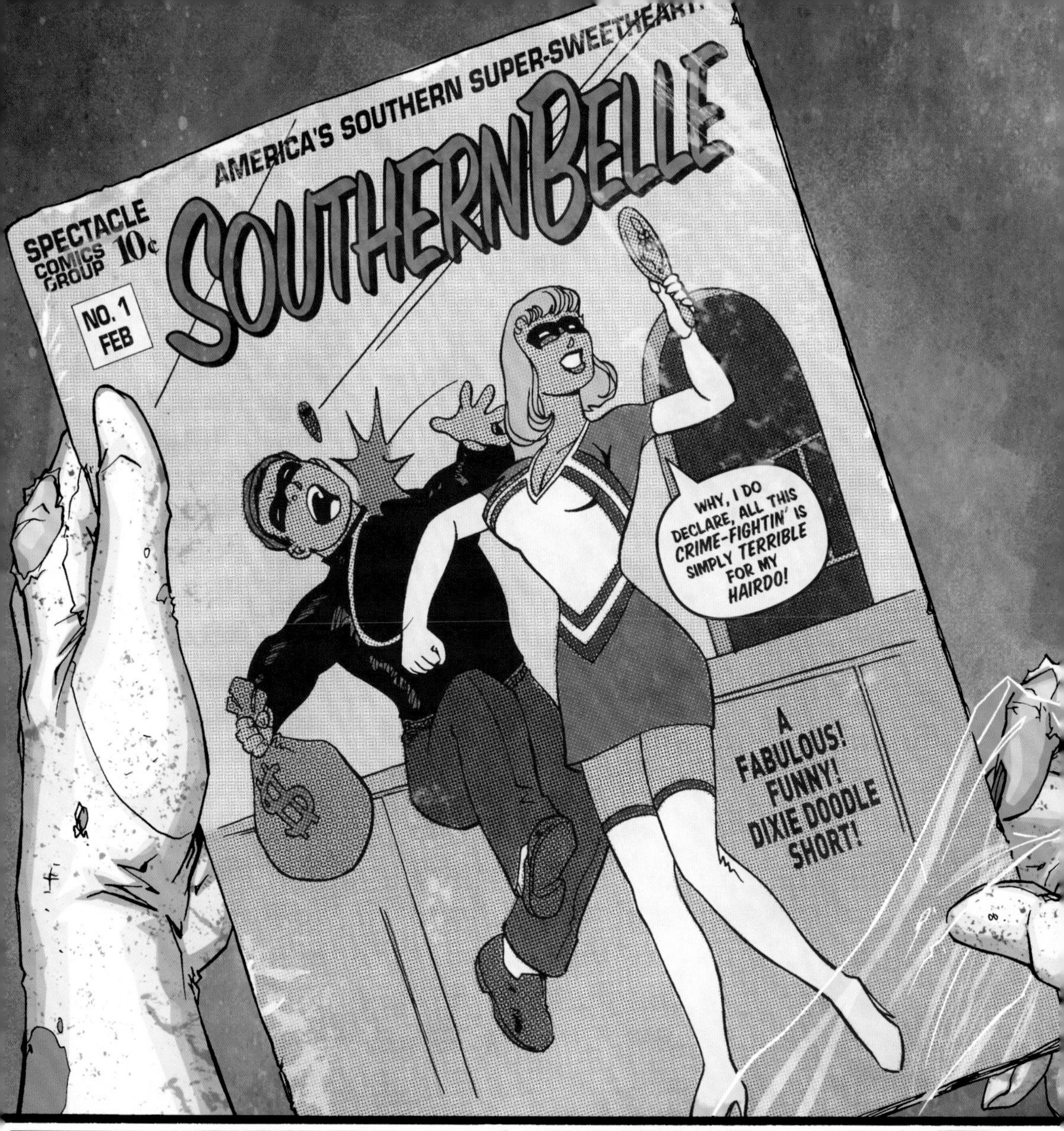
AMERICA'S SOUTHERN SUPER-SWEETHEART!
SOUTHERN BELLE
SPECTACLE COMICS GROUP 10¢
NO. 1 FEB
WHY, I DO DECLARE, ALL THIS CRIME-FIGHTIN' IS SIMPLY TERRIBLE FOR MY HAIRDO!
A FABULOUS! FUNNY! DIXIE DOODLE SHORT!

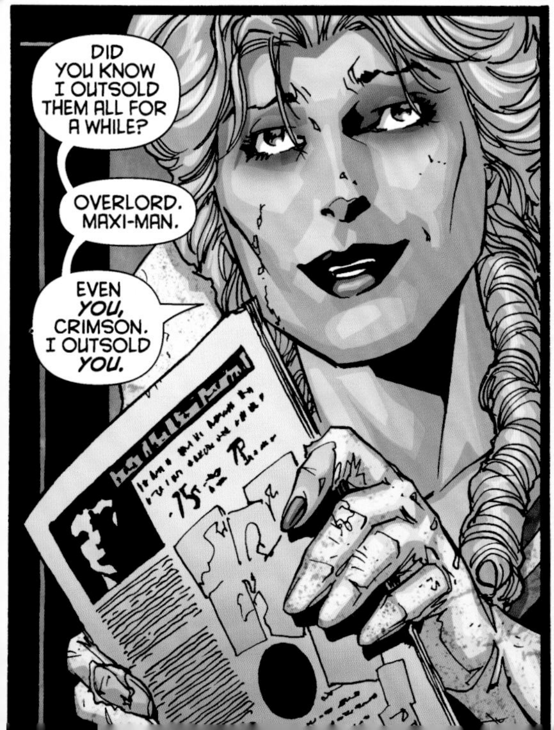
DID YOU KNOW I OUTSOLD THEM ALL FOR A WHILE?
OVERLORD. MAXI-MAN.
EVEN *YOU*, CRIMSON. I OUTSOLD *YOU*.

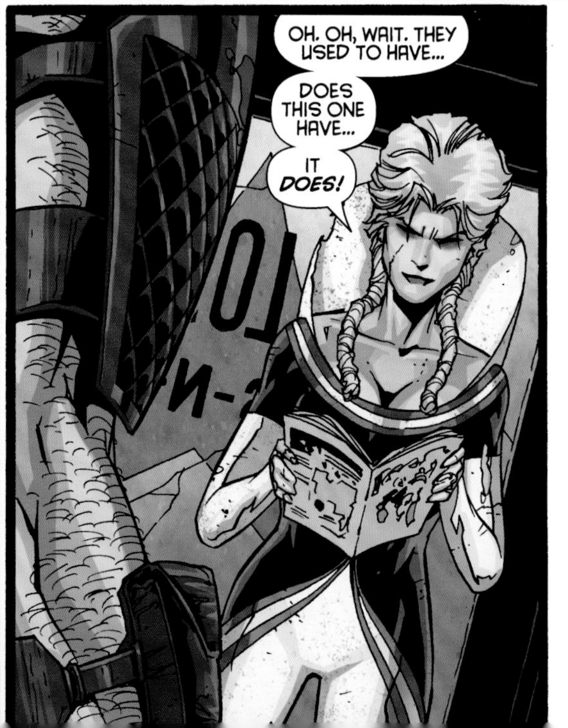
OH. OH, WAIT. THEY USED TO HAVE...
DOES THIS ONE HAVE...
IT *DOES!*

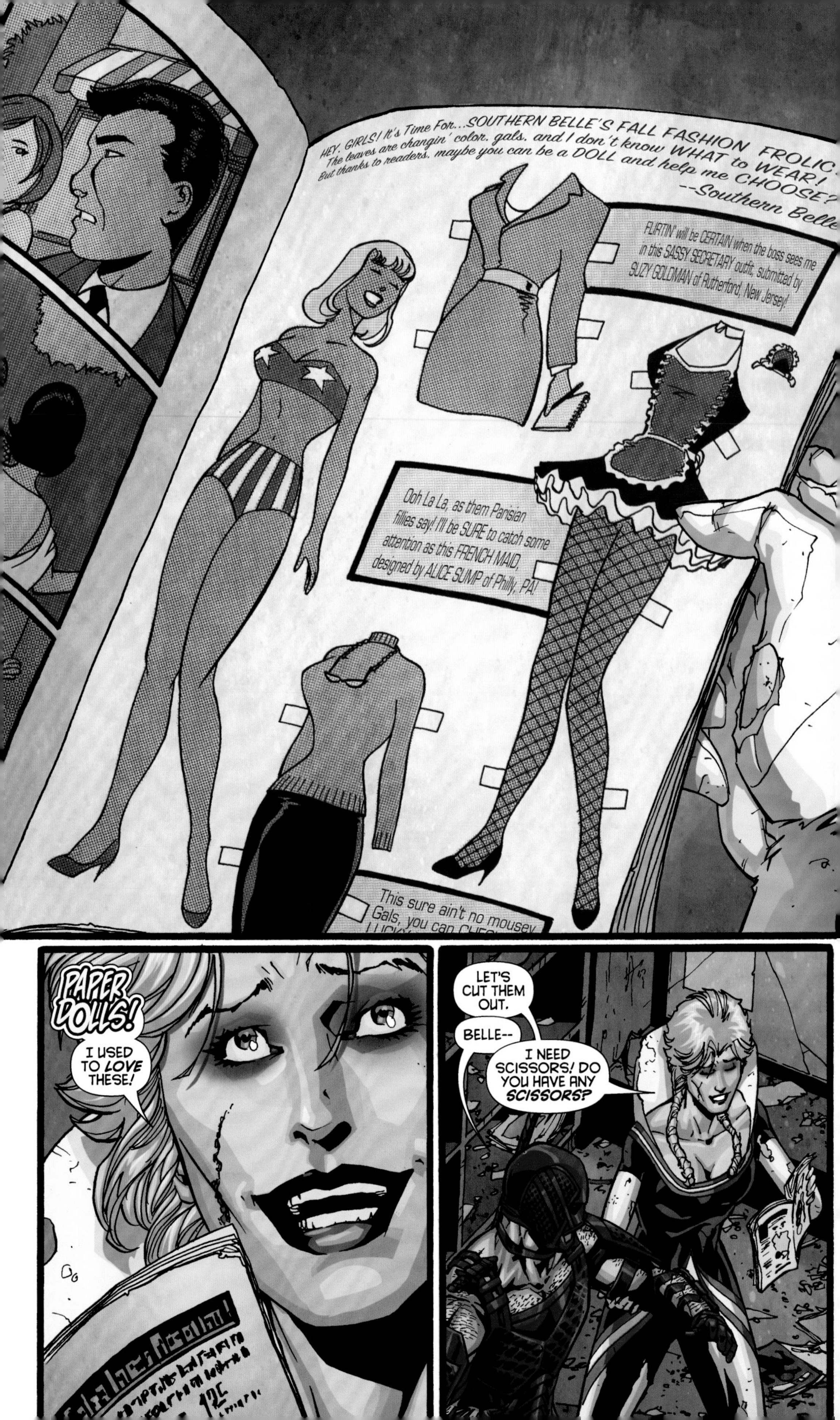

HEY, GIRLS! It's Time For...SOUTHERN BELLE'S FALL FASHION FROLIC!
The leaves are changin' color, gals, and I don't know WHAT to WEAR!
But thanks to readers, maybe you can be a DOLL and help me CHOOSE?
--Southern Belle
FLIRTIN' will be CERTAIN when the boss sees me in this SASSY SECRETARY outfit, submitted by SUZY GOLDMAN of Rutherford, New Jersey!
Ooh La La, as them Parisian fillies say! I'll be SURE to catch some attention as this FRENCH MAID, designed by ALICE SUMP of Philly, PA!
This sure ain't no mousey
Gals, you can
PAPER DOLLS!
I USED TO LOVE THESE!
LET'S CUT THEM OUT.
BELLE--
I NEED SCISSORS! DO YOU HAVE ANY SCISSORS?

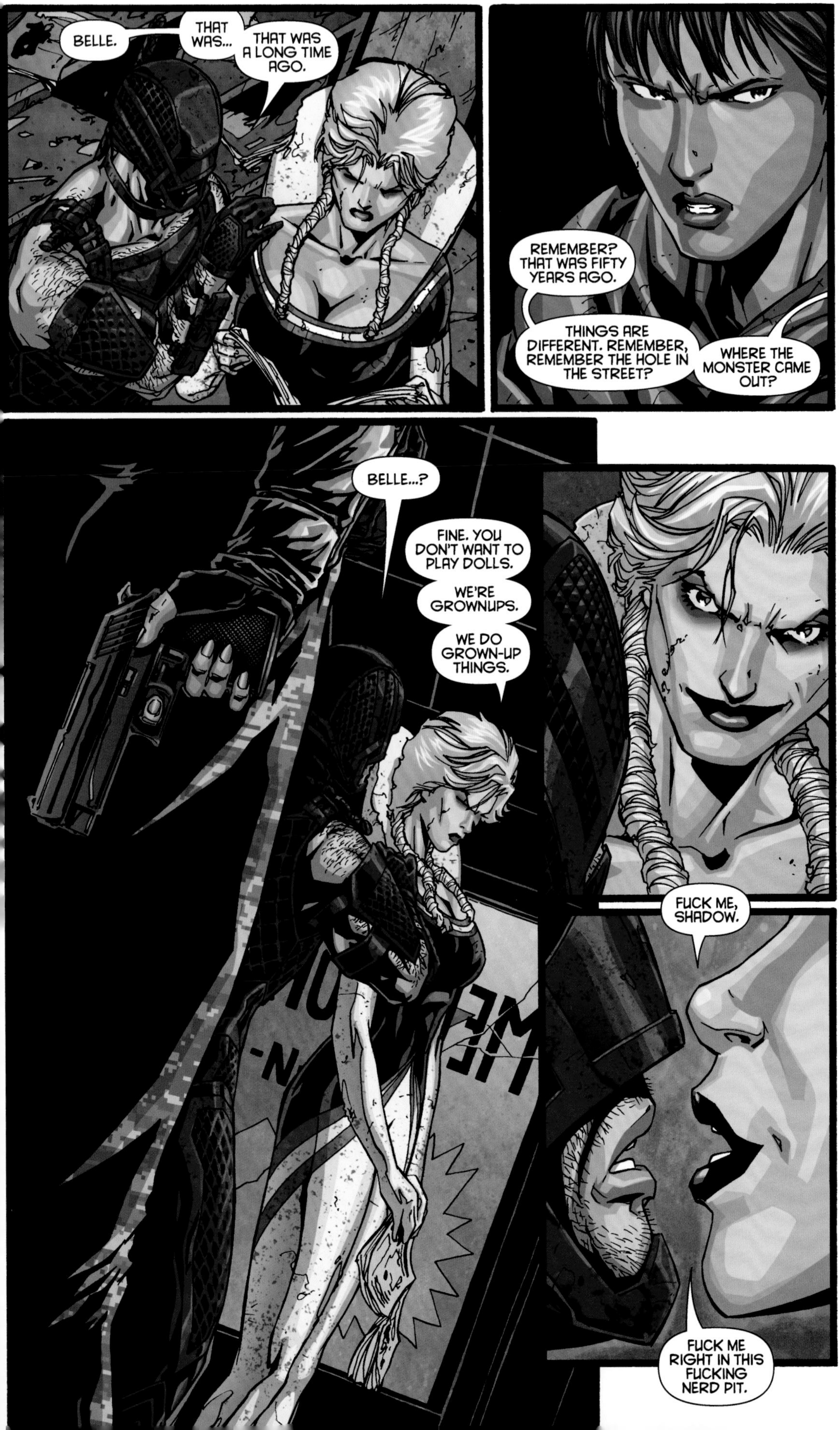
BELLE.
THAT WAS...
THAT WAS A LONG TIME AGO.
REMEMBER? THAT WAS FIFTY YEARS AGO.
THINGS ARE DIFFERENT. REMEMBER, REMEMBER THE HOLE IN THE STREET?
WHERE THE MONSTER CAME OUT?
BELLE...?
FINE. YOU DON'T WANT TO PLAY DOLLS.
WE'RE GROWNUPS.
WE DO GROWN-UP THINGS.
FUCK ME, SHADOW.
FUCK ME RIGHT IN THIS FUCKING NERD PIT.

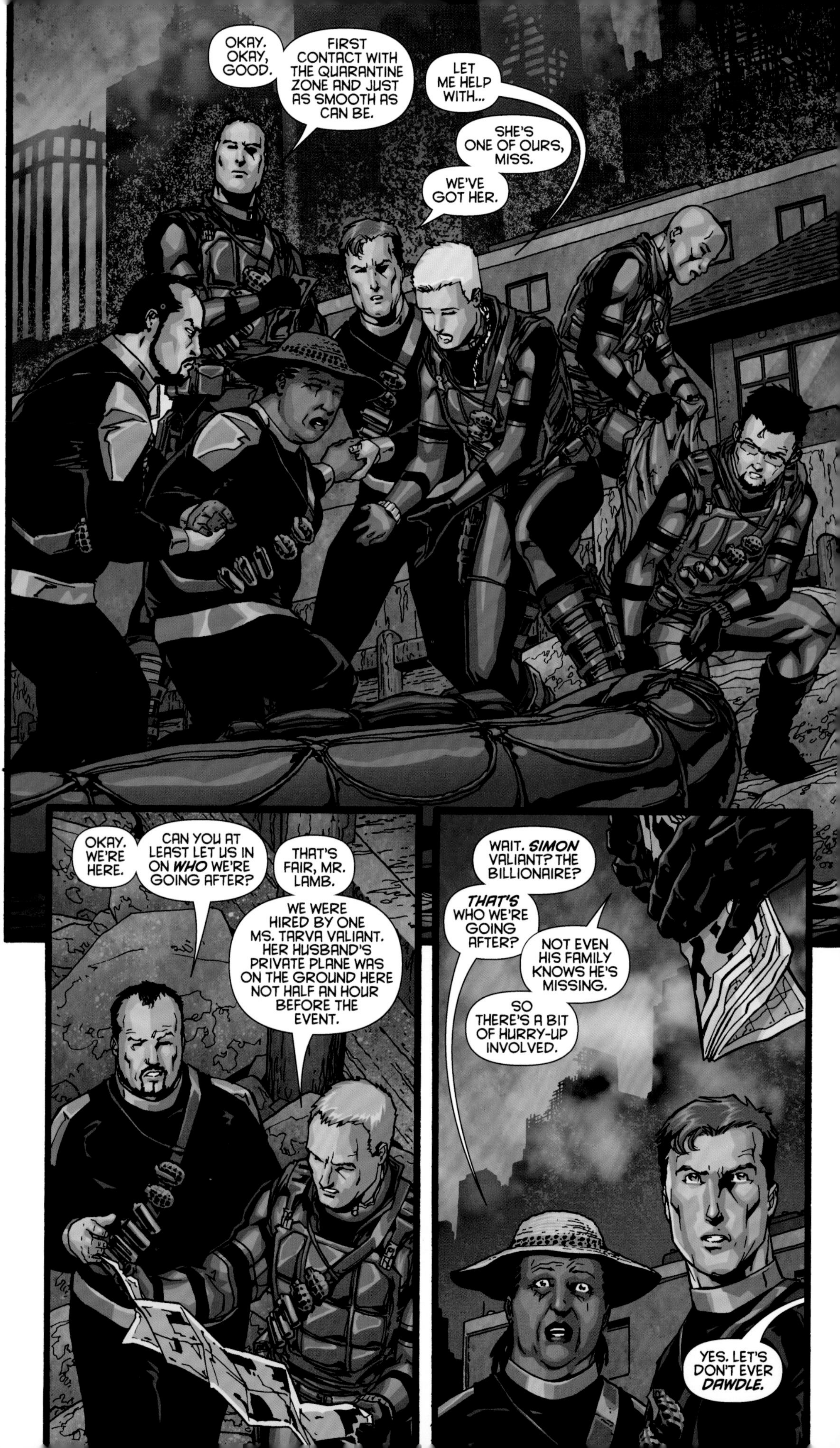
OKAY. OKAY, GOOD.
FIRST CONTACT WITH THE QUARANTINE ZONE AND JUST AS SMOOTH AS CAN BE.
LET ME HELP WITH...
SHE'S ONE OF OURS, MISS.
WE'VE GOT HER.
OKAY. WE'RE HERE.
CAN YOU AT LEAST LET US IN ON WHO WE'RE GOING AFTER?
THAT'S FAIR, MR. LAMB.
WE WERE HIRED BY ONE MS. TARVA VALIANT. HER HUSBAND'S PRIVATE PLANE WAS ON THE GROUND HERE NOT HALF AN HOUR BEFORE THE EVENT.
WAIT. SIMON VALIANT? THE BILLIONAIRE?
THAT'S WHO WE'RE GOING AFTER?
NOT EVEN HIS FAMILY KNOWS HE'S MISSING.
SO THERE'S A BIT OF HURRY-UP INVOLVED.
YES. LET'S DON'T EVER DAWDLE.

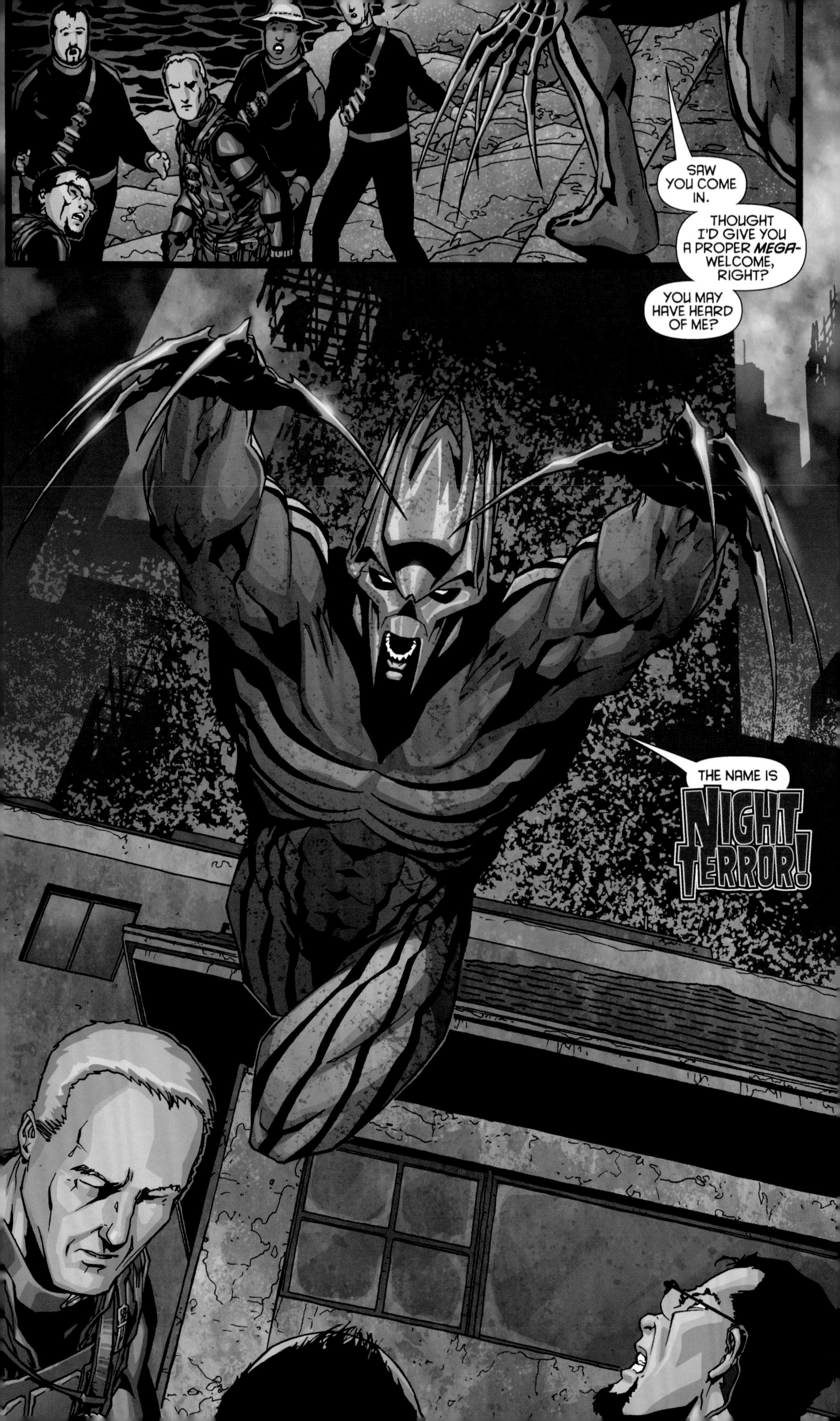

SAW YOU COME IN.
THOUGHT I'D GIVE YOU A PROPER MEGA-WELCOME, RIGHT?
YOU MAY HAVE HEARD OF ME?
THE NAME IS
NIGHT TERROR!

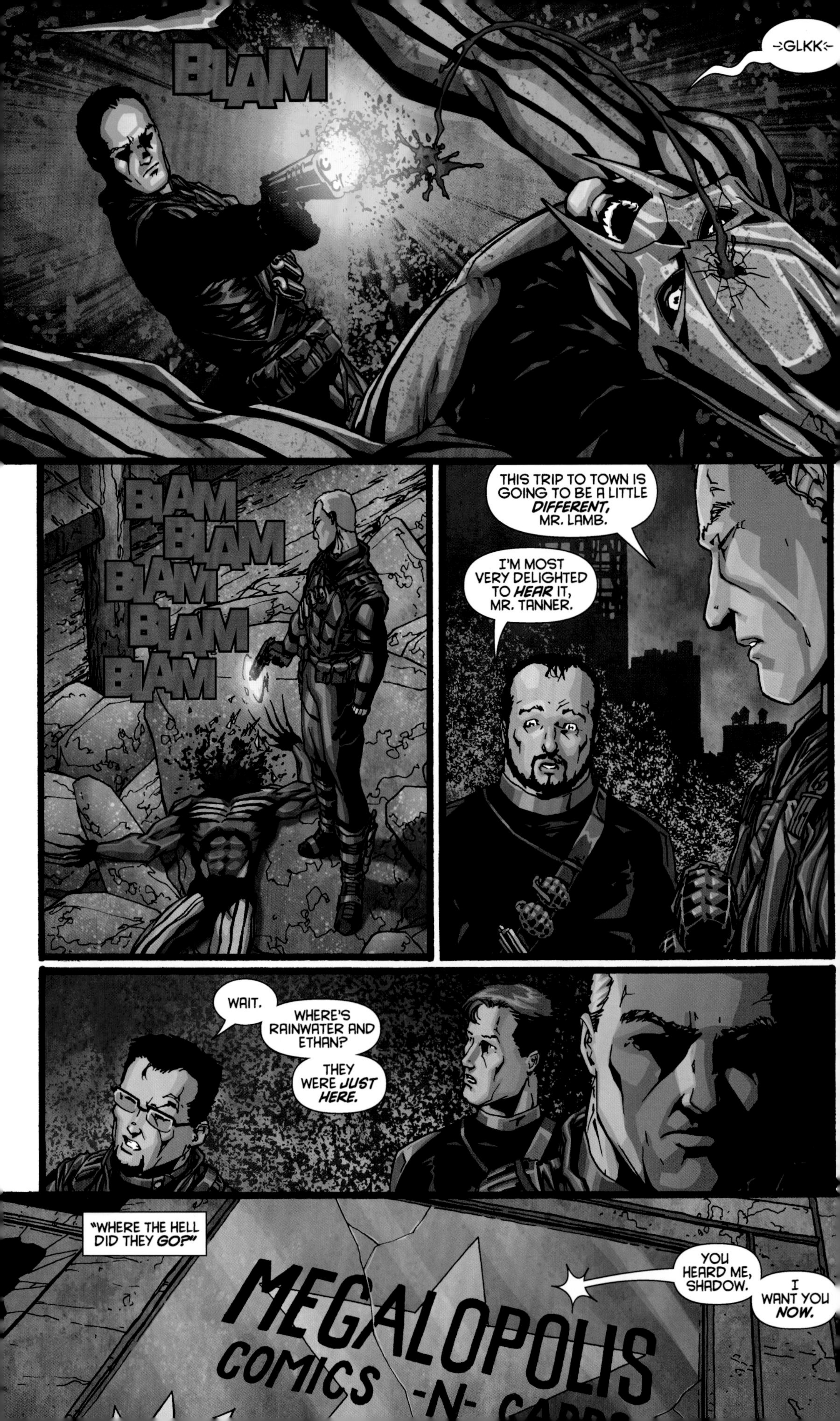

BLAM
-GLKK-
BLAM BLAM BLAM BLAM BLAM
THIS TRIP TO TOWN IS GOING TO BE A LITTLE DIFFERENT, MR. LAMB.
I'M MOST VERY DELIGHTED TO HEAR IT, MR. TANNER.
WAIT.
WHERE'S RAINWATER AND ETHAN?
THEY WERE JUST HERE.
"WHERE THE HELL DID THEY GO?"
MEGALOPOLIS COMICS -N-
YOU HEARD ME, SHADOW.
I WANT YOU NOW.

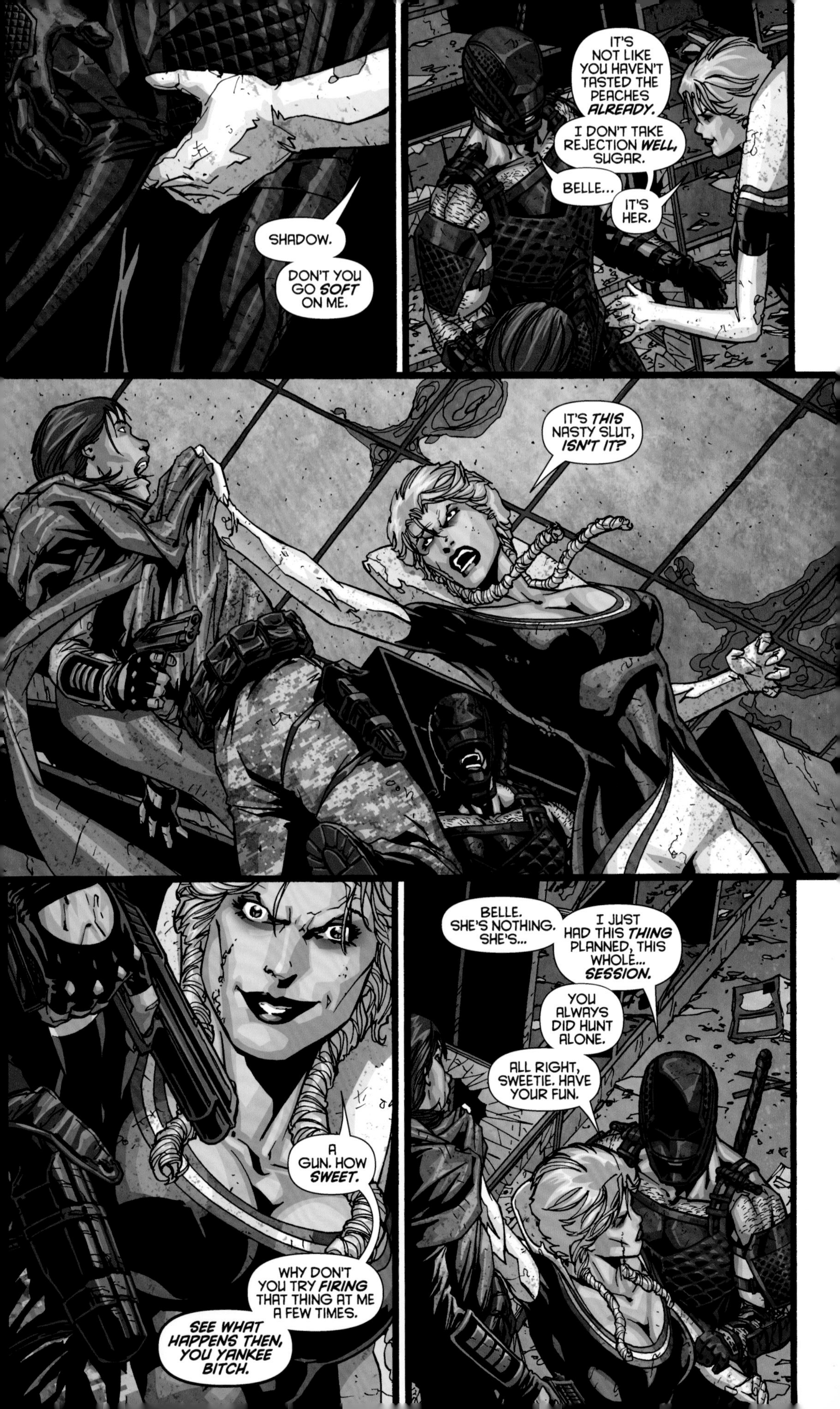
SHADOW.
DON'T YOU GO SOFT ON ME.
IT'S NOT LIKE YOU HAVEN'T TASTED THE PEACHES ALREADY.
I DON'T TAKE REJECTION WELL, SUGAR.
BELLE...
IT'S HER.
IT'S THIS NASTY SLUT, ISN'T IT?
A GUN. HOW SWEET.
WHY DON'T YOU TRY FIRING THAT THING AT ME A FEW TIMES.
SEE WHAT HAPPENS THEN, YOU YANKEE BITCH.
BELLE. SHE'S NOTHING. SHE'S...
I JUST HAD THIS THING PLANNED, THIS WHOLE... SESSION.
YOU ALWAYS DID HUNT ALONE.
ALL RIGHT, SWEETIE. HAVE YOUR FUN.

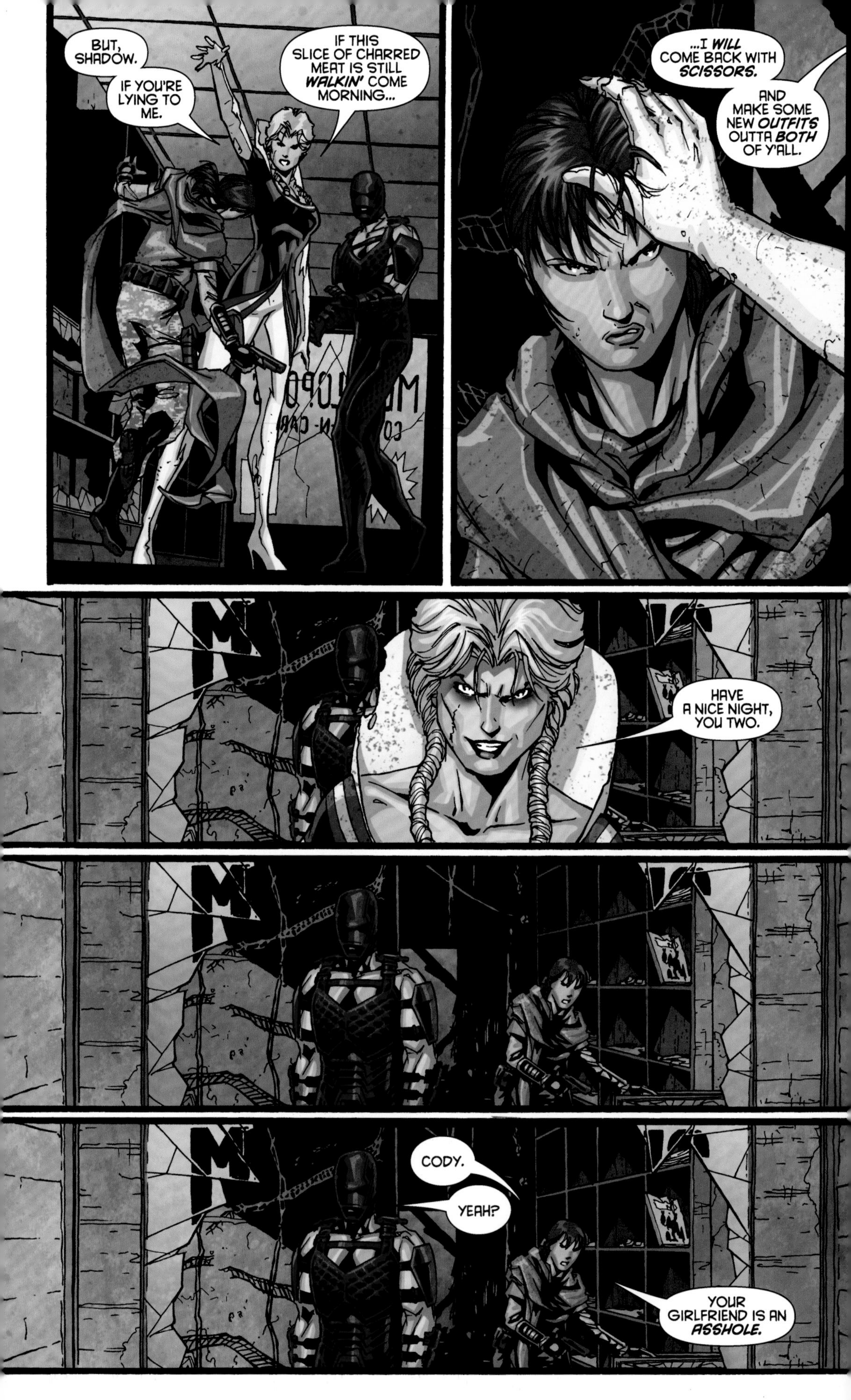
BUT, SHADOW.
IF YOU'RE LYING TO ME.
IF THIS SLICE OF CHARRED MEAT IS STILL *WALKIN'* COME MORNING...
...I *WILL* COME BACK WITH *SCISSORS.*
AND MAKE SOME NEW *OUTFITS* OUTTA *BOTH* OF Y'ALL.
HAVE A NICE NIGHT, YOU TWO.
CODY.
YEAH?
YOUR GIRLFRIEND IS AN *ASSHOLE.*

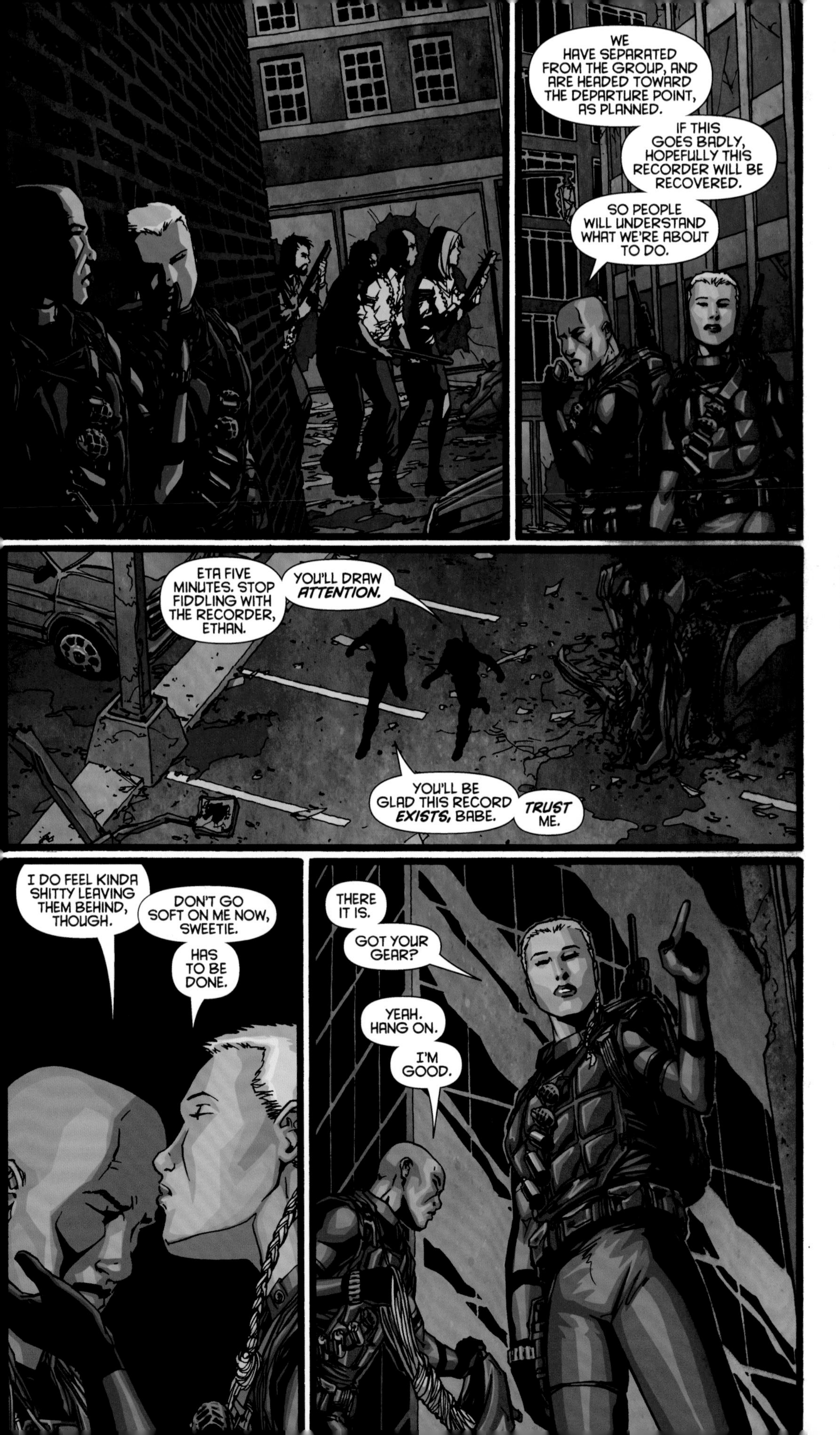
WE HAVE SEPARATED FROM THE GROUP, AND ARE HEADED TOWARD THE DEPARTURE POINT, AS PLANNED.
IF THIS GOES BADLY, HOPEFULLY THIS RECORDER WILL BE RECOVERED.
SO PEOPLE WILL UNDERSTAND WHAT WE'RE ABOUT TO DO.
ETA FIVE MINUTES. STOP FIDDLING WITH THE RECORDER, ETHAN.
YOU'LL DRAW *ATTENTION.*
YOU'LL BE GLAD THIS RECORD *EXISTS,* BABE.
TRUST ME.
I DO FEEL KINDA SHITTY LEAVING THEM BEHIND, THOUGH.
DON'T GO SOFT ON ME NOW, SWEETIE.
HAS TO BE DONE.
THERE IT IS.
GOT YOUR GEAR?
YEAH. HANG ON.
I'M GOOD.

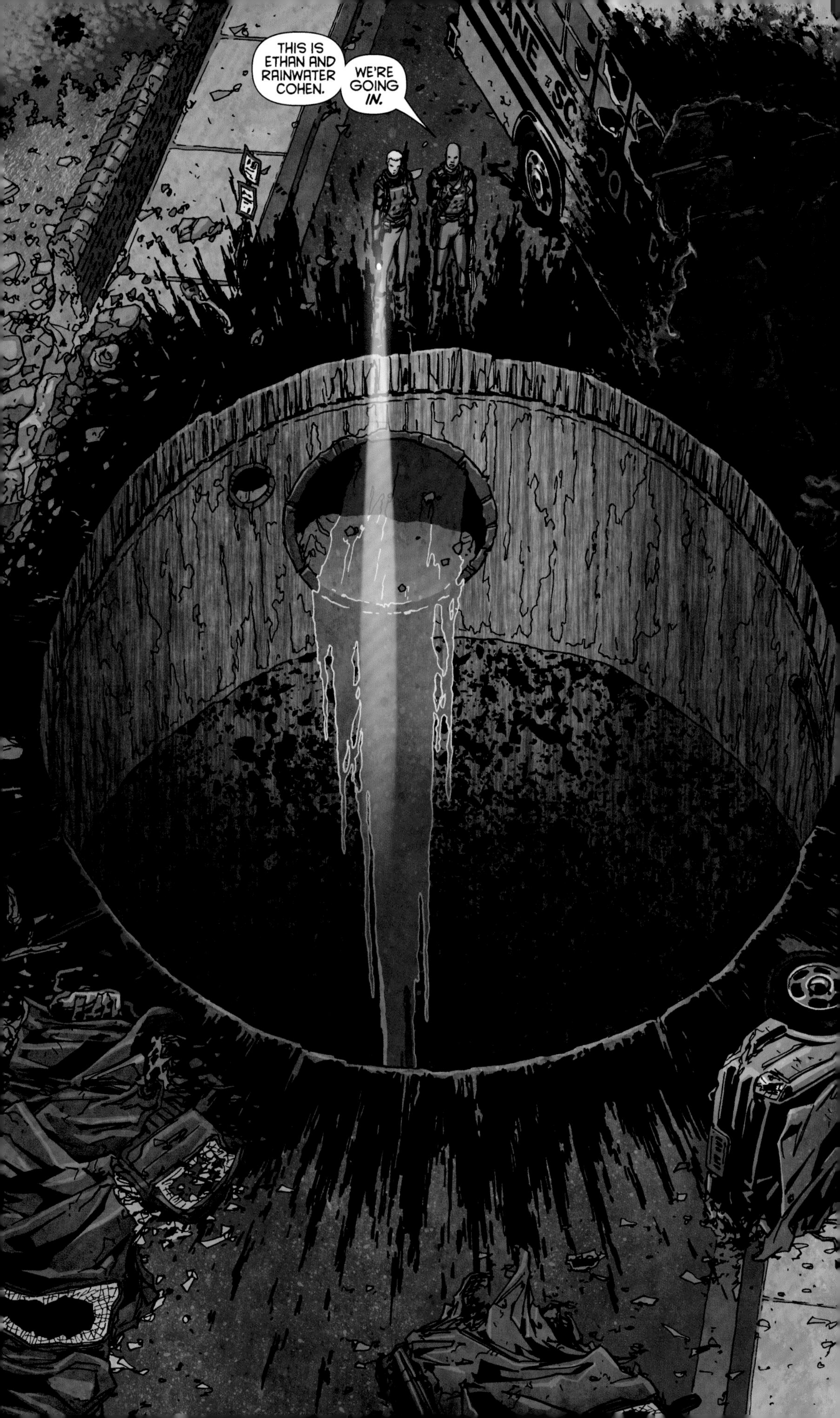
THIS IS ETHAN AND RAINWATER COHEN.
WE'RE GOING *IN.*

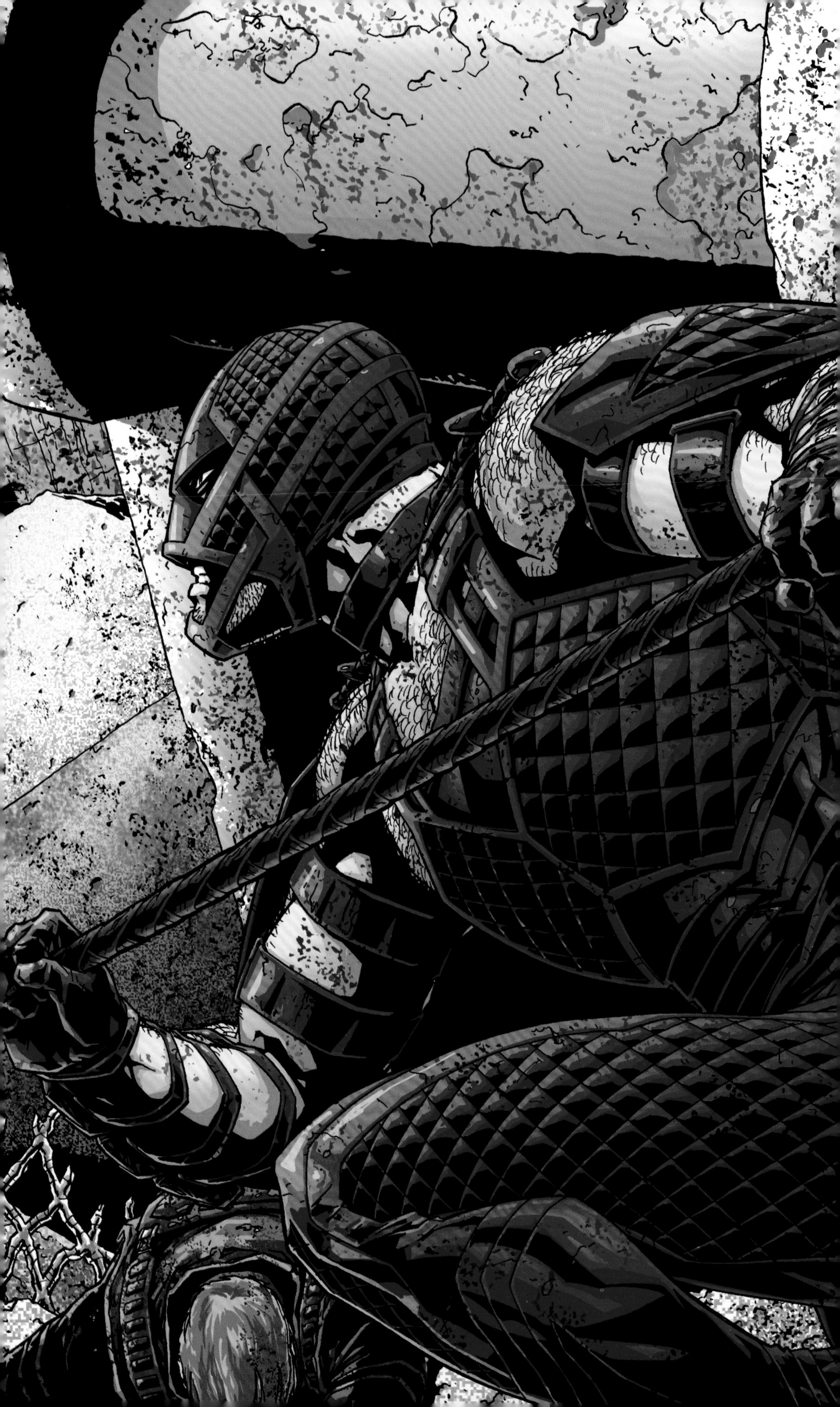

RIDE THE MEGA-RAIL

ALL ABOARD! Rise above the city streets on the Megalopolis elevated railway system. Avoid all the traffic, and ride in luxury and comfort in one of our state-of-the-art trains. Recline, stretch out and relax, and let us do the driving. Eat. Read a good book. Listen to music. Why not take a nap even? But don't forget about the spectacular views of the city skyline outside the window. And who knows, you might even catch a glimpse of one of the city's famous **superheroes!**

Monday–Sun

Northbound Corridor												
Star Ferry Port	7:35a	8:02a	8:25a	9:10a	9:42a	10:26		11:15	11:40	12:14p	26p	12:5
Grande Bay Port	7:57	8:34	8:47	9:59	10:45	11:15	11:46	11:57	58	12:4	1:15
F St/Birnbaum Pl W	8:15	8:52	9:05	10:35	11:03	11:34	12:02p	12:33	1:00	1:33
K St	8:35	9:01	9:25	10:56	11:07	11:32	12:03p	12:3	1:01	1:34
Central Sta.	9:01	9:25	9:47	11:07	11:32	12:17		1:5
Megalopolis Pk	9:17	9:41	10:01	11:17	11:47	12:25	12:5	
James St	9:25	9:52	10:32	11:25	11:58	12:42	1:10	
U St/Stank Ln	9:42	10:05	10:56	11:37	12:11p	12:57	1	2:3
Patton Circle U	9:57	10:15	11:08	11:49	12:26	1:2	2:04	2:3
Heroes Plaza A	10:12	10:37	11:7	12:06p	12:31	1:05	1:3	2:36	2:57
Y St/Lost Point	10:35	11:01	12:11p	12:50	1:29	1:57	
Razor's Pt/Stadium	10:...	11:23	12:11p	12:50		

W Stops weekdays only
A Stops at MEGASTAR Int'l Airport monorail connection
U Stops the third Wednesday of months with a "U" in them

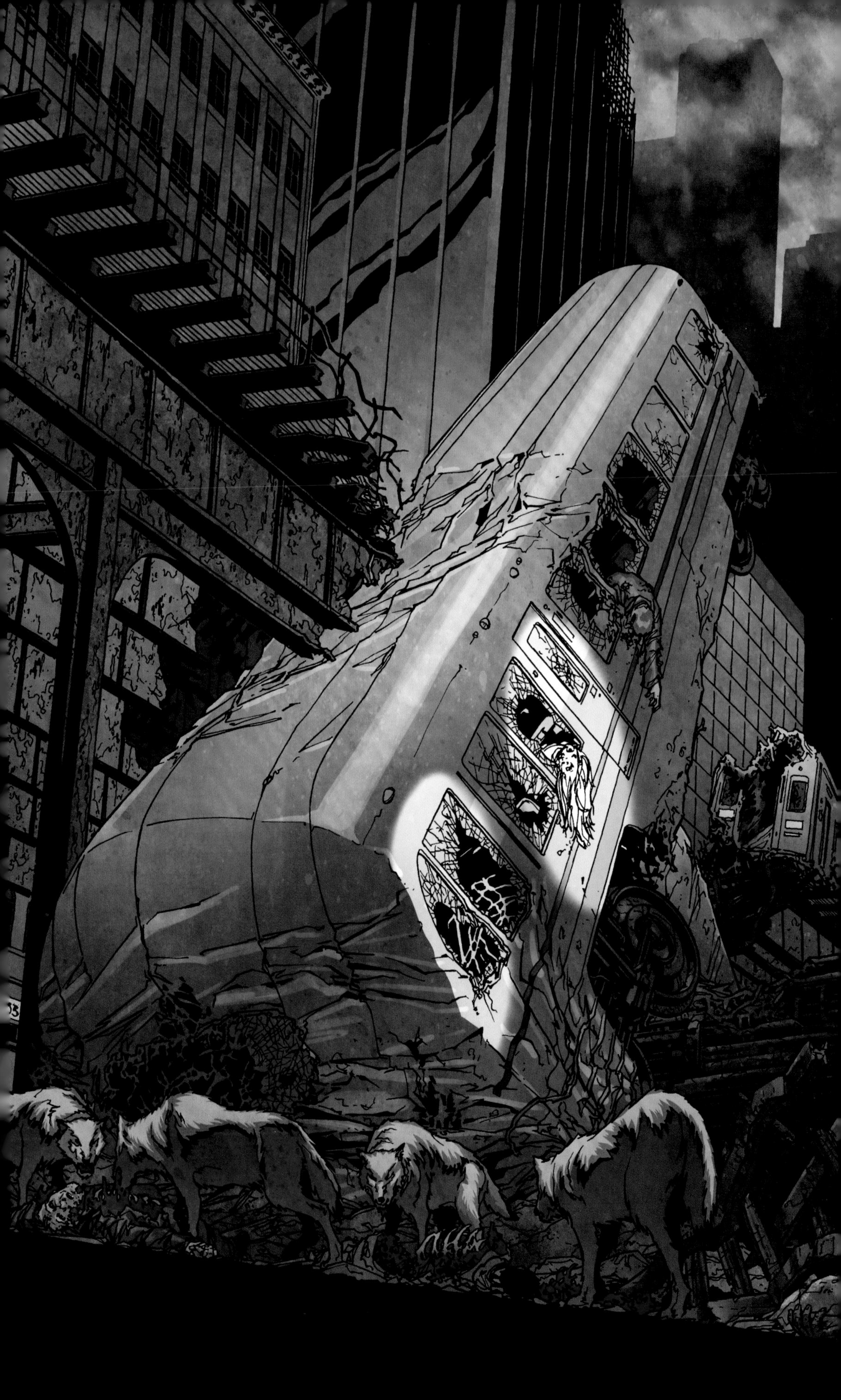

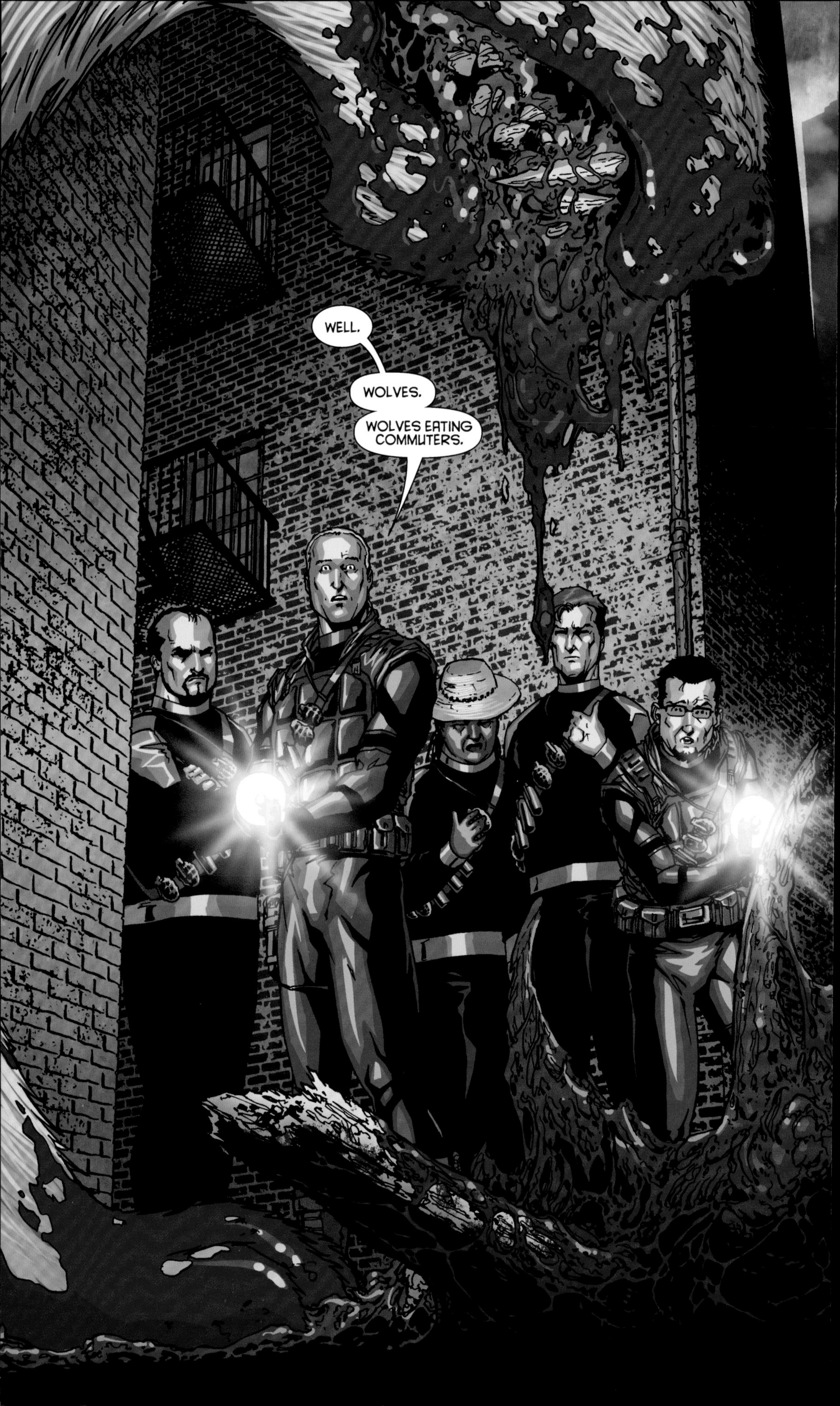
WELL.
WOLVES.
WOLVES EATING COMMUTERS.

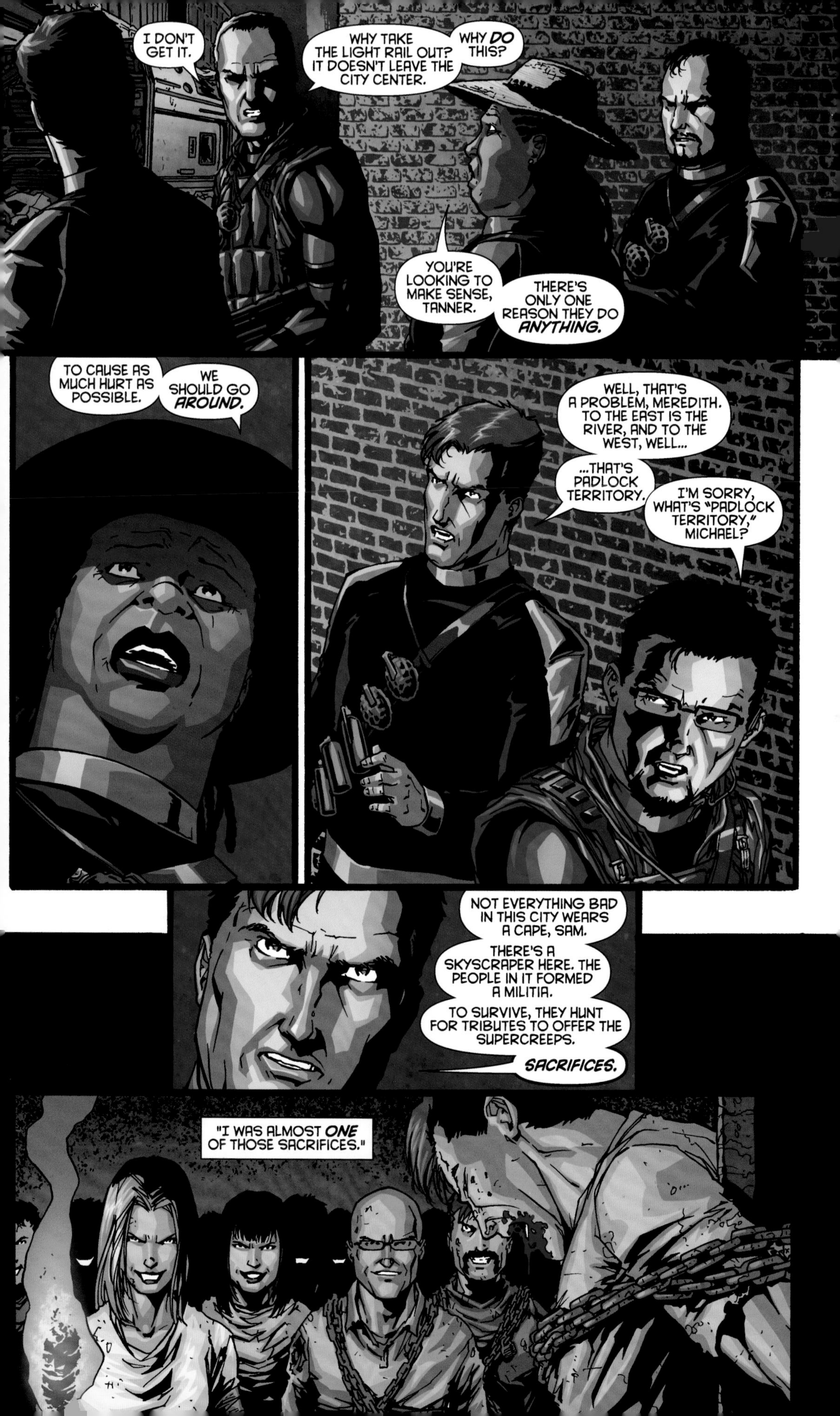
I DON'T GET IT.
WHY TAKE THE LIGHT RAIL OUT? IT DOESN'T LEAVE THE CITY CENTER.
WHY DO THIS?
YOU'RE LOOKING TO MAKE SENSE, TANNER.
THERE'S ONLY ONE REASON THEY DO ANYTHING.
TO CAUSE AS MUCH HURT AS POSSIBLE.
WE SHOULD GO AROUND.
WELL, THAT'S A PROBLEM, MEREDITH. TO THE EAST IS THE RIVER, AND TO THE WEST, WELL...
...THAT'S PADLOCK TERRITORY.
I'M SORRY, WHAT'S "PADLOCK TERRITORY," MICHAEL?
NOT EVERYTHING BAD IN THIS CITY WEARS A CAPE, SAM.
THERE'S A SKYSCRAPER HERE. THE PEOPLE IN IT FORMED A MILITIA.
TO SURVIVE, THEY HUNT FOR TRIBUTES TO OFFER THE SUPERCREEPS.
SACRIFICES.
"I WAS ALMOST ONE OF THOSE SACRIFICES."

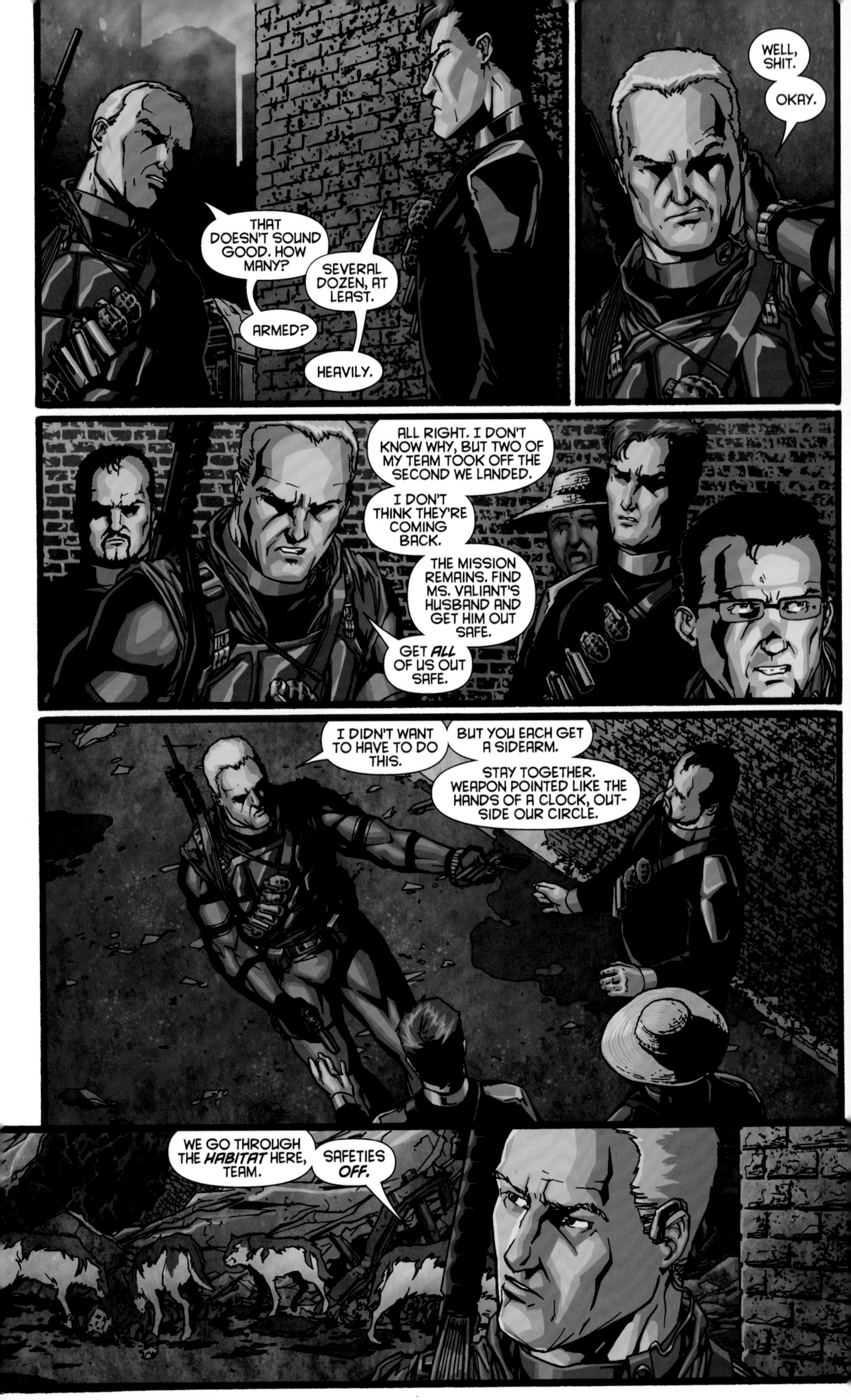
THAT DOESN'T SOUND GOOD. HOW MANY?
SEVERAL DOZEN, AT LEAST.
ARMED?
HEAVILY.
WELL, SHIT.
OKAY.
ALL RIGHT. I DON'T KNOW WHY, BUT TWO OF MY TEAM TOOK OFF THE SECOND WE LANDED.
I DON'T THINK THEY'RE COMING BACK.
THE MISSION REMAINS. FIND MS. VALIANT'S HUSBAND AND GET HIM OUT SAFE.
GET *ALL* OF US OUT SAFE.
I DIDN'T WANT TO HAVE TO DO THIS.
BUT YOU EACH GET A SIDEARM.
STAY TOGETHER. WEAPON POINTED LIKE THE HANDS OF A CLOCK, OUTSIDE OUR CIRCLE.
WE GO THROUGH THE *HABITAT* HERE, TEAM.
SAFETIES *OFF.*

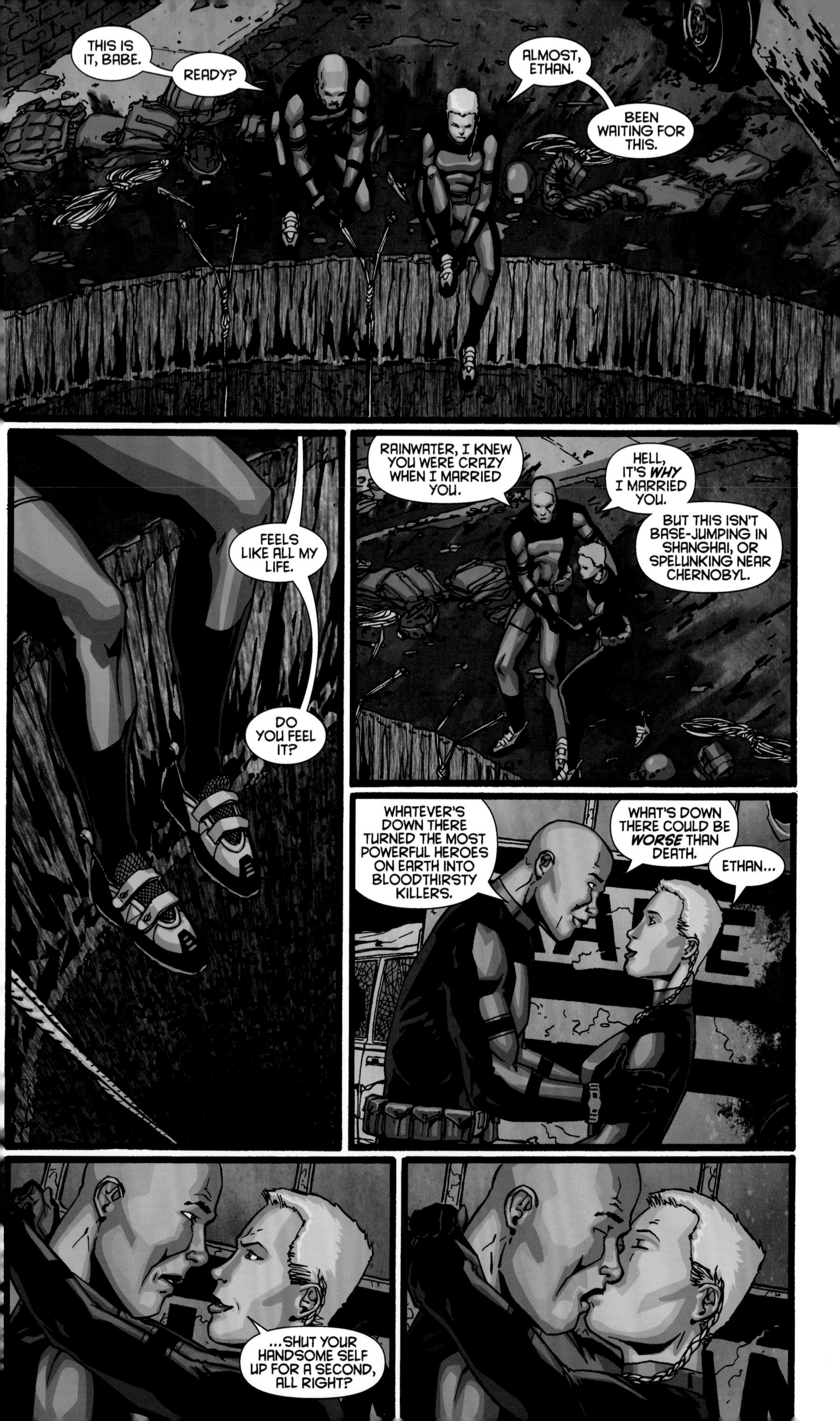
THIS IS IT, BABE.
READY?
ALMOST, ETHAN.
BEEN WAITING FOR THIS.
FEELS LIKE ALL MY LIFE.
DO YOU FEEL IT?
RAINWATER, I KNEW YOU WERE CRAZY WHEN I MARRIED YOU.
HELL, IT'S *WHY* I MARRIED YOU.
BUT THIS ISN'T BASE-JUMPING IN SHANGHAI, OR SPELUNKING NEAR CHERNOBYL.
WHATEVER'S DOWN THERE TURNED THE MOST POWERFUL HEROES ON EARTH INTO BLOODTHIRSTY KILLERS.
WHAT'S DOWN THERE COULD BE *WORSE* THAN DEATH.
ETHAN...
...SHUT YOUR HANDSOME SELF UP FOR A SECOND, ALL RIGHT?

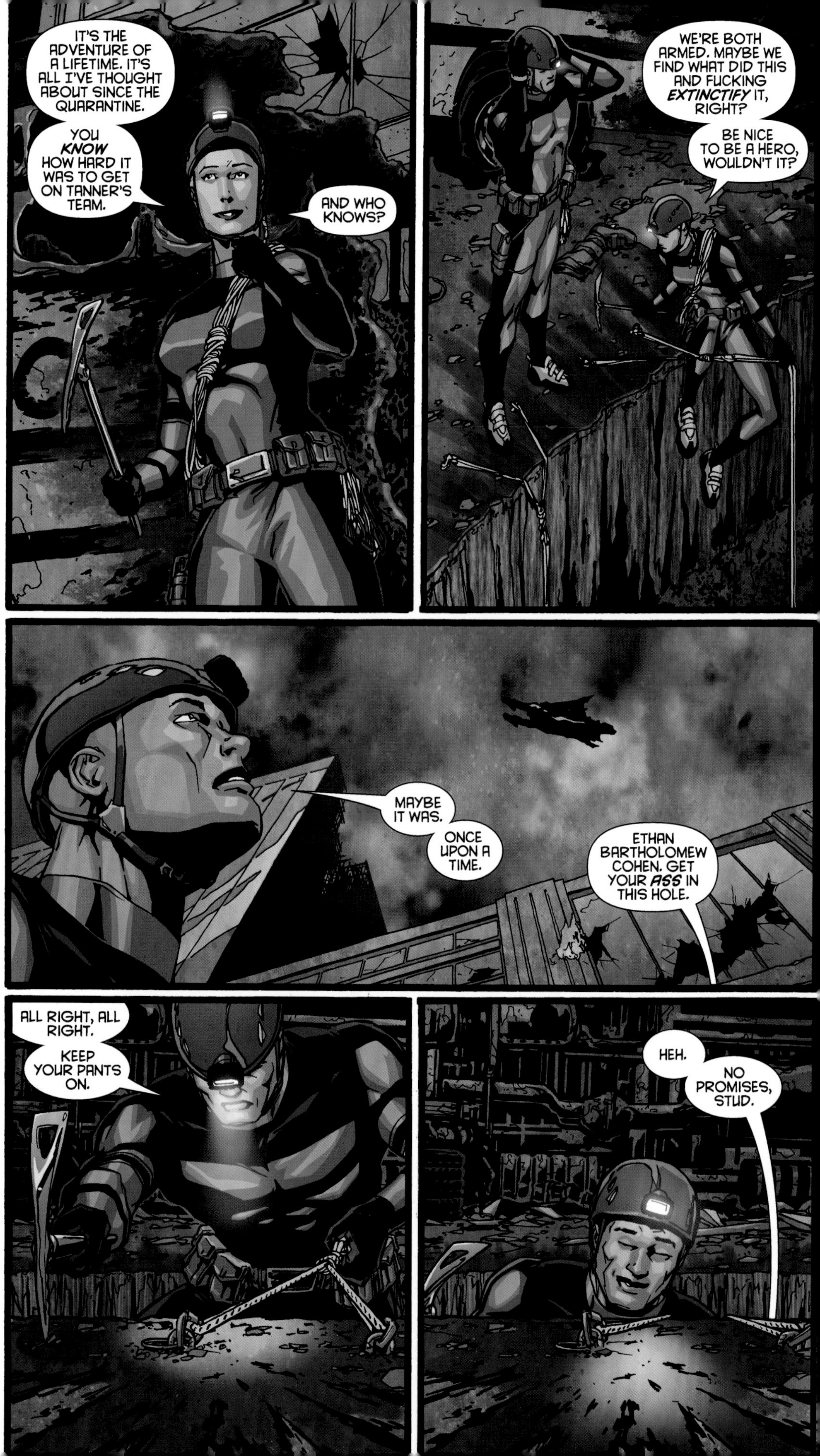
IT'S THE ADVENTURE OF A LIFETIME. IT'S ALL I'VE THOUGHT ABOUT SINCE THE QUARANTINE.
YOU *KNOW* HOW HARD IT WAS TO GET ON TANNER'S TEAM.
AND WHO KNOWS?
WE'RE BOTH ARMED. MAYBE WE FIND WHAT DID THIS AND FUCKING *EXTINCTIFY* IT, RIGHT?
BE NICE TO BE A HERO, WOULDN'T IT?
MAYBE IT WAS.
ONCE UPON A TIME.
ETHAN BARTHOLOMEW COHEN. GET YOUR *ASS* IN THIS HOLE.
ALL RIGHT, ALL RIGHT.
KEEP YOUR PANTS ON.
HEH.
NO PROMISES, STUD.

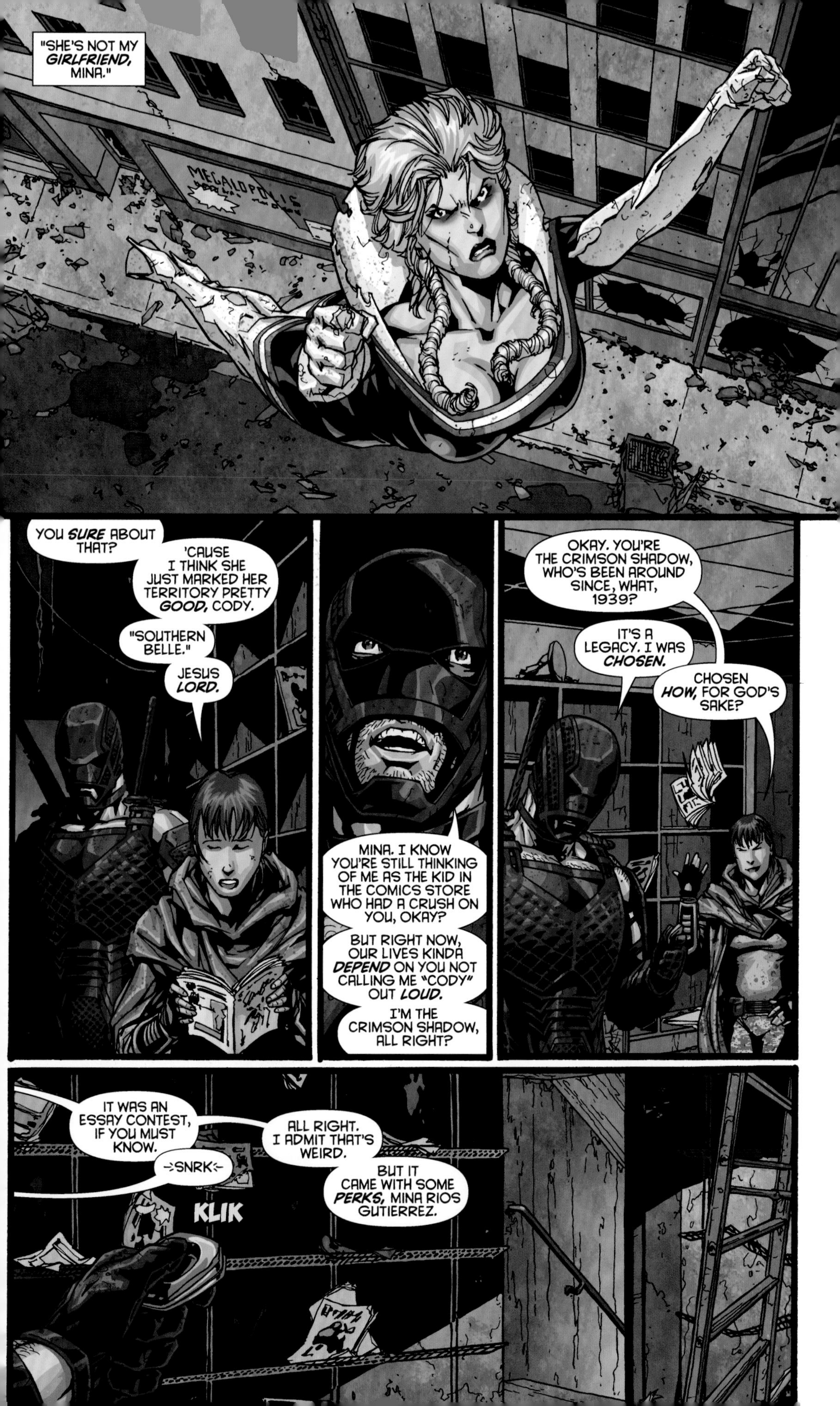
"SHE'S NOT MY GIRLFRIEND, MINA."
MEGALOPOLIS
YOU SURE ABOUT THAT?
'CAUSE I THINK SHE JUST MARKED HER TERRITORY PRETTY GOOD, CODY.
"SOUTHERN BELLE."
JESUS LORD.
MINA. I KNOW YOU'RE STILL THINKING OF ME AS THE KID IN THE COMICS STORE WHO HAD A CRUSH ON YOU, OKAY?
BUT RIGHT NOW, OUR LIVES KINDA DEPEND ON YOU NOT CALLING ME "CODY" OUT LOUD.
I'M THE CRIMSON SHADOW, ALL RIGHT?
OKAY. YOU'RE THE CRIMSON SHADOW, WHO'S BEEN AROUND SINCE, WHAT, 1939?
IT'S A LEGACY. I WAS CHOSEN.
CHOSEN HOW, FOR GOD'S SAKE?
IT WAS AN ESSAY CONTEST, IF YOU MUST KNOW.
->SNRK<-
ALL RIGHT. I ADMIT THAT'S WEIRD.
BUT IT CAME WITH SOME PERKS, MINA RIOS GUTIERREZ.
KLIK

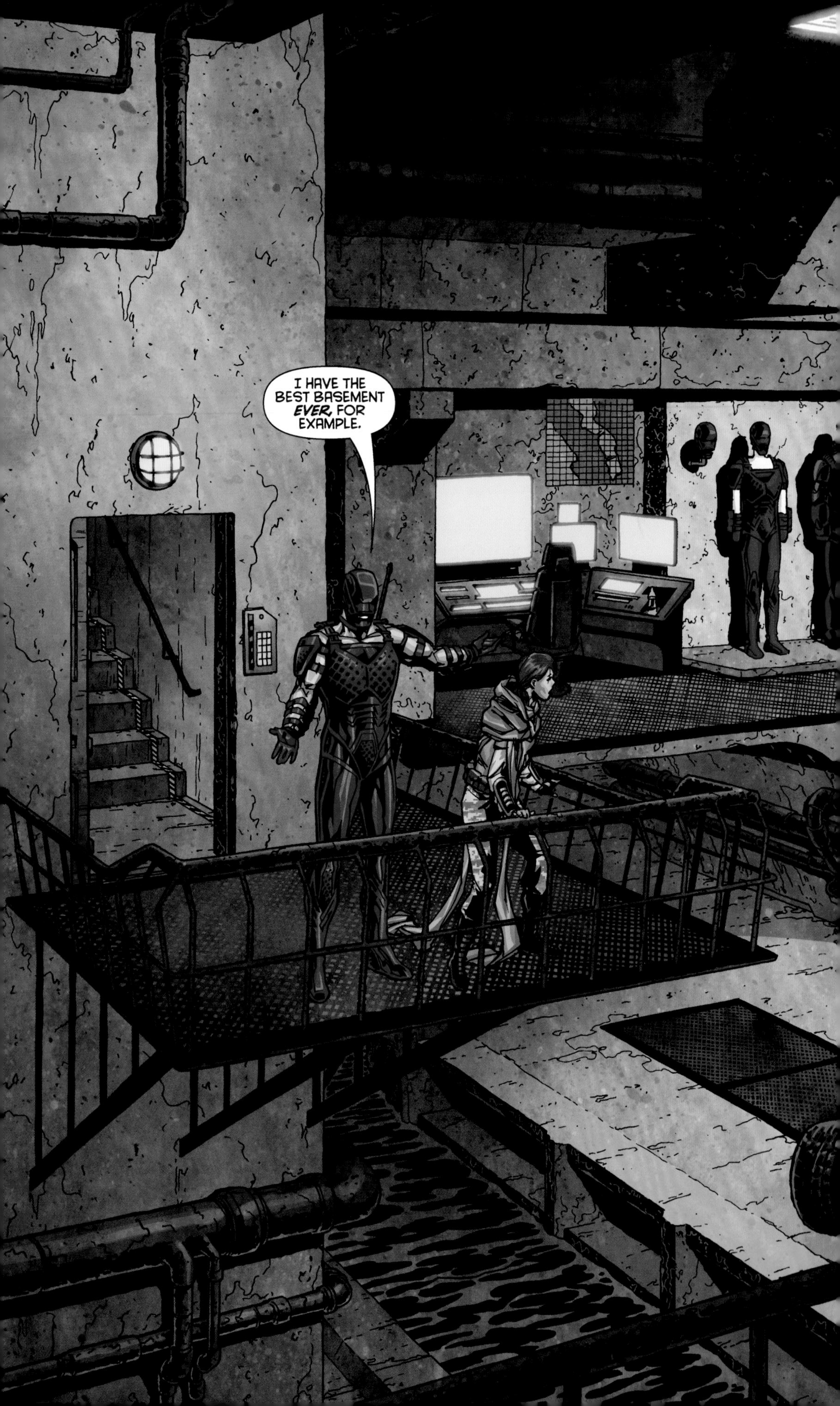
I HAVE THE BEST BASEMENT EVER, FOR EXAMPLE.

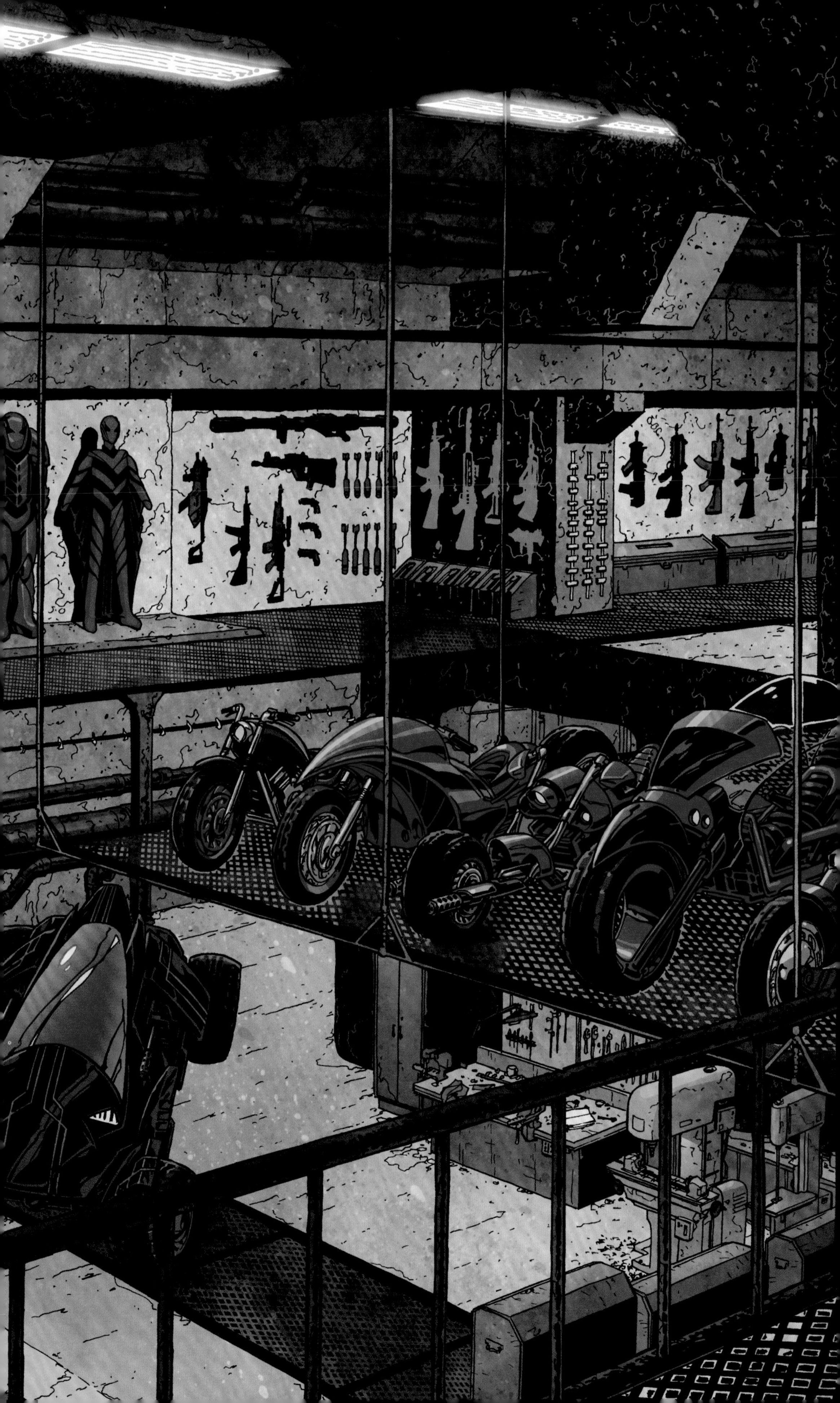

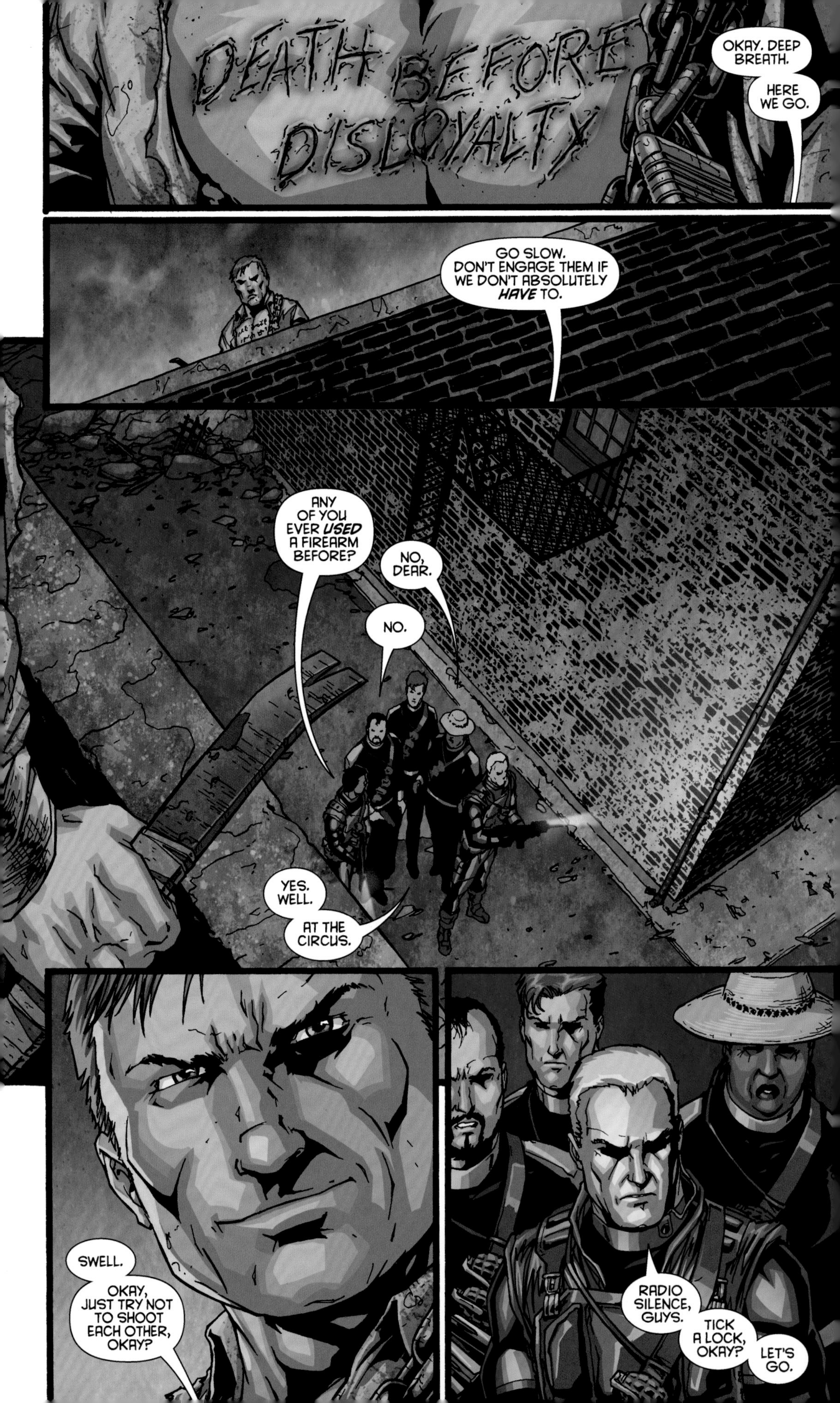

DEATH BEFORE DISLOYALTY
OKAY. DEEP BREATH.
HERE WE GO.
GO SLOW. DON'T ENGAGE THEM IF WE DON'T ABSOLUTELY *HAVE* TO.
ANY OF YOU EVER *USED* A FIREARM BEFORE?
NO, DEAR.
NO.
YES. WELL.
AT THE CIRCUS.
SWELL.
OKAY, JUST TRY NOT TO SHOOT EACH OTHER, OKAY?
RADIO SILENCE, GUYS.
TICK A LOCK, OKAY?
LET'S GO.

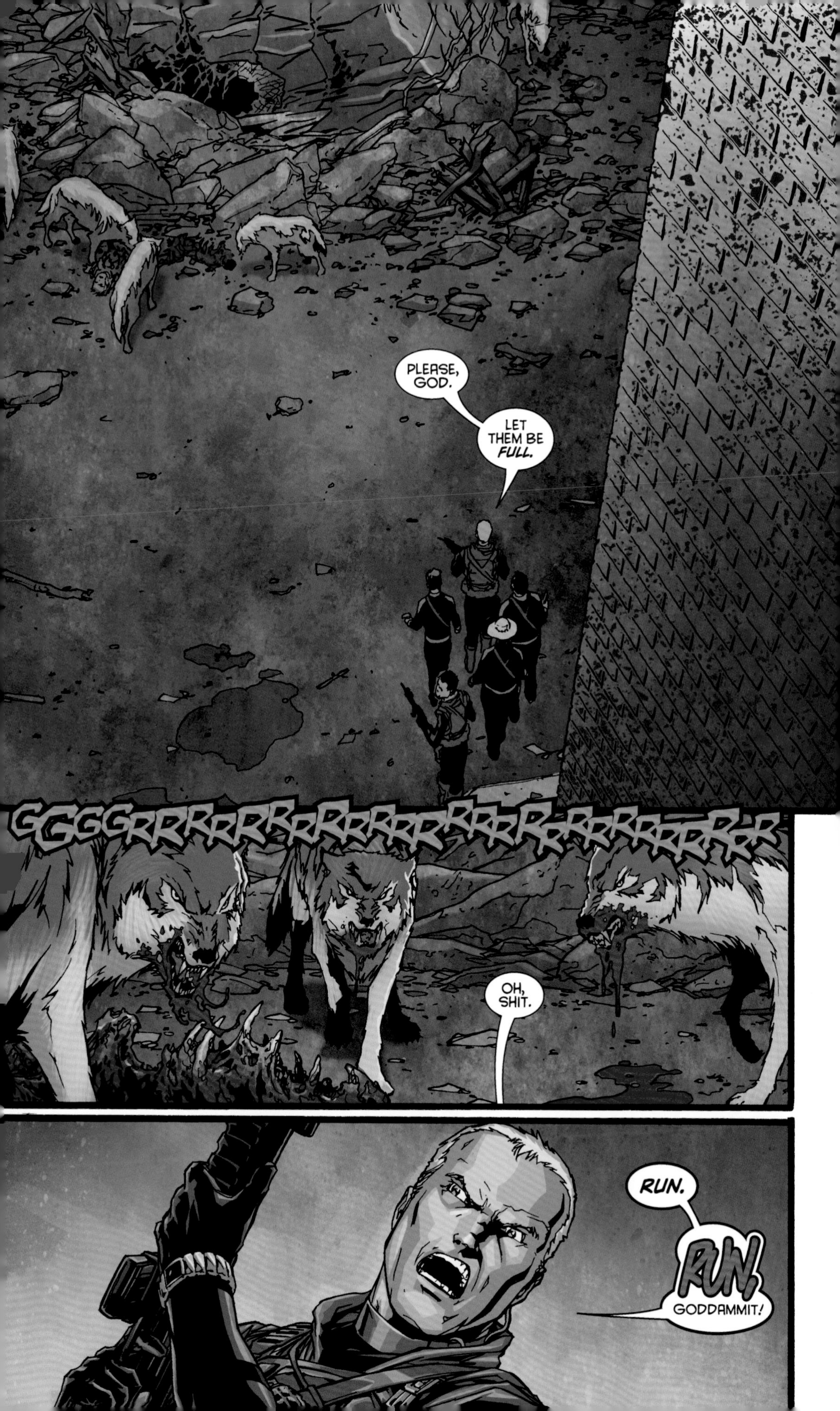
PLEASE, GOD.
LET THEM BE FULL.
GGGGRRRRRRRRRRRRRRRRRRRRRRRRRRRRR
OH, SHIT.
RUN.
RUN, GODDAMMIT!

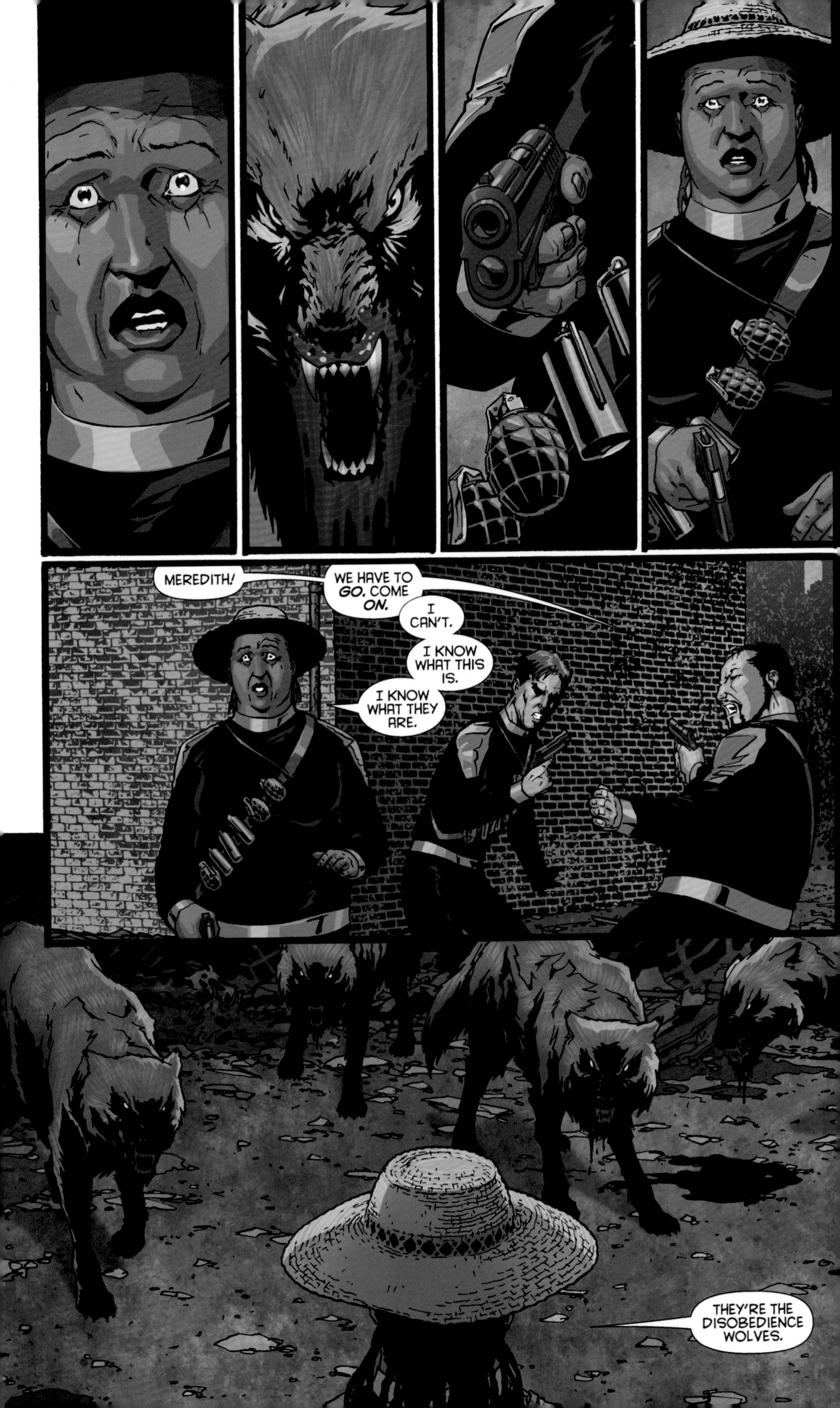
MEREDITH!
WE HAVE TO GO. COME ON.
I CAN'T.
I KNOW WHAT THIS IS.
I KNOW WHAT THEY ARE.
THEY'RE THE DISOBEDIENCE WOLVES.

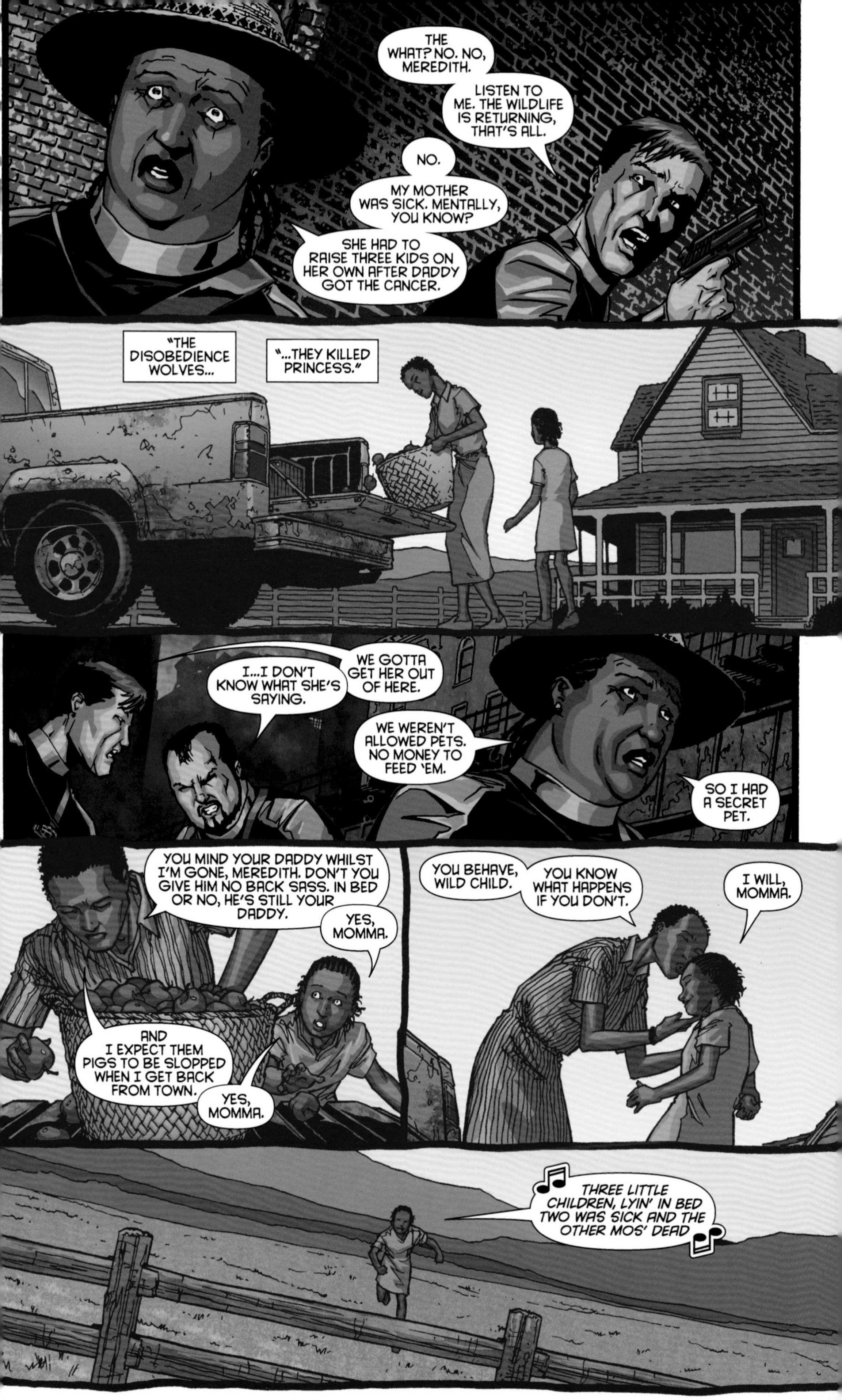
THE WHAT? NO. NO, MEREDITH.
LISTEN TO ME. THE WILDLIFE IS RETURNING, THAT'S ALL.
NO.
MY MOTHER WAS SICK. MENTALLY, YOU KNOW?
SHE HAD TO RAISE THREE KIDS ON HER OWN AFTER DADDY GOT THE CANCER.
"THE DISOBEDIENCE WOLVES...
"...THEY KILLED PRINCESS."
I...I DON'T KNOW WHAT SHE'S SAYING.
WE GOTTA GET HER OUT OF HERE.
WE WEREN'T ALLOWED PETS. NO MONEY TO FEED 'EM.
SO I HAD A SECRET PET.
YOU MIND YOUR DADDY WHILST I'M GONE, MEREDITH. DON'T YOU GIVE HIM NO BACK SASS. IN BED OR NO, HE'S STILL YOUR DADDY.
YES, MOMMA.
AND I EXPECT THEM PIGS TO BE SLOPPED WHEN I GET BACK FROM TOWN.
YES, MOMMA.
YOU BEHAVE, WILD CHILD.
YOU KNOW WHAT HAPPENS IF YOU DON'T.
I WILL, MOMMA.
THREE LITTLE CHILDREN, LYIN' IN BED TWO WAS SICK AND THE OTHER MOS' DEAD

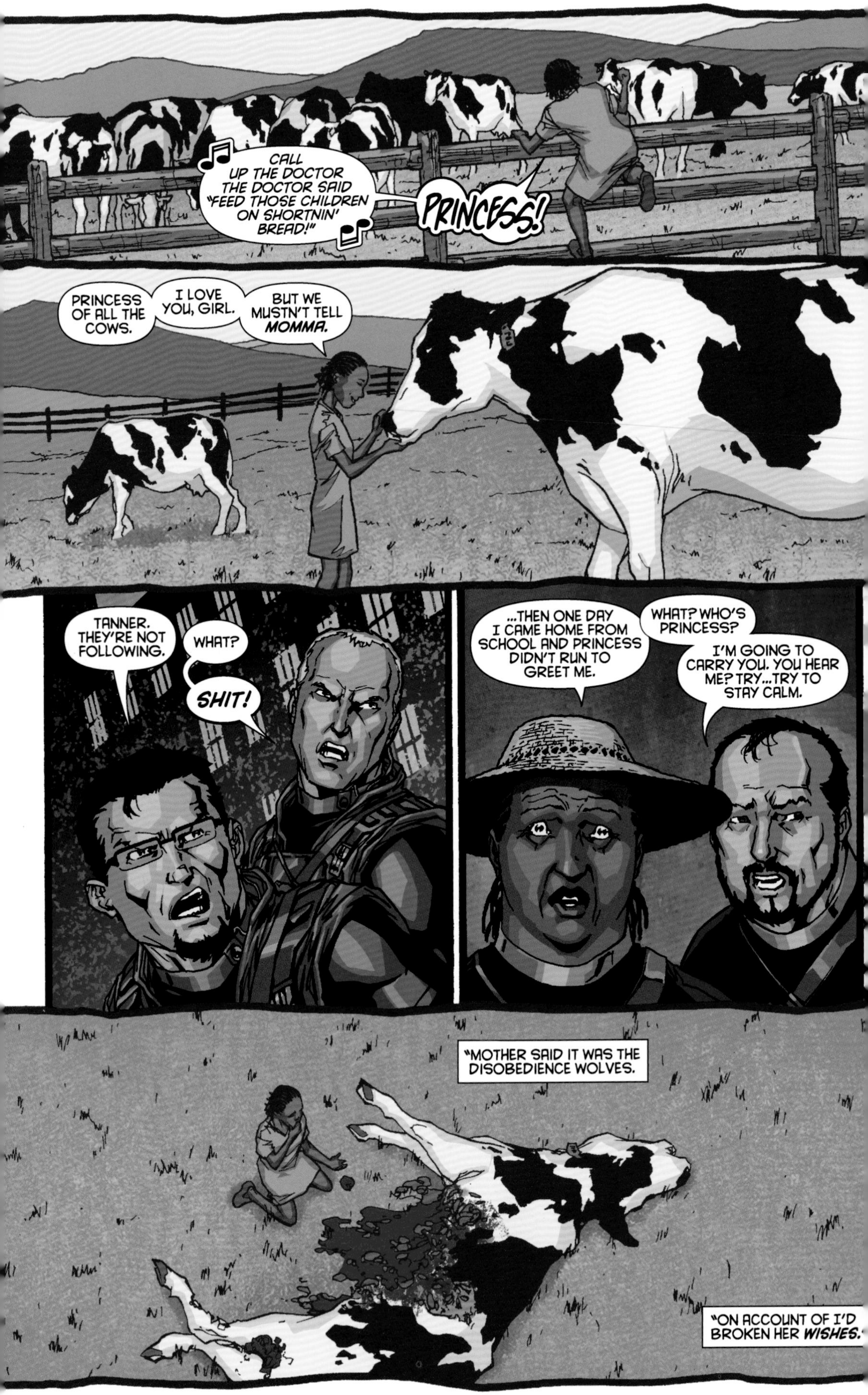
CALL UP THE DOCTOR THE DOCTOR SAID "FEED THOSE CHILDREN ON SHORTNIN' BREAD!"
PRINCESS!
PRINCESS OF ALL THE COWS.
I LOVE YOU, GIRL.
BUT WE MUSTN'T TELL *MOMMA.*
TANNER. THEY'RE NOT FOLLOWING.
WHAT?
SHIT!
...THEN ONE DAY I CAME HOME FROM SCHOOL AND PRINCESS DIDN'T RUN TO GREET ME.
WHAT? WHO'S PRINCESS?
I'M GOING TO CARRY YOU. YOU HEAR ME? TRY...TRY TO STAY CALM.
"MOTHER SAID IT WAS THE DISOBEDIENCE WOLVES.
"ON ACCOUNT OF I'D BROKEN HER *WISHES.*

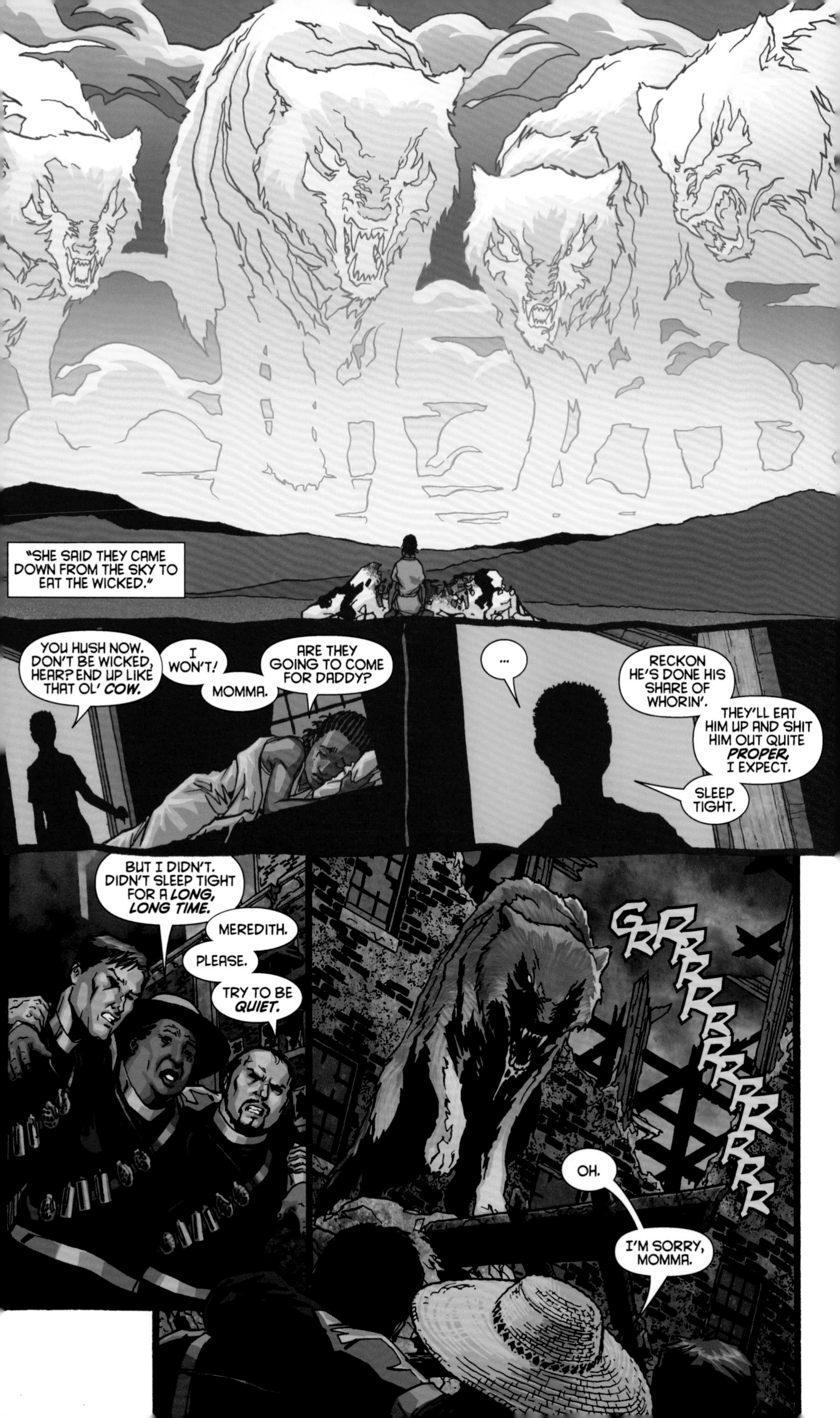
"SHE SAID THEY CAME DOWN FROM THE SKY TO EAT THE WICKED."
YOU HUSH NOW. DON'T BE WICKED, HEAR? END UP LIKE THAT OL' COW.
I WON'T!
MOMMA.
ARE THEY GOING TO COME FOR DADDY?
...
RECKON HE'S DONE HIS SHARE OF WHORIN'.
THEY'LL EAT HIM UP AND SHIT HIM OUT QUITE PROPER, I EXPECT.
SLEEP TIGHT.
BUT I DIDN'T. DIDN'T SLEEP TIGHT FOR A LONG, LONG TIME.
MEREDITH.
PLEASE.
TRY TO BE QUIET.
GRRRRRRRRRRRRR
OH.
I'M SORRY, MOMMA.

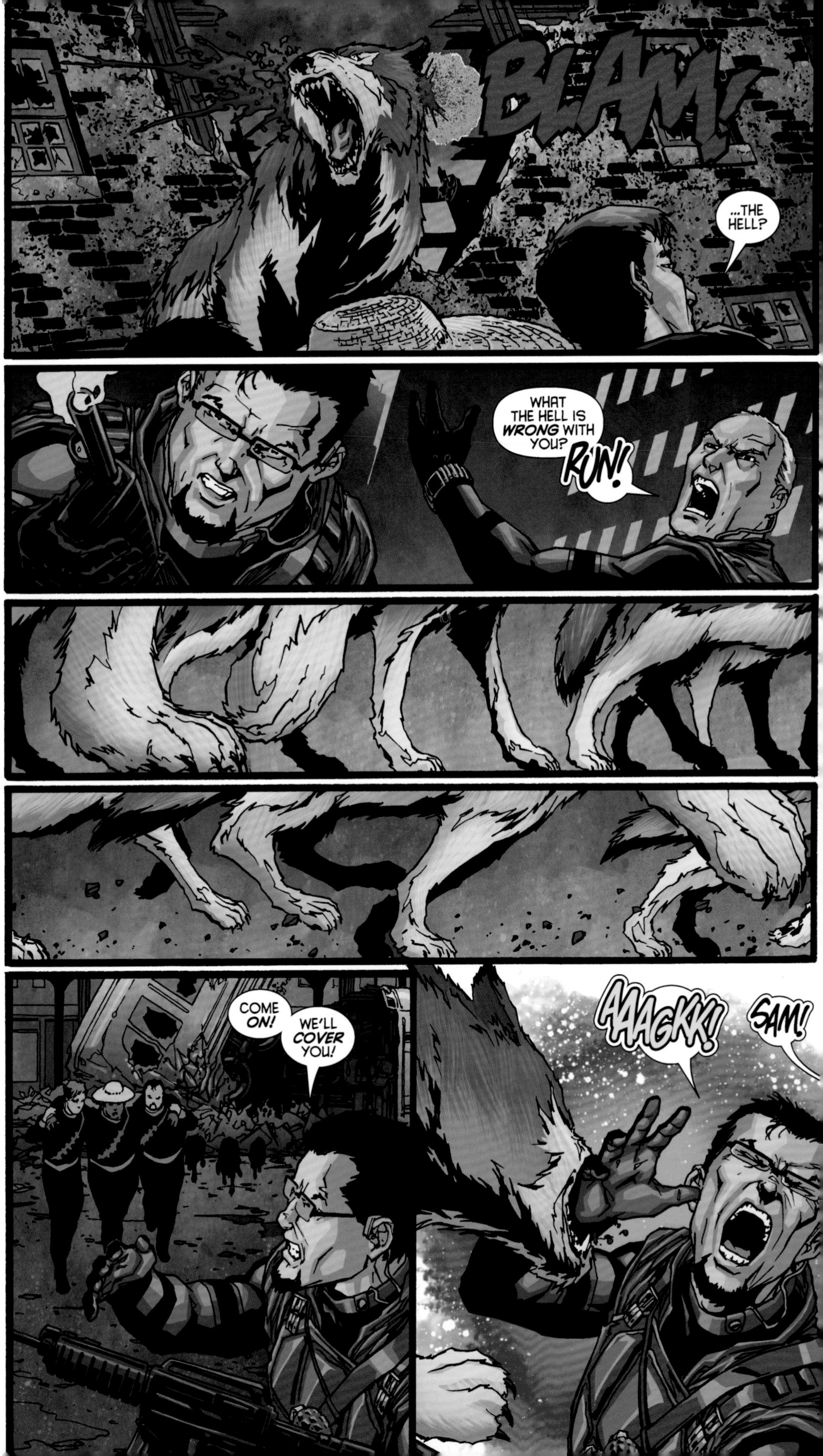
BLAM!
...THE HELL?
WHAT THE HELL IS WRONG WITH YOU?
RUN!
COME ON!
WE'LL COVER YOU!
AAAGKK!
SAM!

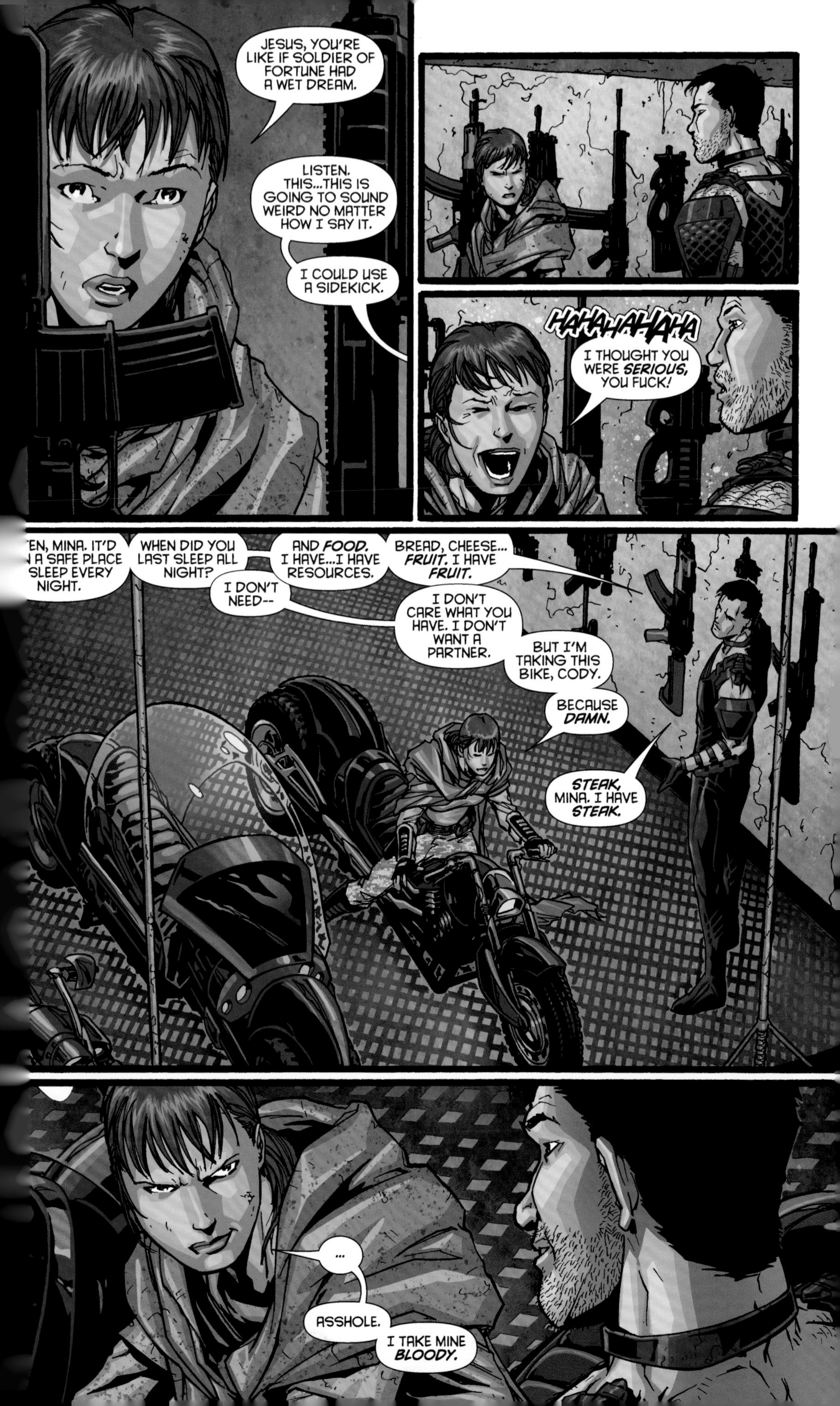

JESUS, YOU'RE LIKE IF SOLDIER OF FORTUNE HAD A WET DREAM.
LISTEN. THIS...THIS IS GOING TO SOUND WEIRD NO MATTER HOW I SAY IT.
I COULD USE A SIDEKICK.
HAHAHAHAHA
I THOUGHT YOU WERE SERIOUS, YOU FUCK!
TEN, MINA. IT'D N A SAFE PLACE SLEEP EVERY NIGHT.
WHEN DID YOU LAST SLEEP ALL NIGHT?
I DON'T NEED--
AND FOOD. I HAVE...I HAVE RESOURCES.
BREAD, CHEESE... FRUIT. I HAVE FRUIT.
I DON'T CARE WHAT YOU HAVE. I DON'T WANT A PARTNER.
BUT I'M TAKING THIS BIKE, CODY.
BECAUSE DAMN.
STEAK, MINA. I HAVE STEAK.
...
ASSHOLE.
I TAKE MINE BLOODY.

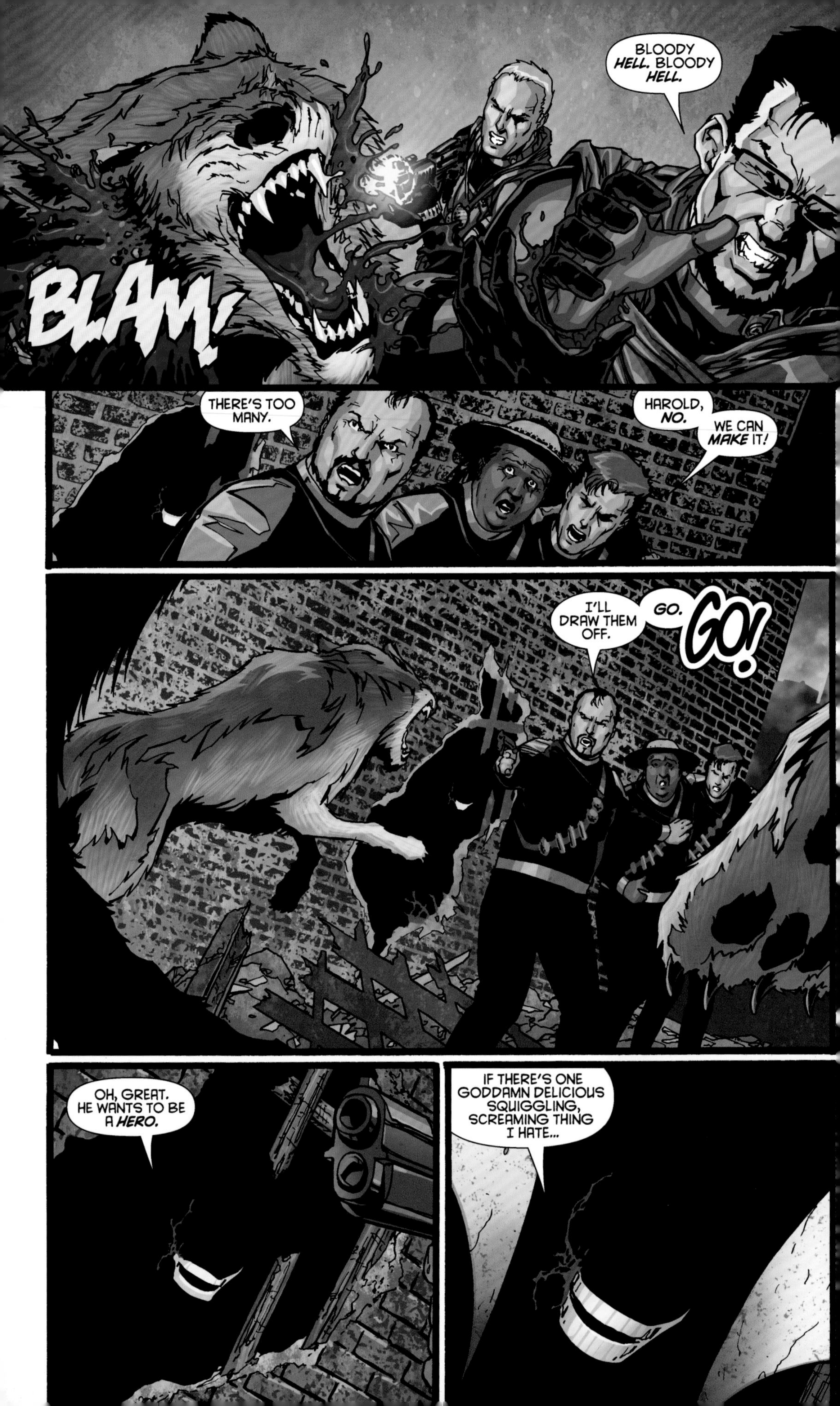
BLAM!
BLOODY HELL. BLOODY HELL.
THERE'S TOO MANY.
HAROLD, NO.
WE CAN MAKE IT!
I'LL DRAW THEM OFF.
GO.
GO!
OH, GREAT. HE WANTS TO BE A HERO.
IF THERE'S ONE GODDAMN DELICIOUS SQUIGGLING, SCREAMING THING I HATE...

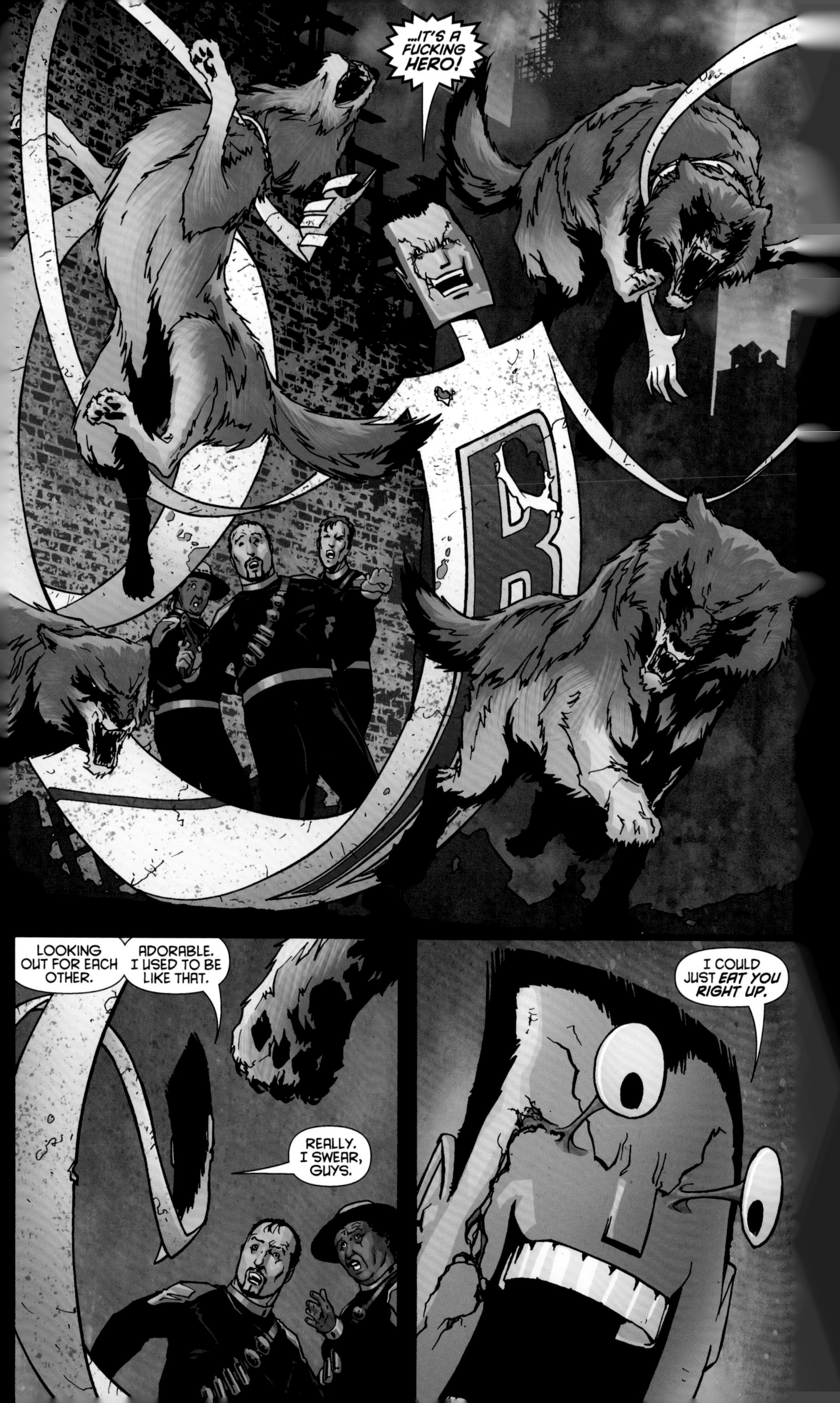

...IT'S A FUCKING HERO!
LOOKING OUT FOR EACH OTHER.
ADORABLE. I USED TO BE LIKE THAT.
REALLY. I SWEAR, GUYS.
I COULD JUST EAT YOU RIGHT UP.

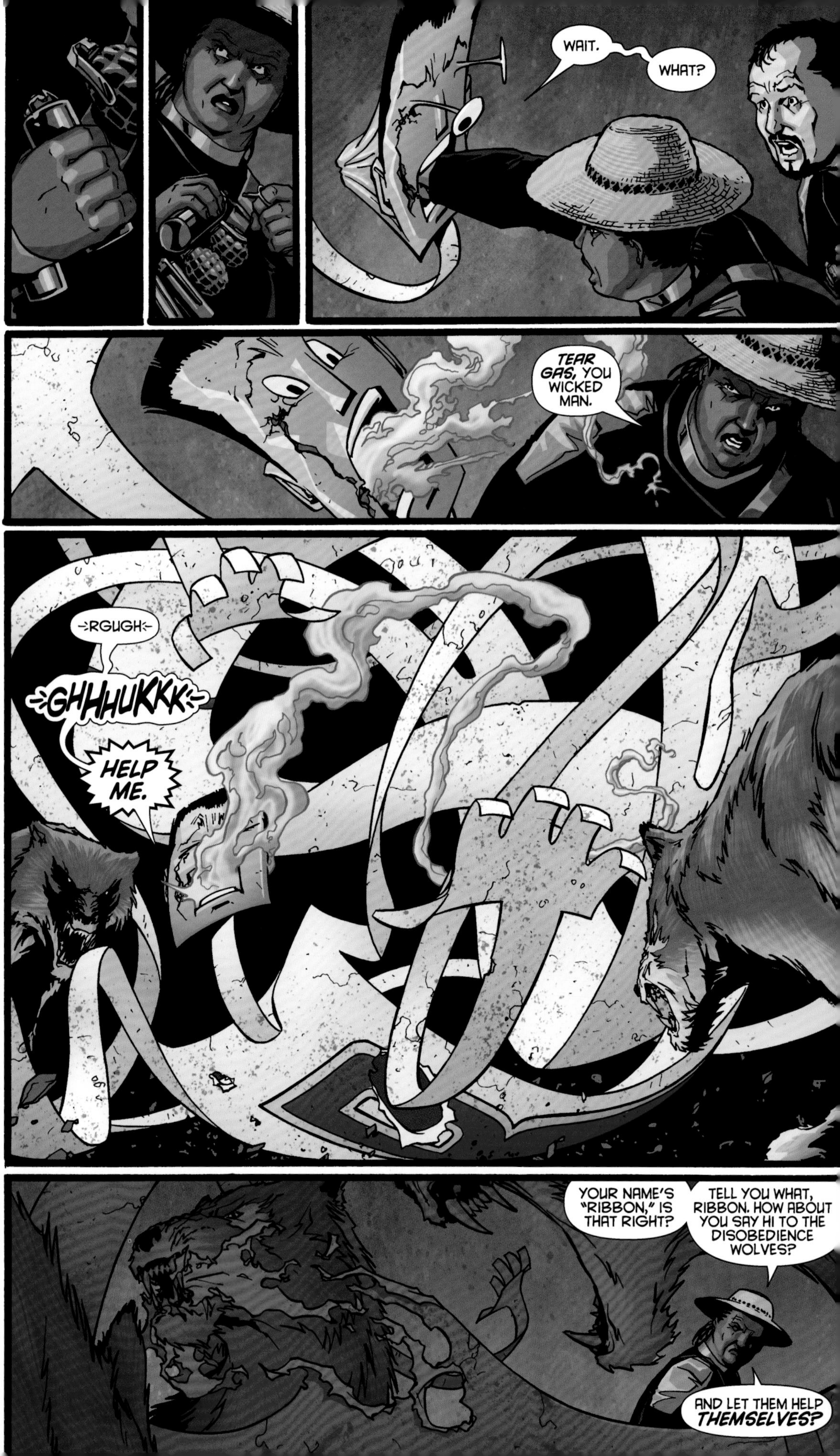
WAIT.
WHAT?
TEAR GAS, YOU WICKED MAN.
-RGUGH-
-GHHHUKKK-
HELP ME.
YOUR NAME'S "RIBBON," IS THAT RIGHT?
TELL YOU WHAT, RIBBON. HOW ABOUT YOU SAY HI TO THE DISOBEDIENCE WOLVES?
AND LET THEM HELP *THEMSELVES?*

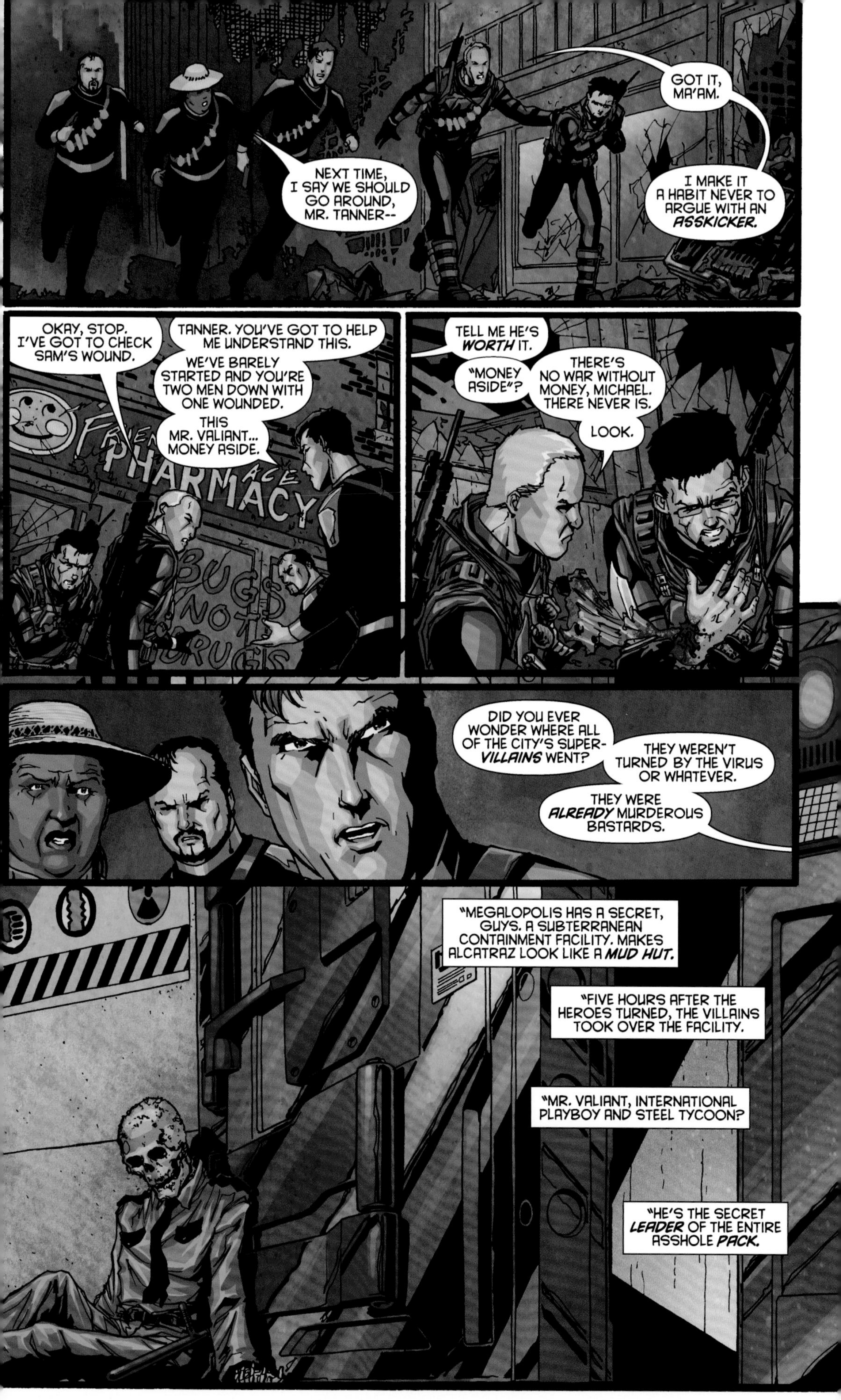

NEXT TIME, I SAY WE SHOULD GO AROUND, MR. TANNER--
GOT IT, MA'AM.
I MAKE IT A HABIT NEVER TO ARGUE WITH AN *ASSKICKER.*
OKAY, STOP. I'VE GOT TO CHECK SAM'S WOUND.
TANNER. YOU'VE GOT TO HELP ME UNDERSTAND THIS.
WE'VE BARELY STARTED AND YOU'RE TWO MEN DOWN WITH ONE WOUNDED.
THIS MR. VALIANT... MONEY ASIDE.
PHARMACY
ACE
BUGS NOT DRUGS
TELL ME HE'S *WORTH* IT.
"MONEY ASIDE"?
THERE'S NO WAR WITHOUT MONEY, MICHAEL. THERE NEVER IS.
LOOK.
DID YOU EVER WONDER WHERE ALL OF THE CITY'S SUPER-*VILLAINS* WENT?
THEY WEREN'T TURNED BY THE VIRUS OR WHATEVER.
THEY WERE *ALREADY* MURDEROUS BASTARDS.
"MEGALOPOLIS HAS A SECRET, GUYS. A SUBTERRANEAN CONTAINMENT FACILITY. MAKES ALCATRAZ LOOK LIKE A *MUD HUT.*
"FIVE HOURS AFTER THE HEROES TURNED, THE VILLAINS TOOK OVER THE FACILITY.
"MR. VALIANT, INTERNATIONAL PLAYBOY AND STEEL TYCOON?
"HE'S THE SECRET *LEADER* OF THE ENTIRE ASSHOLE *PACK.*

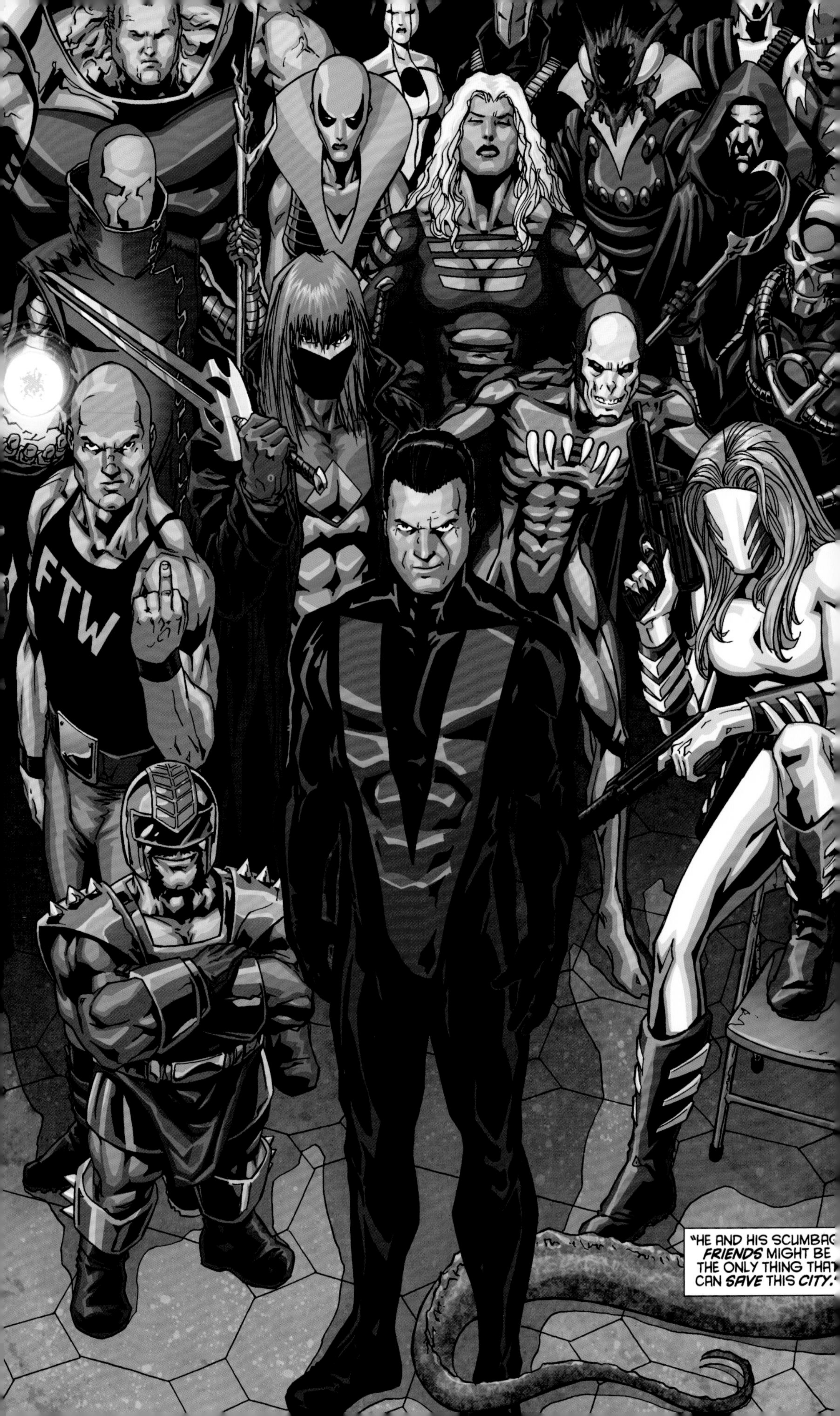
FTW
"HE AND HIS SCUMBAG FRIENDS MIGHT BE THE ONLY THING THAT CAN SAVE THIS CITY."

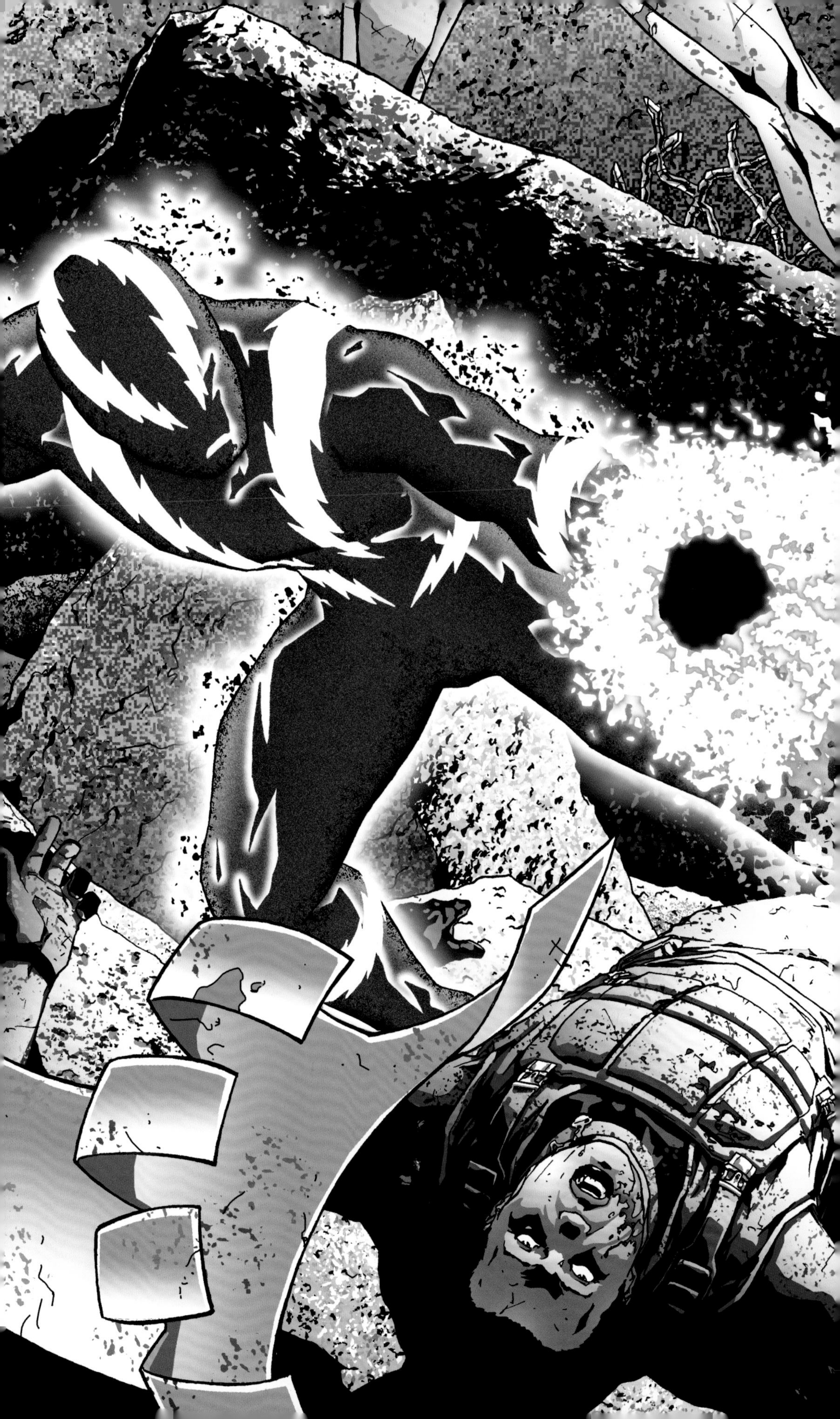

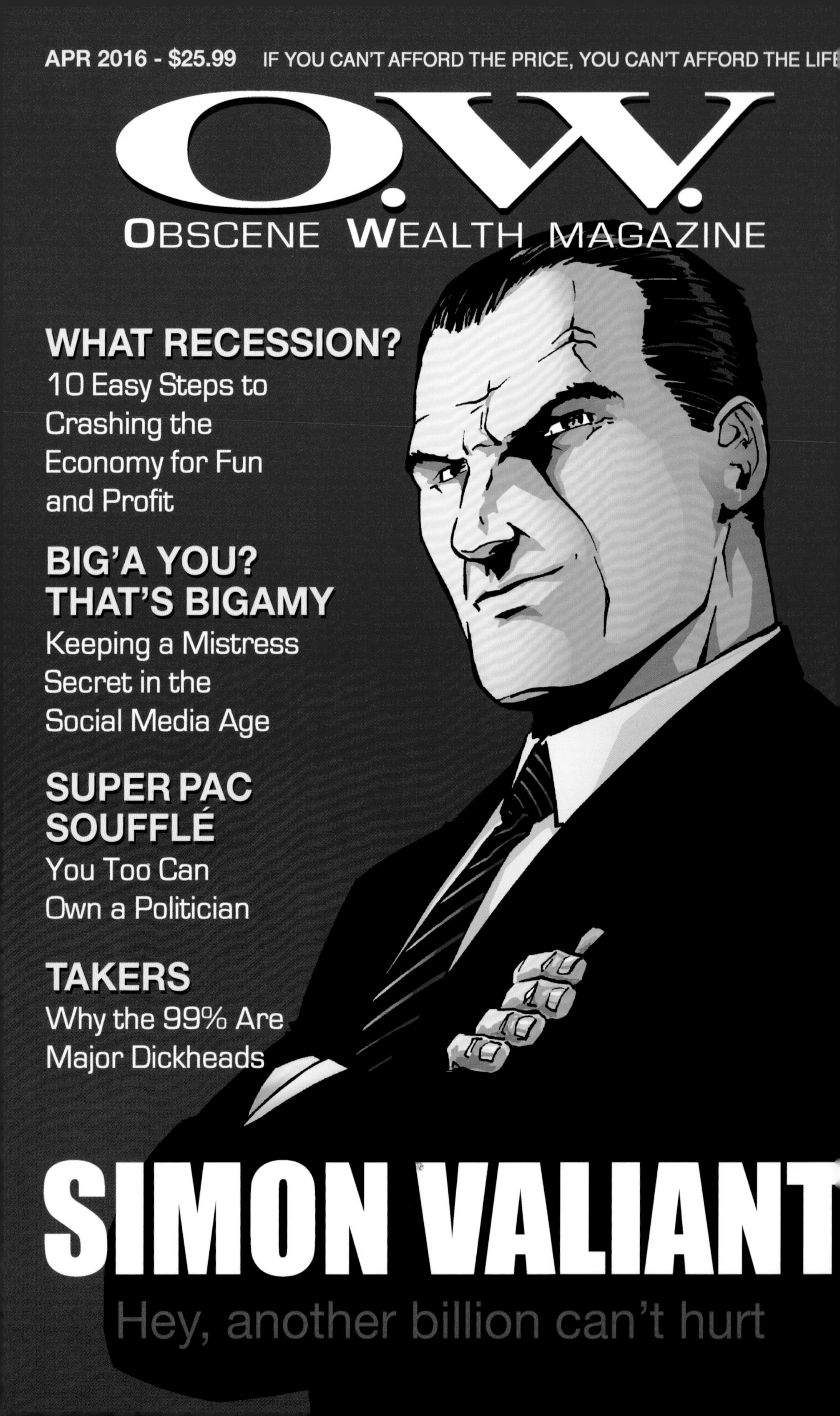
APR 2016 - $25.99
IF YOU CAN'T AFFORD THE PRICE, YOU CAN'T AFFORD THE LIFE
O.W.
OBSCENE WEALTH MAGAZINE
WHAT RECESSION?
10 Easy Steps to Crashing the Economy for Fun and Profit
BIG'A YOU? THAT'S BIGAMY
Keeping a Mistress Secret in the Social Media Age
SUPER PAC SOUFFLÉ
You Too Can Own a Politician
TAKERS
Why the 99% Are Major Dickheads
SIMON VALIANT
Hey, another billion can't hurt

WAKE UP, SLEEPYHEAD.

THERE YOU ARE. I'M AFRAID YOU'VE *OVERSLEPT*, RIP VAN WINKLE.

I KNEW THERE WAS STILL GRANITE IN YOUR PANTS.

THE OTHERS DIDN'T BELIEVE ME.

THEY SAID WE SHOULD HAVE LEFT YOU AT THE BOTTOM OF THE WAKAMA RIVER.

OH, BUT I'M FORGETTIN' MY MANNERS, SUGAR BEAR.

WOULD YOU LIKE A BITE?

SUIT YOUR-SELF. NEVER LET IT BE SAID THAT SOUTHERN BELLE SENT A HANDSOME MAN AWAY *PECKISH*.

OR MAYBE... MAYBE YOU'RE HUNGRY FOR SOMETHIN' A LITTLE *MEATIER*.

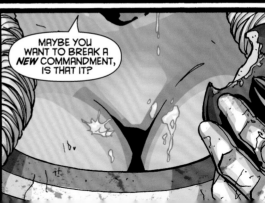

MAYBE YOU WANT TO BREAK A *NEW* COMMANDMENT, IS THAT IT?

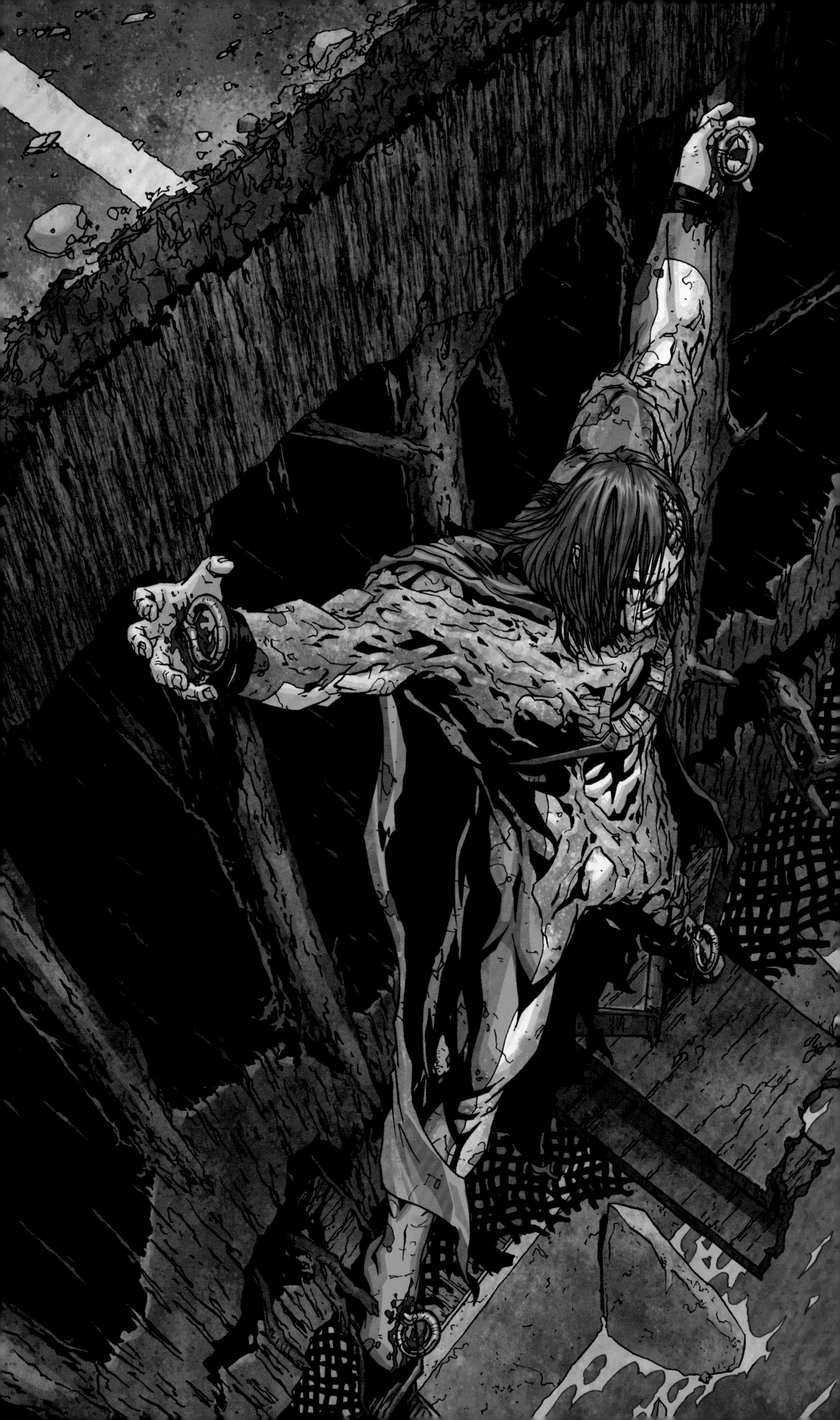

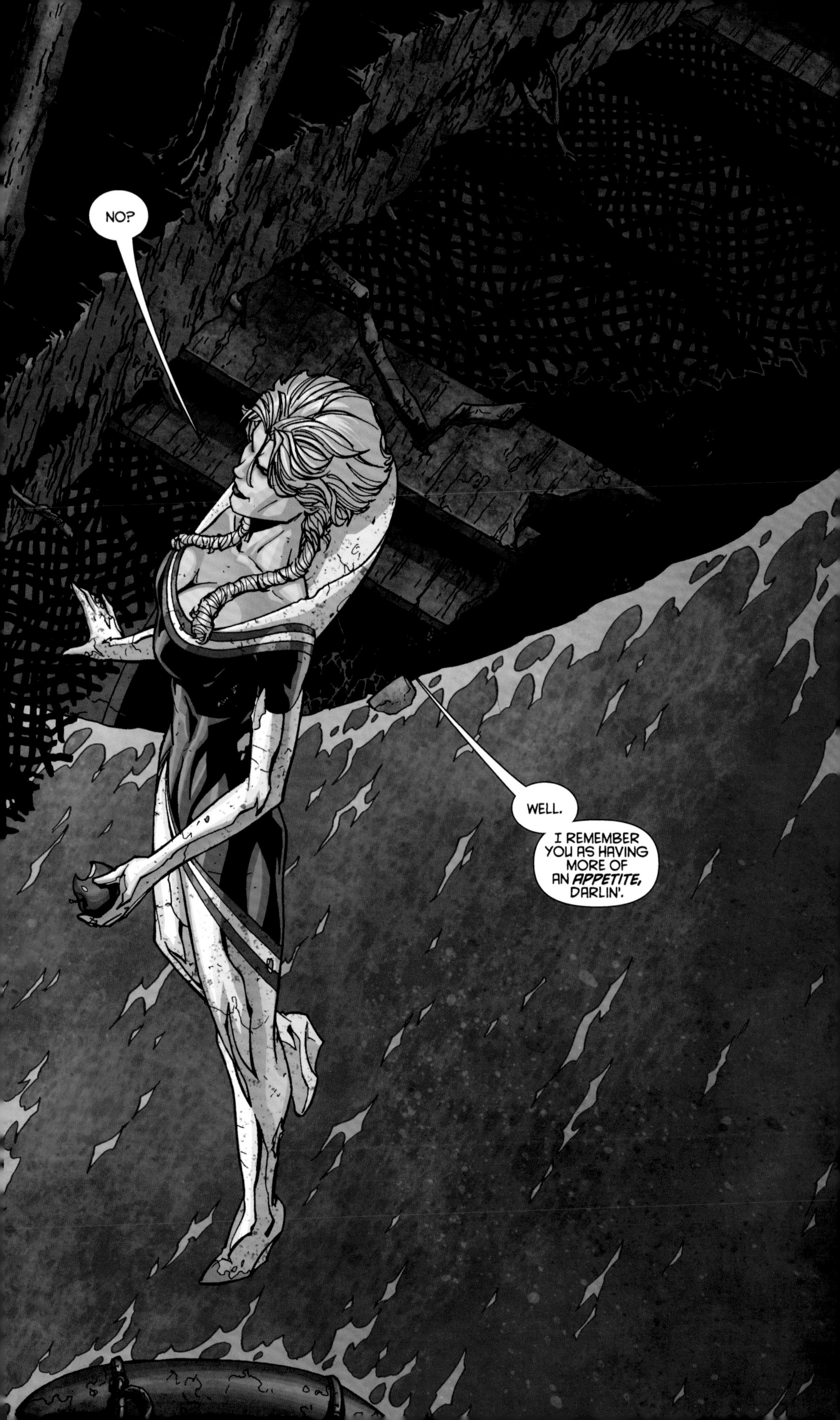
NO?
WELL.
I REMEMBER YOU AS HAVING MORE OF AN *APPETITE,* DARLIN'.

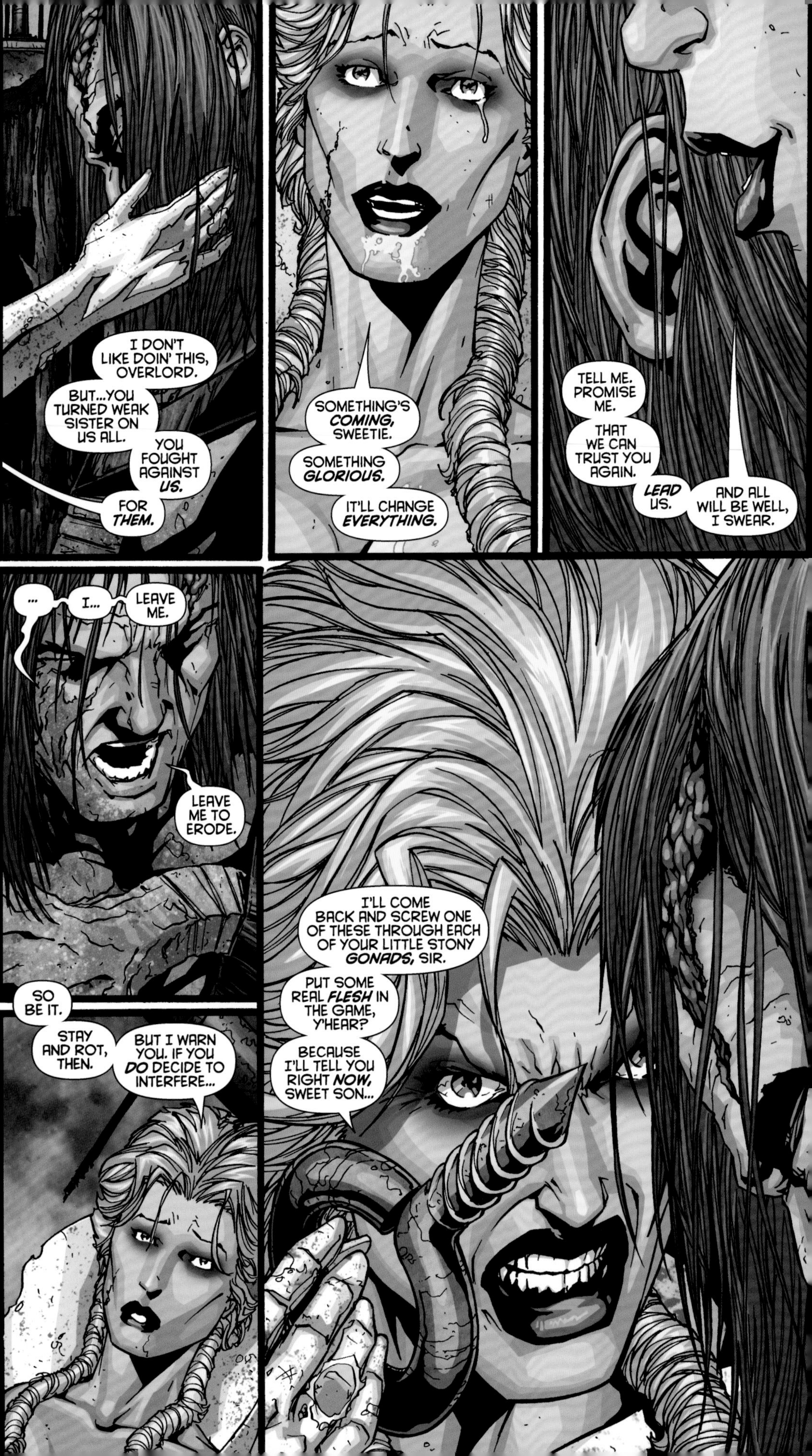
I DON'T LIKE DOIN' THIS, OVERLORD.
BUT...YOU TURNED WEAK SISTER ON US ALL.
YOU FOUGHT AGAINST *US.*
FOR *THEM.*
SOMETHING'S *COMING,* SWEETIE.
SOMETHING *GLORIOUS.*
IT'LL CHANGE *EVERYTHING.*
TELL ME. PROMISE ME.
THAT WE CAN TRUST YOU AGAIN.
LEAD US.
AND ALL WILL BE WELL, I SWEAR.
...
I...
LEAVE ME.
LEAVE ME TO ERODE.
SO BE IT.
STAY AND ROT, THEN.
BUT I WARN YOU. IF YOU *DO* DECIDE TO INTERFERE...
I'LL COME BACK AND SCREW ONE OF THESE THROUGH EACH OF YOUR LITTLE STONY *GONADS,* SIR.
PUT SOME REAL *FLESH* IN THE GAME, Y'HEAR?
BECAUSE I'LL TELL YOU RIGHT *NOW,* SWEET SON...

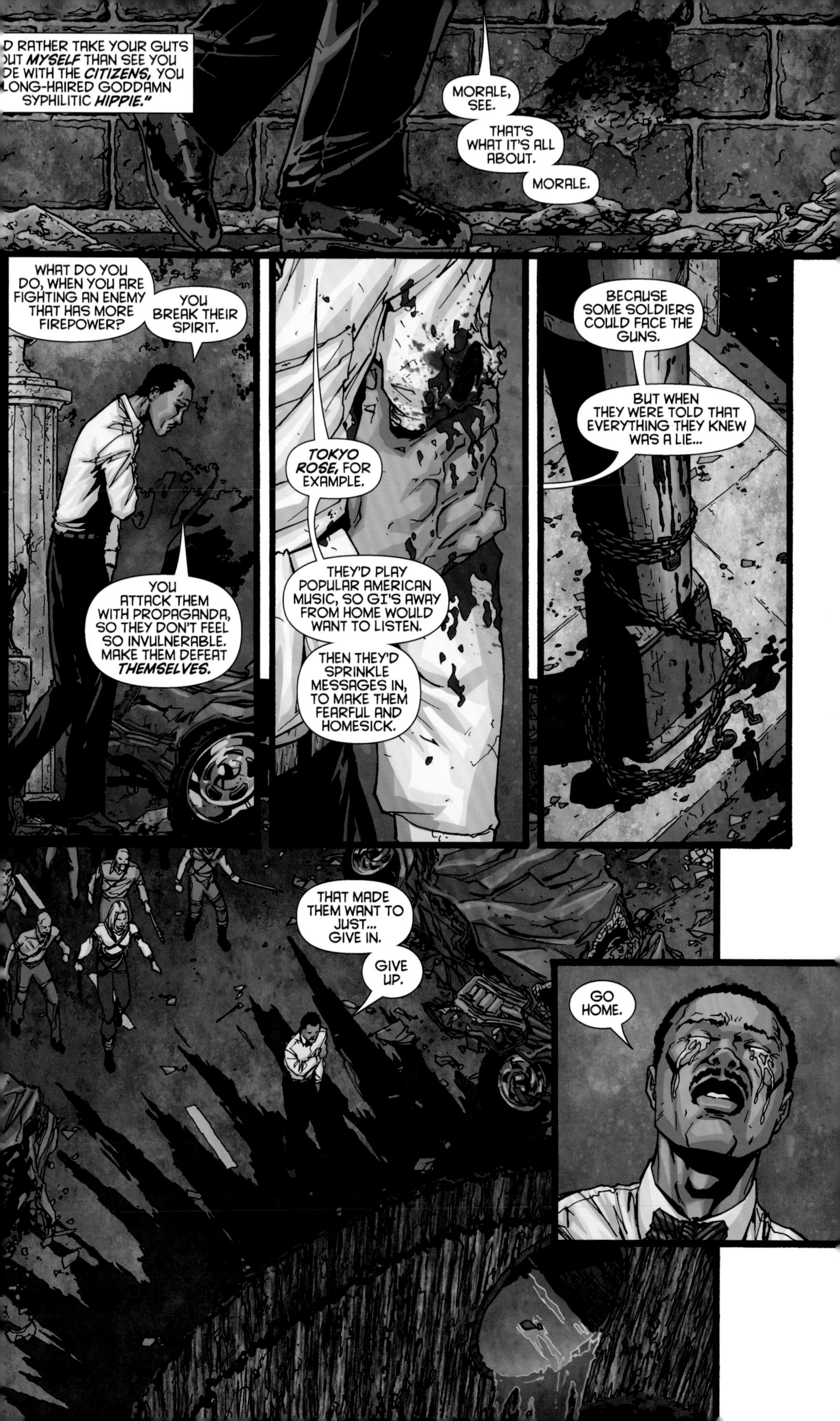
D RATHER TAKE YOUR GUTS
OUT MYSELF THAN SEE YOU
DE WITH THE CITIZENS, YOU
LONG-HAIRED GODDAMN
SYPHILITIC HIPPIE."
MORALE, SEE.
THAT'S WHAT IT'S ALL ABOUT.
MORALE.
WHAT DO YOU DO, WHEN YOU ARE FIGHTING AN ENEMY THAT HAS MORE FIREPOWER?
YOU BREAK THEIR SPIRIT.
YOU ATTACK THEM WITH PROPAGANDA, SO THEY DON'T FEEL SO INVULNERABLE. MAKE THEM DEFEAT THEMSELVES.
TOKYO ROSE, FOR EXAMPLE.
THEY'D PLAY POPULAR AMERICAN MUSIC, SO GI'S AWAY FROM HOME WOULD WANT TO LISTEN.
THEN THEY'D SPRINKLE MESSAGES IN, TO MAKE THEM FEARFUL AND HOMESICK.
BECAUSE SOME SOLDIERS COULD FACE THE GUNS.
BUT WHEN THEY WERE TOLD THAT EVERYTHING THEY KNEW WAS A LIE...
THAT MADE THEM WANT TO JUST... GIVE IN.
GIVE UP.
GO HOME.

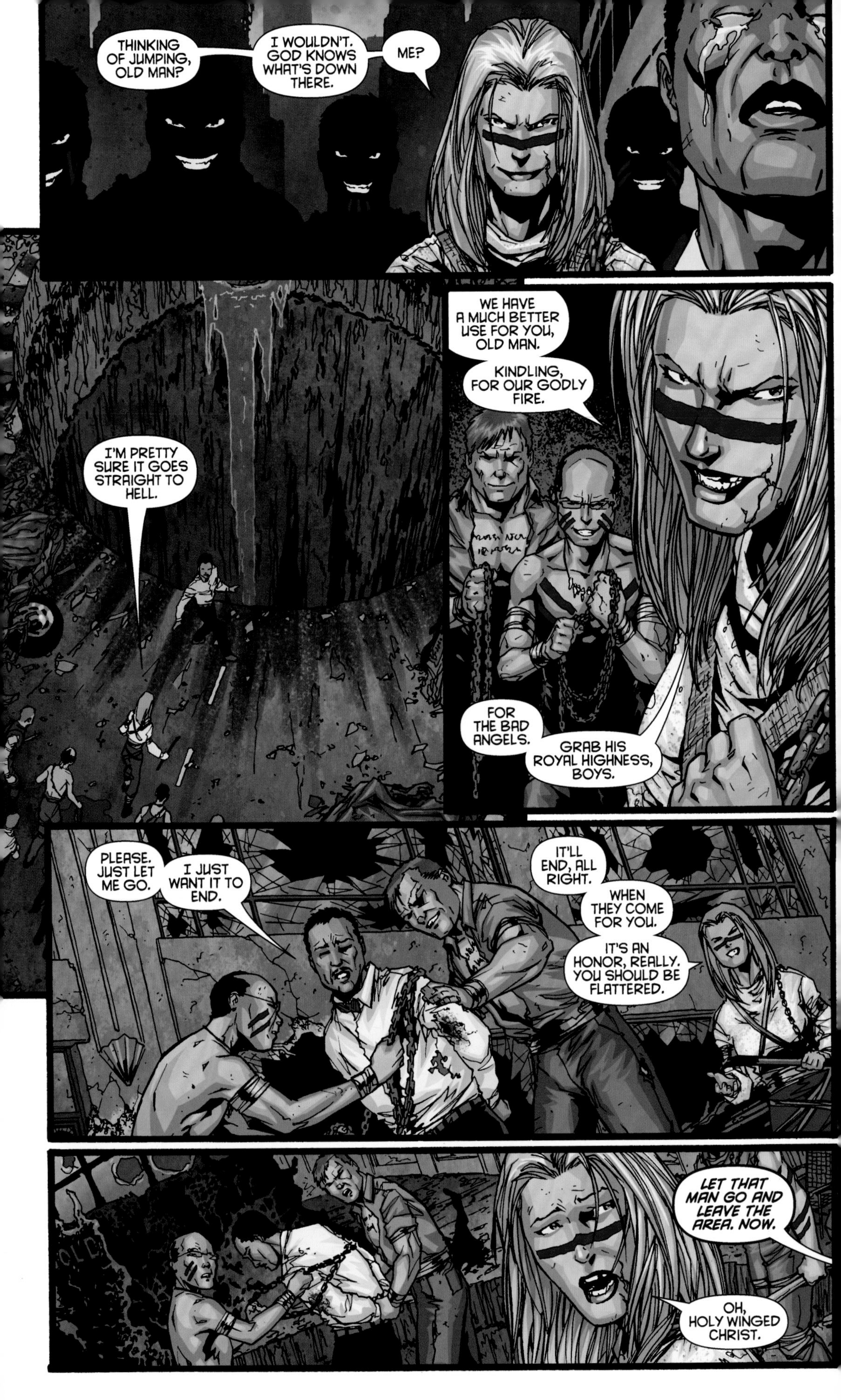
THINKING OF JUMPING, OLD MAN?
I WOULDN'T. GOD KNOWS WHAT'S DOWN THERE.
ME?
I'M PRETTY SURE IT GOES STRAIGHT TO HELL.
WE HAVE A MUCH BETTER USE FOR YOU, OLD MAN.
KINDLING, FOR OUR GODLY FIRE.
FOR THE BAD ANGELS.
GRAB HIS ROYAL HIGHNESS, BOYS.
PLEASE. JUST LET ME GO.
I JUST WANT IT TO END.
IT'LL END, ALL RIGHT.
WHEN THEY COME FOR YOU.
IT'S AN HONOR, REALLY. YOU SHOULD BE FLATTERED.
LET THAT MAN GO AND LEAVE THE AREA. NOW.
OH, HOLY WINGED CHRIST.

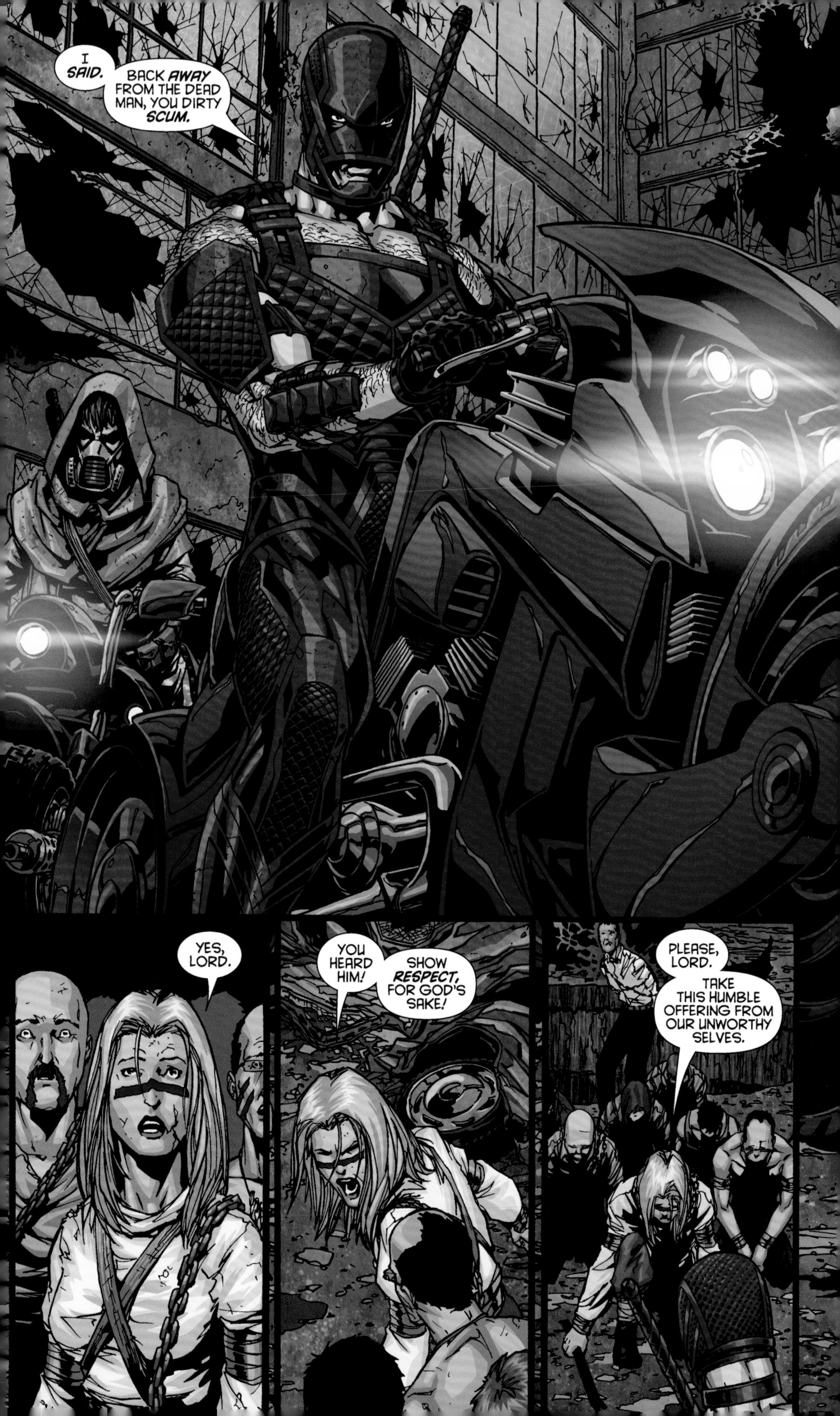
I SAID.
BACK AWAY FROM THE DEAD MAN, YOU DIRTY SCUM.
YES, LORD.
YOU HEARD HIM!
SHOW RESPECT, FOR GOD'S SAKE!
PLEASE, LORD.
TAKE THIS HUMBLE OFFERING FROM OUR UNWORTHY SELVES.

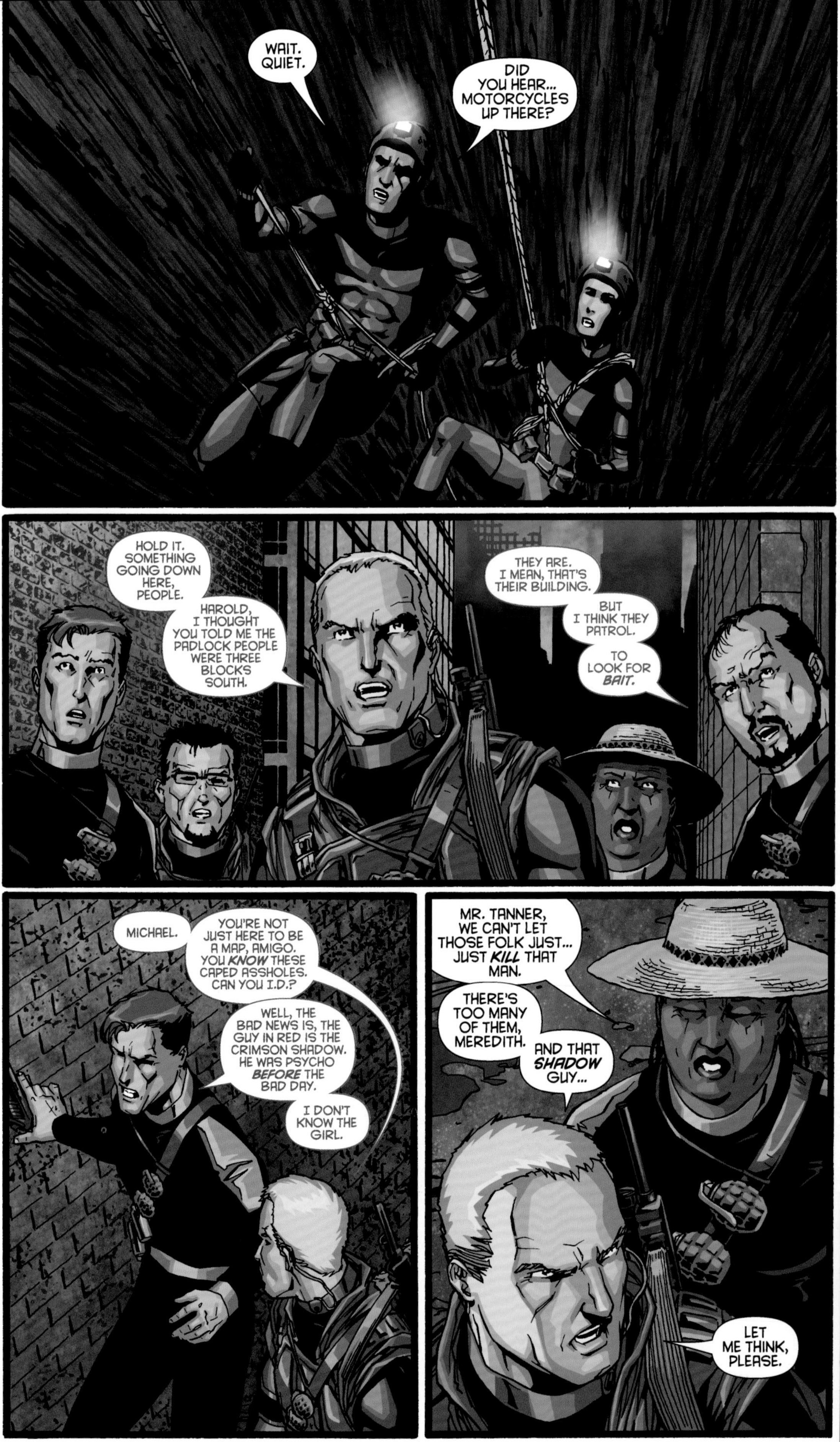
WAIT. QUIET.
DID YOU HEAR... MOTORCYCLES UP THERE?
HOLD IT. SOMETHING GOING DOWN HERE, PEOPLE.
HAROLD, I THOUGHT YOU TOLD ME THE PADLOCK PEOPLE WERE THREE BLOCKS SOUTH.
THEY ARE. I MEAN, THAT'S THEIR BUILDING.
BUT I THINK THEY PATROL.
TO LOOK FOR BAIT.
MICHAEL.
YOU'RE NOT JUST HERE TO BE A MAP, AMIGO. YOU KNOW THESE CAPED ASSHOLES. CAN YOU I.D.?
WELL, THE BAD NEWS IS, THE GUY IN RED IS THE CRIMSON SHADOW. HE WAS PSYCHO BEFORE THE BAD DAY.
I DON'T KNOW THE GIRL.
MR. TANNER, WE CAN'T LET THOSE FOLK JUST... JUST KILL THAT MAN.
THERE'S TOO MANY OF THEM, MEREDITH.
AND THAT SHADOW GUY...
LET ME THINK, PLEASE.

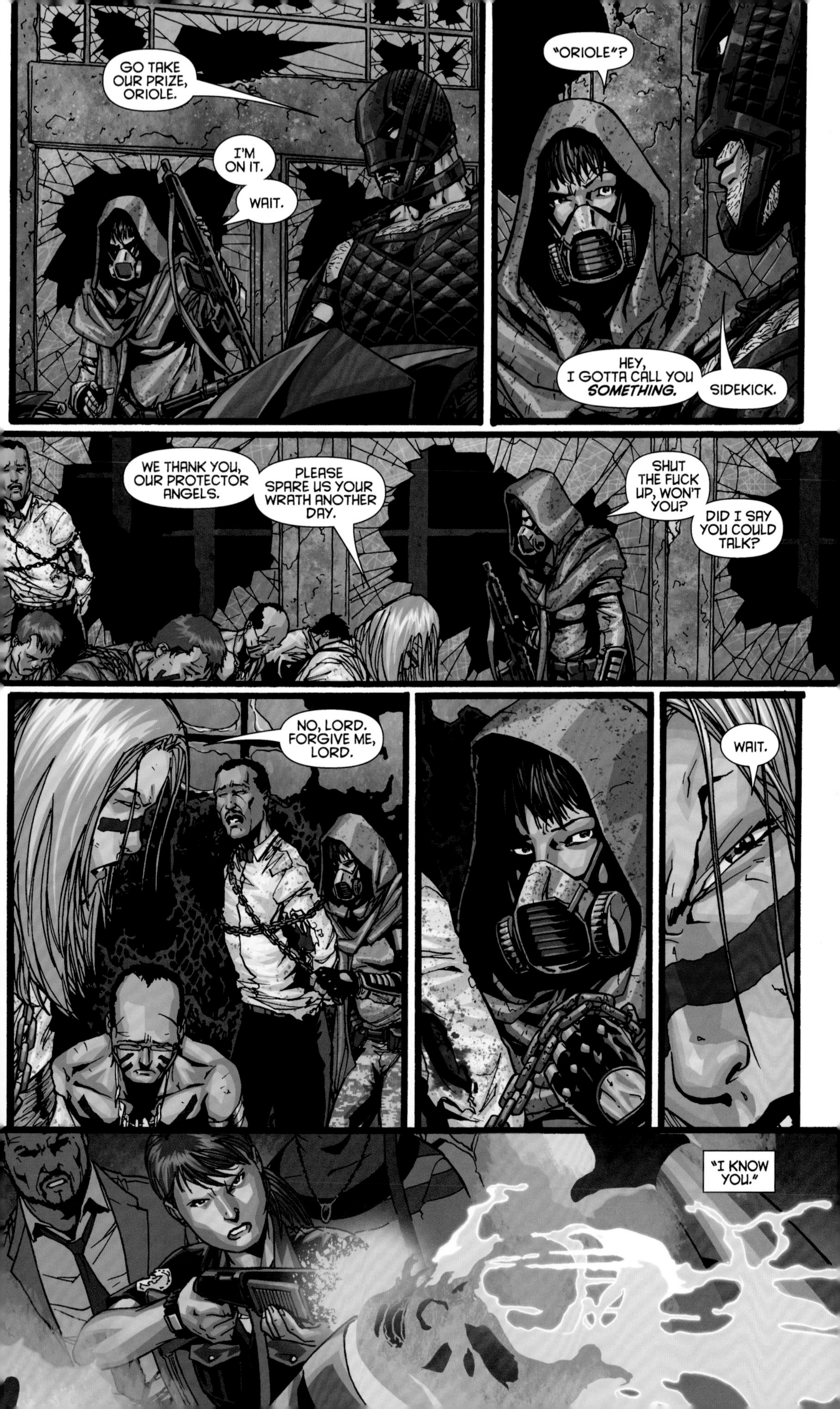
GO TAKE OUR PRIZE, ORIOLE.
I'M ON IT.
WAIT.
"ORIOLE"?
HEY, I GOTTA CALL YOU *SOMETHING.*
SIDEKICK.
WE THANK YOU, OUR PROTECTOR ANGELS.
PLEASE SPARE US YOUR WRATH ANOTHER DAY.
SHUT THE FUCK UP, WON'T YOU?
DID I SAY YOU COULD TALK?
NO, LORD. FORGIVE ME, LORD.
WAIT.
"I KNOW YOU."

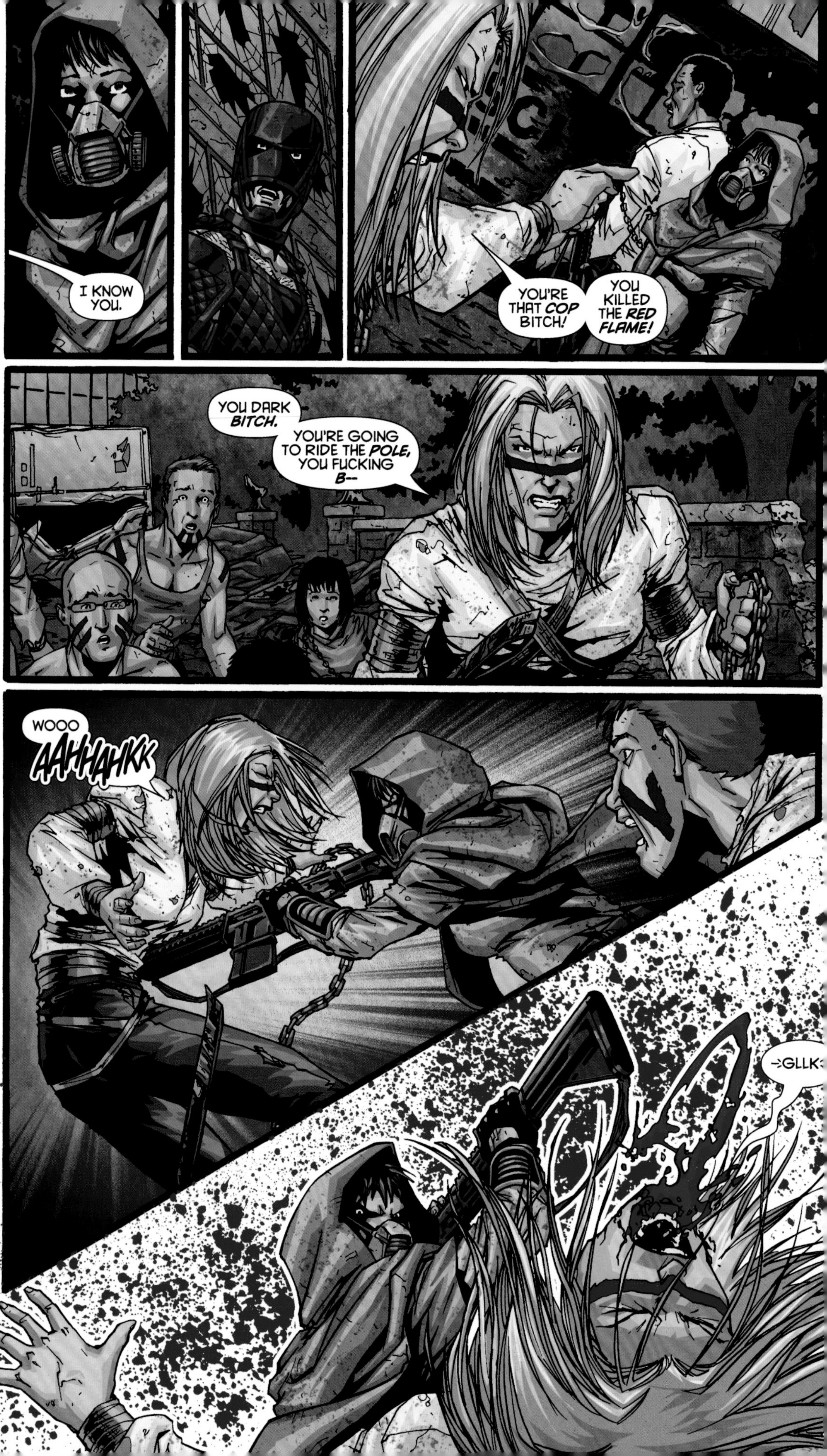
I KNOW YOU.
YOU'RE THAT COP BITCH!
YOU KILLED THE RED FLAME!
YOU DARK BITCH.
YOU'RE GOING TO RIDE THE POLE, YOU FUCKING B--
WOOO AAHHAHKK
-GLLK-

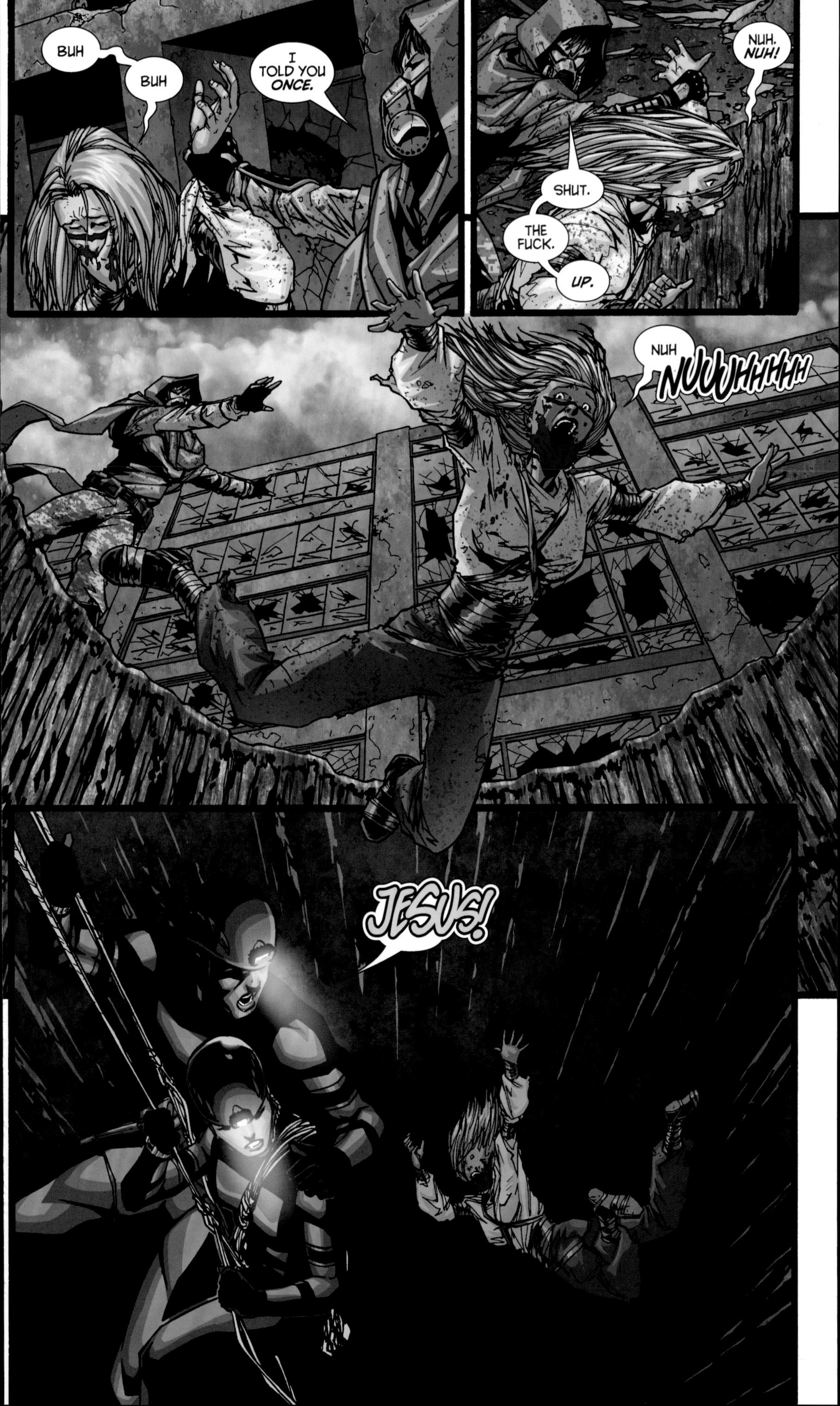
BUH
BUH
I TOLD YOU ONCE.
NUH, NUH!
SHUT.
THE FUCK.
UP.
NUH
NUUUHHHHH
JESUS!

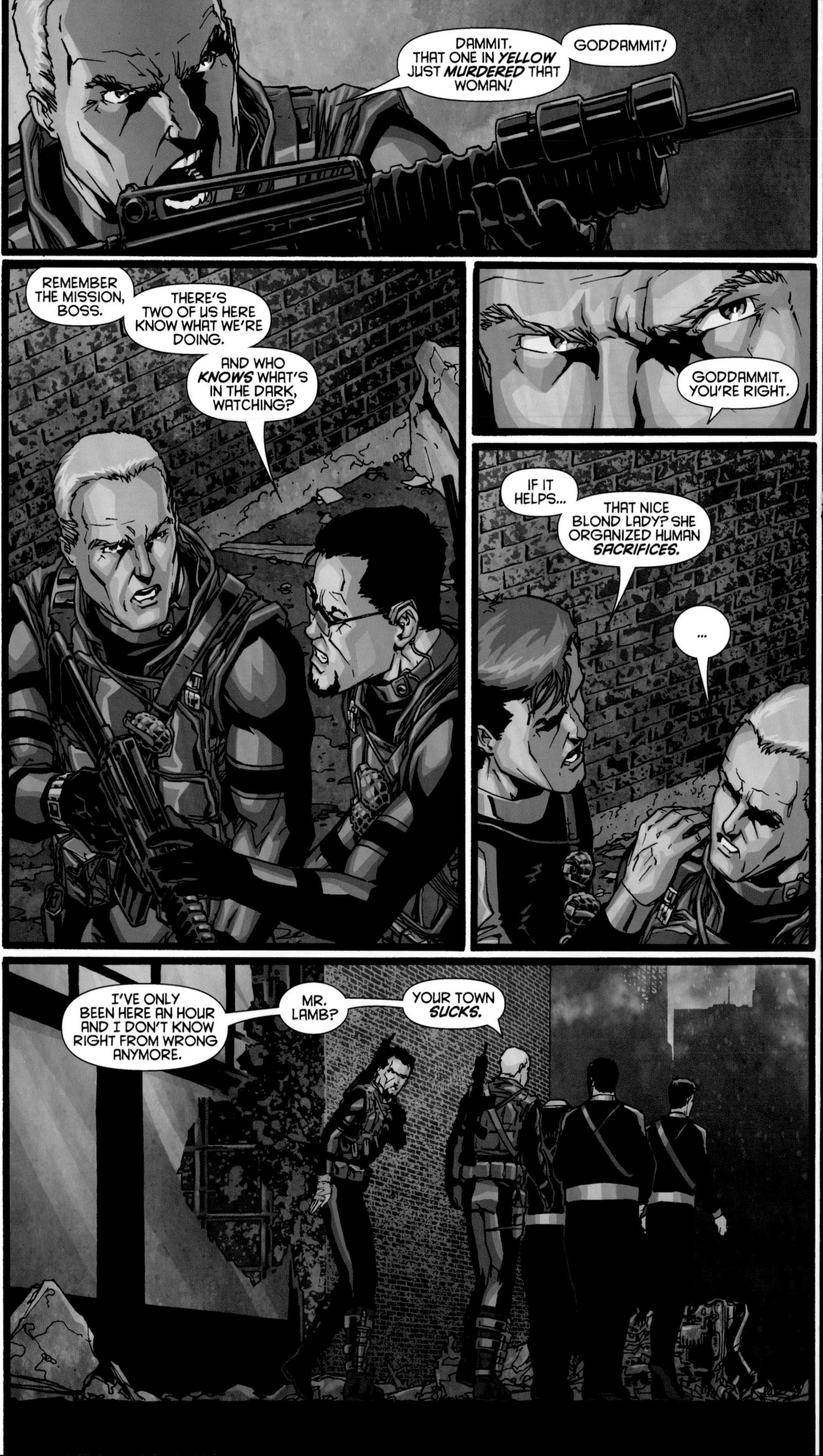

DAMMIT. THAT ONE IN *YELLOW* JUST *MURDERED* THAT WOMAN!
GODDAMMIT!
REMEMBER THE MISSION, BOSS.
THERE'S TWO OF US HERE KNOW WHAT WE'RE DOING.
AND WHO *KNOWS* WHAT'S IN THE DARK, WATCHING?
GODDAMMIT. YOU'RE RIGHT.
IF IT HELPS...
THAT NICE BLOND LADY? SHE ORGANIZED HUMAN *SACRIFICES.*
...
I'VE ONLY BEEN HERE AN HOUR AND I DON'T KNOW RIGHT FROM WRONG ANYMORE.
MR. LAMB?
YOUR TOWN *SUCKS.*

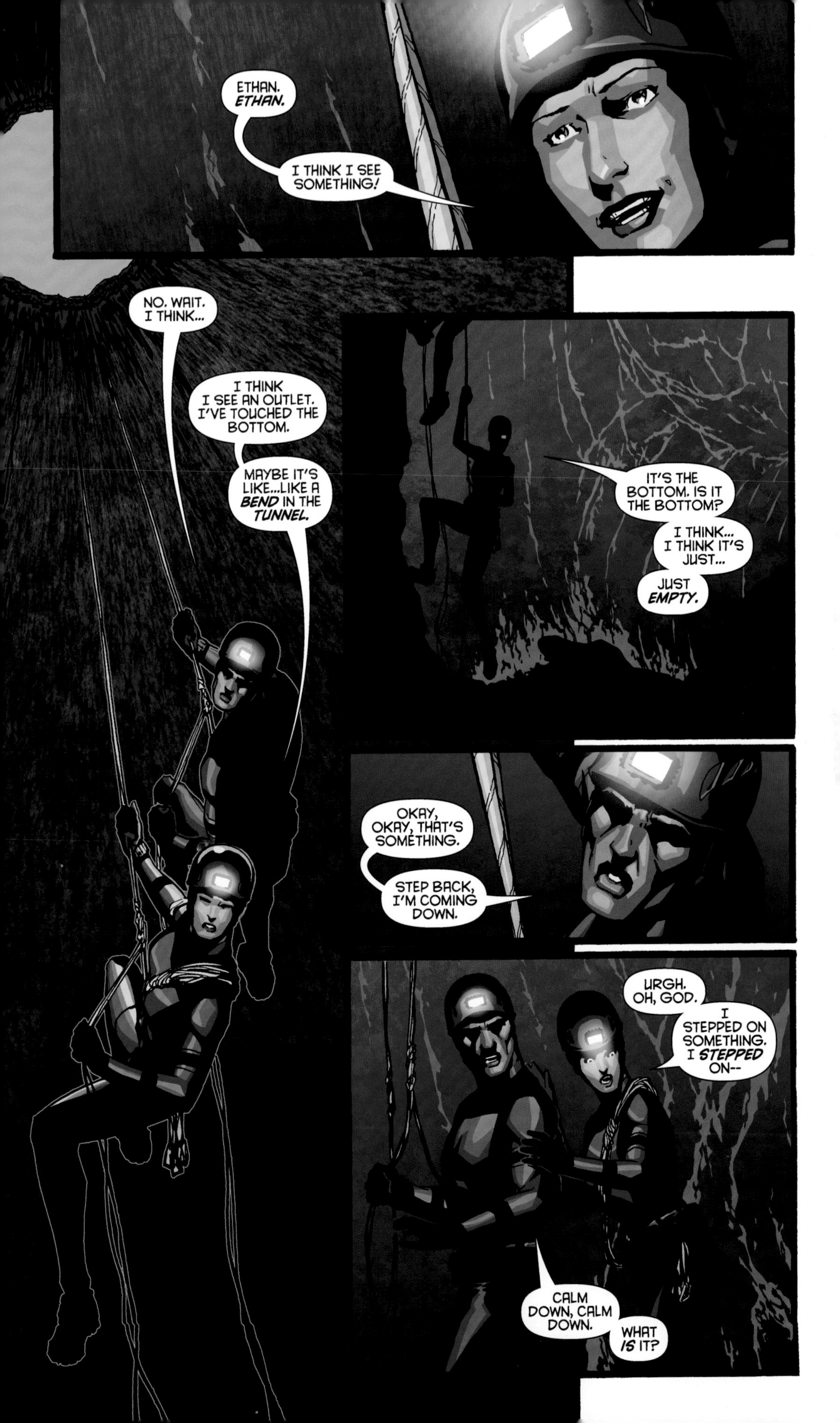
ETHAN. ETHAN.
I THINK I SEE SOMETHING!
NO. WAIT. I THINK...
I THINK I SEE AN OUTLET. I'VE TOUCHED THE BOTTOM.
MAYBE IT'S LIKE...LIKE A BEND IN THE TUNNEL.
IT'S THE BOTTOM. IS IT THE BOTTOM?
I THINK... I THINK IT'S JUST...
JUST EMPTY.
OKAY, OKAY, THAT'S SOMETHING.
STEP BACK, I'M COMING DOWN.
URGH. OH, GOD.
I STEPPED ON SOMETHING. I STEPPED ON--
CALM DOWN, CALM DOWN.
WHAT IS IT?

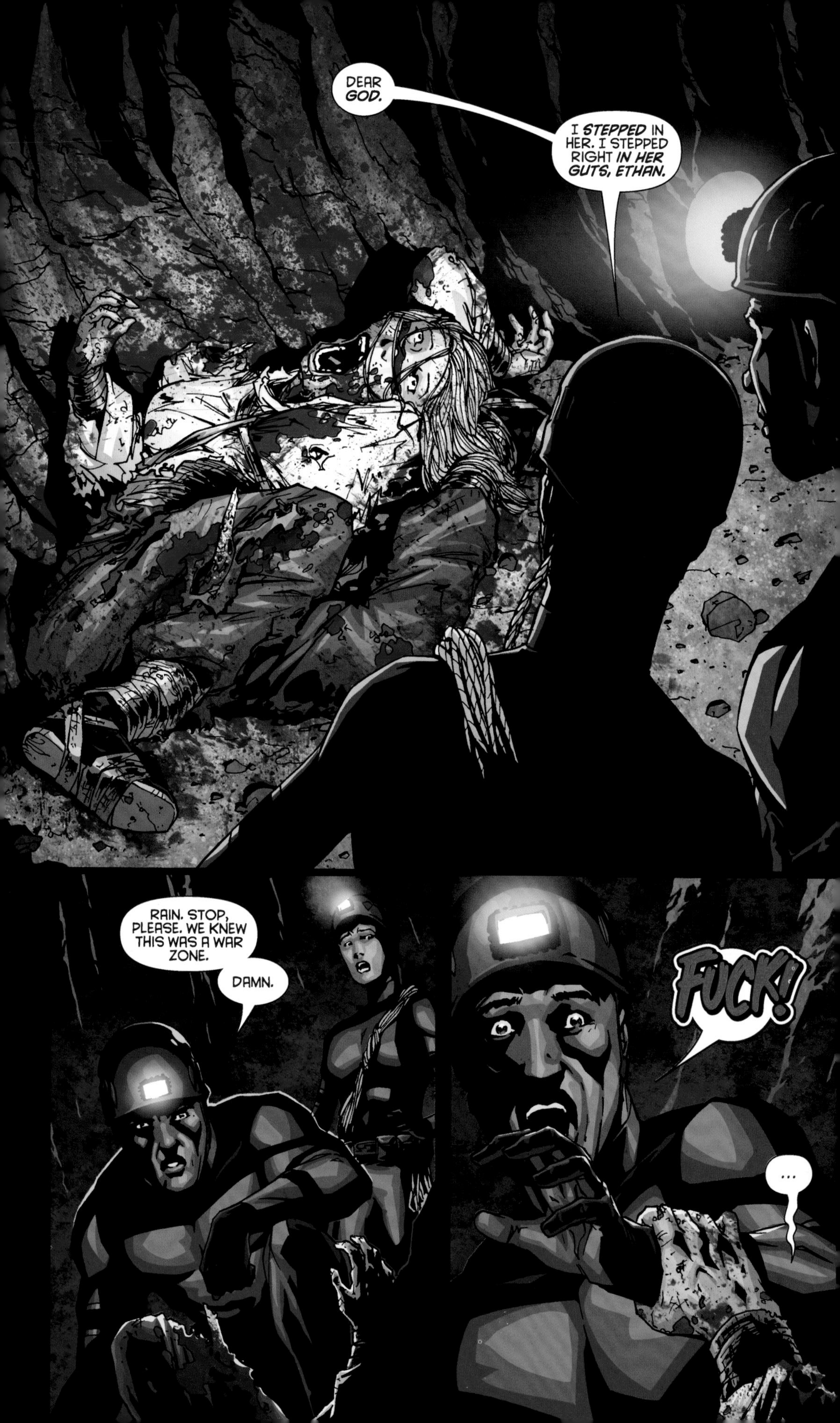
DEAR GOD.
I STEPPED IN HER. I STEPPED RIGHT IN HER GUTS, ETHAN.
RAIN. STOP, PLEASE. WE KNEW THIS WAS A WAR ZONE.
DAMN.
FUCK!
...

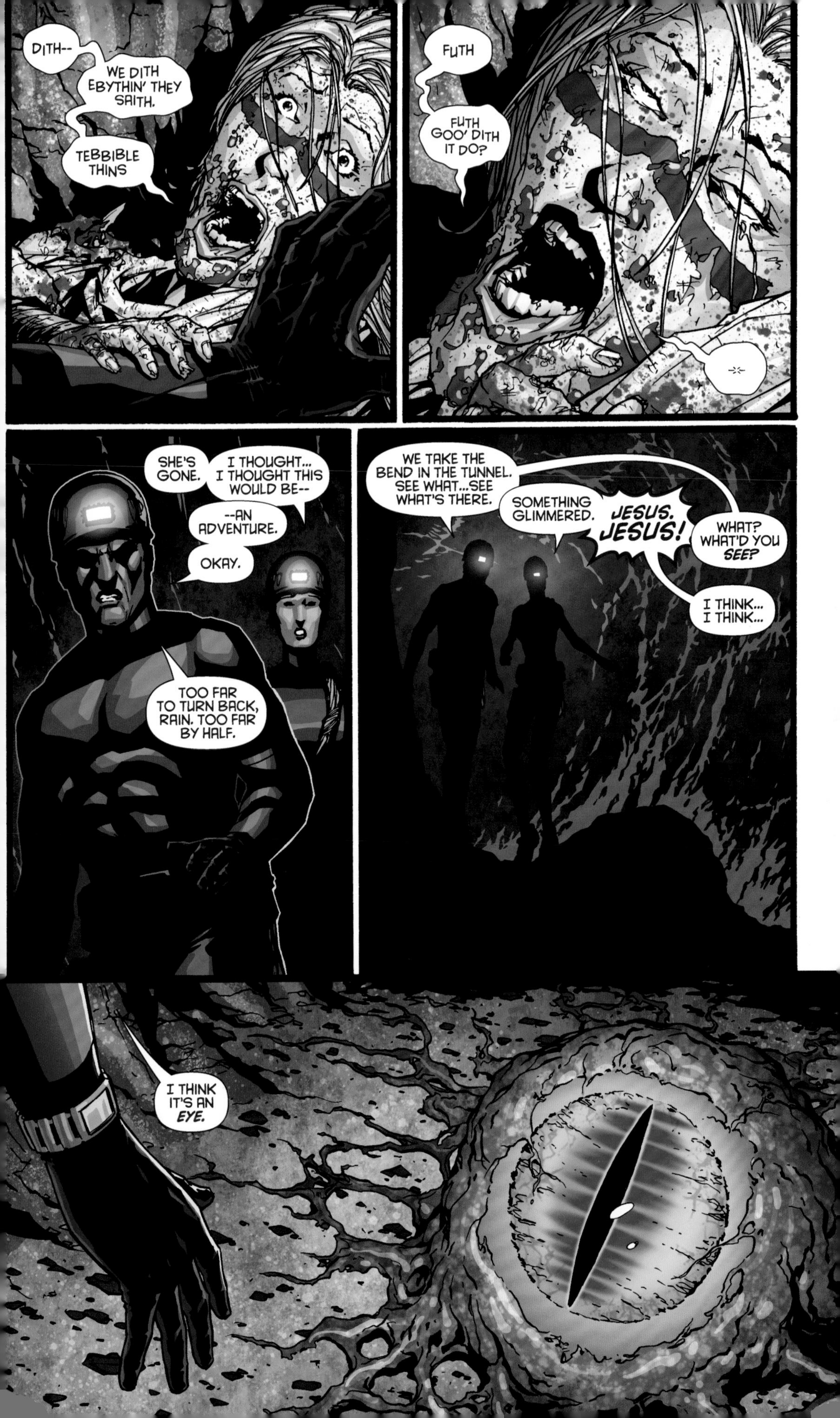
DITH--
WE DITH EBYTHIN' THEY SAITH.
TEBBIBLE THINS
FUTH
FUTH GOO' DITH IT DO?
SHE'S GONE.
I THOUGHT... I THOUGHT THIS WOULD BE--
--AN ADVENTURE.
OKAY.
TOO FAR TO TURN BACK, RAIN. TOO FAR BY HALF.
WE TAKE THE BEND IN THE TUNNEL. SEE WHAT...SEE WHAT'S THERE.
SOMETHING GLIMMERED.
JESUS. JESUS!
WHAT? WHAT'D YOU SEE?
I THINK... I THINK...
I THINK IT'S AN EYE.

SENATOR BELL: Now, Colonel Culver, I want to speak about something very frankly, here. And I feel it is in the best interests of this committee, and indeed the entire country, if I do not pussyfoot about with polite language, do you understand?

CULVER: I do, Senator.

CULVER: I believe we are all here in the interests of patriotism

SENATOR BELL: You seem unwell, Colonel. Do you need a recess?

CULVER: I do not, thank you, ma'am.

SENATOR BELL: Very good.

SENATOR BELL: Colonel, I wish to speak of the skin of the quarantine zone. I want to understand how, with our complete military resources, how that perimeter could be so porous as to allow

CULVER: Ma'am, if I may, I disagree with that assessment.

CULVER: Our remit was to prevent citizens from LEAVING the perimeter not to keep lunatics from trying to get back IN.

SENATOR BELL: So as to ALLOW, Colonel Culver...a party of ARMED MERCENARIES into the restricted zone, under the noses of yourself and your command.

CULVER: Perhaps...

CULVER: I am being advised by counsel, Senator.

CULVER: Perhaps a brief recess is indeed in order.

CULVER: With the committee's kind permission.

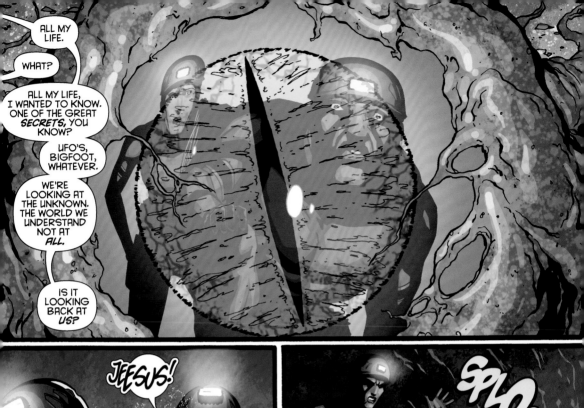

ALL MY LIFE.

WHAT?

ALL MY LIFE, I WANTED TO KNOW. ONE OF THE GREAT *SECRETS*, YOU KNOW?

UFO'S, BIGFOOT, WHATEVER.

WE'RE LOOKING AT THE UNKNOWN. THE WORLD WE UNDERSTAND NOT AT *ALL*.

IS IT LOOKING BACK AT *US*?

JEESUS!

FFTTSSSS

OOK UT.

SPLOOOOSH

GODDAMMIT.

ARE YOU OKAY? RAIN, ARE YOU ALL RIGHT?

...GOT IN MY *MOUTH*.

GOOD GOD, THAT'S *REVOLTING*.

DO WE TURN BACK?

NO.

NO, BABY, WE DON'T.

SENATOR BELL: If we may continue...

CULVER: Yes, ma'am, thank you, Senator.

SENATOR BELL: I guess what I'm trying to ask, Culver, is how, with the personnel and surveillance resources at your disposal, a group of ARMED paramilitary activists were able to breach your guideposts?

CULVER: It's as I said, Senator. We were told to abate any flow of citizens OUTWARD.

CULVER: If someone really, REALLY wants to jump into the tiger pit at the zoo, no amount of CAMERAS is going to stop them.

SENATOR BELL: But ARMED militia men, with VERY shady pasts...?

CULVER: We told the populace the approved story, Senator. The entire WORLD was told that the area was TOXIC and INFECTED and LETHAL.

CULVER: What happened to those people, those occupiers, was tragic. Horrific.

CULVER: But it was NOT our FAULT.

SENATOR: Colonel Culver, our mission is not to find "fault."

CULVER: Tanks make a poor fence, Senator. They might stop a bus.

CULVER: They don't stop a small RAFT in the middle of the NIGHT.

SENATOR BELL: And because of that...

CULVER: ...people died. Yes.

CULVER: People died.

CULVER: A lot of people died.

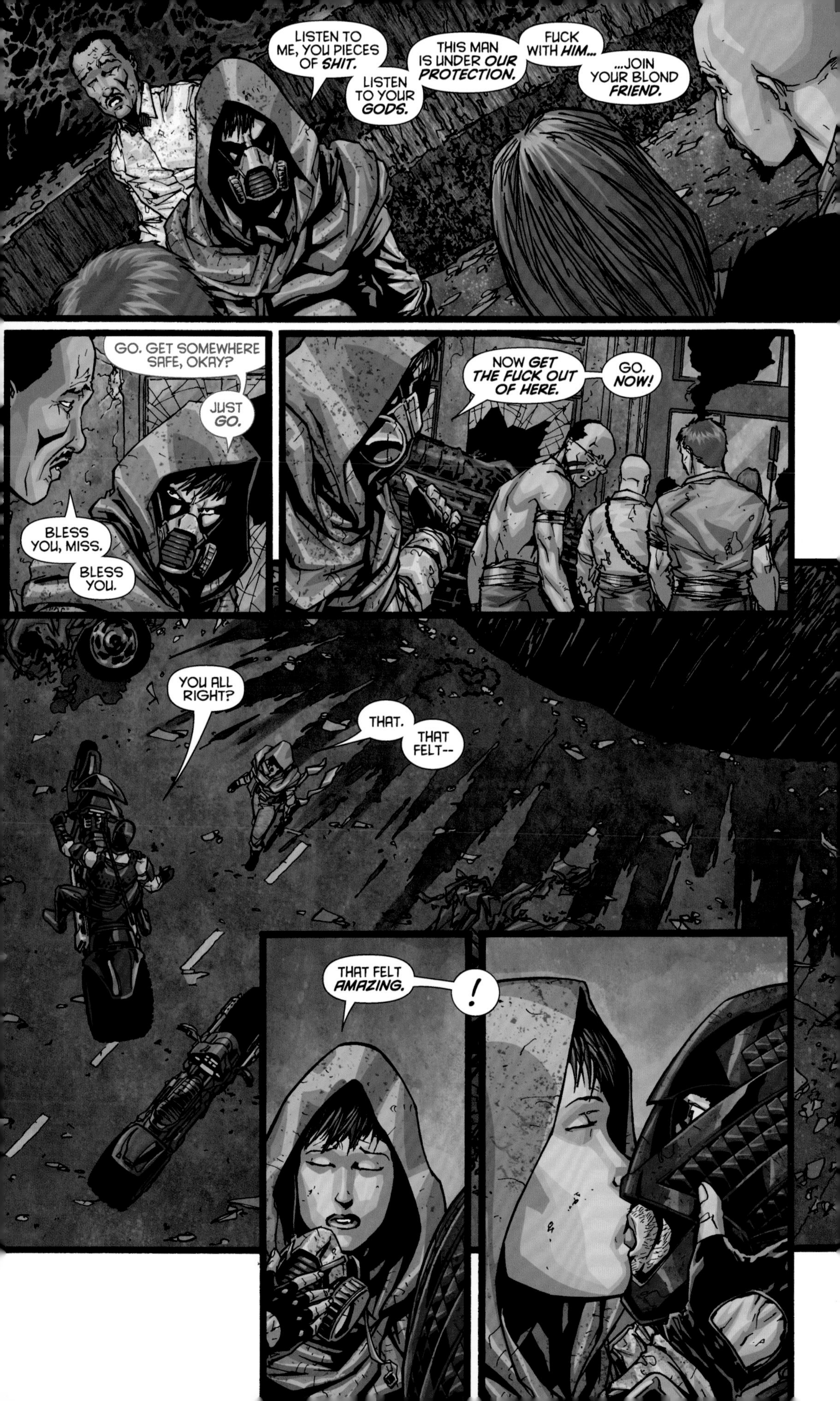
LISTEN TO ME, YOU PIECES OF *SHIT.*
LISTEN TO YOUR *GODS.*
THIS MAN IS UNDER *OUR PROTECTION.*
FUCK WITH *HIM...*
...JOIN YOUR BLOND *FRIEND.*
GO. GET SOMEWHERE SAFE, OKAY?
JUST *GO.*
BLESS YOU, MISS.
BLESS YOU.
NOW *GET THE FUCK OUT OF HERE.*
GO. *NOW!*
YOU ALL RIGHT?
THAT.
THAT FELT--
THAT FELT *AMAZING.*
!

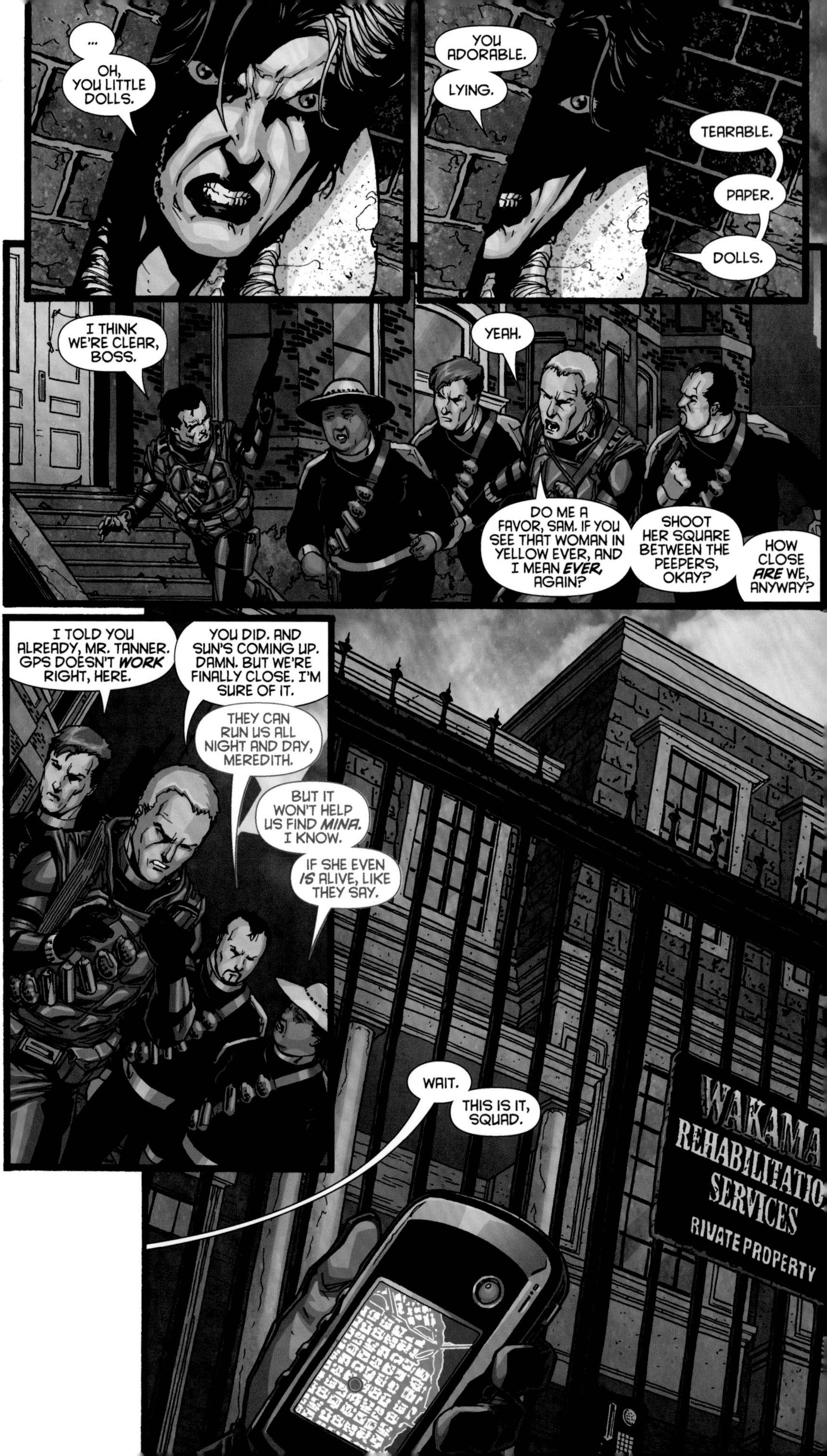
...
OH, YOU LITTLE DOLLS.
YOU ADORABLE.
LYING.
TEARABLE.
PAPER.
DOLLS.
I THINK WE'RE CLEAR, BOSS.
YEAH.
DO ME A FAVOR, SAM. IF YOU SEE THAT WOMAN IN YELLOW EVER, AND I MEAN *EVER*, AGAIN?
SHOOT HER SQUARE BETWEEN THE PEEPERS, OKAY?
HOW CLOSE *ARE* WE, ANYWAY?
I TOLD YOU ALREADY, MR. TANNER. GPS DOESN'T *WORK* RIGHT, HERE.
YOU DID. AND SUN'S COMING UP. DAMN. BUT WE'RE FINALLY CLOSE. I'M SURE OF IT.
THEY CAN RUN US ALL NIGHT AND DAY, MEREDITH.
BUT IT WON'T HELP US FIND *MINA*. I KNOW.
IF SHE EVEN *IS* ALIVE, LIKE THEY SAY.
WAIT.
THIS IS IT, SQUAD.
WAKAMA
REHABILITATIO
SERVICES
RIVATE PROPERTY

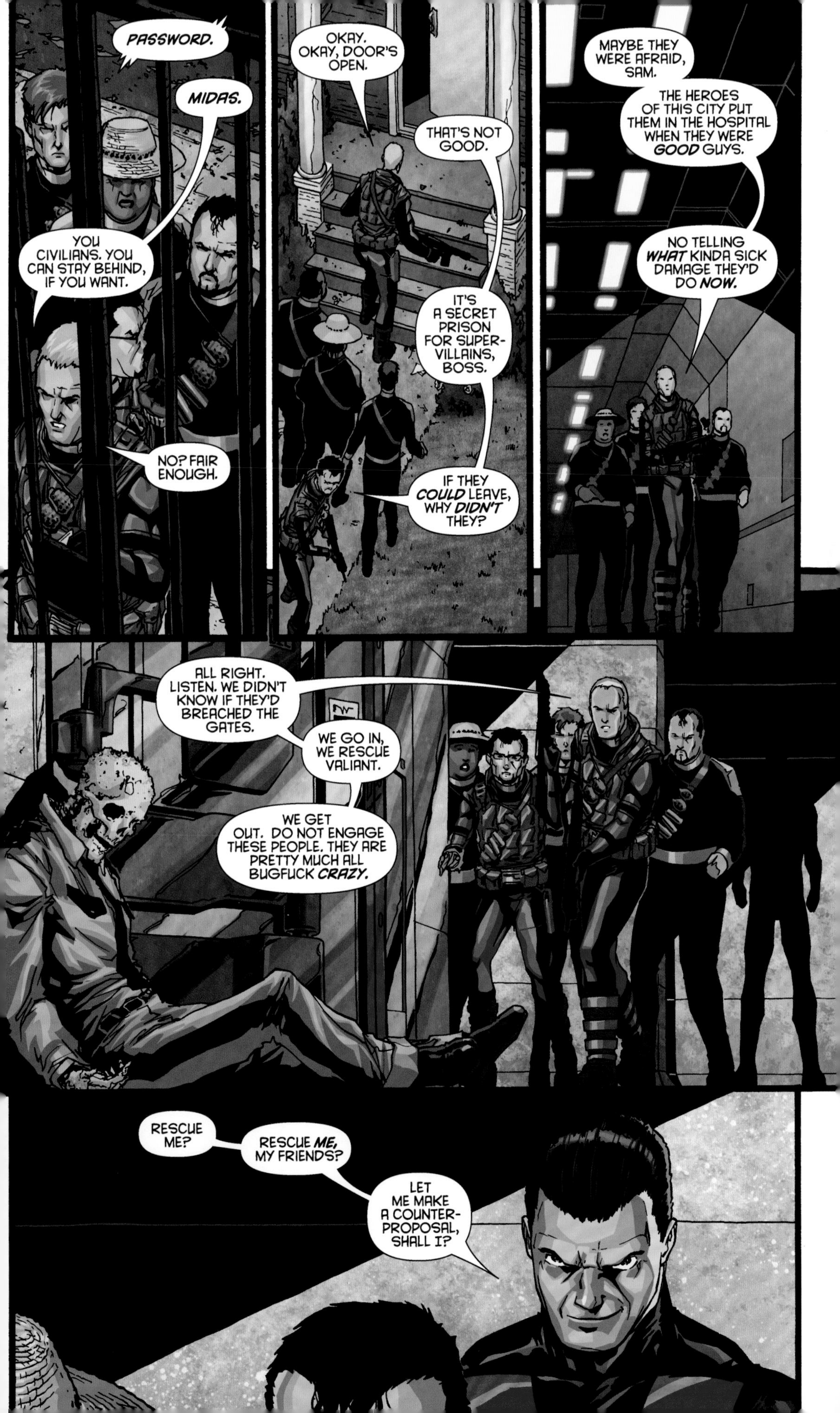
PASSWORD.
MIDAS.
YOU CIVILIANS. YOU CAN STAY BEHIND, IF YOU WANT.
NO? FAIR ENOUGH.
OKAY. OKAY, DOOR'S OPEN.
THAT'S NOT GOOD.
IT'S A SECRET PRISON FOR SUPER-VILLAINS, BOSS.
IF THEY COULD LEAVE, WHY DIDN'T THEY?
MAYBE THEY WERE AFRAID, SAM.
THE HEROES OF THIS CITY PUT THEM IN THE HOSPITAL WHEN THEY WERE GOOD GUYS.
NO TELLING WHAT KINDA SICK DAMAGE THEY'D DO NOW.
ALL RIGHT. LISTEN. WE DIDN'T KNOW IF THEY'D BREACHED THE GATES.
WE GO IN, WE RESCUE VALIANT.
WE GET OUT. DO NOT ENGAGE THESE PEOPLE. THEY ARE PRETTY MUCH ALL BUGFUCK CRAZY.
RESCUE ME?
RESCUE ME, MY FRIENDS?
LET ME MAKE A COUNTER-PROPOSAL, SHALL I?

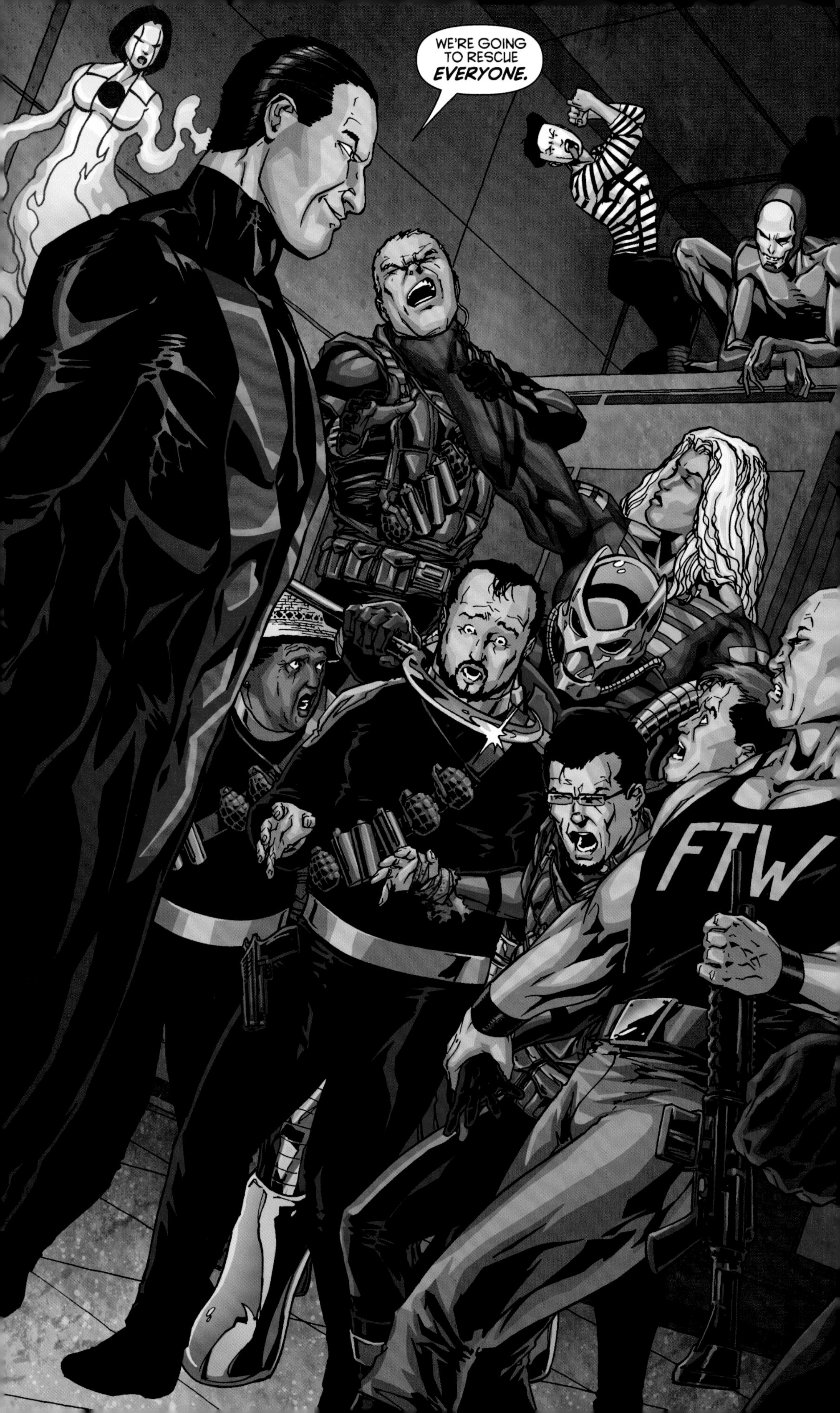
WE'RE GOING TO RESCUE EVERYONE.
FTW

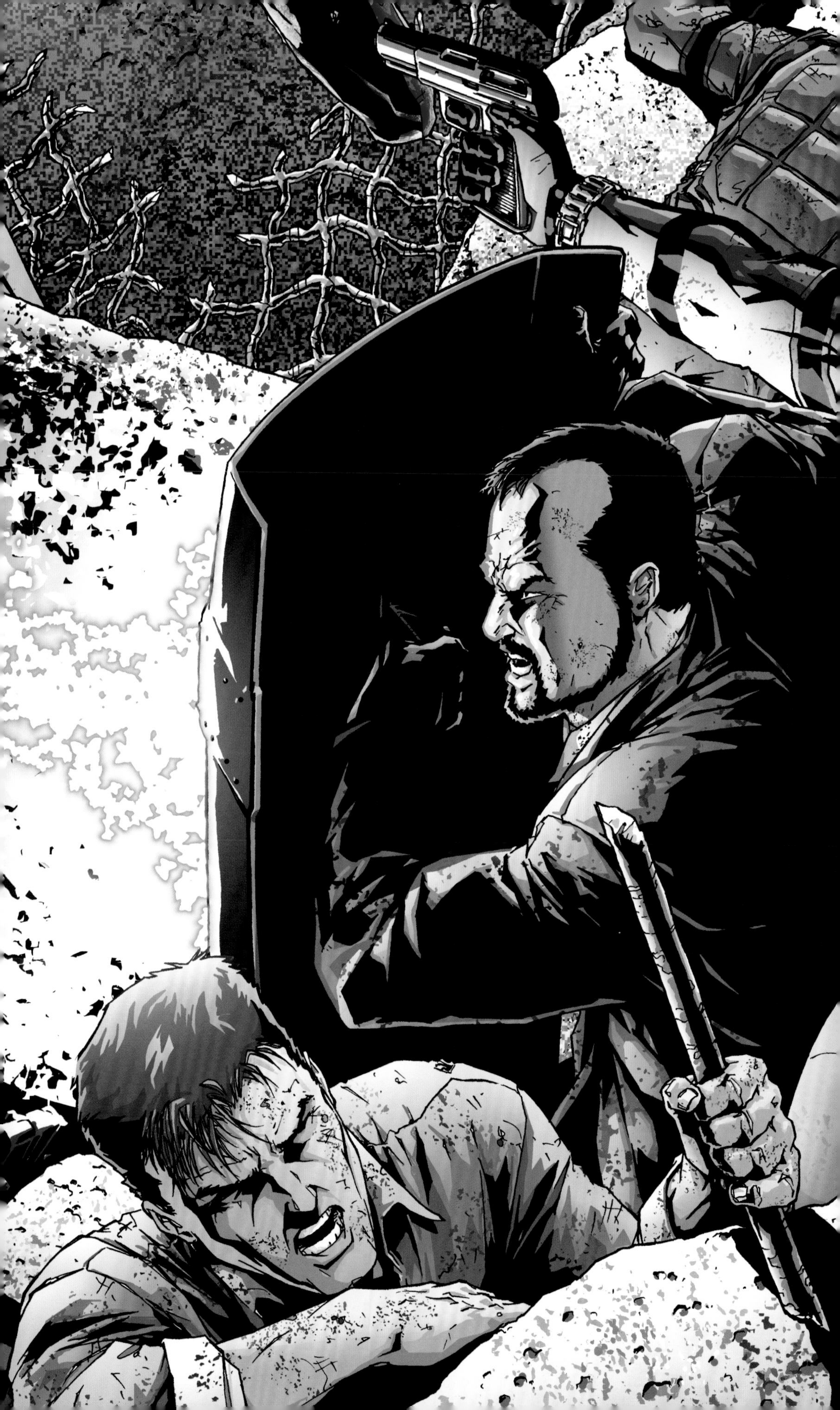

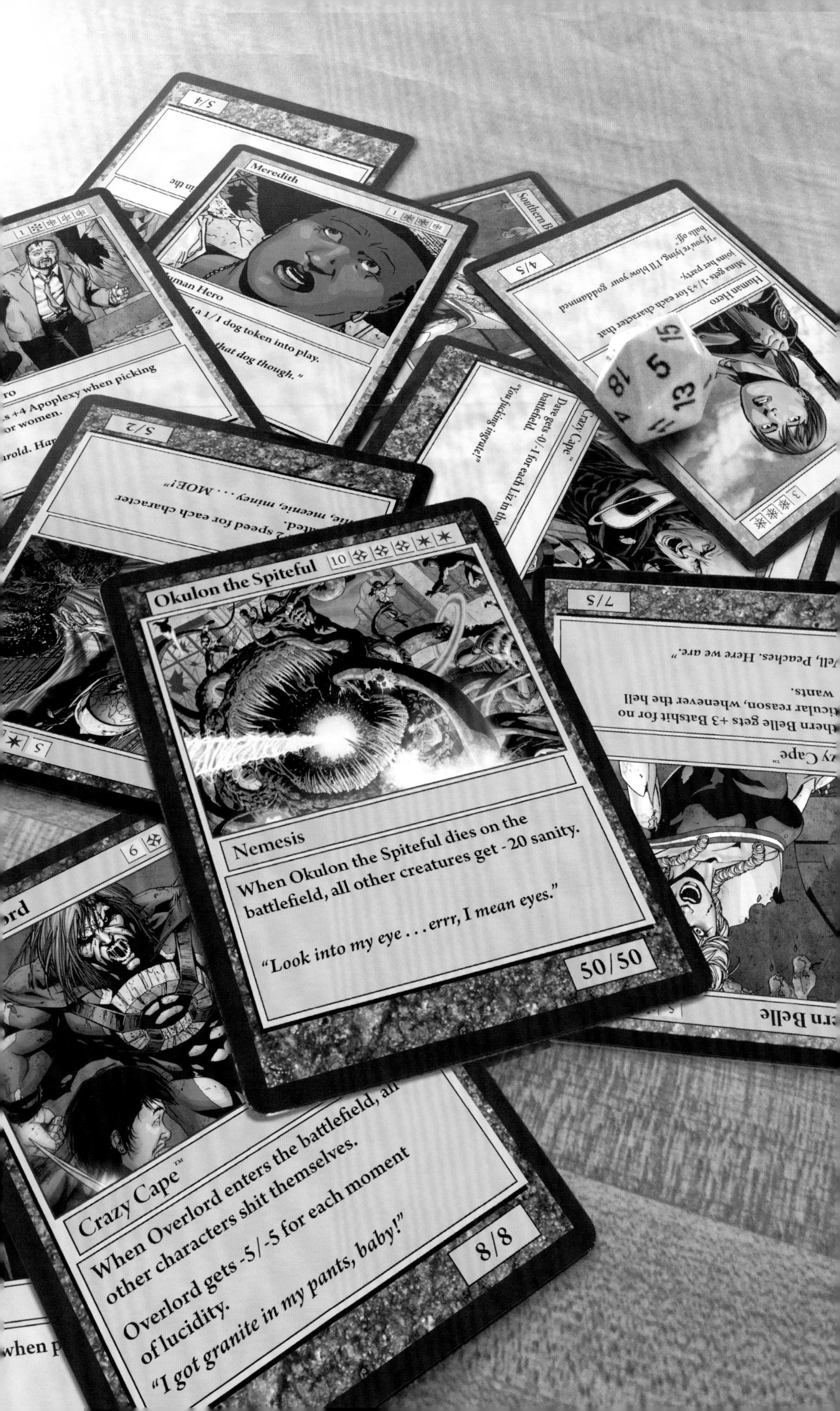

Okulon the Spiteful
10
Nemesis
When Okulon the Spiteful dies on the battlefield, all other creatures get - 20 sanity.
"Look into my eye . . . errr, I mean eyes."
50/50
Crazy Cape™
When Overlord enters the battlefield, all other characters shit themselves.
Overlord gets -5/-5 for each moment of lucidity.
"I got granite in my pants, baby!"
8/8
Meredith
Human Hero
Crazy Cape™
Dave gets -0/-1 for each Liv in the battlefield.
"You fucking ingrate!"
Human Hero
Mina gets -1/+3 for each character that joins her party.
"If you're lying, I'll blow your goddamned balls off."
4/5
5/4
5/2
7/5

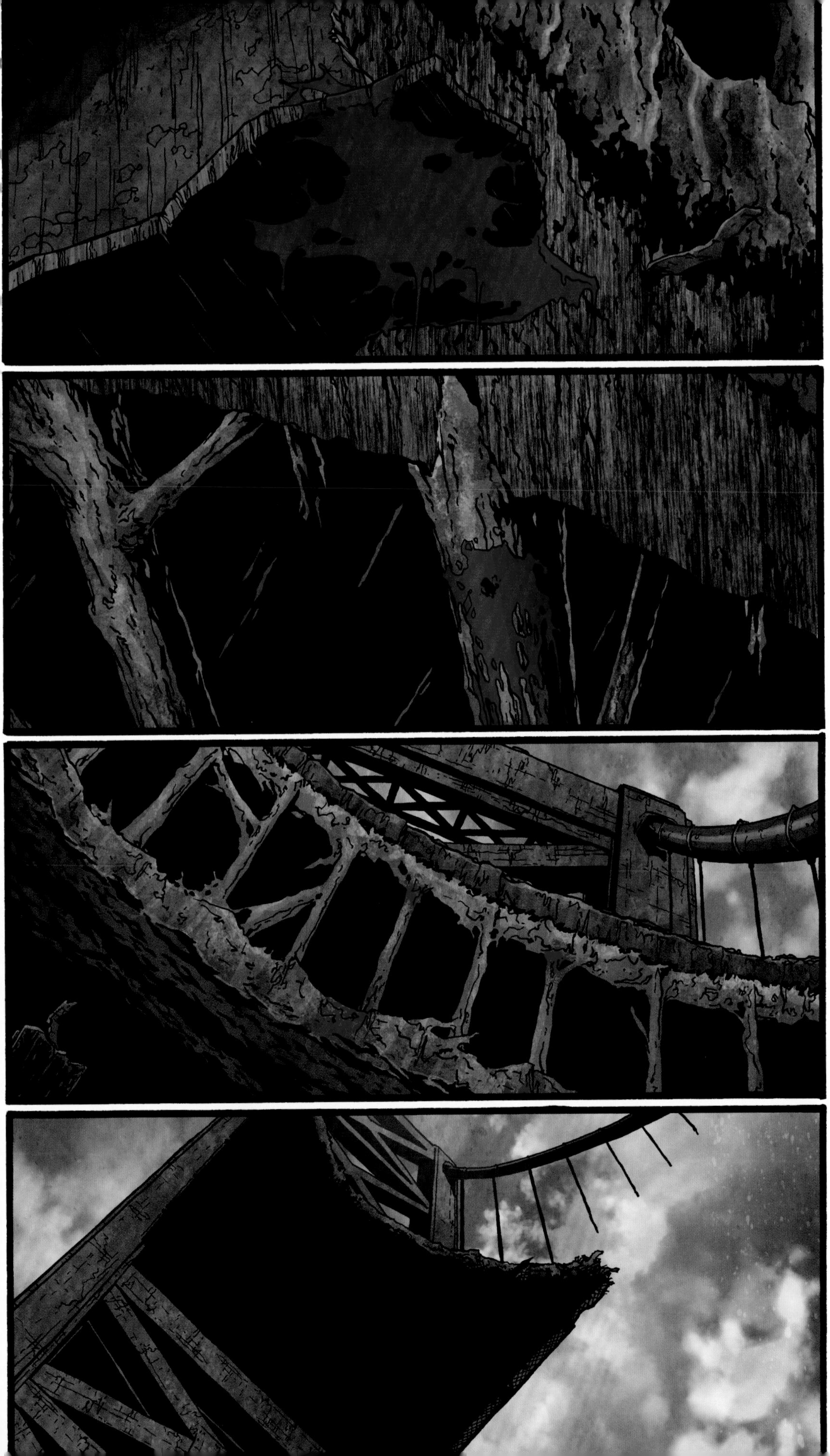

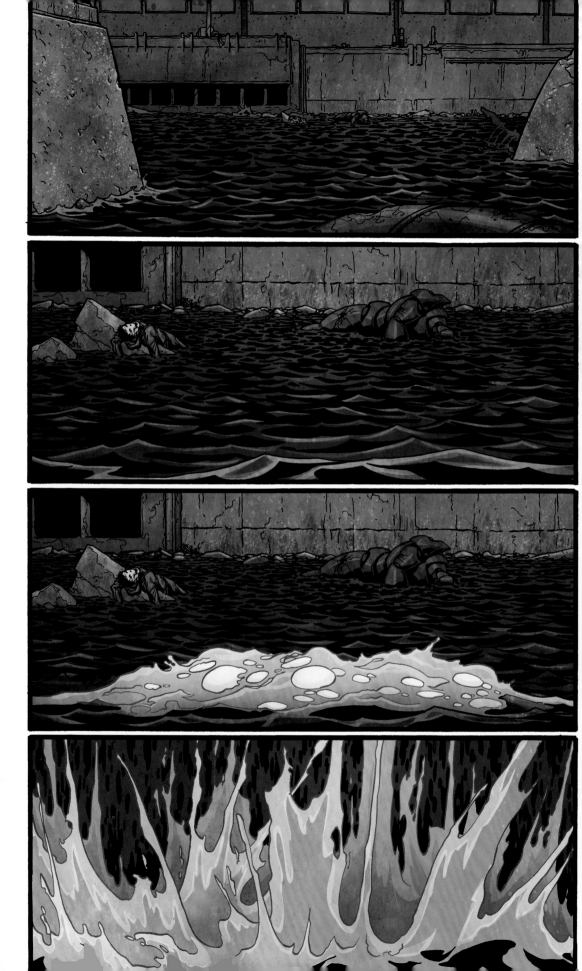

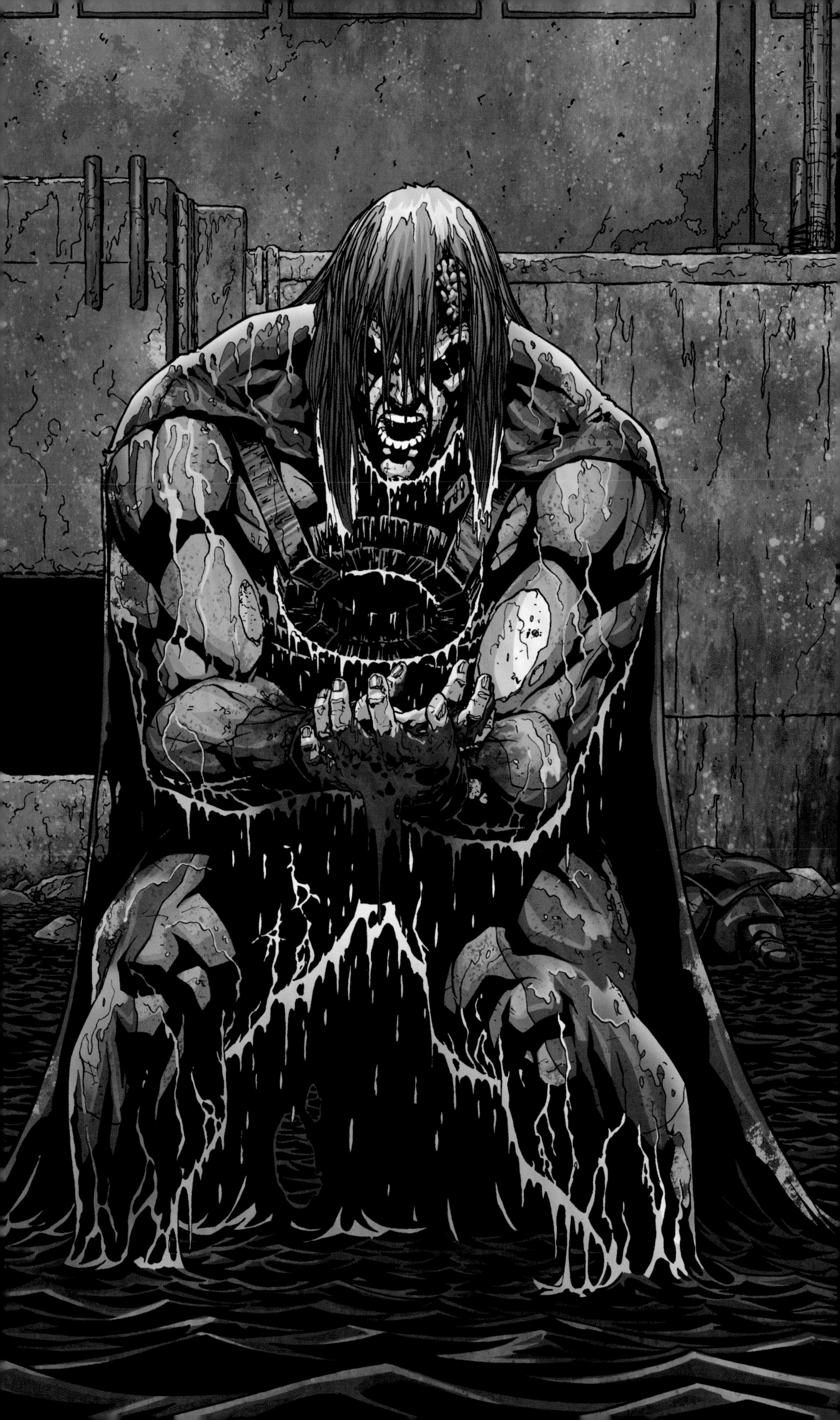

SENATOR BELL: Colonel Culver, this committee would like to ask about--

COLONEL CULVER (coughs heavily, counsel pours a glass of water, which the colonel drinks, seemingly recovering): Ma'am. Pardon.

SENATOR BELL: Are you unwell, sir?

COLONEL CULVER: I haven't had a proper night's sleep in a bit, Senator.

SENATOR BELL: Are you able to continue?

COLONEL CULVER: I am.

SENATOR BELL: Outstanding. I have here a transcript of a statement you made to journalists on the evening following the first military attempt to enter the quarantine zone. Are you familiar with this document?

COLONEL CULVER: I am, ma'am. I may have been somewhat optimistic.

SENATOR BELL: You state, and I quote, "We're the most powerful military in the world. I think we can pacify a few freaks in Jazzercise outfits."

COLONEL CULVER: As I said, I may have been optimistic.

SENATOR BELL: And did something cause you to lose your optimism, Colonel?

COLONEL CULVER: Yes. I lost my optimism when they sent our first tank back to us, crushed to the size of a cocker spaniel.

SENATOR BELL: I...I see.

COLONEL CULVER: With the crew still inside.

SENATOR BELL: Let's move on.

COLONEL CULVER: Then they got MEAN.

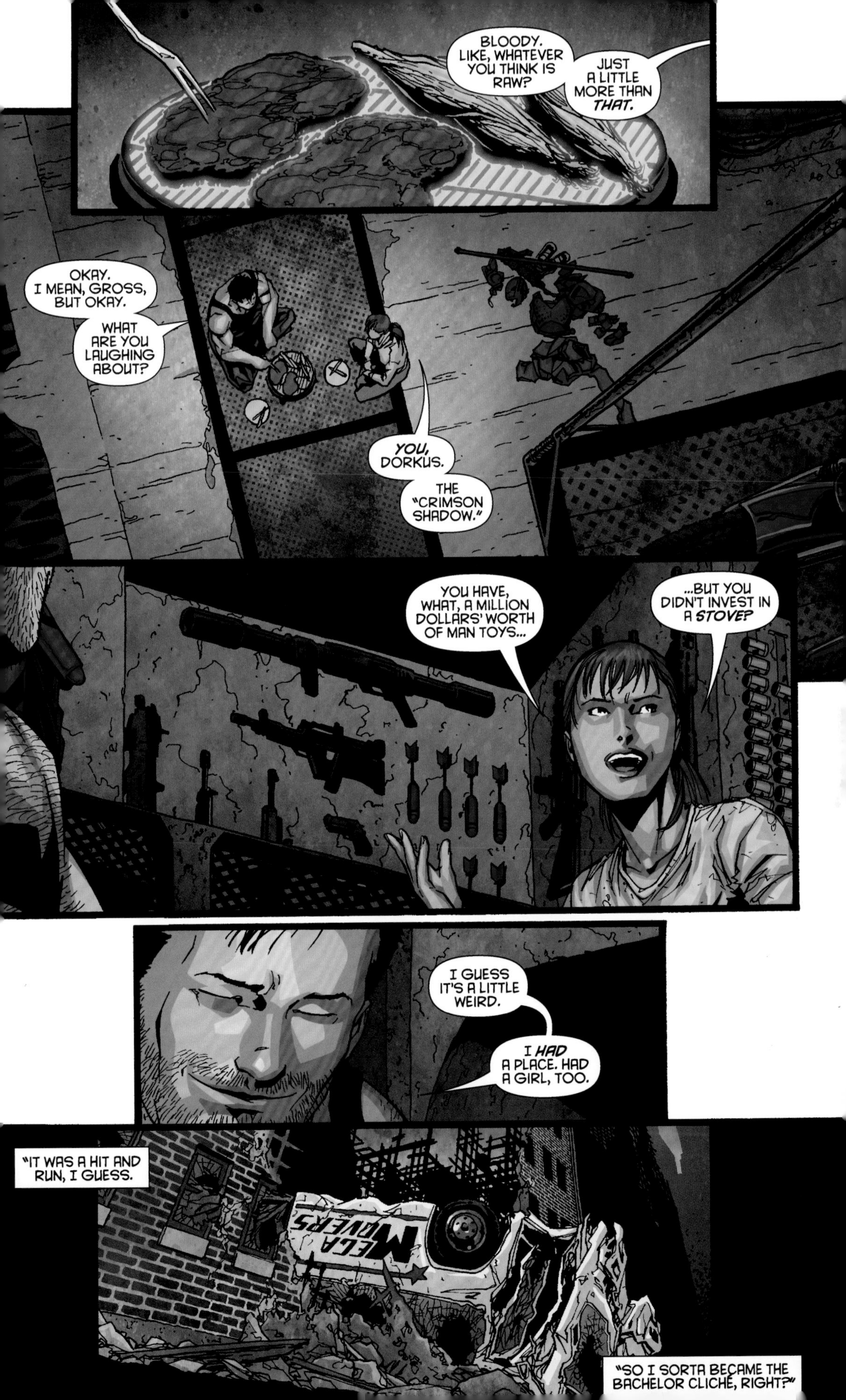
BLOODY. LIKE, WHATEVER YOU THINK IS RAW?
JUST A LITTLE MORE THAN *THAT.*
OKAY. I MEAN, GROSS, BUT OKAY.
WHAT ARE YOU LAUGHING ABOUT?
YOU, DORKUS.
THE "CRIMSON SHADOW."
YOU HAVE, WHAT, A MILLION DOLLARS' WORTH OF MAN TOYS...
...BUT YOU DIDN'T INVEST IN A *STOVE?*
I GUESS IT'S A LITTLE WEIRD.
I *HAD* A PLACE. HAD A GIRL, TOO.
"IT WAS A HIT AND RUN, I GUESS.
MEGA MOVERS
"SO I SORTA BECAME THE BACHELOR CLICHÉ, RIGHT?"

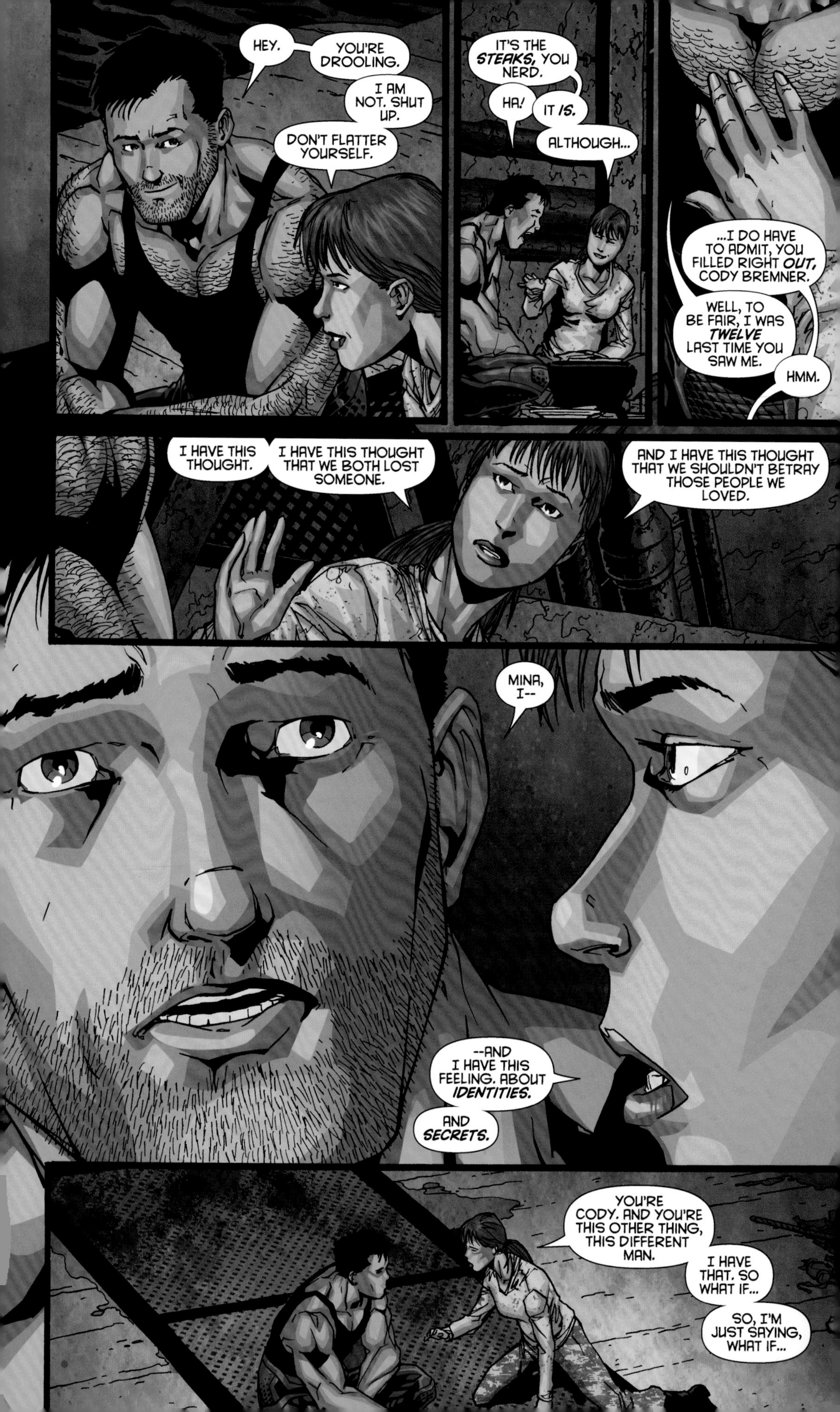
HEY.
YOU'RE DROOLING.
I AM NOT. SHUT UP.
DON'T FLATTER YOURSELF.
IT'S THE STEAKS, YOU NERD.
HA!
IT IS.
ALTHOUGH...
...I DO HAVE TO ADMIT, YOU FILLED RIGHT OUT, CODY BREMNER.
WELL, TO BE FAIR, I WAS TWELVE LAST TIME YOU SAW ME.
HMM.
I HAVE THIS THOUGHT.
I HAVE THIS THOUGHT THAT WE BOTH LOST SOMEONE.
AND I HAVE THIS THOUGHT THAT WE SHOULDN'T BETRAY THOSE PEOPLE WE LOVED.
MINA, I--
--AND I HAVE THIS FEELING. ABOUT IDENTITIES.
AND SECRETS.
YOU'RE CODY. AND YOU'RE THIS OTHER THING, THIS DIFFERENT MAN.
I HAVE THAT. SO WHAT IF...
SO, I'M JUST SAYING, WHAT IF...

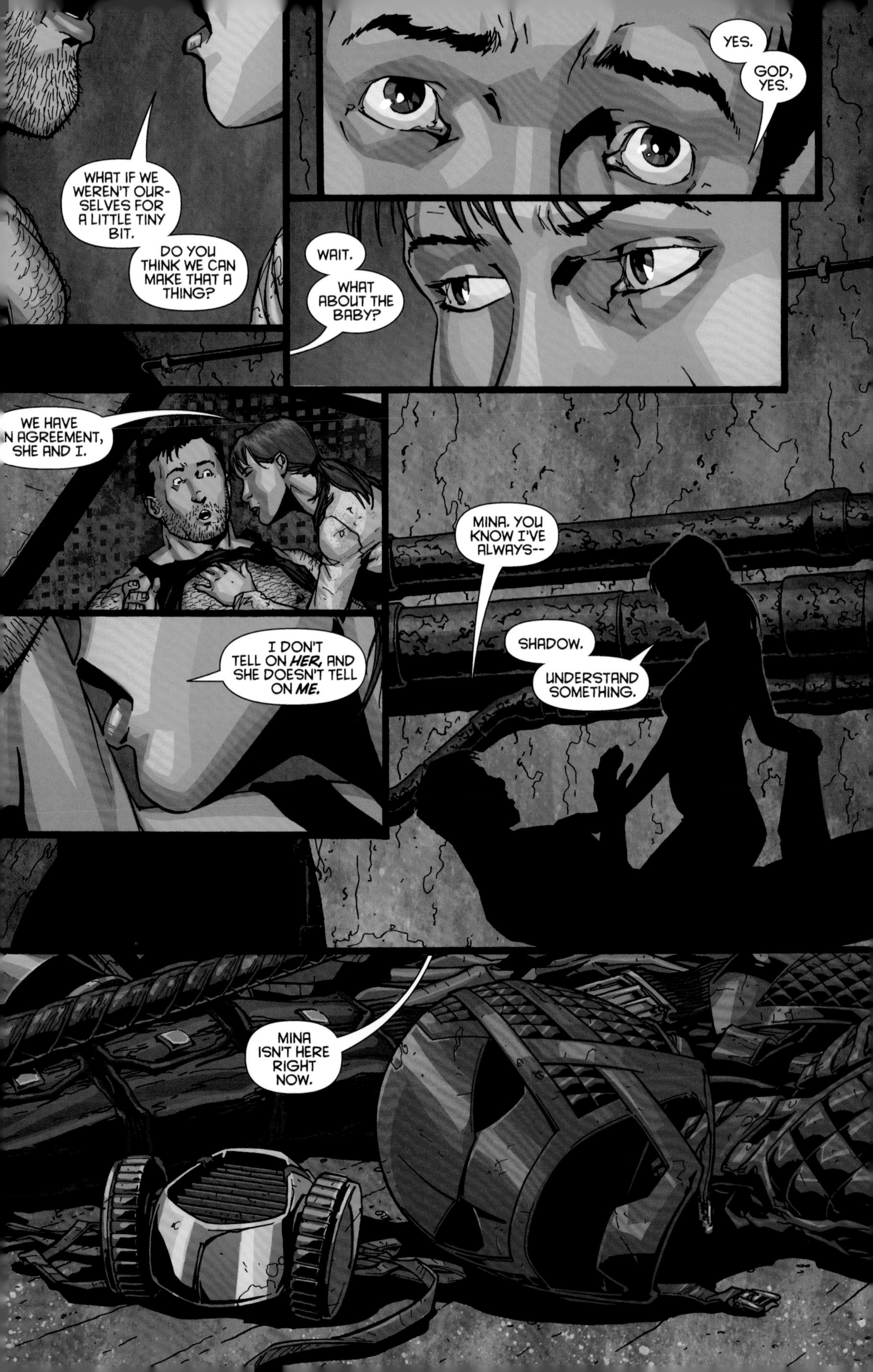
WHAT IF WE WEREN'T OUR-SELVES FOR A LITTLE TINY BIT.
DO YOU THINK WE CAN MAKE THAT A THING?
YES.
GOD, YES.
WAIT.
WHAT ABOUT THE BABY?
WE HAVE N AGREEMENT, SHE AND I.
I DON'T TELL ON HER, AND SHE DOESN'T TELL ON ME.
MINA. YOU KNOW I'VE ALWAYS--
SHADOW.
UNDERSTAND SOMETHING.
MINA ISN'T HERE RIGHT NOW.

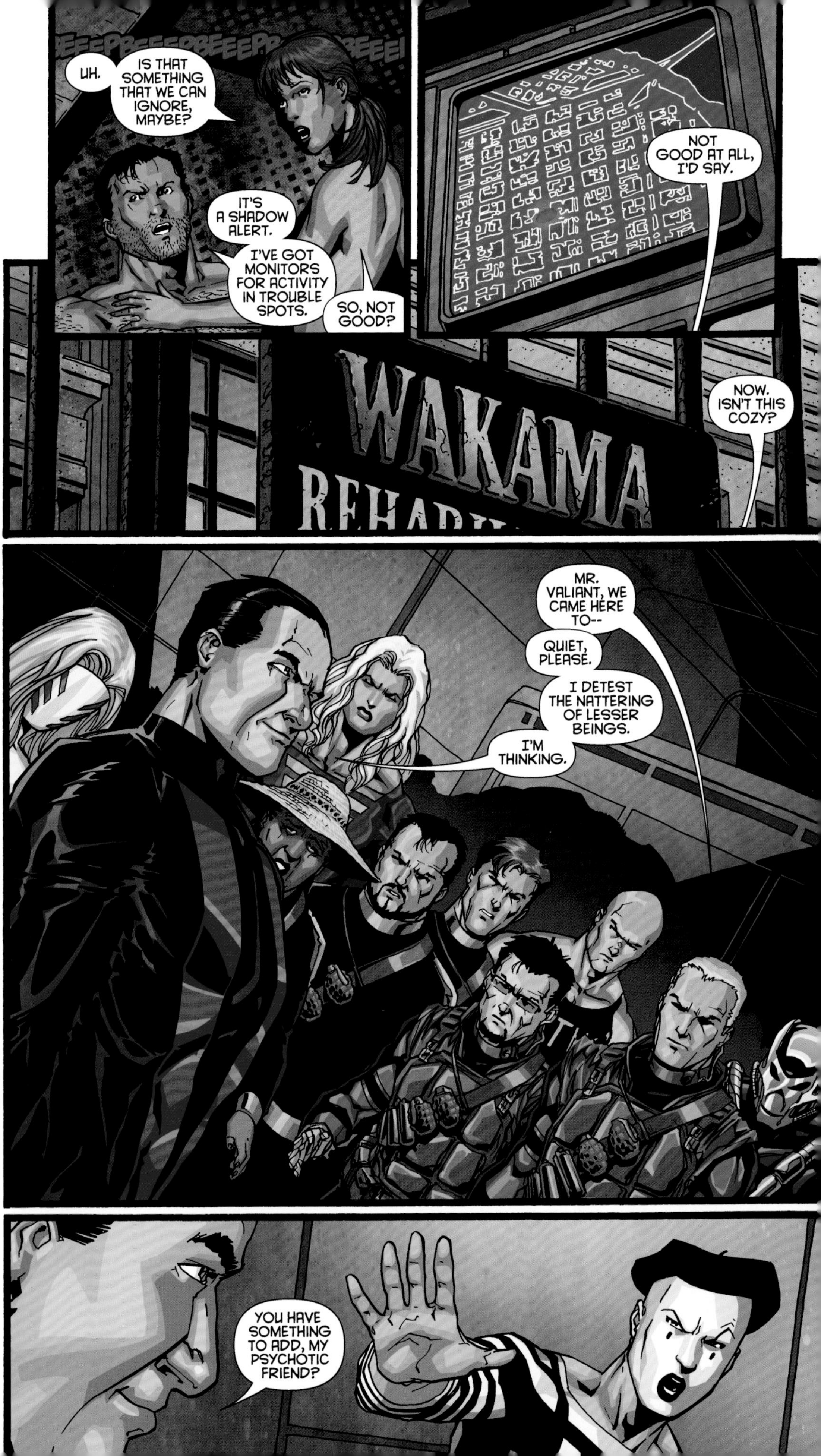
BEEEPBEEEPBEEEPBEEEPBEEEI
UH.
IS THAT SOMETHING THAT WE CAN IGNORE, MAYBE?
IT'S A SHADOW ALERT.
I'VE GOT MONITORS FOR ACTIVITY IN TROUBLE SPOTS.
SO, NOT GOOD?
NOT GOOD AT ALL, I'D SAY.
WAKAMA
NOW. ISN'T THIS COZY?
MR. VALIANT, WE CAME HERE TO--
QUIET, PLEASE.
I DETEST THE NATTERING OF LESSER BEINGS.
I'M THINKING.
YOU HAVE SOMETHING TO ADD, MY PSYCHOTIC FRIEND?

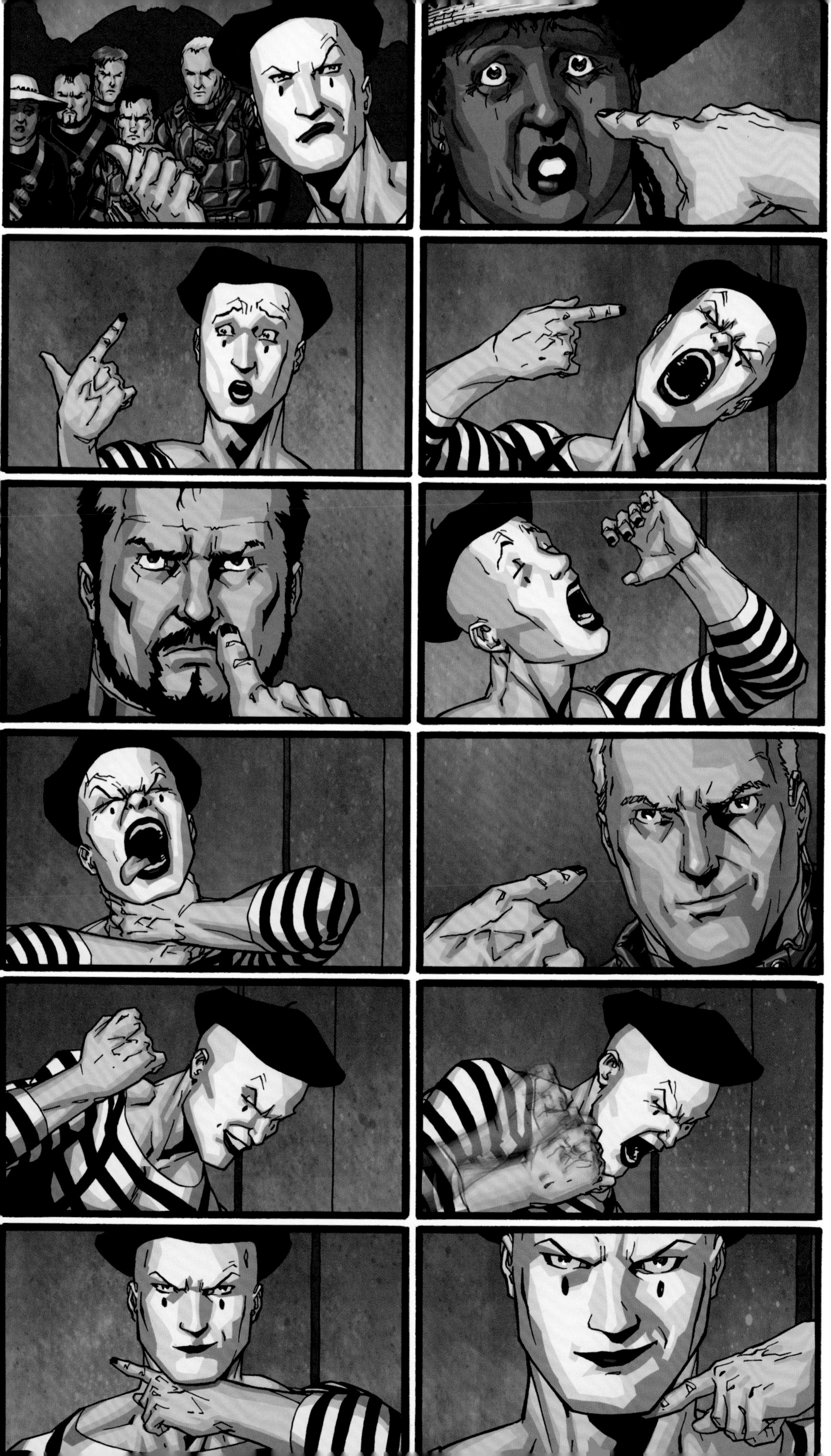

I HATE MIMES.

EVERYONE DOES.

YOUR POINT IS WELL TAKEN, MIME MASTER.

IT POSSIBLY *WOULD* BE A GOOD DEAL MORE PRUDENT TO DISPOSE OF THE ARMED GROUP THAT SHOWED UP ON OUR DOORSTEP UNANNOUNCED.

YOU'RE CLEARLY THE LEADER.

WHAT SAY *YOU* TO MY PALE COMPANION'S PROPOSAL?

QUICKLY NOW.

TICK TOCK.

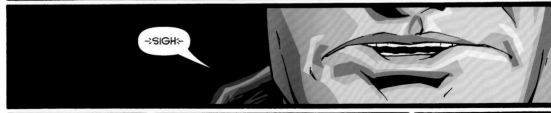

⊰SIGH⊱

OH, DEAR.

MR. VALIANT.

YOUR SUPERMODEL *WIFE* SEEMS TO THINK YOU'RE WORTH SAVING.

I MYSELF REMAIN UNCONVINCED.

BUT SHE IS PAYING ME ONE *HELL* OF A LOT OF MONEY TO SEE YOU HOME SAFELY.

AND IT'S MY PLAN TO COLLECT.

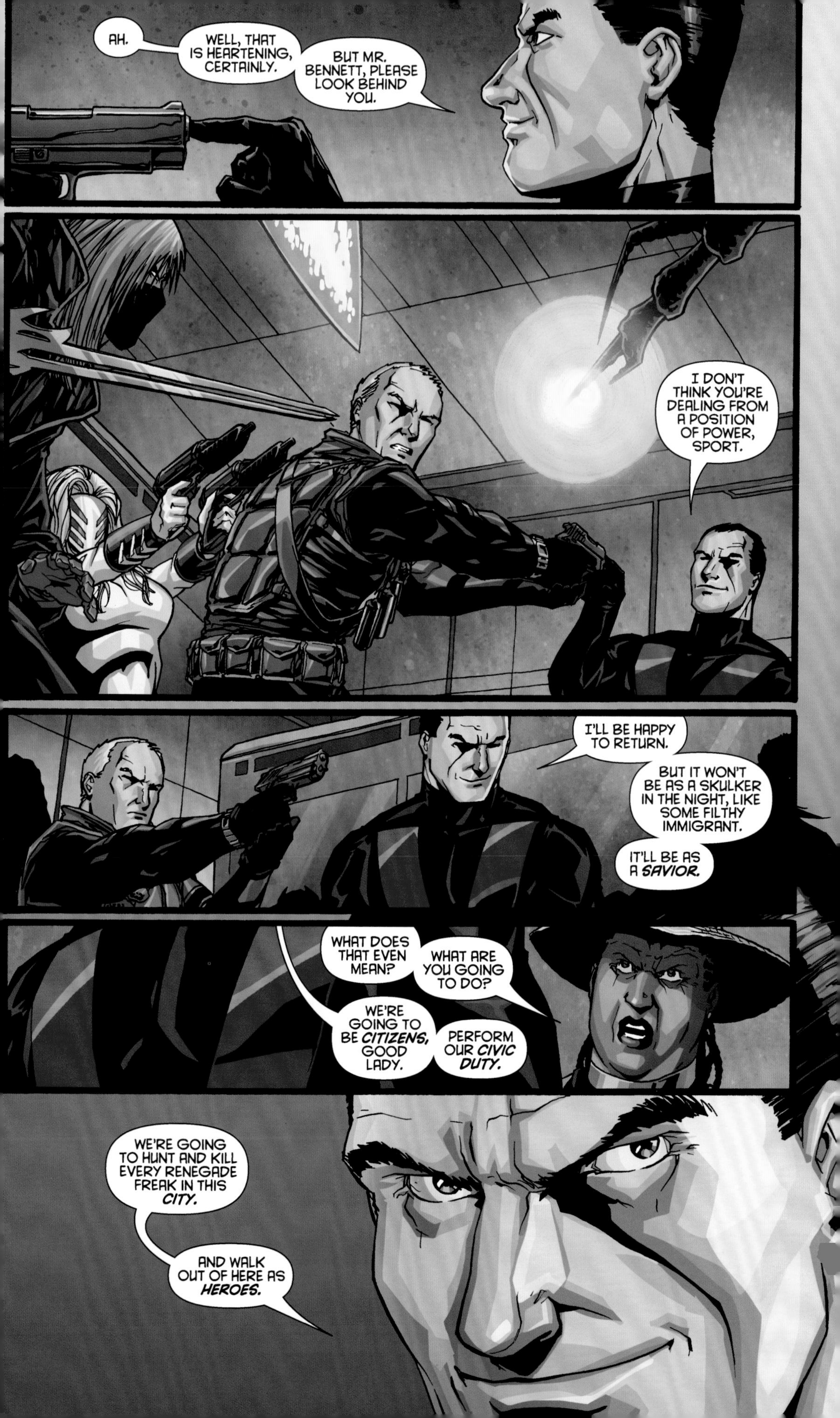
AH.
WELL, THAT IS HEARTENING, CERTAINLY.
BUT MR. BENNETT, PLEASE LOOK BEHIND YOU.
I DON'T THINK YOU'RE DEALING FROM A POSITION OF POWER, SPORT.
I'LL BE HAPPY TO RETURN.
BUT IT WON'T BE AS A SKULKER IN THE NIGHT, LIKE SOME FILTHY IMMIGRANT.
IT'LL BE AS A *SAVIOR.*
WHAT DOES THAT EVEN MEAN?
WHAT ARE YOU GOING TO DO?
WE'RE GOING TO BE *CITIZENS,* GOOD LADY.
PERFORM OUR *CIVIC DUTY.*
WE'RE GOING TO HUNT AND KILL EVERY RENEGADE FREAK IN THIS *CITY.*
AND WALK OUT OF HERE AS *HEROES.*

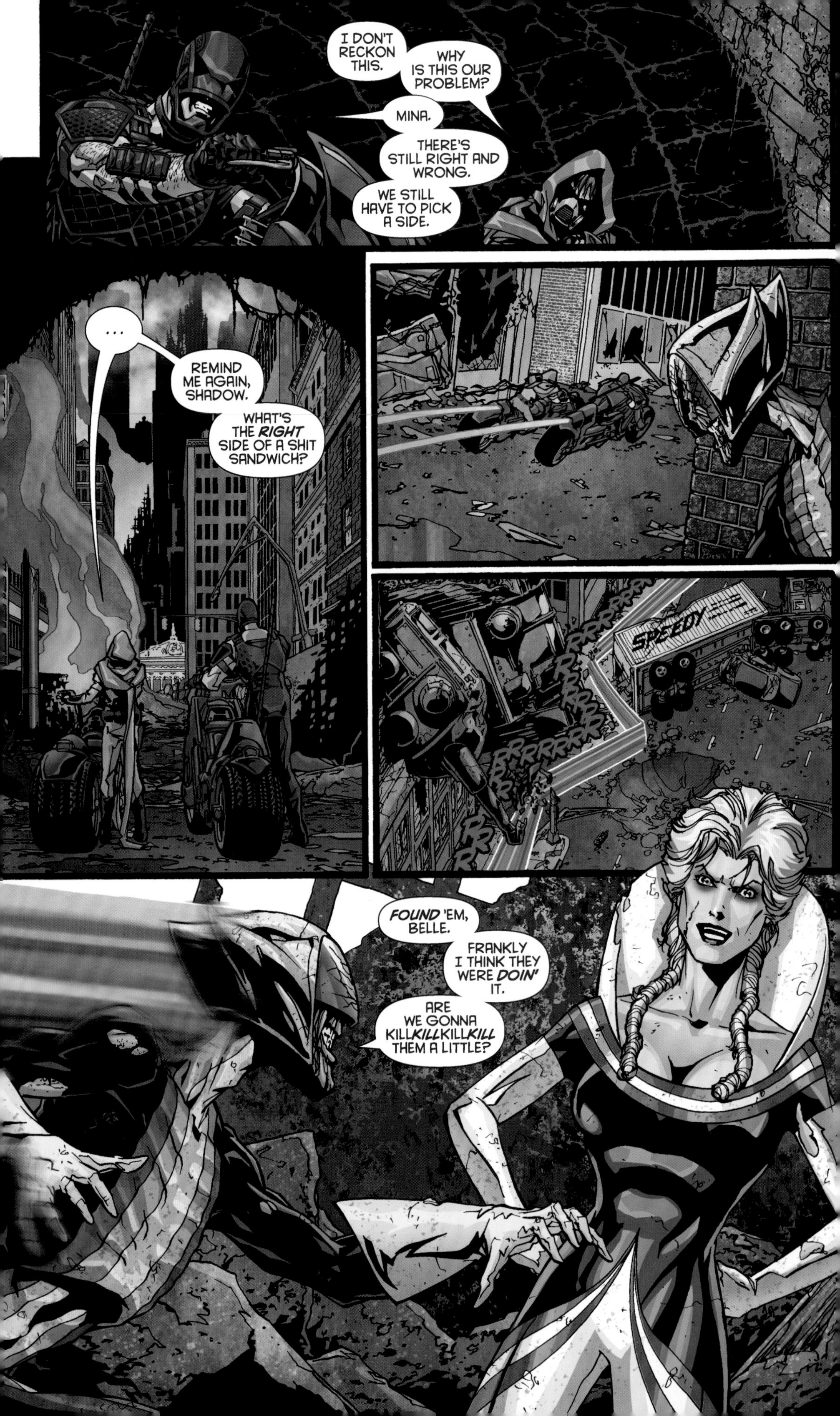
I DON'T RECKON THIS.
WHY IS THIS OUR PROBLEM?
MINA.
THERE'S STILL RIGHT AND WRONG.
WE STILL HAVE TO PICK A SIDE.
...
REMIND ME AGAIN, SHADOW.
WHAT'S THE **RIGHT** SIDE OF A SHIT SANDWICH?
SPEEDY
RRRRRRRRRRRRRRRRRRRK
FOUND 'EM, BELLE.
FRANKLY I THINK THEY WERE **DOIN'** IT.
ARE WE GONNA KILL**KILL**KILL**KILL** THEM A LITTLE?

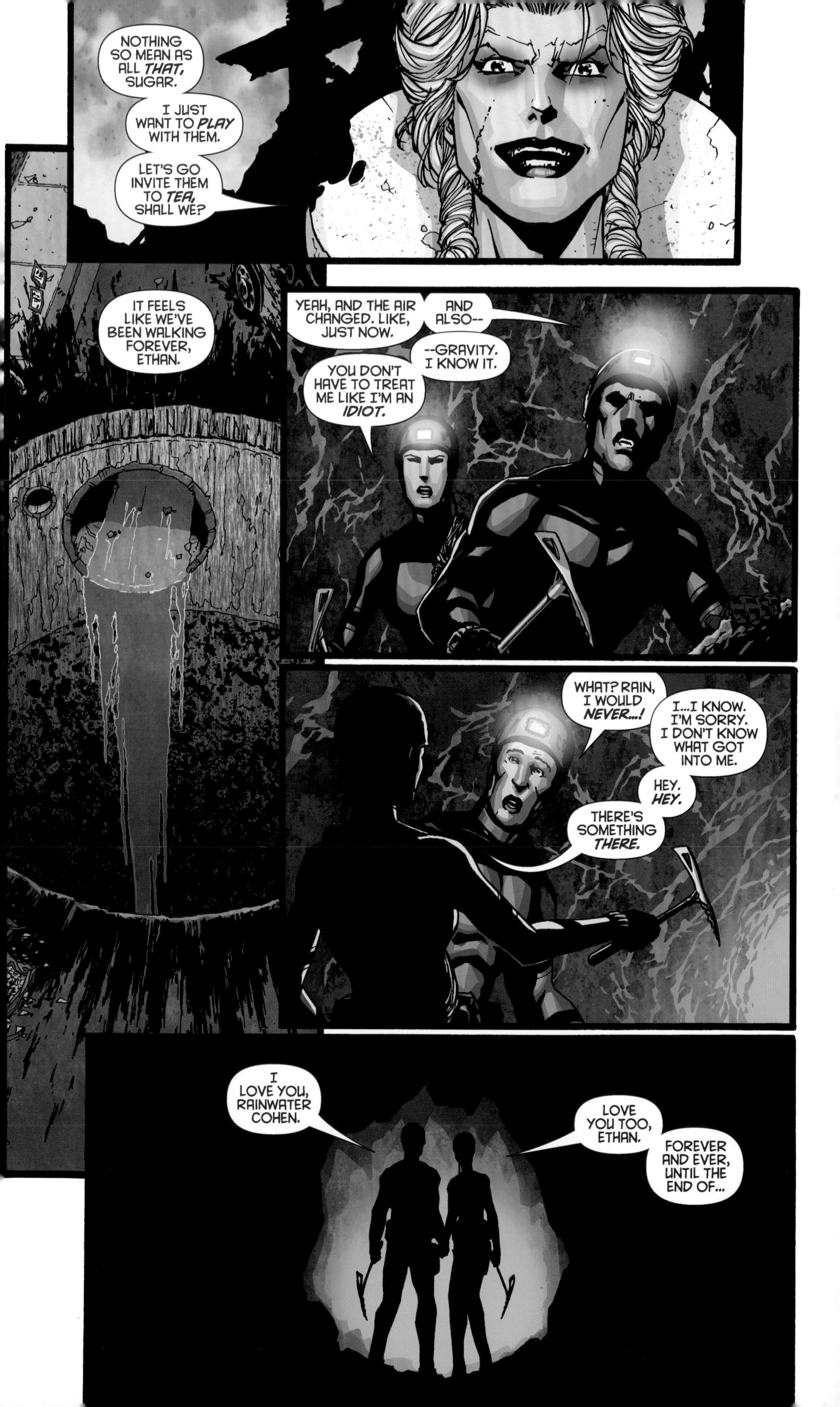
NOTHING SO MEAN AS ALL THAT, SUGAR.
I JUST WANT TO PLAY WITH THEM.
LET'S GO INVITE THEM TO TEA, SHALL WE?
IT FEELS LIKE WE'VE BEEN WALKING FOREVER, ETHAN.
YEAH, AND THE AIR CHANGED. LIKE, JUST NOW.
AND ALSO--
--GRAVITY. I KNOW IT.
YOU DON'T HAVE TO TREAT ME LIKE I'M AN IDIOT.
WHAT? RAIN, I WOULD NEVER...!
I...I KNOW. I'M SORRY. I DON'T KNOW WHAT GOT INTO ME.
HEY. HEY.
THERE'S SOMETHING THERE.
I LOVE YOU, RAINWATER COHEN.
LOVE YOU TOO, ETHAN.
FOREVER AND EVER, UNTIL THE END OF...

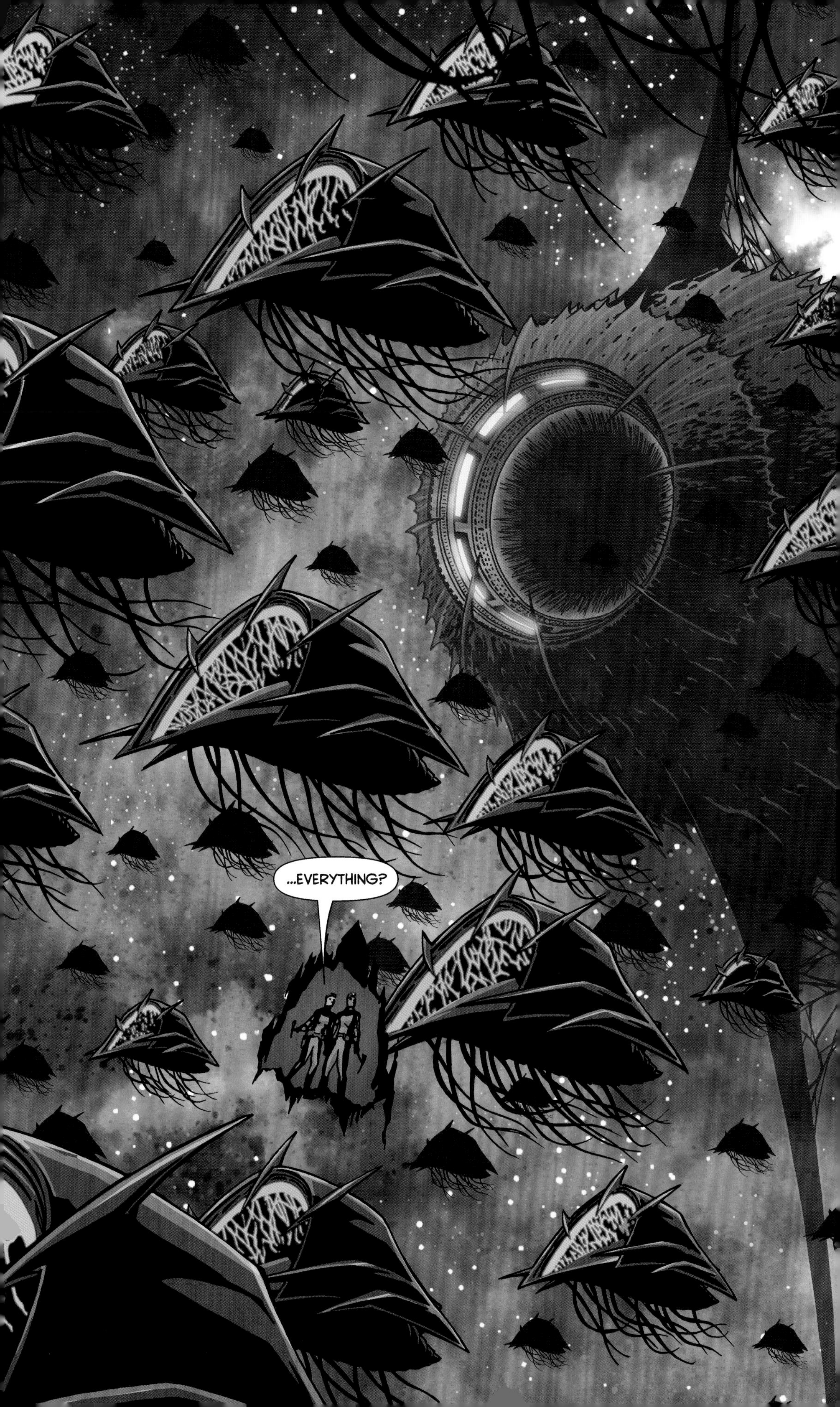
...EVERYTHING?

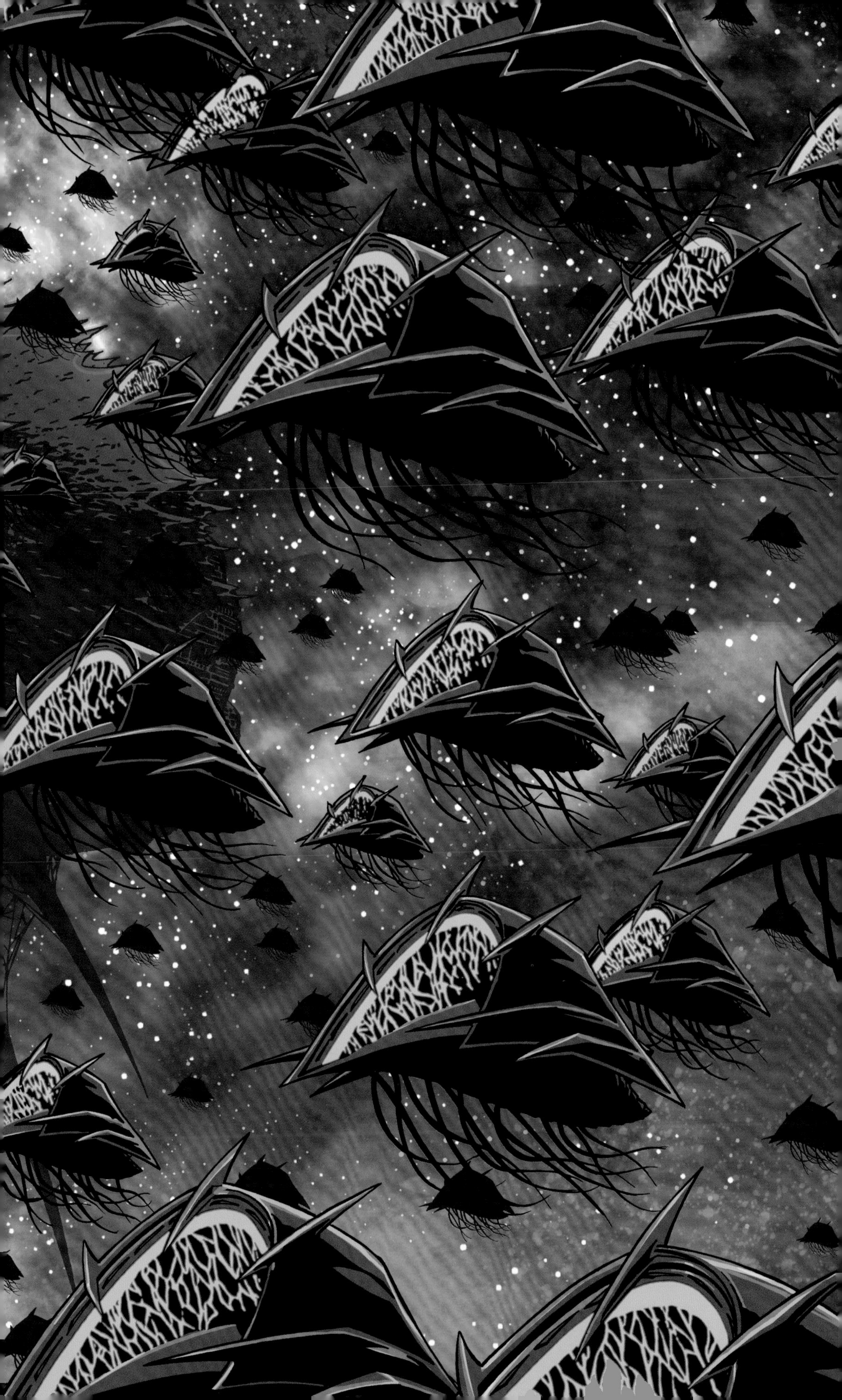

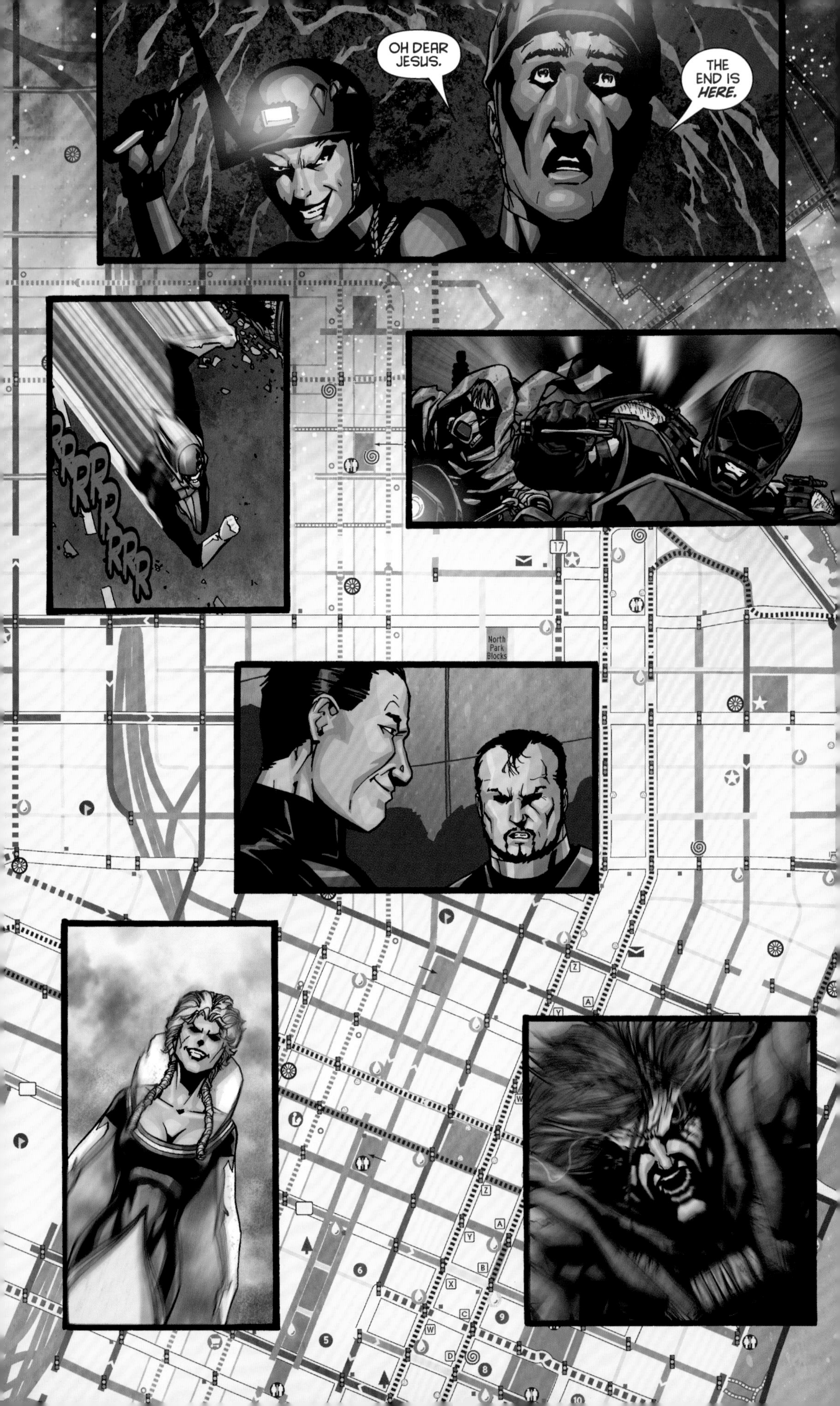
OH DEAR JESUS.
THE END IS HERE.
17
North Park Blocks

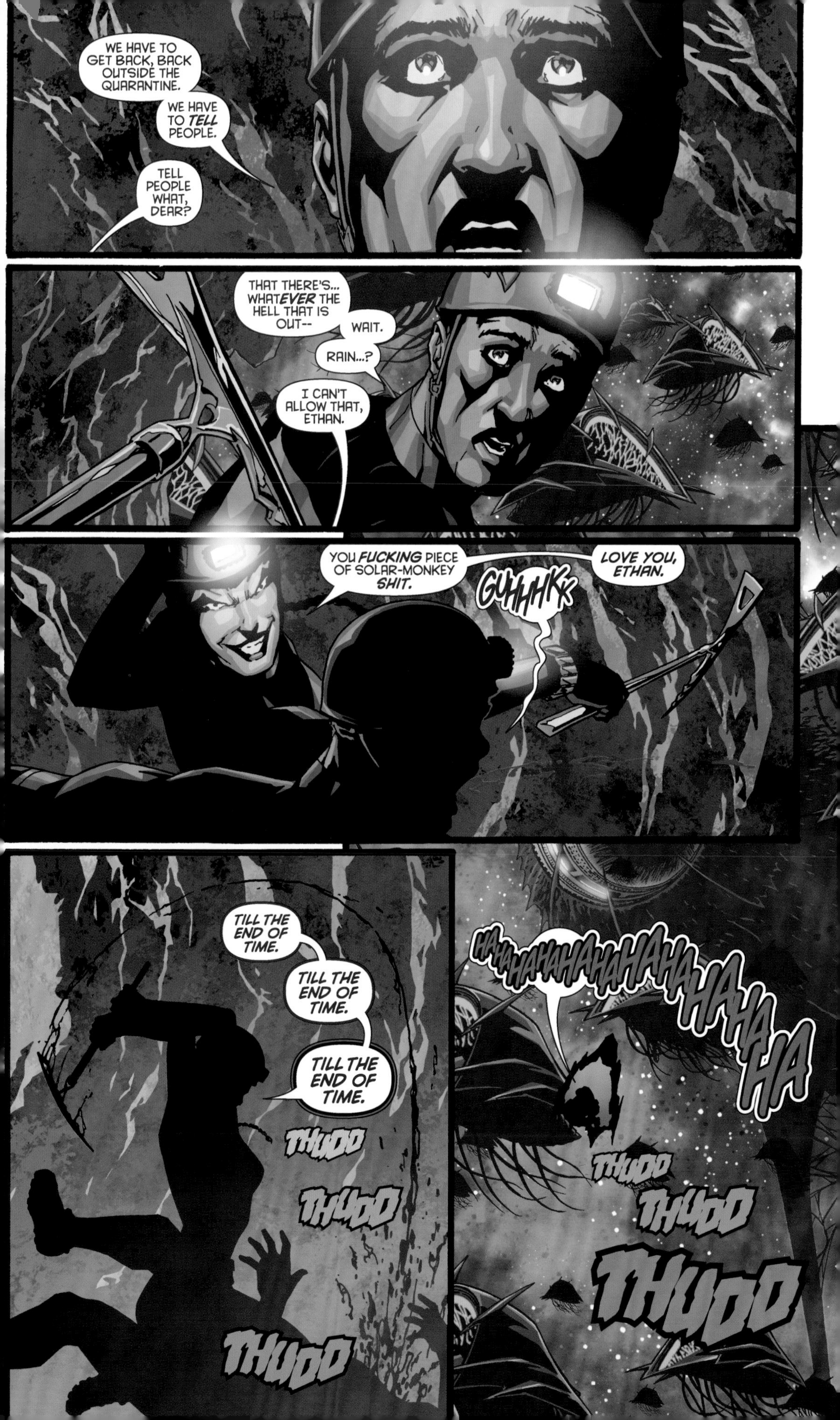

WE HAVE TO GET BACK, BACK OUTSIDE THE QUARANTINE.
WE HAVE TO TELL PEOPLE.
TELL PEOPLE WHAT, DEAR?
THAT THERE'S... WHATEVER THE HELL THAT IS OUT--
WAIT.
RAIN...?
I CAN'T ALLOW THAT, ETHAN.
YOU FUCKING PIECE OF SOLAR-MONKEY SHIT.
LOVE YOU, ETHAN.
GUHHHKK
TILL THE END OF TIME.
TILL THE END OF TIME.
TILL THE END OF TIME.
THUDD
THUDD
THUDD
HAHAHAHAHAHAHAHAHAHAHAHAHA
THUDD
THUDD
THUDD

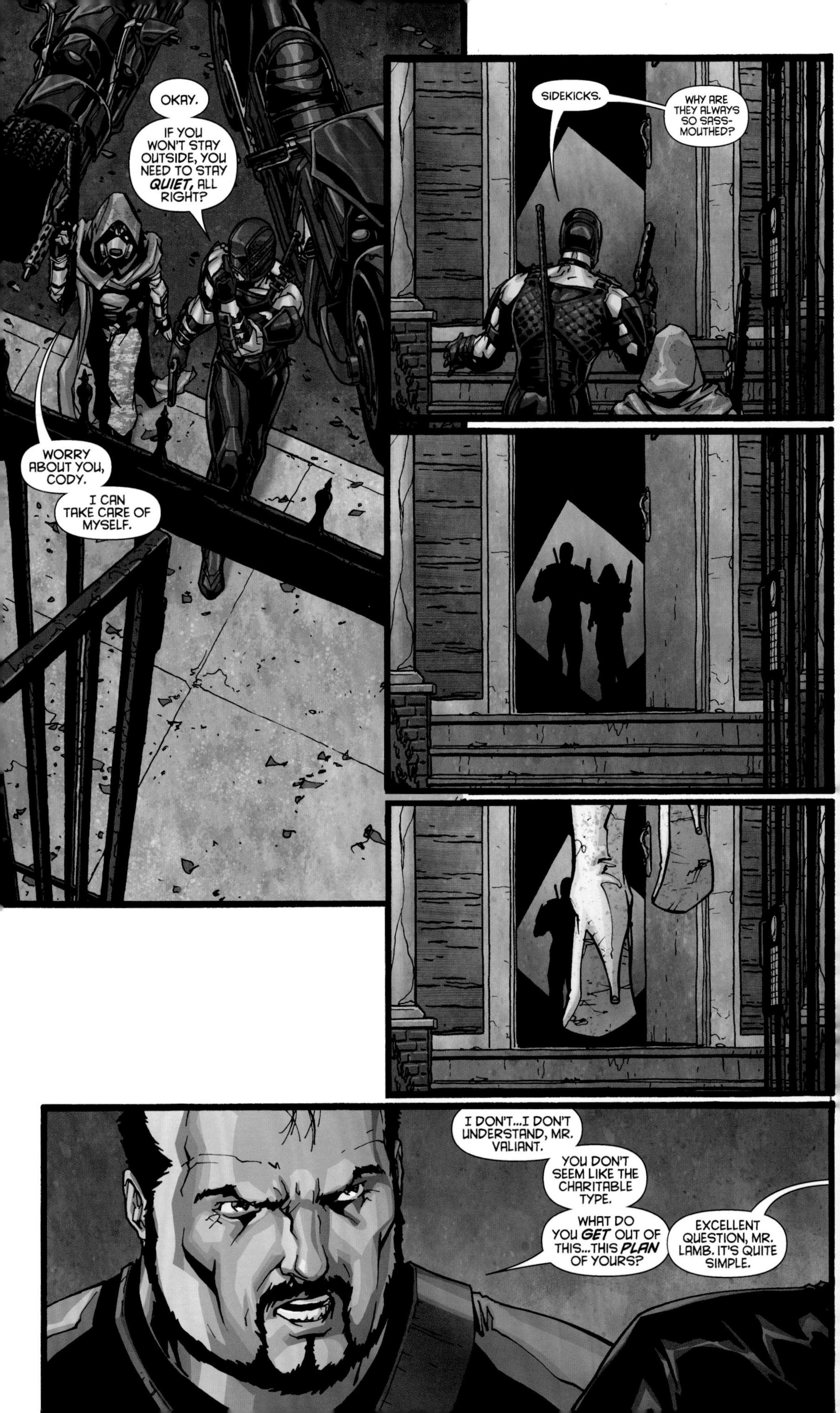
OKAY.
IF YOU WON'T STAY OUTSIDE, YOU NEED TO STAY QUIET, ALL RIGHT?
WORRY ABOUT YOU, CODY.
I CAN TAKE CARE OF MYSELF.
SIDEKICKS.
WHY ARE THEY ALWAYS SO SASS-MOUTHED?
I DON'T...I DON'T UNDERSTAND, MR. VALIANT.
YOU DON'T SEEM LIKE THE CHARITABLE TYPE.
WHAT DO YOU GET OUT OF THIS...THIS PLAN OF YOURS?
EXCELLENT QUESTION, MR. LAMB. IT'S QUITE SIMPLE.

CLEMENCY.

HOW MANY CITIZENS HAVE YOU *PERSONALLY* KILLED, WIDOWER?

I HONESTLY HAVE NO IDEA, VALIANT.

TRIPLE DIGITS, CERTAINLY.

YOU SEE? WHAT'S A PRESIDENTIAL PARDON, MORE OR LESS, COMPARED TO THE LIBERATION OF ONE OF AMERICA'S GREATEST CITIES?

THEY'LL THROW US A *PARADE.* I'LL BE FUCKING *MAYOR.*

AND BEYOND THAT, FRANKLY...

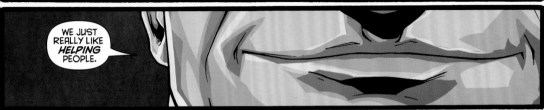

WE JUST REALLY LIKE *HELPING* PEOPLE.

BULLSHIT. EVERYONE *AWFUL* SAYS THAT. NO ONE *GOOD.*

YOU'RE ALL *WOLVES.*

DISOBEDIENT WOLVES!

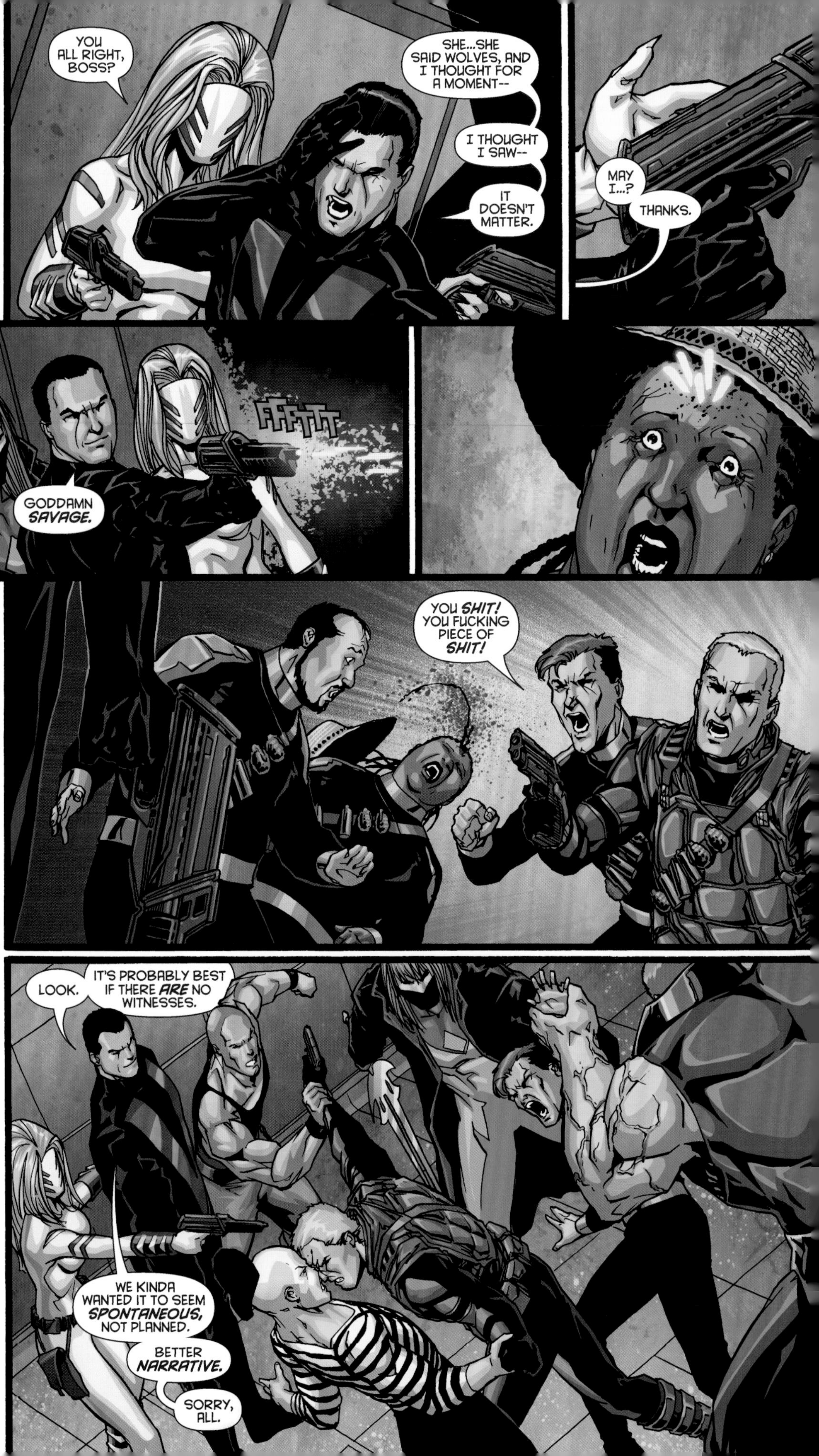
YOU ALL RIGHT, BOSS?
SHE...SHE SAID WOLVES, AND I THOUGHT FOR A MOMENT--
I THOUGHT I SAW--
IT DOESN'T MATTER.
MAY I...?
THANKS.
GODDAMN *SAVAGE.*
FFFTTT
YOU *SHIT!* YOU FUCKING PIECE OF *SHIT!*
LOOK.
IT'S PROBABLY BEST IF THERE *ARE* NO WITNESSES.
WE KINDA WANTED IT TO SEEM *SPONTANEOUS,* NOT PLANNED.
BETTER *NARRATIVE.*
SORRY, ALL.

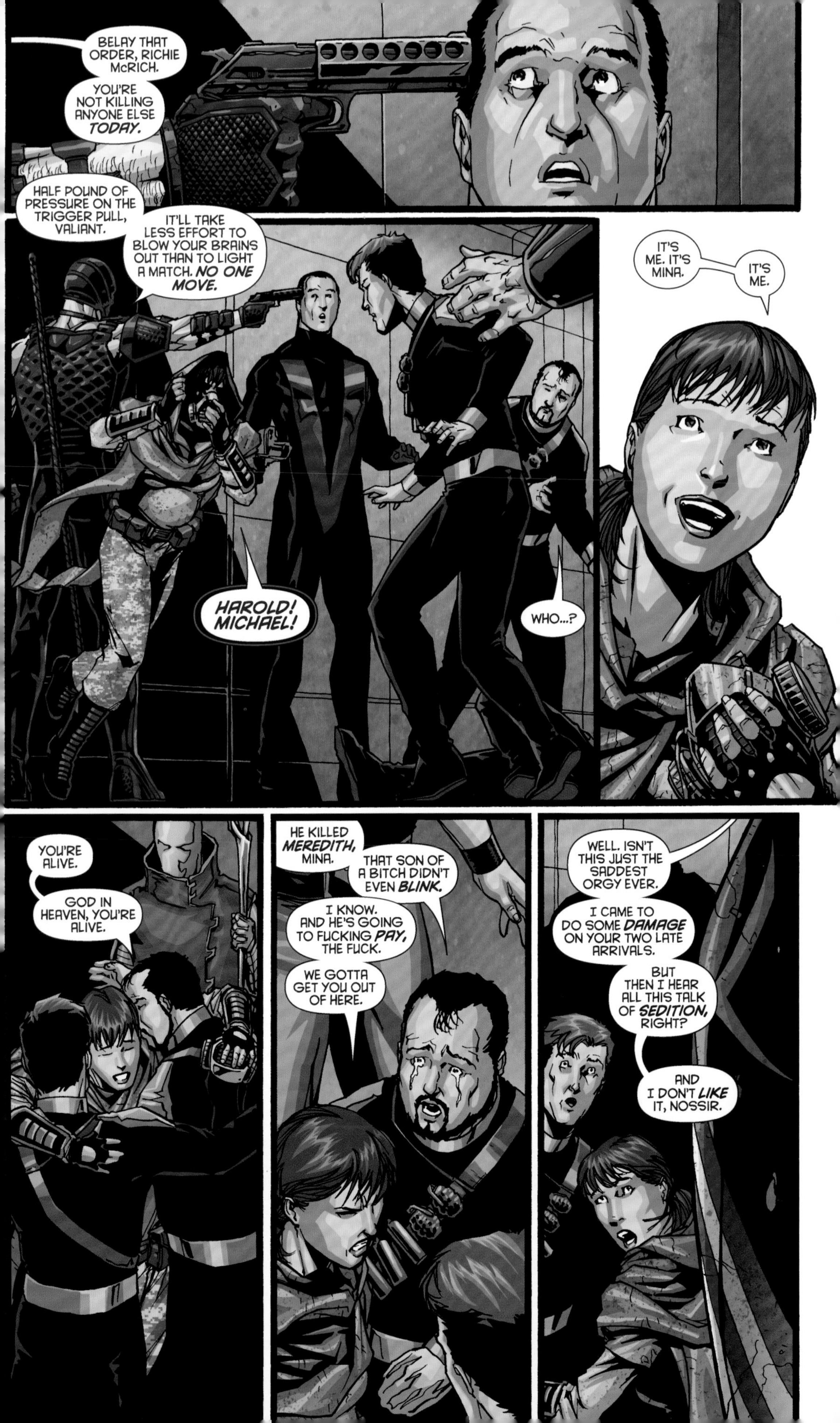
BELAY THAT ORDER, RICHIE McRICH.
YOU'RE NOT KILLING ANYONE ELSE TODAY.
HALF POUND OF PRESSURE ON THE TRIGGER PULL, VALIANT.
IT'LL TAKE LESS EFFORT TO BLOW YOUR BRAINS OUT THAN TO LIGHT A MATCH. NO ONE MOVE.
HAROLD! MICHAEL!
WHO...?
IT'S ME. IT'S MINA.
IT'S ME.
YOU'RE ALIVE.
GOD IN HEAVEN, YOU'RE ALIVE.
HE KILLED MEREDITH, MINA.
THAT SON OF A BITCH DIDN'T EVEN BLINK.
I KNOW. AND HE'S GOING TO FUCKING PAY, THE FUCK.
WE GOTTA GET YOU OUT OF HERE.
WELL. ISN'T THIS JUST THE SADDEST ORGY EVER.
I CAME TO DO SOME DAMAGE ON YOUR TWO LATE ARRIVALS.
BUT THEN I HEAR ALL THIS TALK OF SEDITION, RIGHT?
AND I DON'T LIKE IT, NOSSIR.

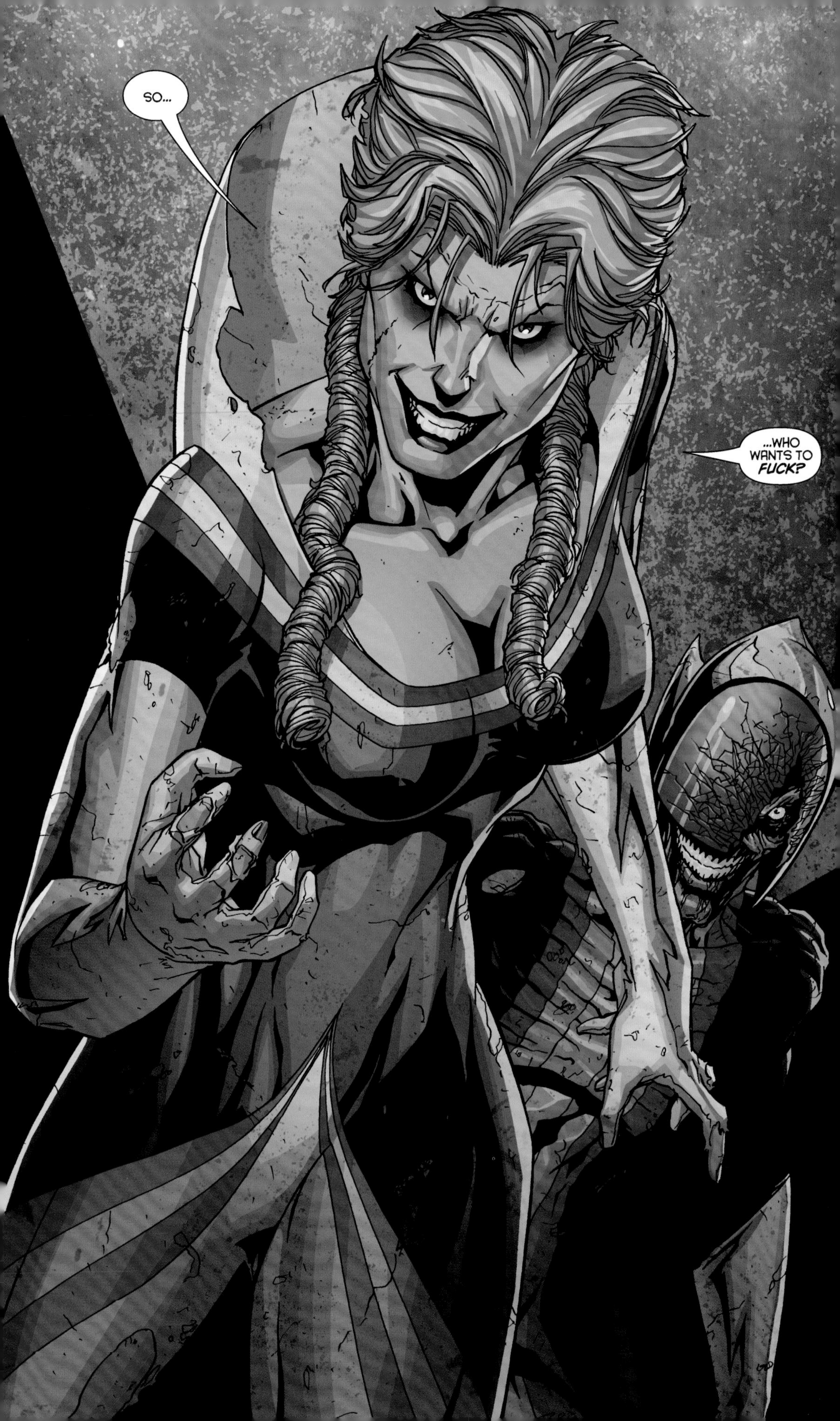
SO...
...WHO WANTS TO *FUCK?*

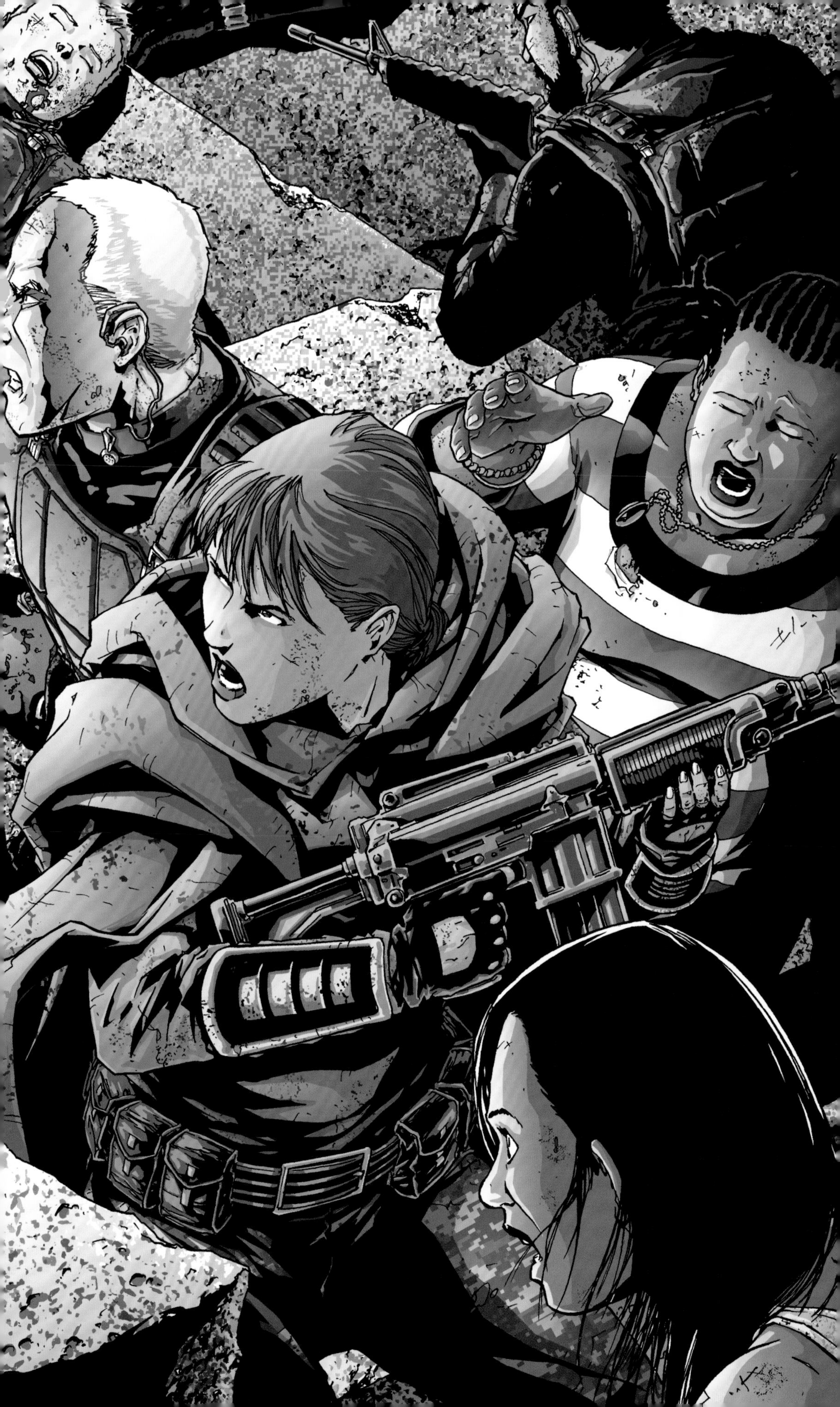

IT HAD TO HAPPEN!!!
Presented by
BENNY'S FOR EATS
Megalopolis' Best Eats
(currently under renovation)
THE RUMBLE IN THE RUBBLE
CHAMPIONSHIP FIGHT
SOUTHERN BELLE
VS
OVERLORD
MAN OF GRANITE
FRI 19TH AUG
THE BRAWL TO SETTLE IT ALL
NO PUNCHES PULLED ★ NO STRUCTURES SPARED
DOORS BLOWN 10:00 PM
BE THERE & BE DEAD
SCREAMING ROOM ONLY
★RINGSIDE IS WHERE IT'S AT ★ NO HOME TV ★ NO RADIO ★ NO ESCAPE ★★

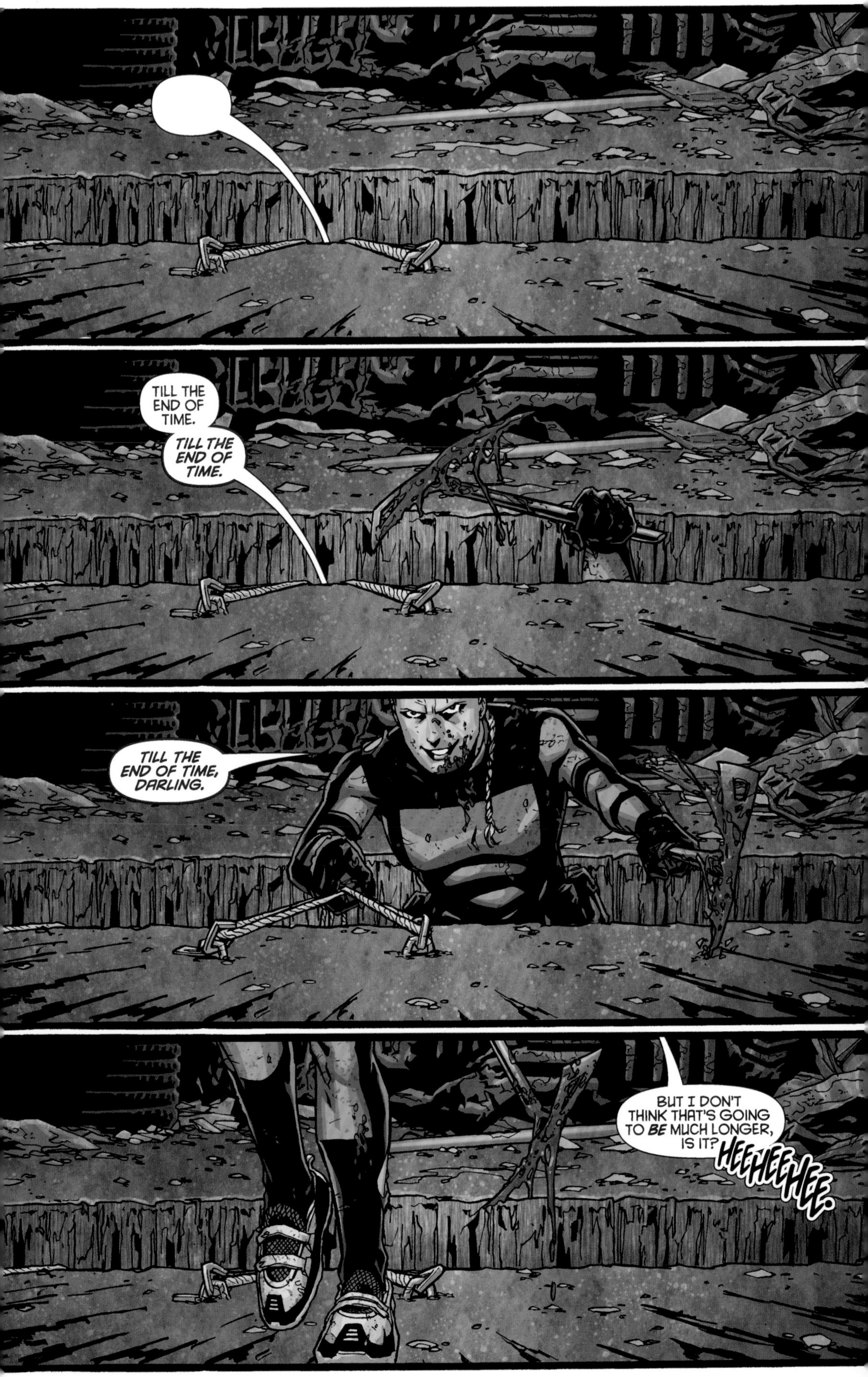
TILL THE END OF TIME.
TILL THE END OF TIME.
TILL THE END OF TIME, DARLING.
BUT I DON'T THINK THAT'S GOING TO BE MUCH LONGER, IS IT?
HEEHEEHEE.

THE SEATTLE LIBERTY
SENATE SHAM?

SENATOR BELL: Colonel Culver, I want to remind you of two oaths at this time.

COLONEL CULVER: Ma'am?

SENATOR BELL: The oath of service you took upon joining the military, and the oath you took with your hand on the Bible at the beginning of this exculpatory process.

COLONEL CULVER: Ma'am, I am fully aware of those oaths, I assure you.

SENATOR BELL: Are you aware of an allegation made in this morning's *Liberty*, regarding the state of your health, Colonel?

COLONEL CULVER: I am.

SENATOR BELL: And are these allegations accurate, Colonel?

COLONEL CULVER: I wish that they were NOT, Senator Bell.

SENATOR BELL: And I will ask you again, Colonel.

SENATOR BELL: Who gave the command for you to send the troops over the quarantine line, into a city that somehow breeds more megahuman individuals than the rest of the world COMBINED?

COLONEL CULVER: . . .

COLONEL CULVER: I do not recall, Senator.

SENATOR BELL: Do you expect this committee to believe that? That an officer of your distinguished record would suddenly FORGET the chain of command?

COLONEL CULVER: I have been in this chair for three days, ma'am. This is my fourth appearance before the committee and the remaining life I have can be measured in weeks, if not days.

COLONEL CULVER: What you believe is not very important at this time, if madam will forgive me for saying.

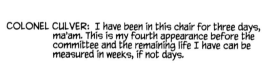

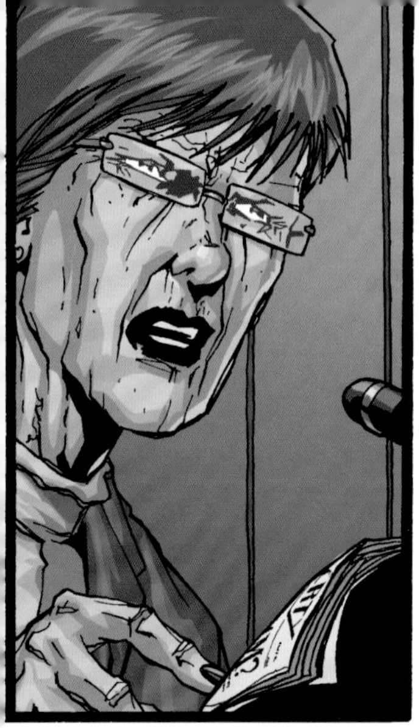

SENATOR BELL: This journalist alleges that you are a sacrificial GOAT, sir. Are you aware of that?

SENATOR BELL: They say you're being made a willing PATSY.

SENATOR BELL: Because you won't be around to face any CHARGES for the debacle that occurred during that unauthorized action.

SENATOR BELL: What say you to that, Colonel?

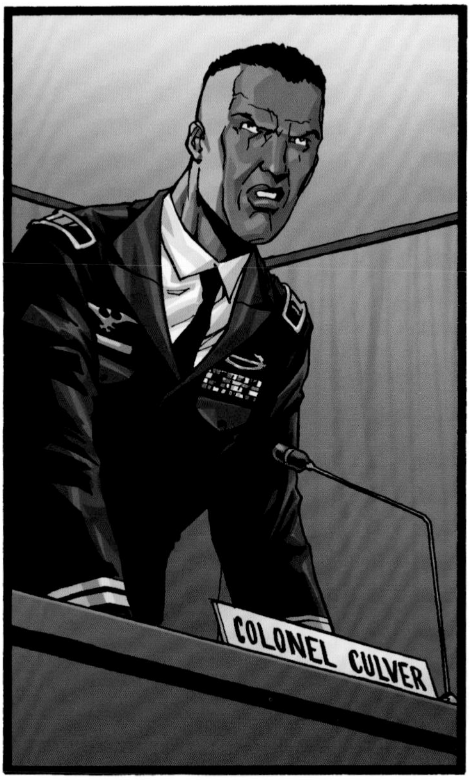
COLONEL CULVER

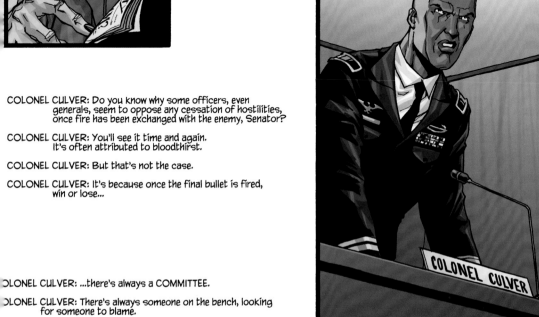

COLONEL CULVER: Do you know why some officers, even generals, seem to oppose any cessation of hostilities, once fire has been exchanged with the enemy, Senator?

COLONEL CULVER: You'll see it time and again. It's often attributed to bloodthirst.

COLONEL CULVER: But that's not the case.

COLONEL CULVER: It's because once the final bullet is fired, win or lose...

COLONEL CULVER: ...there's always a COMMITTEE.

COLONEL CULVER: There's always someone on the bench, looking for someone to blame.

COLONEL CULVER: Looking for a bit of GLORY they never EARNED.

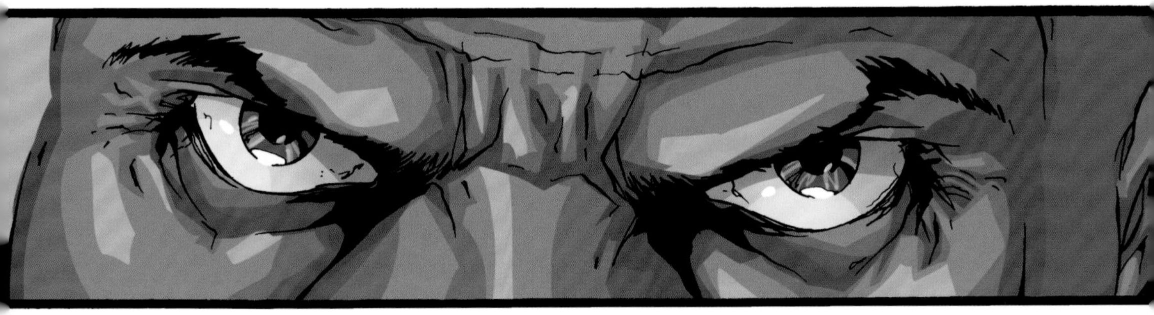

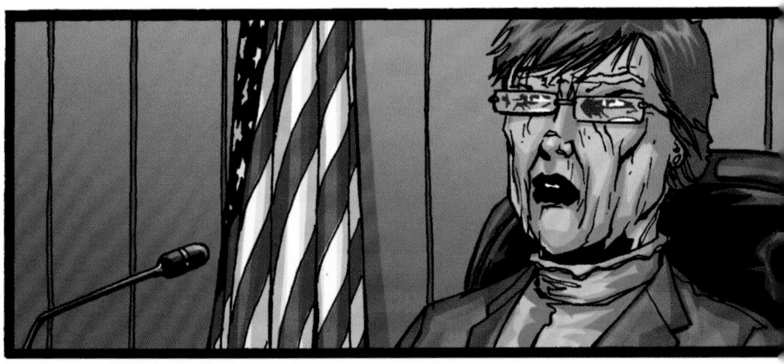

COLONEL CULVER: If the fire never stops burning...

COLONEL CULVER: ...no one stops to arrest the FIREFIGHTERS.

COLONEL CULVER: Because the truth IS, Senator...you NEED us.

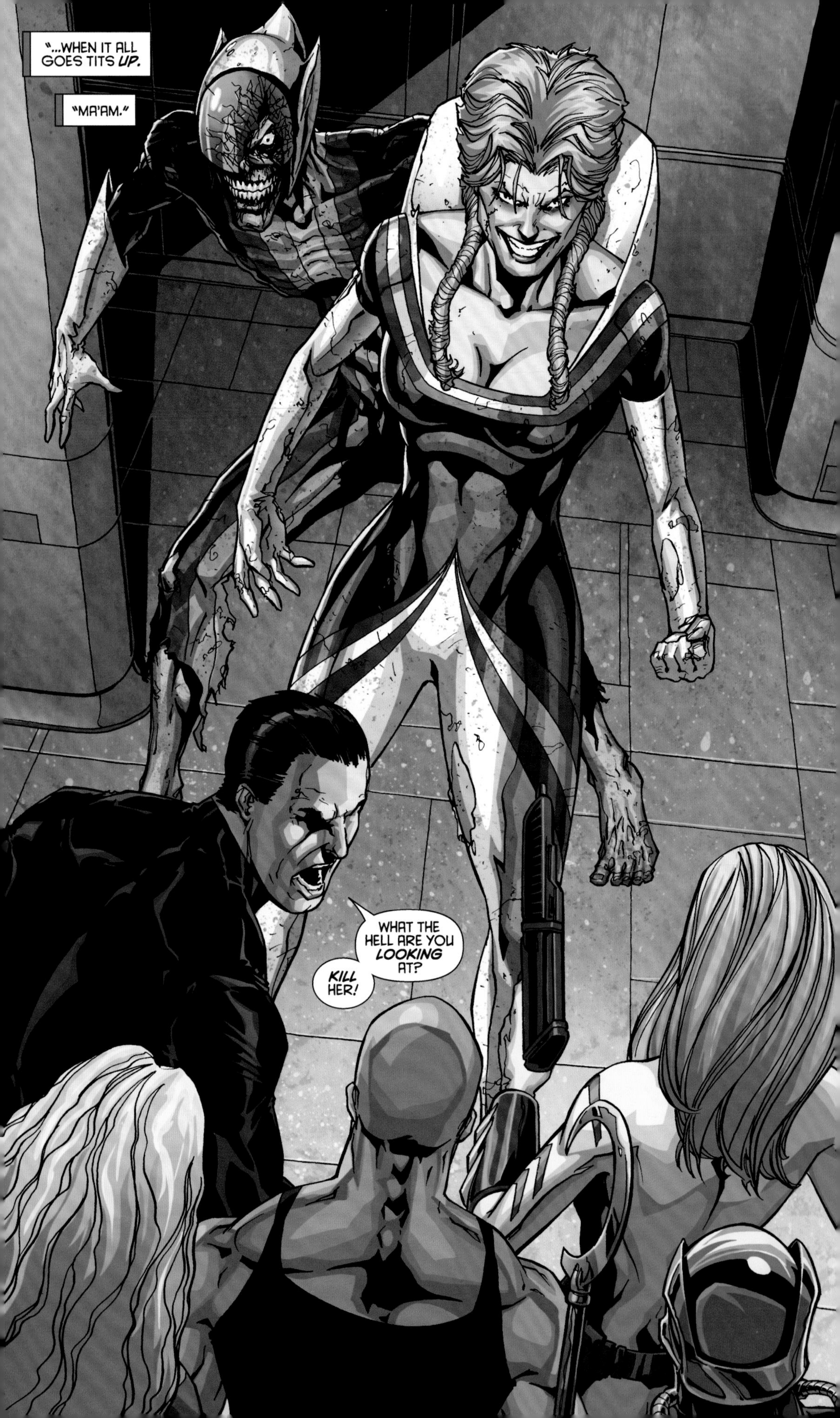
"...WHEN IT ALL GOES TITS *UP.*
"MA'AM."
WHAT THE HELL ARE YOU *LOOKING* AT?
KILL HER!

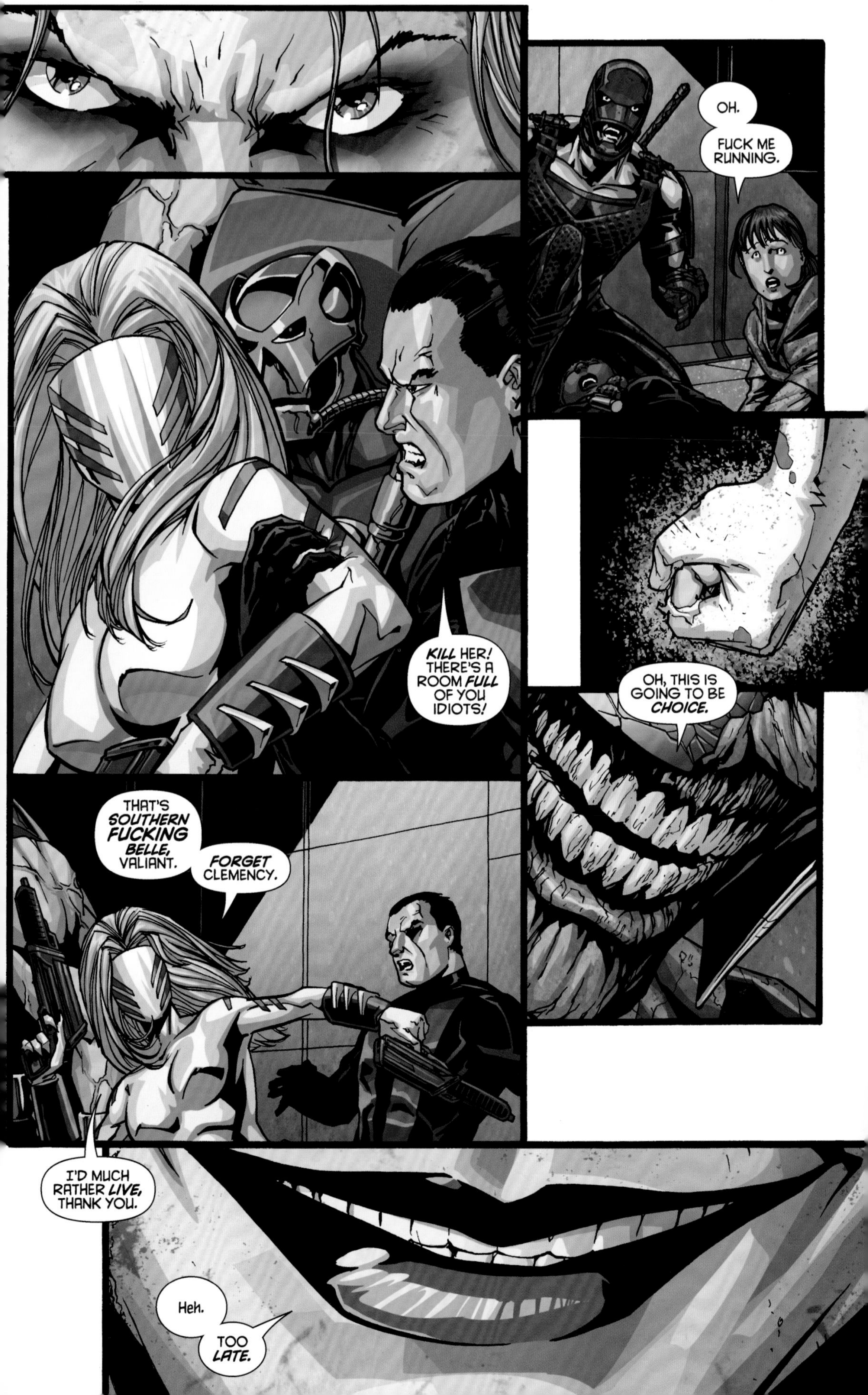

OH.
FUCK ME RUNNING.
KILL HER! THERE'S A ROOM FULL OF YOU IDIOTS!
OH, THIS IS GOING TO BE CHOICE.
THAT'S SOUTHERN FUCKING BELLE, VALIANT.
FORGET CLEMENCY.
I'D MUCH RATHER LIVE, THANK YOU.
Heh.
TOO LATE.

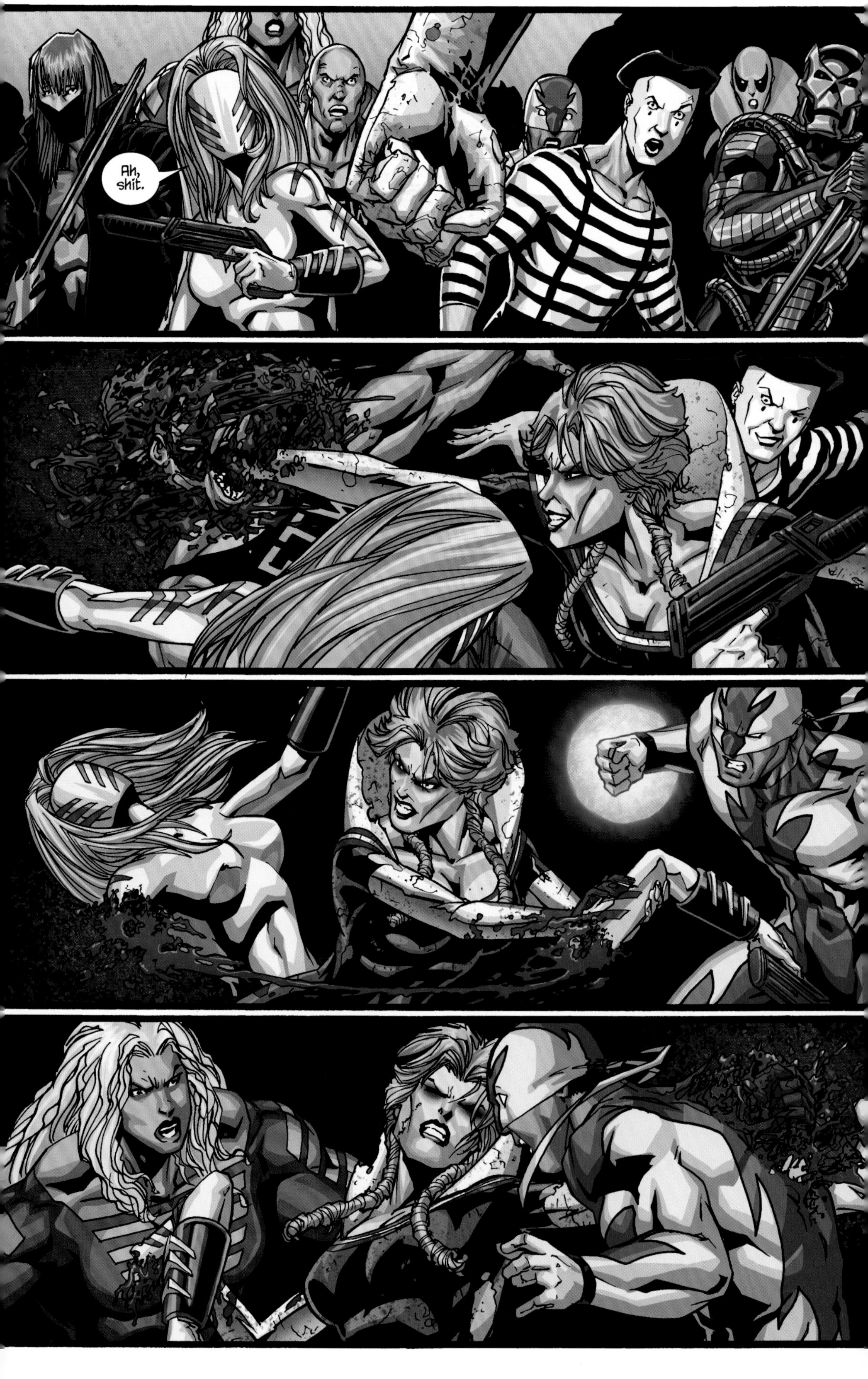
Ah, shit.

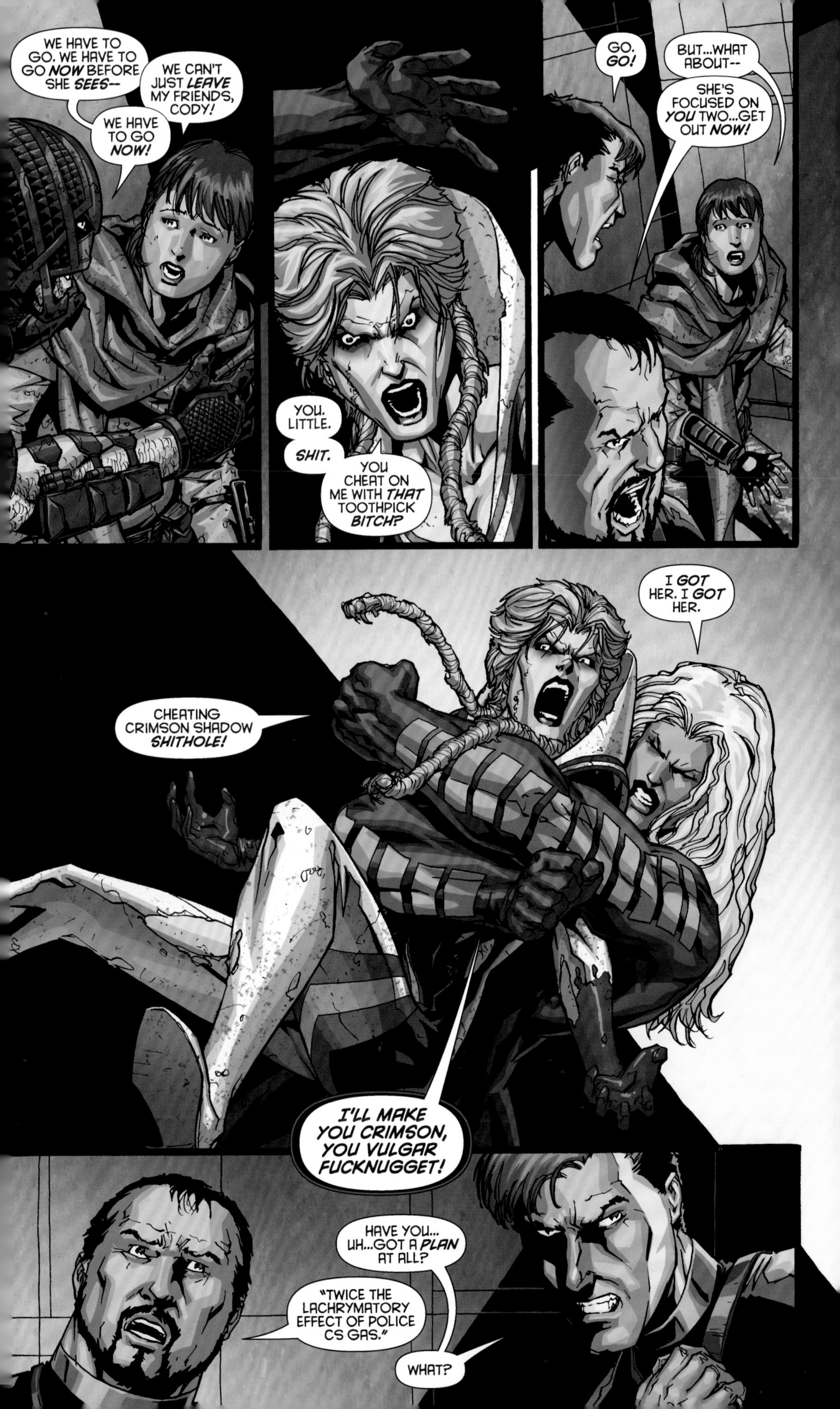
WE HAVE TO GO. WE HAVE TO GO NOW BEFORE SHE SEES--
WE CAN'T JUST LEAVE MY FRIENDS, CODY!
WE HAVE TO GO NOW!
YOU. LITTLE.
SHIT.
YOU CHEAT ON ME WITH THAT TOOTHPICK BITCH?
GO. GO!
BUT...WHAT ABOUT--
SHE'S FOCUSED ON YOU TWO...GET OUT NOW!
I GOT HER. I GOT HER.
CHEATING CRIMSON SHADOW SHITHOLE!
I'LL MAKE YOU CRIMSON, YOU VULGAR FUCKNUGGET!
HAVE YOU... UH...GOT A PLAN AT ALL?
"TWICE THE LACHRYMATORY EFFECT OF POLICE CS GAS."
WHAT?

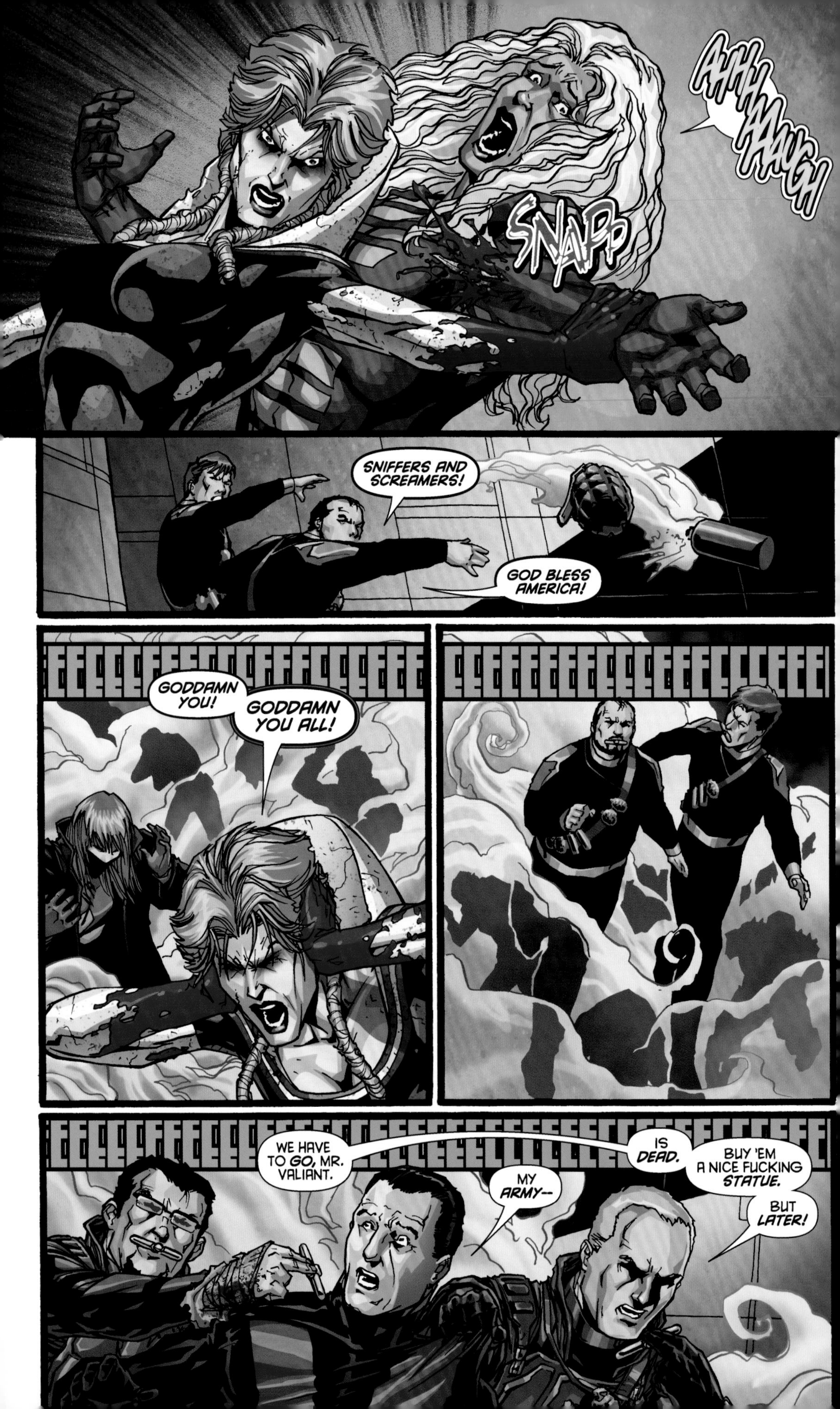
AHHHAAAUGH
SNAPP
SNIFFERS AND SCREAMERS!
GOD BLESS AMERICA!
EEEEEEEEEEEEEEEEEEEEE
GODDAMN YOU!
GODDAMN YOU ALL!
EEEEEEEEEEEEEEEEEEEEEEEE
EEEEEEEEEEEEEEEEEEEEEEEEEEEEEEEEEE
WE HAVE TO GO, MR. VALIANT.
MY ARMY--
IS DEAD.
BUY 'EM A NICE FUCKING STATUE.
BUT LATER!

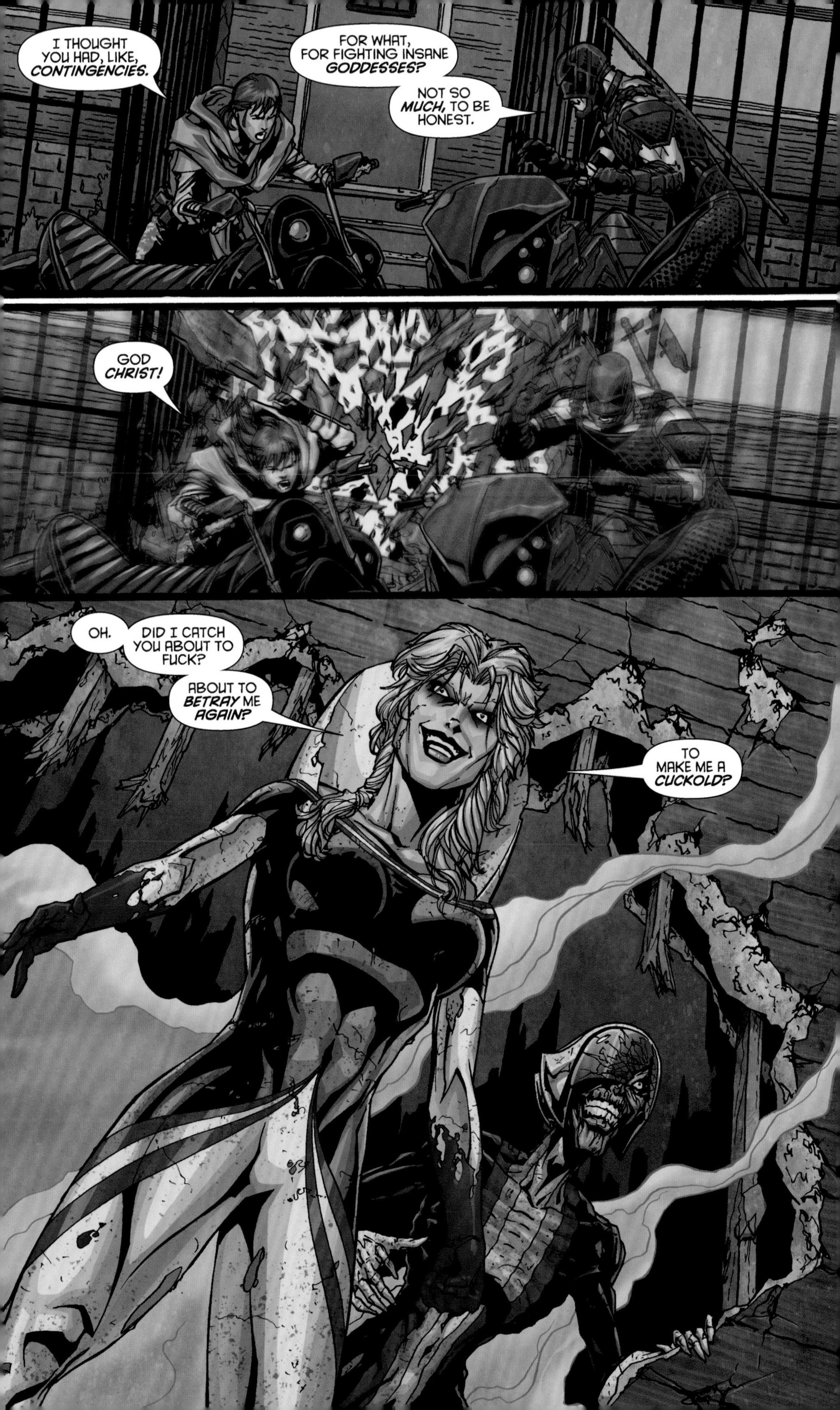
I THOUGHT YOU HAD, LIKE, CONTINGENCIES.
FOR WHAT, FOR FIGHTING INSANE GODDESSES?
NOT SO MUCH, TO BE HONEST.
GOD CHRIST!
OH.
DID I CATCH YOU ABOUT TO FUCK?
ABOUT TO BETRAY ME AGAIN?
TO MAKE ME A CUCKOLD?

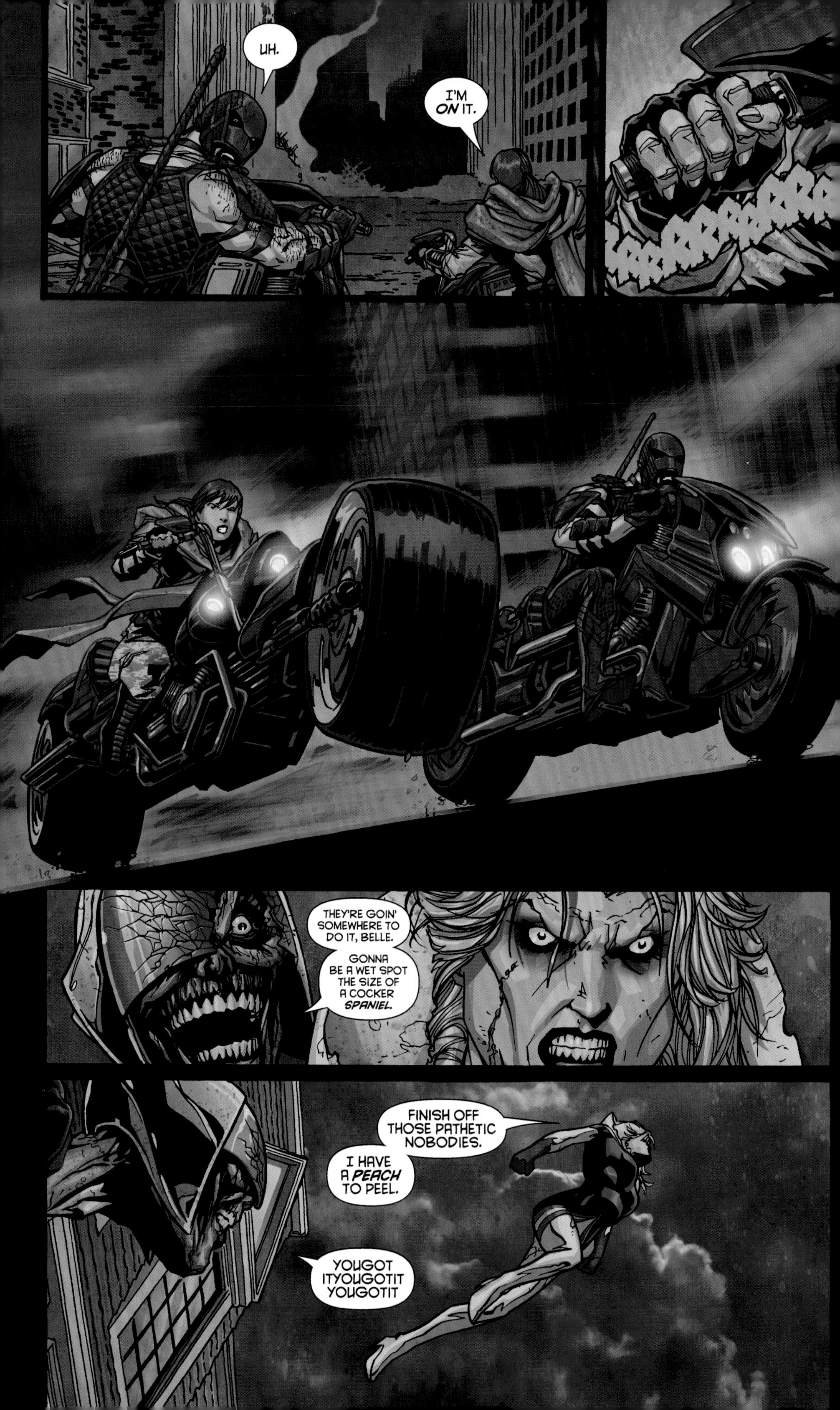
UH.
I'M ON IT.
THEY'RE GOIN' SOMEWHERE TO DO IT, BELLE.
GONNA BE A WET SPOT THE SIZE OF A COCKER SPANIEL.
FINISH OFF THOSE PATHETIC NOBODIES.
I HAVE A PEACH TO PEEL.
YOUGOT ITYOUGOTIT YOUGOTIT

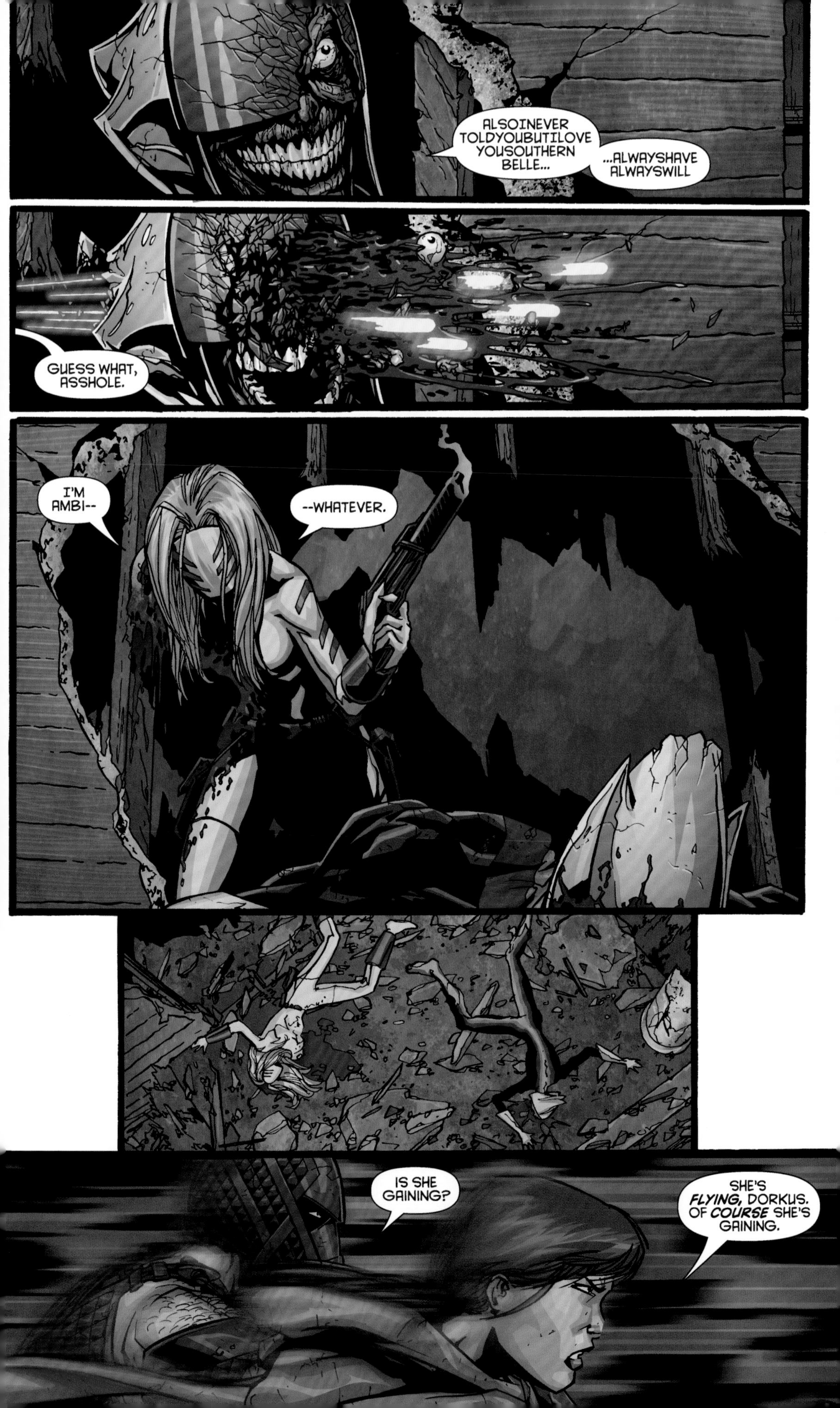
ALSOINEVER TOLDYOUBUTILOVE YOUSOUTHERN BELLE...
...ALWAYSHAVE ALWAYSWILL
GUESS WHAT, ASSHOLE.
I'M AMBI--
--WHATEVER.
IS SHE GAINING?
SHE'S *FLYING,* DORKUS. OF *COURSE* SHE'S GAINING.

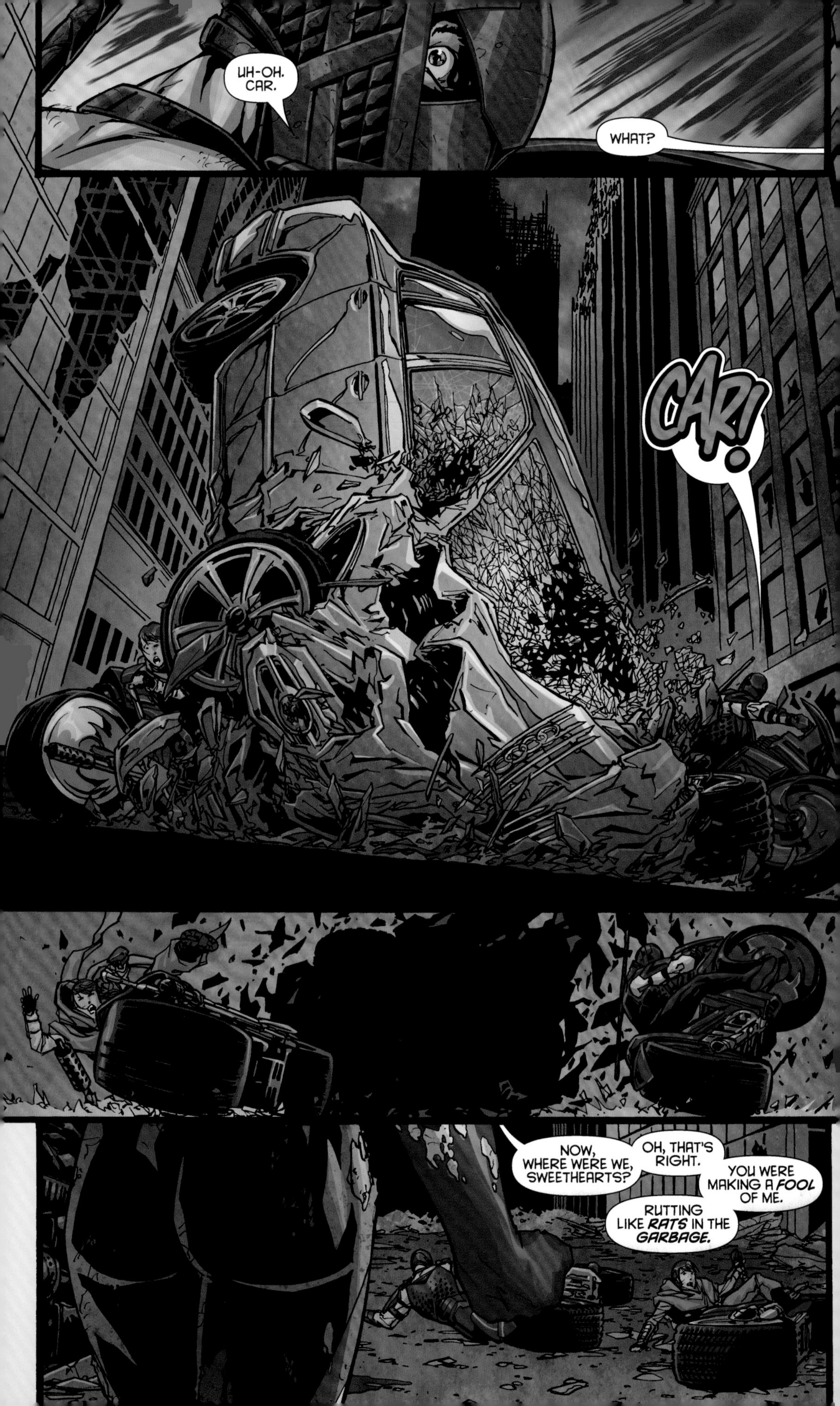
UH-OH. CAR.
WHAT?
CAR!
NOW, WHERE WERE WE, SWEETHEARTS?
OH, THAT'S RIGHT.
YOU WERE MAKING A *FOOL* OF ME.
RUTTING LIKE *RATS* IN THE *GARBAGE.*

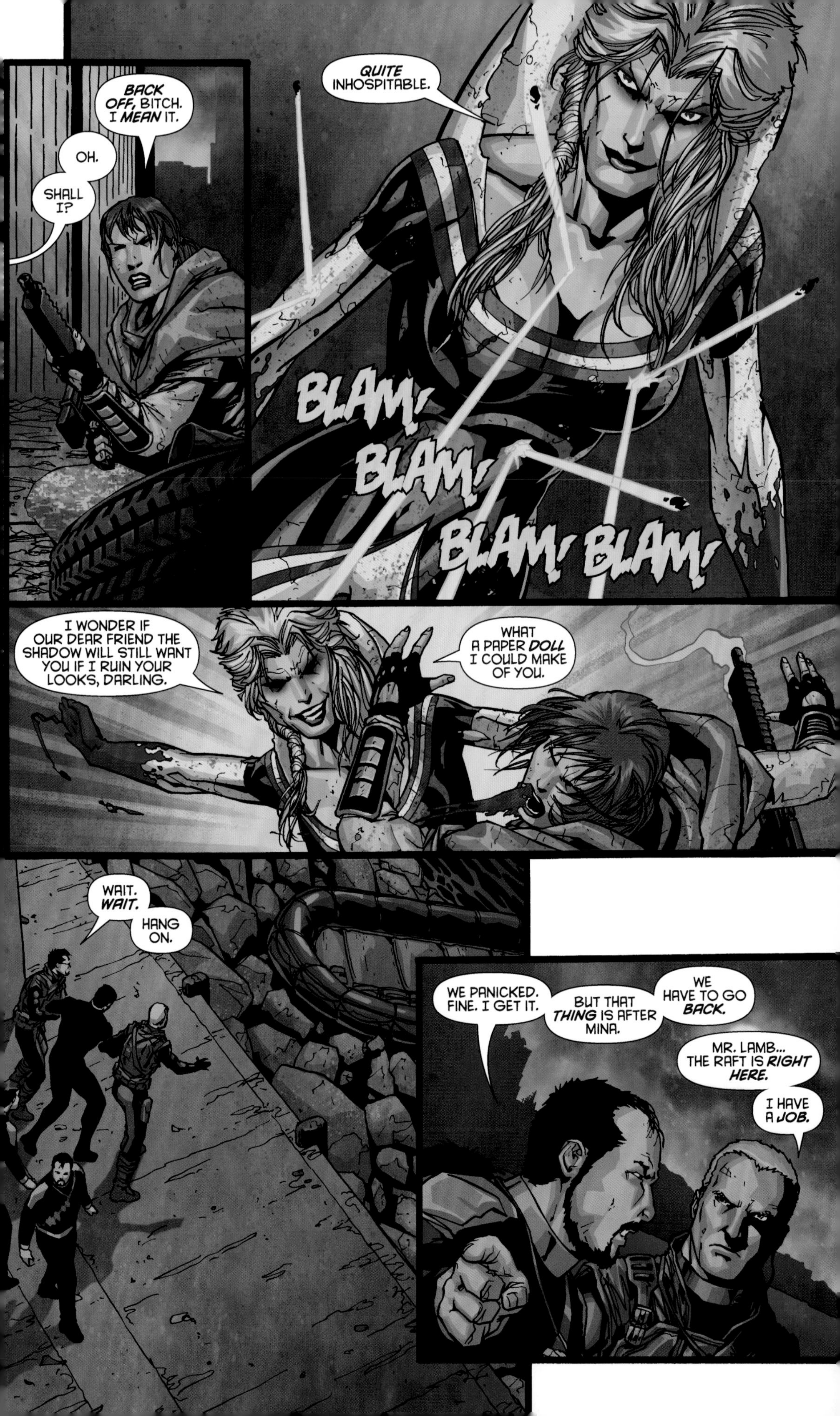
BACK OFF, BITCH. I MEAN IT.
OH.
SHALL I?
QUITE INHOSPITABLE.
BLAM! BLAM! BLAM! BLAM!
I WONDER IF OUR DEAR FRIEND THE SHADOW WILL STILL WANT YOU IF I RUIN YOUR LOOKS, DARLING.
WHAT A PAPER DOLL I COULD MAKE OF YOU.
WAIT. WAIT.
HANG ON.
WE PANICKED. FINE. I GET IT.
BUT THAT THING IS AFTER MINA.
WE HAVE TO GO BACK.
MR. LAMB... THE RAFT IS RIGHT HERE.
I HAVE A JOB.

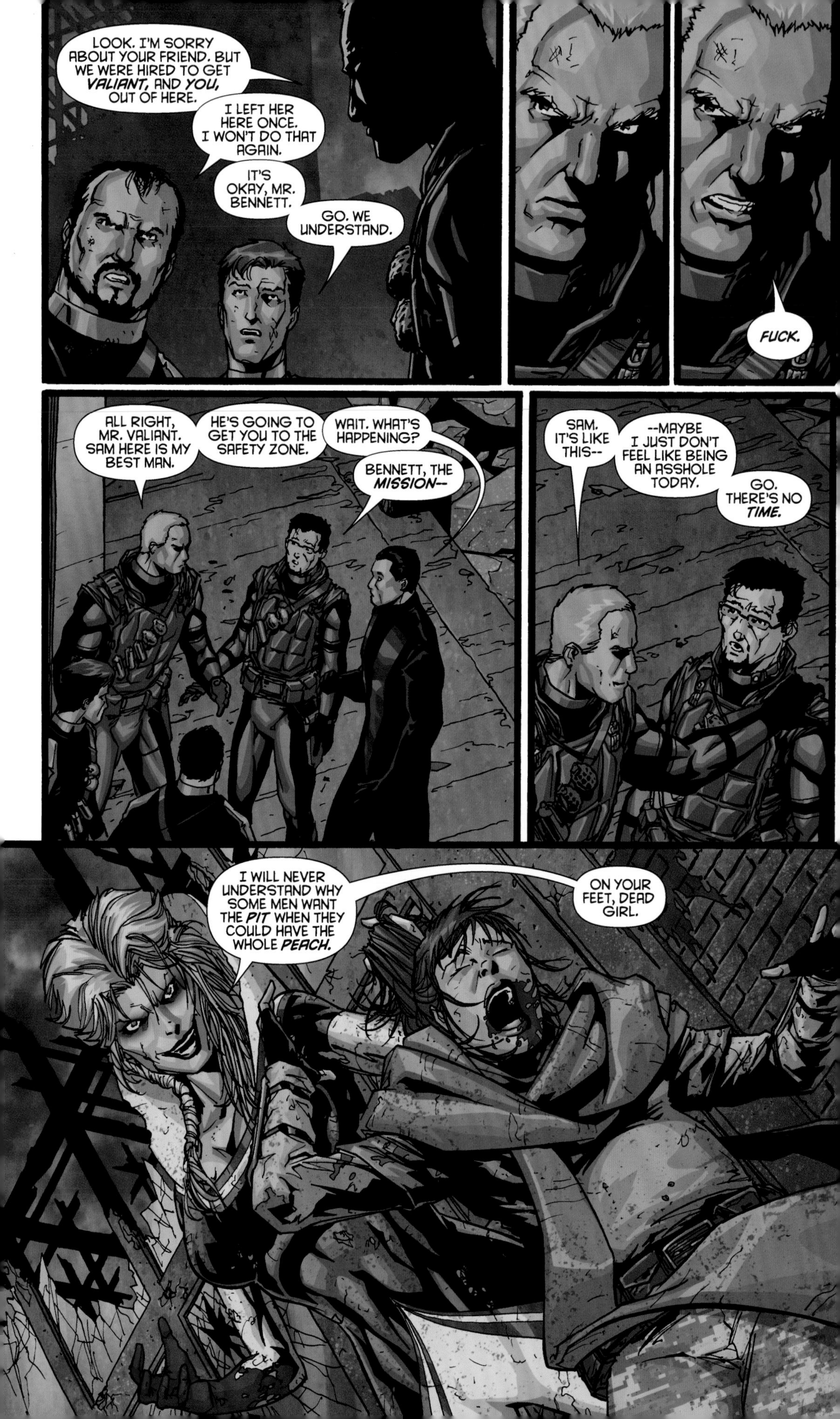
LOOK. I'M SORRY ABOUT YOUR FRIEND. BUT WE WERE HIRED TO GET VALIANT, AND YOU, OUT OF HERE.
I LEFT HER HERE ONCE. I WON'T DO THAT AGAIN.
IT'S OKAY, MR. BENNETT.
GO. WE UNDERSTAND.
FUCK.
ALL RIGHT, MR. VALIANT. SAM HERE IS MY BEST MAN.
HE'S GOING TO GET YOU TO THE SAFETY ZONE.
WAIT. WHAT'S HAPPENING?
BENNETT, THE MISSION--
SAM. IT'S LIKE THIS--
--MAYBE I JUST DON'T FEEL LIKE BEING AN ASSHOLE TODAY.
GO. THERE'S NO TIME.
I WILL NEVER UNDERSTAND WHY SOME MEN WANT THE PIT WHEN THEY COULD HAVE THE WHOLE PEACH.
ON YOUR FEET, DEAD GIRL.

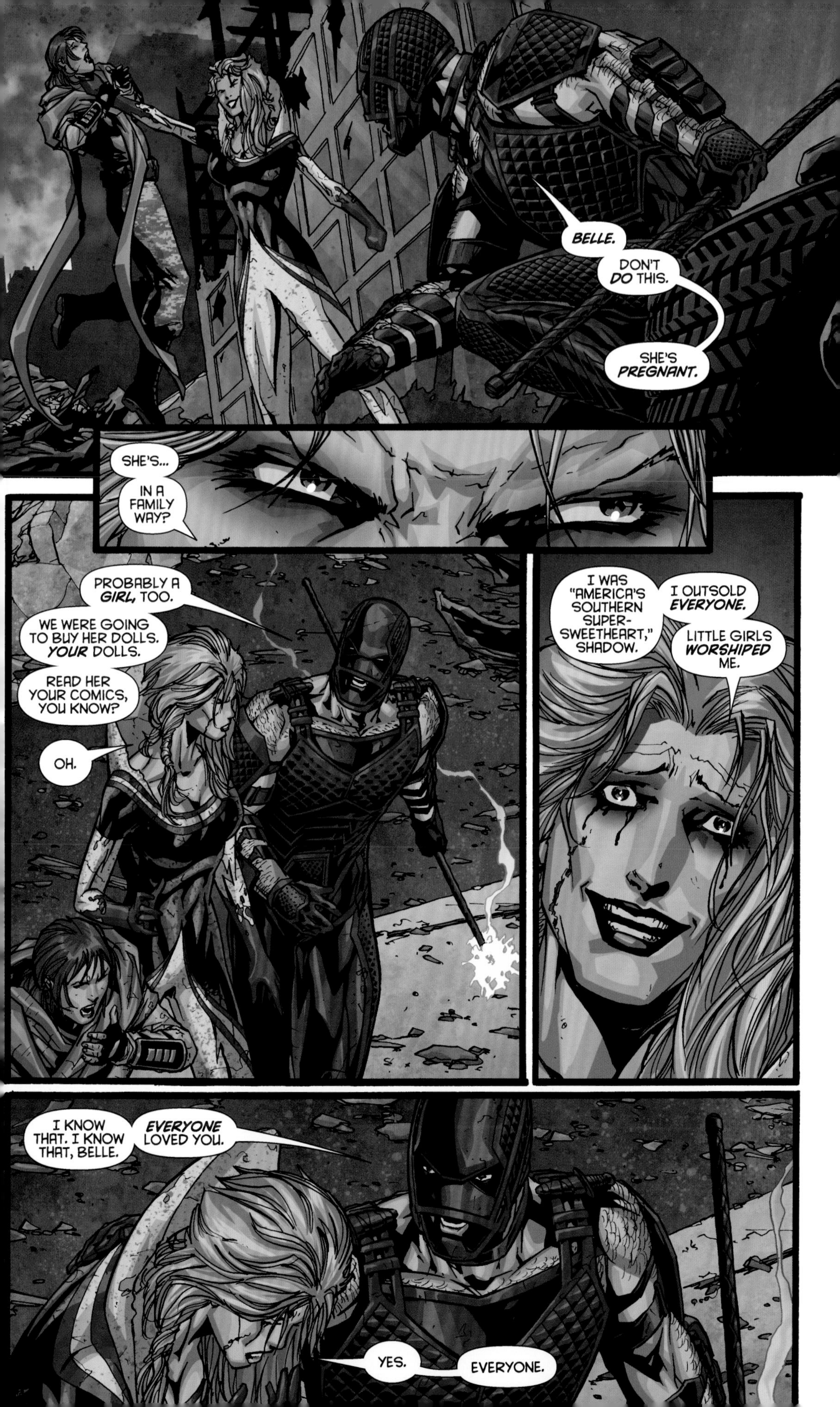
BELLE.
DON'T DO THIS.
SHE'S PREGNANT.
SHE'S...
IN A FAMILY WAY?
PROBABLY A GIRL, TOO.
WE WERE GOING TO BUY HER DOLLS. YOUR DOLLS.
READ HER YOUR COMICS, YOU KNOW?
OH.
I WAS "AMERICA'S SOUTHERN SUPER-SWEETHEART," SHADOW.
I OUTSOLD EVERYONE.
LITTLE GIRLS WORSHIPED ME.
I KNOW THAT. I KNOW THAT, BELLE.
EVERYONE LOVED YOU.
YES.
EVERYONE.

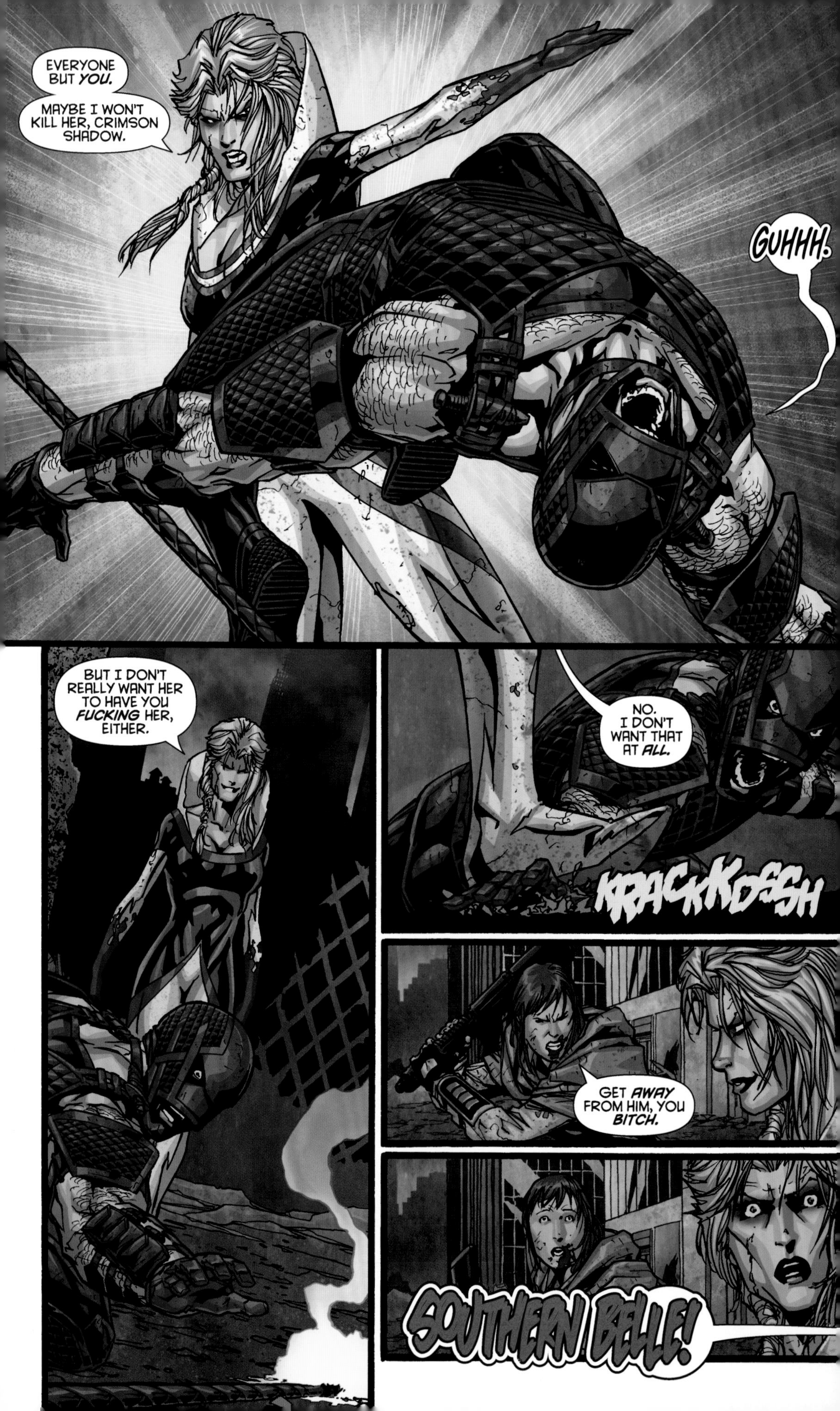
EVERYONE BUT *YOU.*
MAYBE I WON'T KILL HER, CRIMSON SHADOW.
GUHHH.
BUT I DON'T REALLY WANT HER TO HAVE YOU *FUCKING* HER, EITHER.
NO. I DON'T WANT THAT AT *ALL.*
KRACKKOSSH
GET *AWAY* FROM HIM, YOU *BITCH.*
SOUTHERN BELLE!

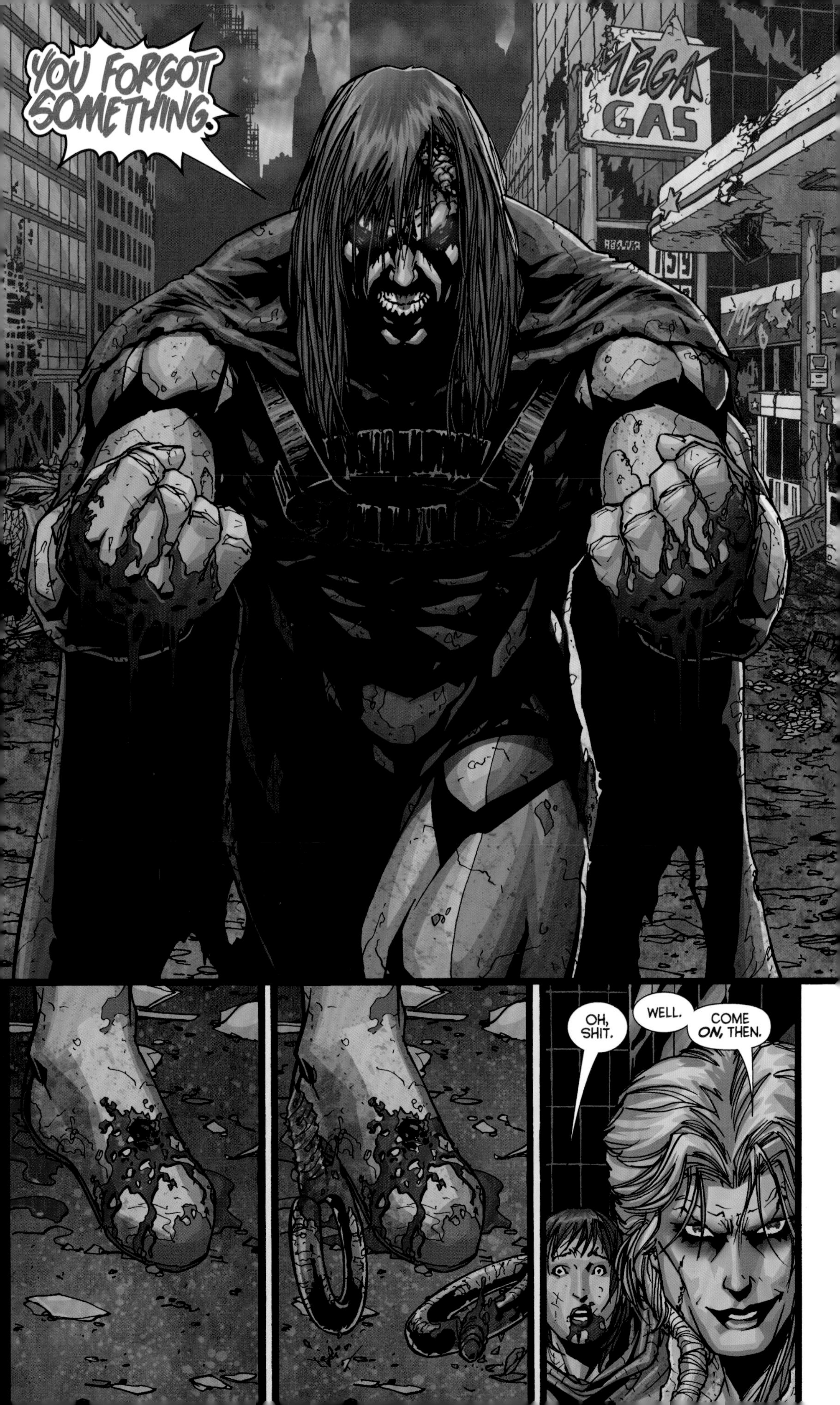

YOU FORGOT SOMETHING.
OH, SHIT.
WELL.
COME ON, THEN.

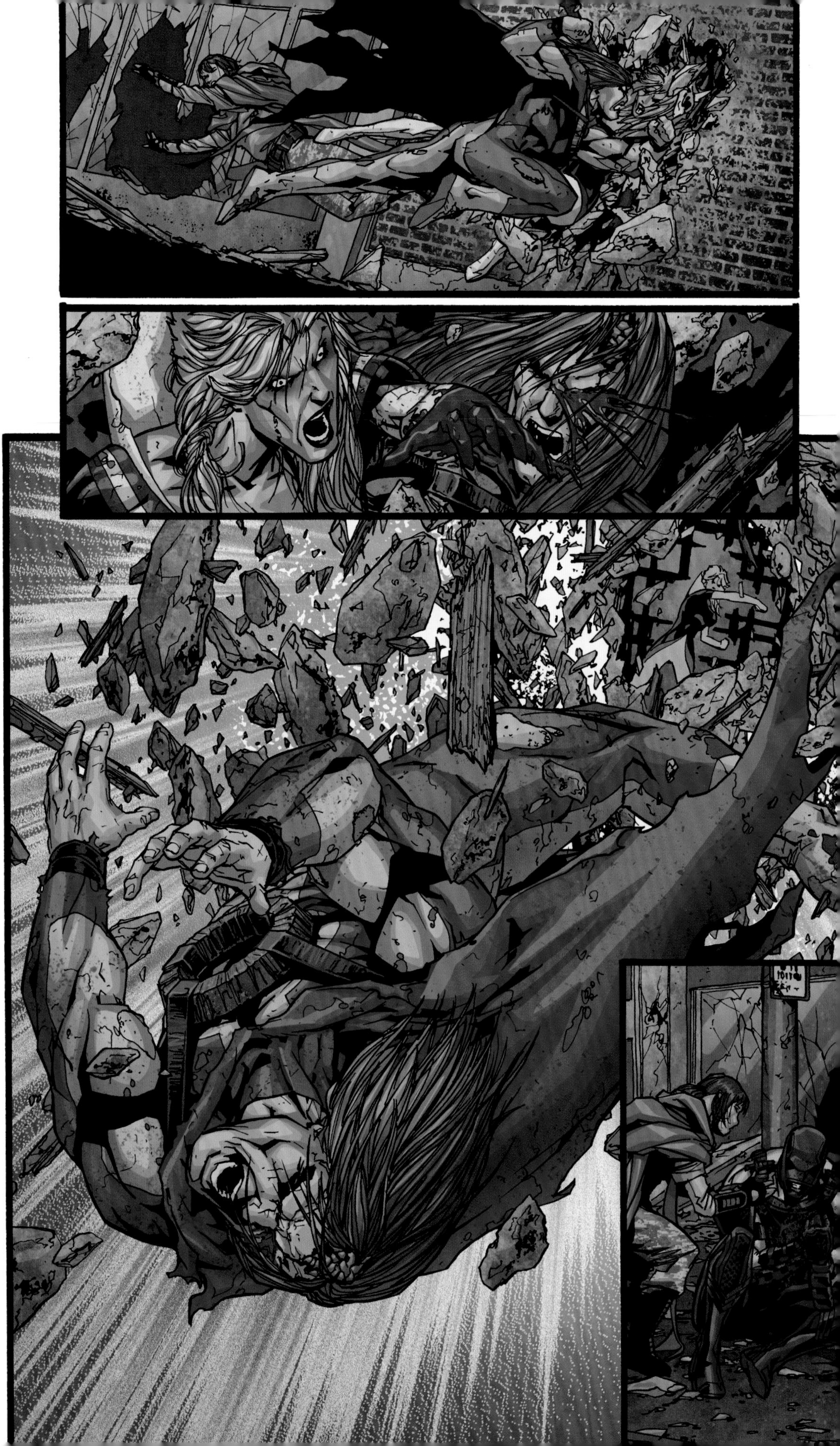

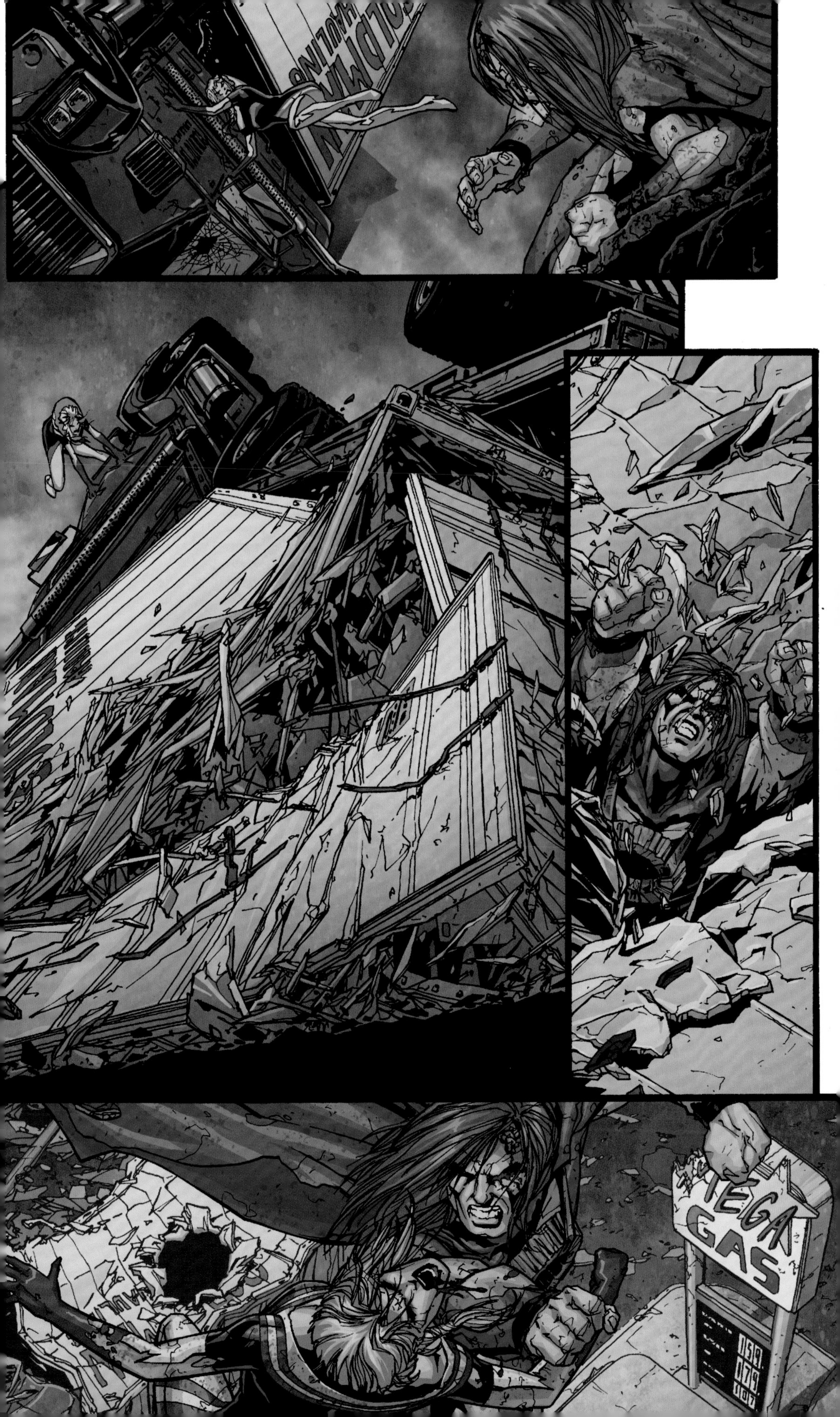
GAS

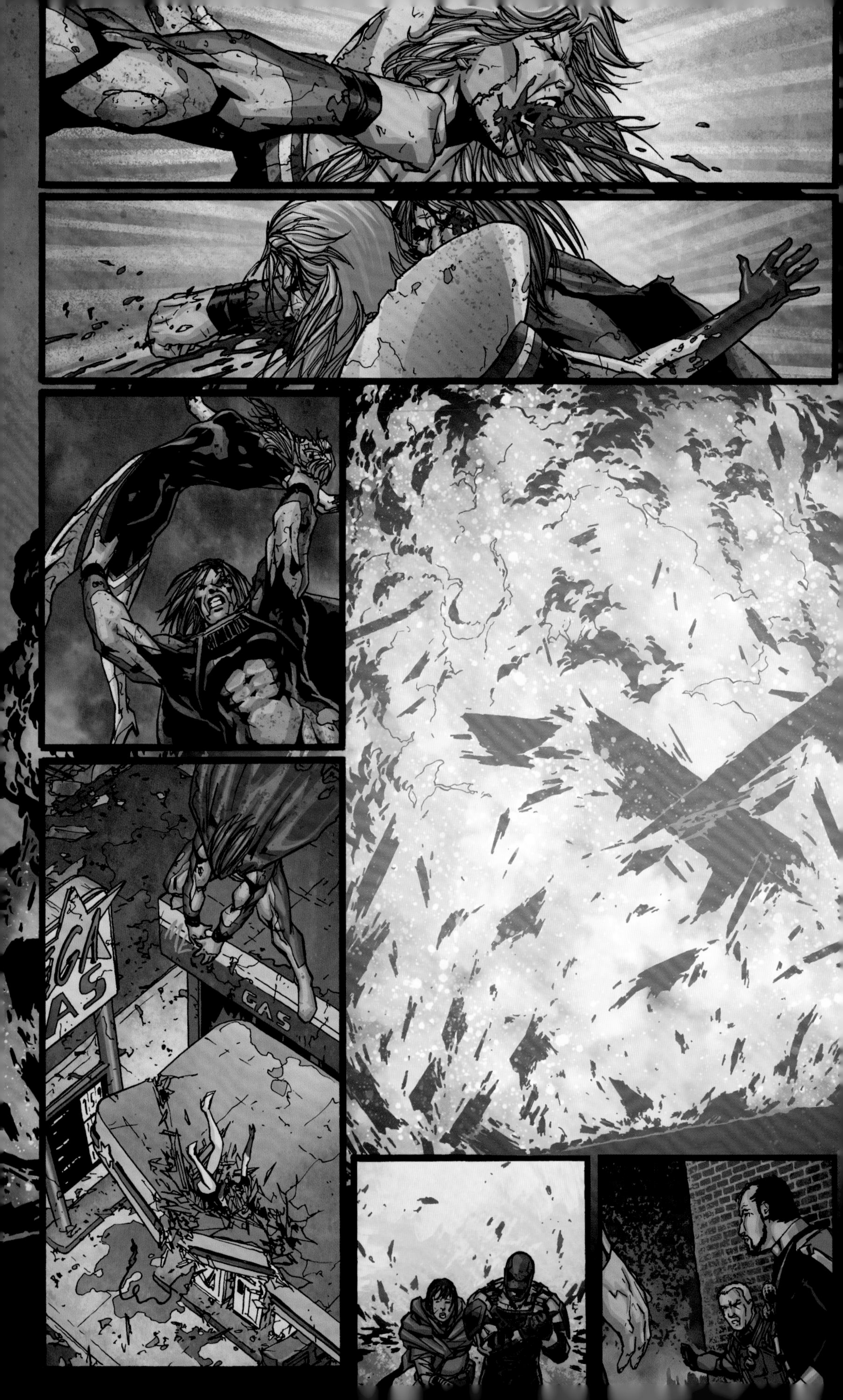
GAS

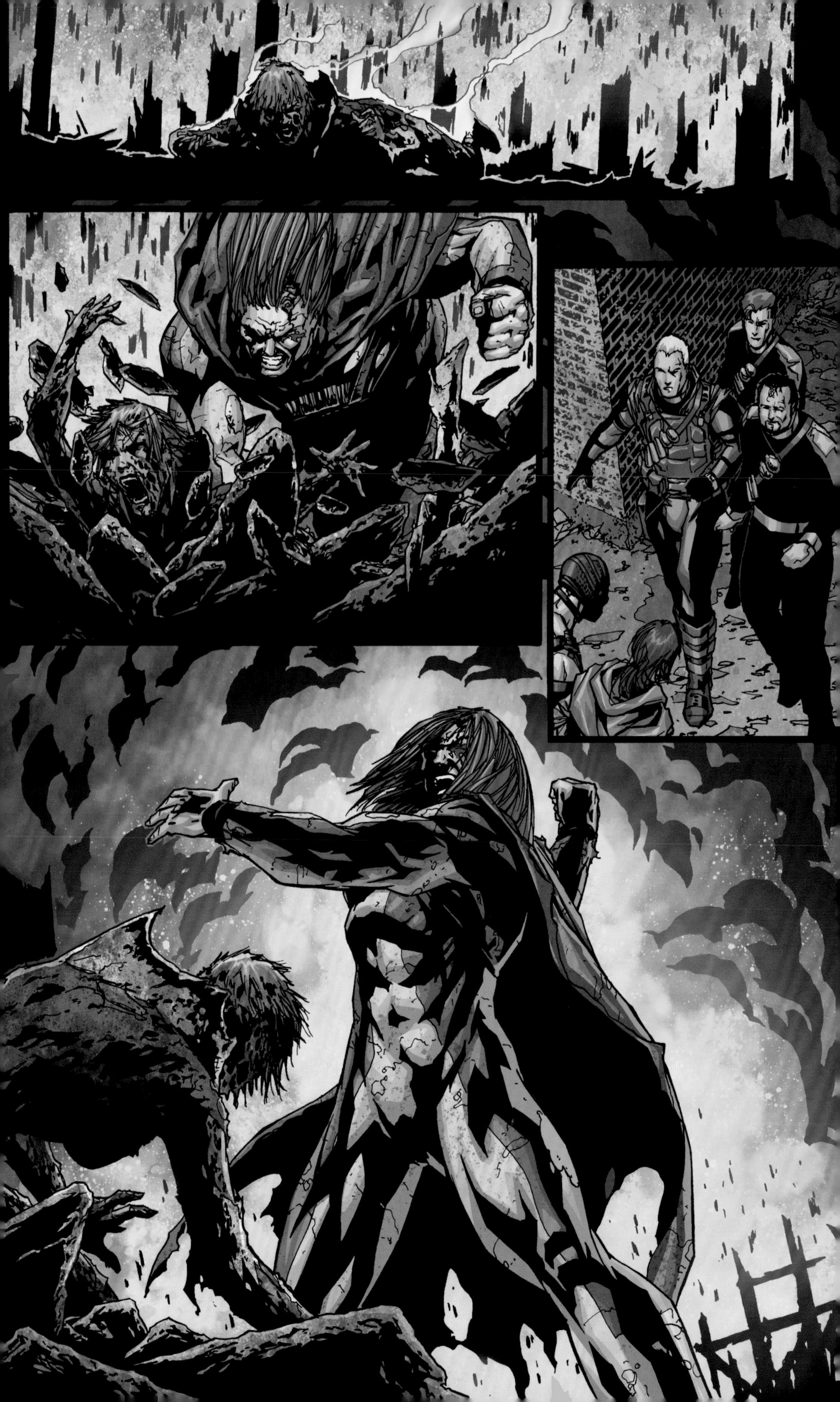

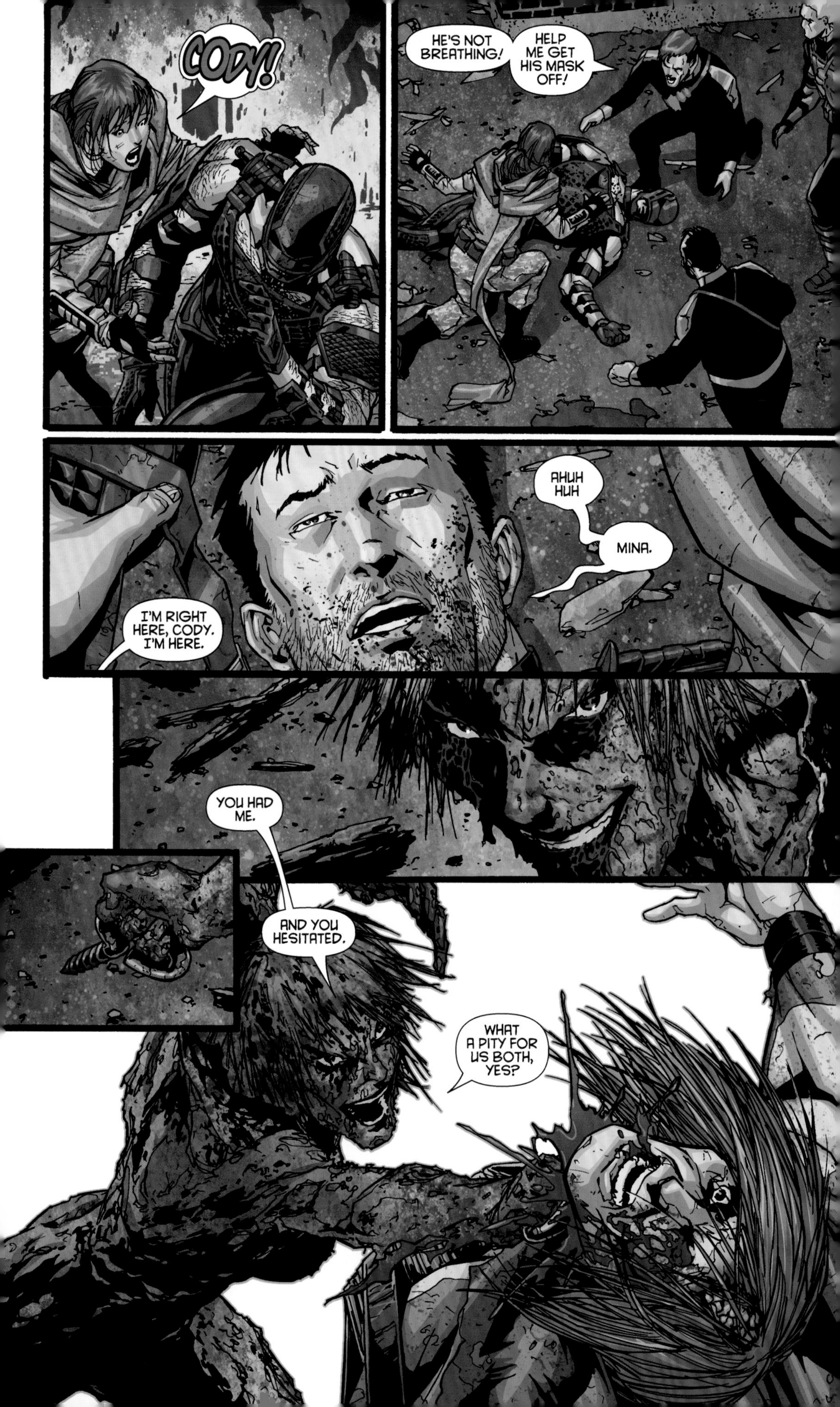
CODY!
HE'S NOT BREATHING!
HELP ME GET HIS MASK OFF!
AHUH HUH
MINA.
I'M RIGHT HERE, CODY. I'M HERE.
YOU HAD ME.
AND YOU HESITATED.
WHAT A PITY FOR US BOTH, YES?

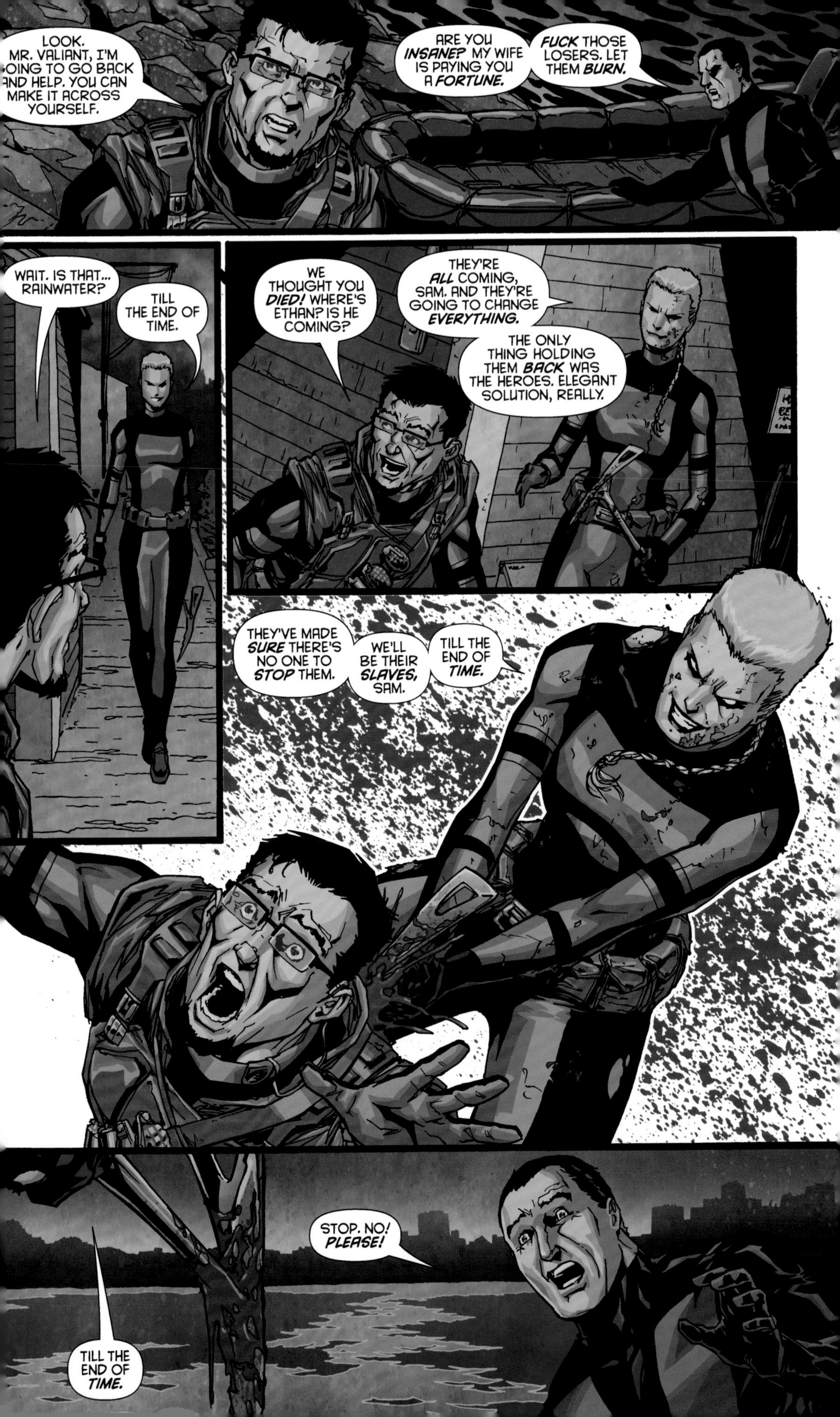
LOOK. MR. VALIANT, I'M GOING TO GO BACK AND HELP. YOU CAN MAKE IT ACROSS YOURSELF.
ARE YOU *INSANE?* MY WIFE IS PAYING YOU A *FORTUNE.*
FUCK THOSE LOSERS. LET THEM *BURN.*
WAIT. IS THAT... RAINWATER?
TILL THE END OF TIME.
WE THOUGHT YOU *DIED!* WHERE'S ETHAN? IS HE COMING?
THEY'RE *ALL* COMING, SAM. AND THEY'RE GOING TO CHANGE *EVERYTHING.*
THE ONLY THING HOLDING THEM *BACK* WAS THE HEROES. ELEGANT SOLUTION, REALLY.
THEY'VE MADE *SURE* THERE'S NO ONE TO *STOP* THEM.
WE'LL BE THEIR *SLAVES,* SAM.
TILL THE END OF *TIME.*
STOP. NO! *PLEASE!*
TILL THE END OF *TIME.*

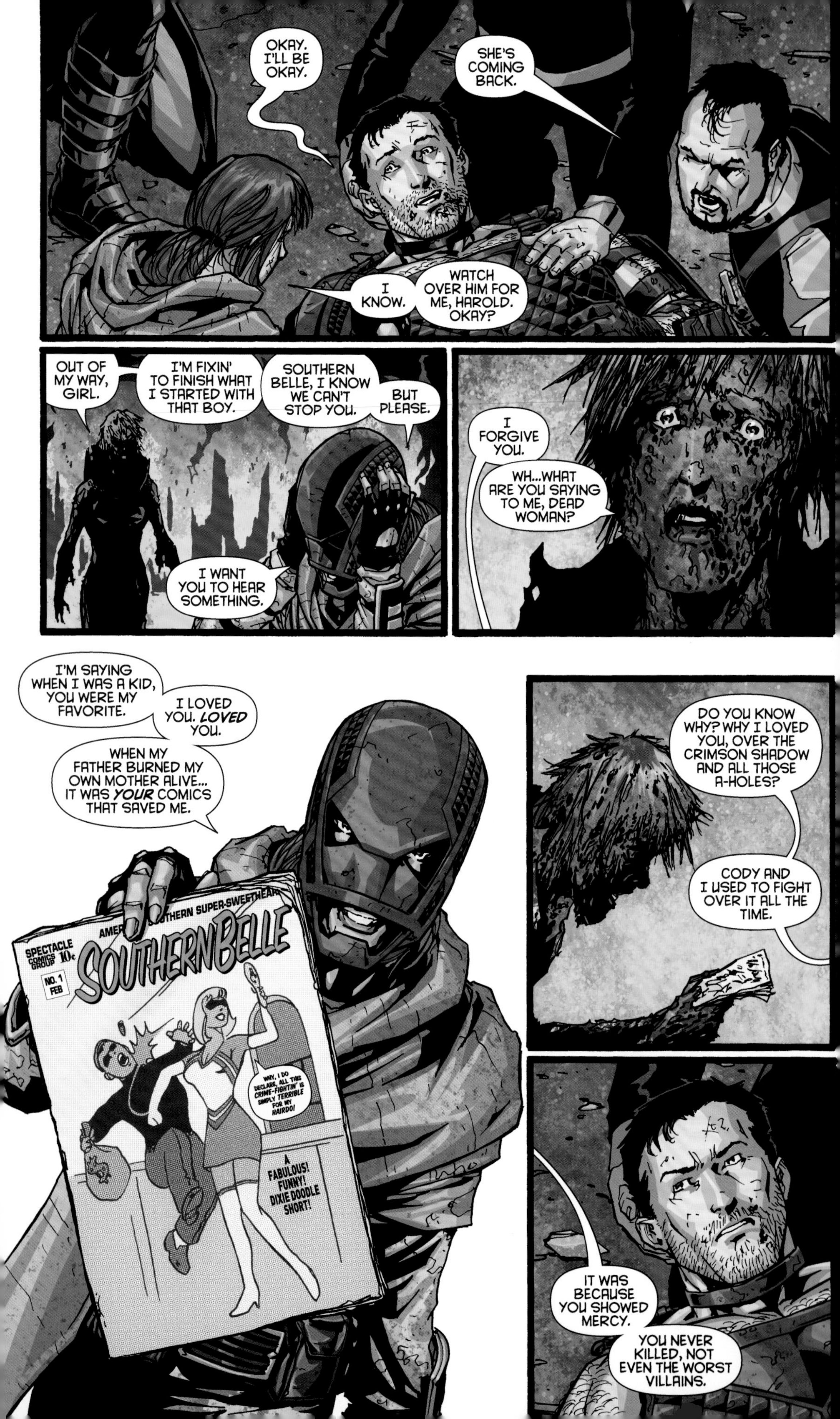
OKAY. I'LL BE OKAY.
SHE'S COMING BACK.
I KNOW.
WATCH OVER HIM FOR ME, HAROLD. OKAY?
OUT OF MY WAY, GIRL.
I'M FIXIN' TO FINISH WHAT I STARTED WITH THAT BOY.
SOUTHERN BELLE, I KNOW WE CAN'T STOP YOU.
BUT PLEASE.
I WANT YOU TO HEAR SOMETHING.
I FORGIVE YOU.
WH...WHAT ARE YOU SAYING TO ME, DEAD WOMAN?
I'M SAYING WHEN I WAS A KID, YOU WERE MY FAVORITE.
I LOVED YOU. *LOVED* YOU.
WHEN MY FATHER BURNED MY OWN MOTHER ALIVE... IT WAS *YOUR* COMICS THAT SAVED ME.
SPECTACLE COMICS GROUP 10¢
NO. 1 FEB
SOUTHERN SUPER-SWEETHEART
SOUTHERN BELLE
WHY, I DO DECLARE, ALL THIS CRIME-FIGHTIN' IS SIMPLY TERRIBLE FOR MY HAIRDO!
A FABULOUS! FUNNY! DIXIE DOODLE SHORT!
DO YOU KNOW WHY? WHY I LOVED YOU, OVER THE CRIMSON SHADOW AND ALL THOSE A-HOLES?
CODY AND I USED TO FIGHT OVER IT ALL THE TIME.
IT WAS BECAUSE YOU SHOWED MERCY.
YOU NEVER KILLED, NOT EVEN THE WORST VILLAINS.

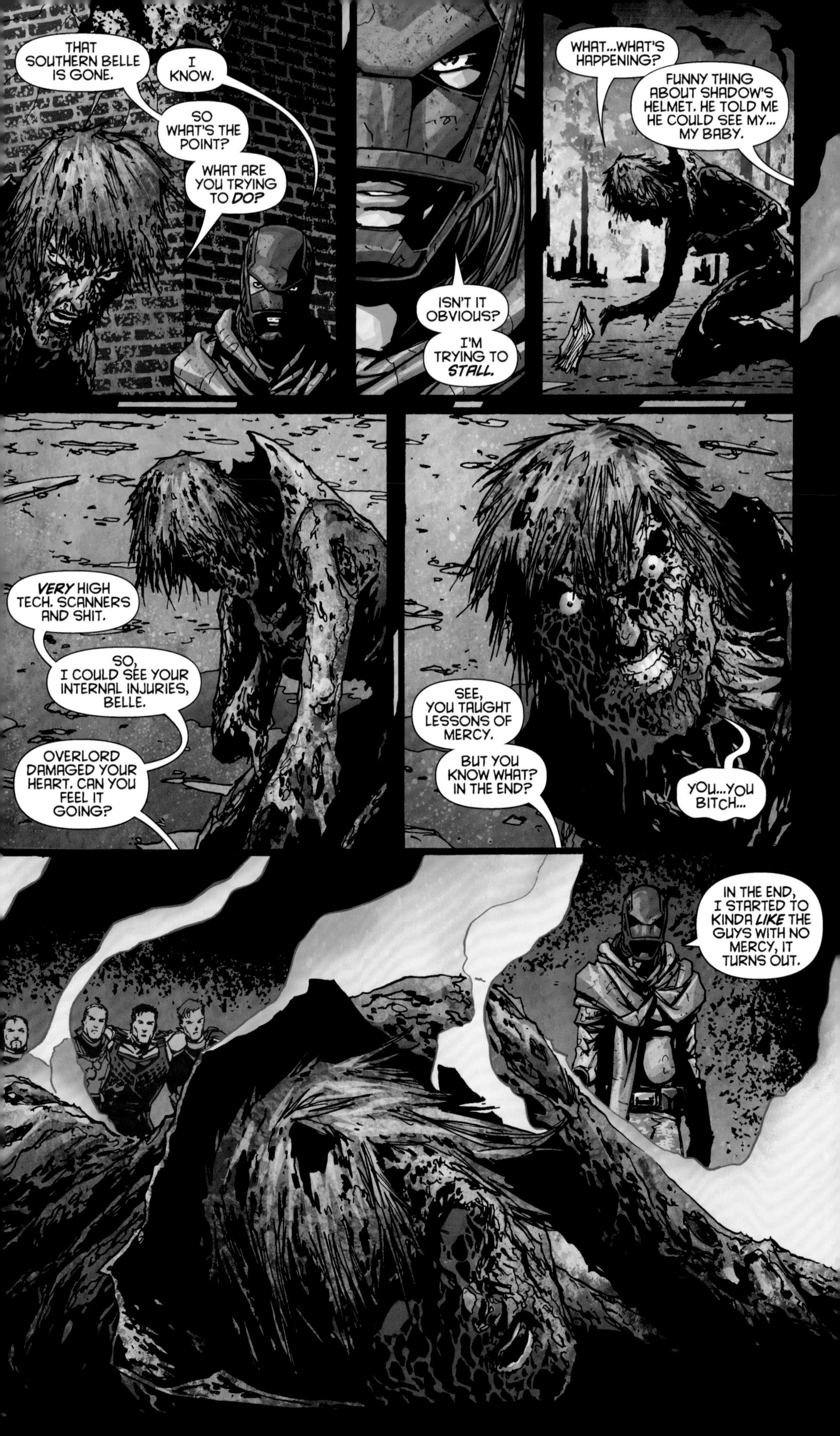
THAT SOUTHERN BELLE IS GONE.
I KNOW.
SO WHAT'S THE POINT?
WHAT ARE YOU TRYING TO *DO?*
ISN'T IT OBVIOUS?
I'M TRYING TO ***STALL.***
WHAT...WHAT'S HAPPENING?
FUNNY THING ABOUT SHADOW'S HELMET. HE TOLD ME HE COULD SEE MY... MY BABY.
VERY HIGH TECH. SCANNERS AND SHIT.
SO, I COULD SEE YOUR INTERNAL INJURIES, BELLE.
OVERLORD DAMAGED YOUR HEART. CAN YOU FEEL IT GOING?
SEE, YOU TAUGHT LESSONS OF MERCY.
BUT YOU KNOW WHAT? IN THE END?
YOU...YOU BITCH...
IN THE END, I STARTED TO KINDA *LIKE* THE GUYS WITH NO MERCY, IT TURNS OUT.

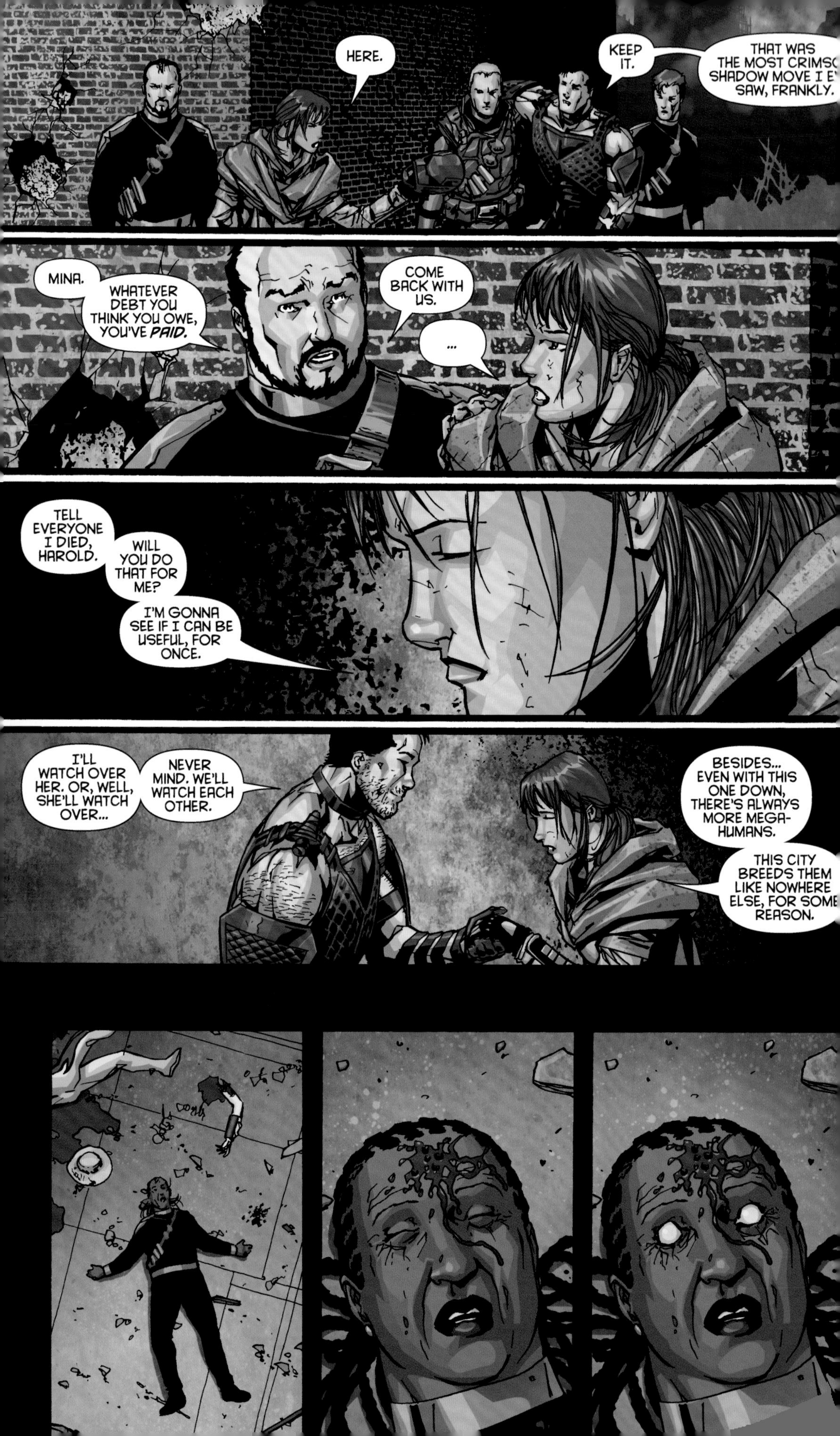
HERE.
KEEP IT.
THAT WAS THE MOST CRIMSO SHADOW MOVE I E SAW, FRANKLY.
MINA.
WHATEVER DEBT YOU THINK YOU OWE, YOU'VE *PAID.*
COME BACK WITH US.
...
TELL EVERYONE I DIED, HAROLD.
WILL YOU DO THAT FOR ME?
I'M GONNA SEE IF I CAN BE USEFUL, FOR ONCE.
I'LL WATCH OVER HER. OR, WELL, SHE'LL WATCH OVER...
NEVER MIND. WE'LL WATCH EACH OTHER.
BESIDES... EVEN WITH THIS ONE DOWN, THERE'S ALWAYS MORE MEGA-HUMANS.
THIS CITY BREEDS THEM LIKE NOWHERE ELSE, FOR SOME REASON.

Leaving Megalopolis **started as a crowdfunded venture created by Gail Simone and J. Calafiore. The campaign was hugely successful, raising more than three times its goal of $34,000. One of the stretch goals was an eight-page digital comic, "Finding Megalopolis: Fleet Sees a Rainbow."**

For the first time in print, here's a look at the story behind one of the "heroes" of Megalopolis, the psychotic speedster FLEET!

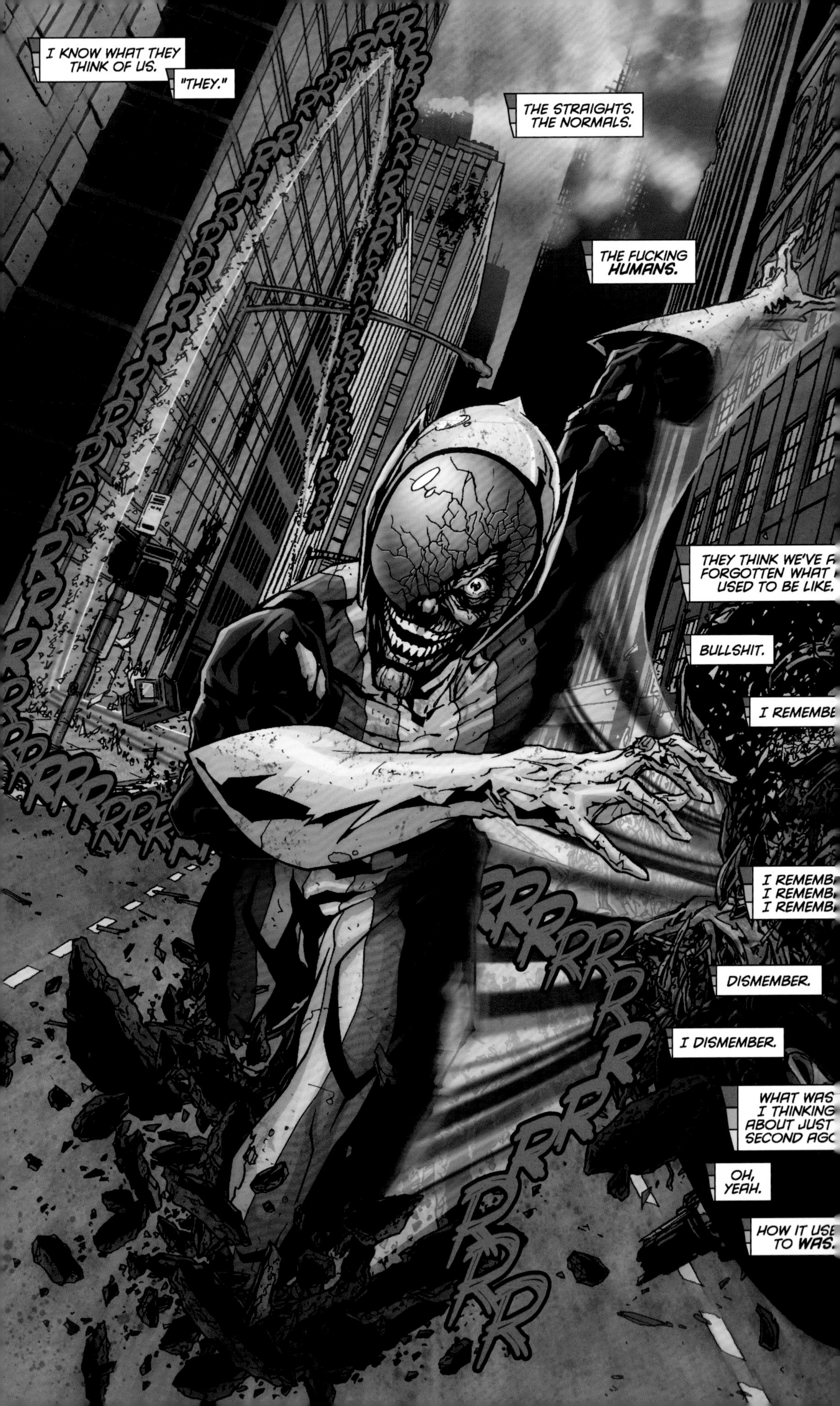
I KNOW WHAT THEY THINK OF US.
"THEY."
THE STRAIGHTS. THE NORMALS.
THE FUCKING *HUMANS.*
THEY THINK WE'VE
FORGOTTEN WHAT
USED TO BE LIKE.
BULLSHIT.
I REMEMBE
I REMEMB
I REMEMB
I REMEMB
DISMEMBER.
I DISMEMBER.
WHAT WAS
I THINKING
ABOUT JUST
SECOND AG
OH, YEAH.
HOW IT USE
TO *WAS.*

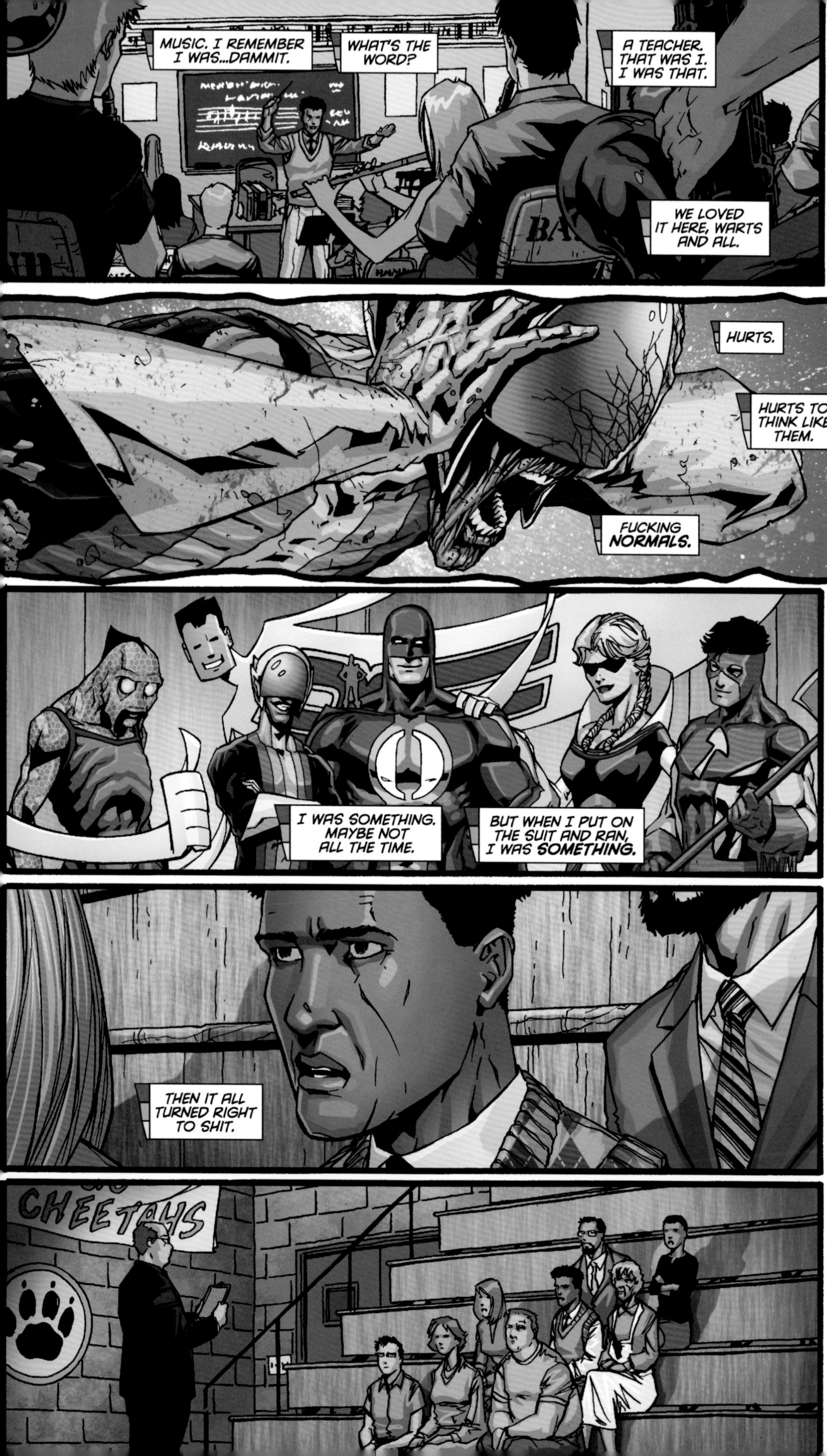
MUSIC. I REMEMBER I WAS...DAMMIT.
WHAT'S THE WORD?
A TEACHER. THAT WAS I. I WAS THAT.
WE LOVED IT HERE, WARTS AND ALL.
HURTS.
HURTS TO THINK LIKE THEM.
FUCKING **NORMALS.**
I WAS SOMETHING. MAYBE NOT ALL THE TIME.
BUT WHEN I PUT ON THE SUIT AND RAN, I WAS **SOMETHING.**
THEN IT ALL TURNED RIGHT TO SHIT.
CHEETAHS

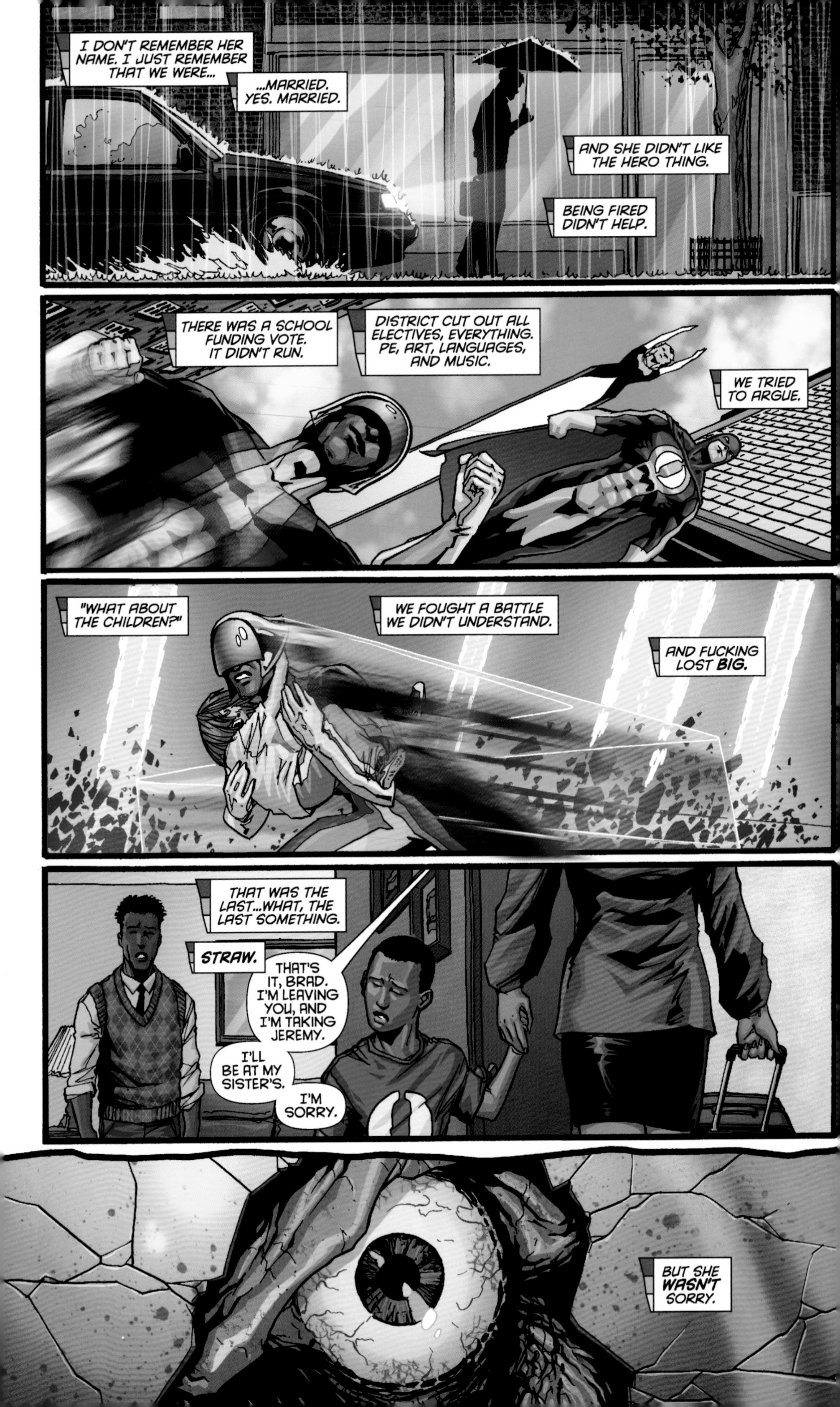
I DON'T REMEMBER HER NAME. I JUST REMEMBER THAT WE WERE...
...MARRIED. YES. MARRIED.
AND SHE DIDN'T LIKE THE HERO THING.
BEING FIRED DIDN'T HELP.
THERE WAS A SCHOOL FUNDING VOTE. IT DIDN'T RUN.
DISTRICT CUT OUT ALL ELECTIVES, EVERYTHING. PE, ART, LANGUAGES, AND MUSIC.
WE TRIED TO ARGUE.
"WHAT ABOUT THE CHILDREN?"
WE FOUGHT A BATTLE WE DIDN'T UNDERSTAND.
AND FUCKING LOST **BIG.**
THAT WAS THE LAST...WHAT, THE LAST SOMETHING.
STRAW.
THAT'S IT, BRAD. I'M LEAVING YOU, AND I'M TAKING JEREMY.
I'LL BE AT MY SISTER'S.
I'M SORRY.
BUT SHE **WASN'T** SORRY.

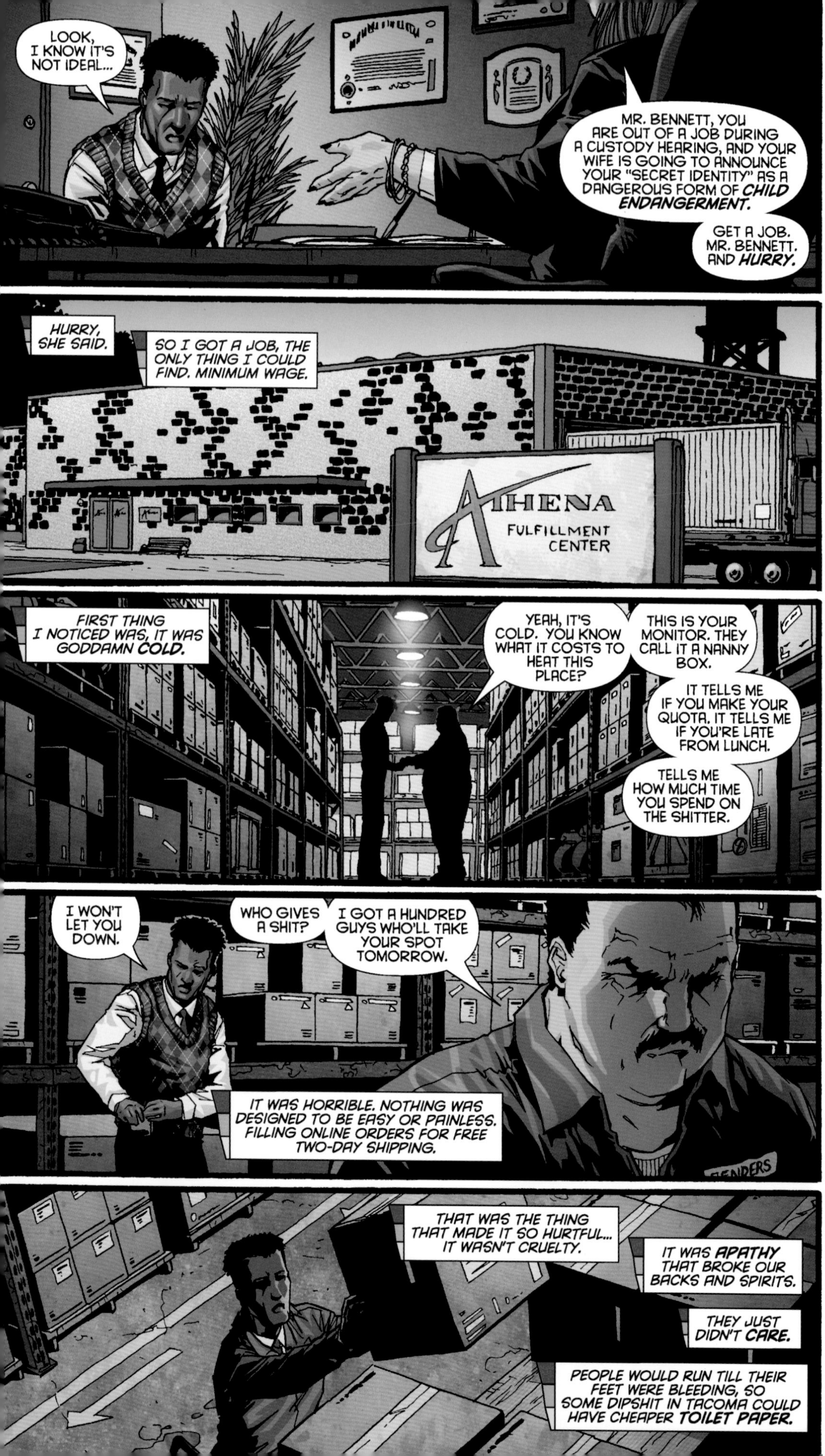
LOOK, I KNOW IT'S NOT IDEAL...
MR. BENNETT, YOU ARE OUT OF A JOB DURING A CUSTODY HEARING, AND YOUR WIFE IS GOING TO ANNOUNCE YOUR "SECRET IDENTITY" AS A DANGEROUS FORM OF CHILD ENDANGERMENT.
GET A JOB. MR. BENNETT. AND HURRY.
HURRY, SHE SAID.
SO I GOT A JOB, THE ONLY THING I COULD FIND. MINIMUM WAGE.
ATHENA FULFILLMENT CENTER
FIRST THING I NOTICED WAS, IT WAS GODDAMN COLD.
YEAH, IT'S COLD. YOU KNOW WHAT IT COSTS TO HEAT THIS PLACE?
THIS IS YOUR MONITOR. THEY CALL IT A NANNY BOX.
IT TELLS ME IF YOU MAKE YOUR QUOTA. IT TELLS ME IF YOU'RE LATE FROM LUNCH.
TELLS ME HOW MUCH TIME YOU SPEND ON THE SHITTER.
I WON'T LET YOU DOWN.
WHO GIVES A SHIT?
I GOT A HUNDRED GUYS WHO'LL TAKE YOUR SPOT TOMORROW.
IT WAS HORRIBLE. NOTHING WAS DESIGNED TO BE EASY OR PAINLESS. FILLING ONLINE ORDERS FOR FREE TWO-DAY SHIPPING.
FLENDERS
THAT WAS THE THING THAT MADE IT SO HURTFUL... IT WASN'T CRUELTY.
IT WAS APATHY THAT BROKE OUR BACKS AND SPIRITS.
THEY JUST DIDN'T CARE.
PEOPLE WOULD RUN TILL THEIR FEET WERE BLEEDING, SO SOME DIPSHIT IN TACOMA COULD HAVE CHEAPER TOILET PAPER.

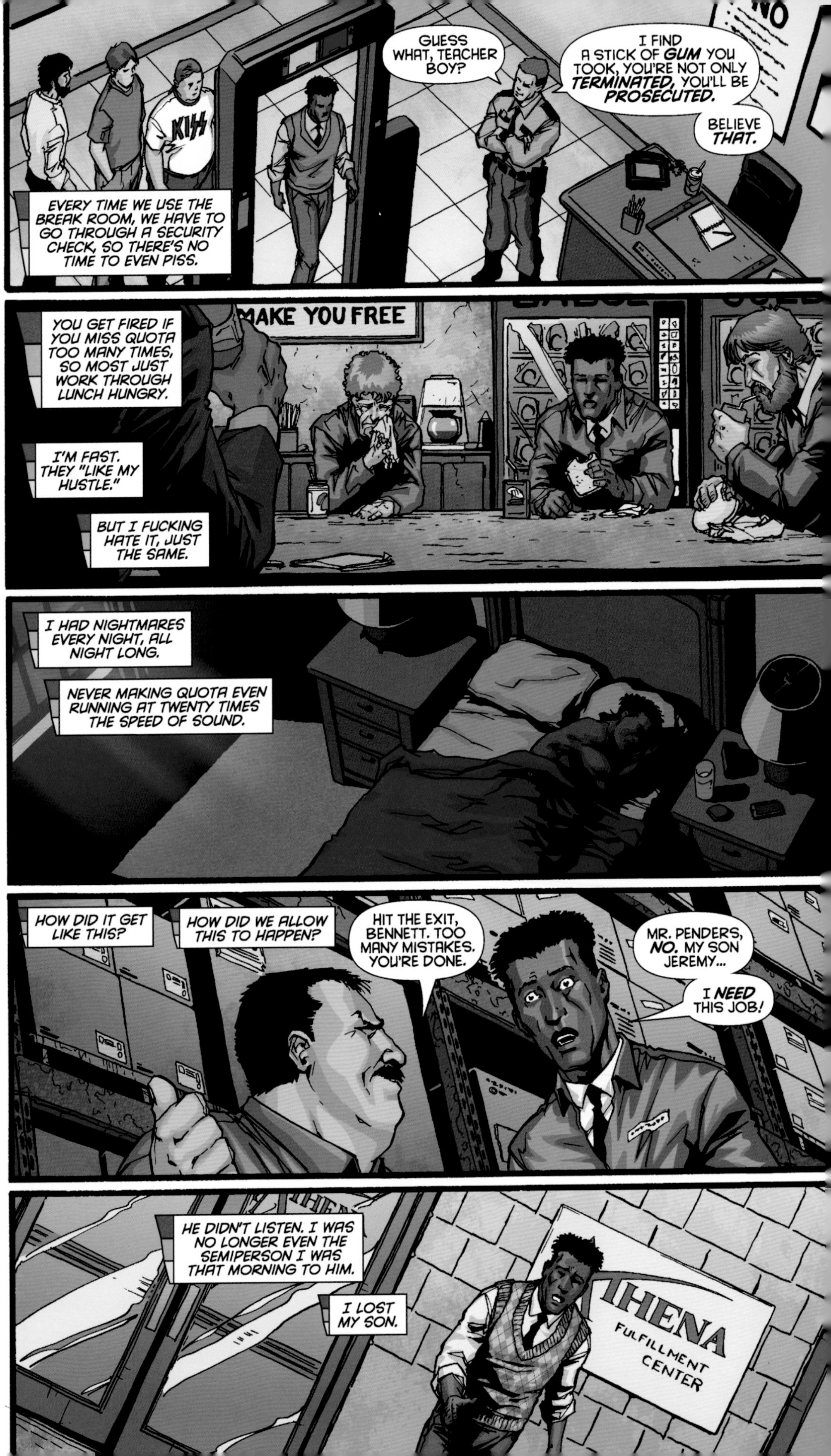
EVERY TIME WE USE THE BREAK ROOM, WE HAVE TO GO THROUGH A SECURITY CHECK, SO THERE'S NO TIME TO EVEN PISS.
GUESS WHAT, TEACHER BOY?
I FIND A STICK OF GUM YOU TOOK, YOU'RE NOT ONLY TERMINATED, YOU'LL BE PROSECUTED.
BELIEVE THAT.
NO
KISS
MAKE YOU FREE
YOU GET FIRED IF YOU MISS QUOTA TOO MANY TIMES, SO MOST JUST WORK THROUGH LUNCH HUNGRY.
I'M FAST. THEY "LIKE MY HUSTLE."
BUT I FUCKING HATE IT, JUST THE SAME.
I HAD NIGHTMARES EVERY NIGHT, ALL NIGHT LONG.
NEVER MAKING QUOTA EVEN RUNNING AT TWENTY TIMES THE SPEED OF SOUND.
HOW DID IT GET LIKE THIS?
HOW DID WE ALLOW THIS TO HAPPEN?
HIT THE EXIT, BENNETT. TOO MANY MISTAKES. YOU'RE DONE.
MR. PENDERS, NO. MY SON JEREMY...
I NEED THIS JOB!
HE DIDN'T LISTEN. I WAS NO LONGER EVEN THE SEMIPERSON I WAS THAT MORNING TO HIM.
I LOST MY SON.
THENA FULFILLMENT CENTER

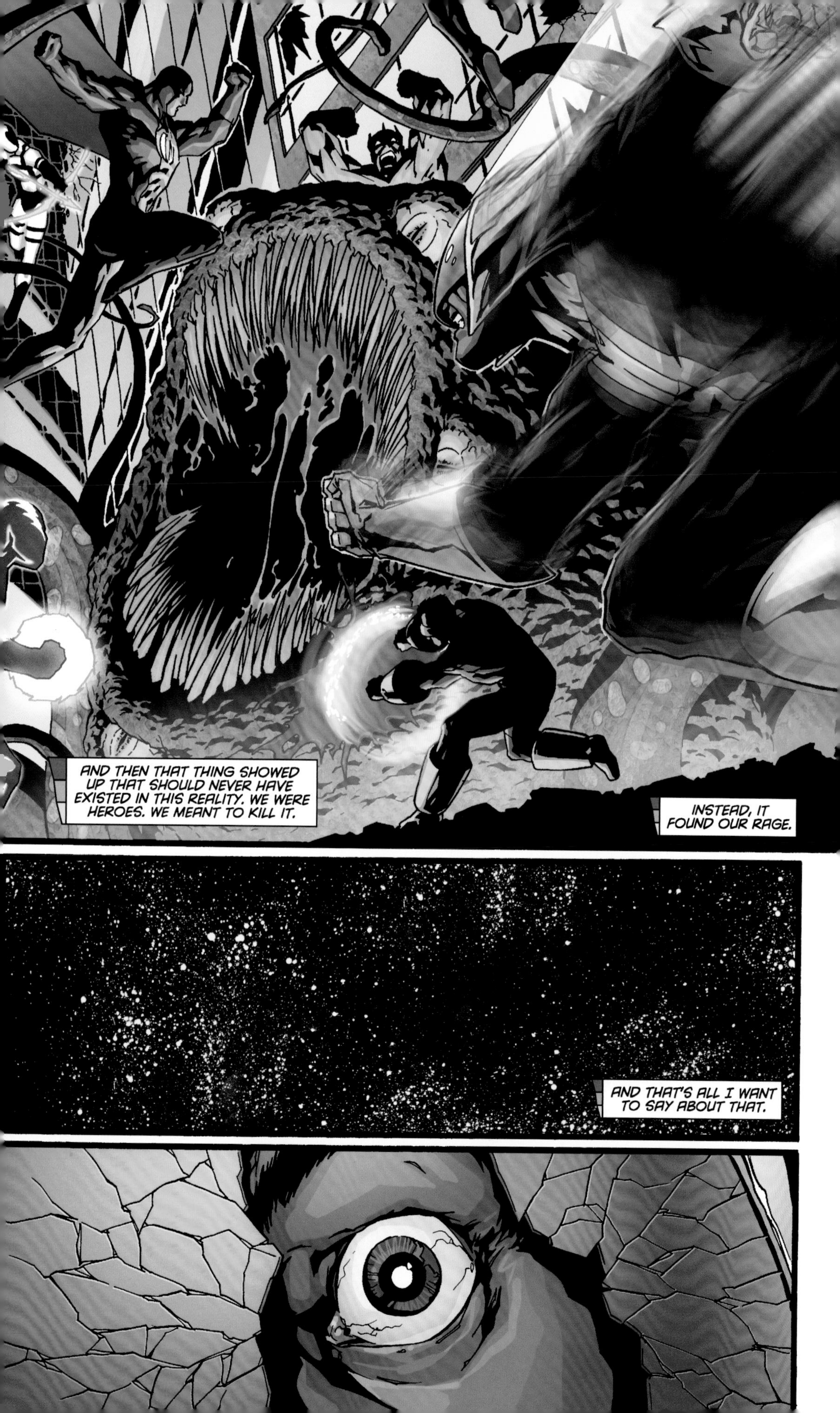
AND THEN THAT THING SHOWED UP THAT SHOULD NEVER HAVE EXISTED IN THIS REALITY. WE WERE HEROES. WE MEANT TO KILL IT.
INSTEAD, IT FOUND OUR RAGE.
AND THAT'S ALL I WANT TO SAY ABOUT THAT.

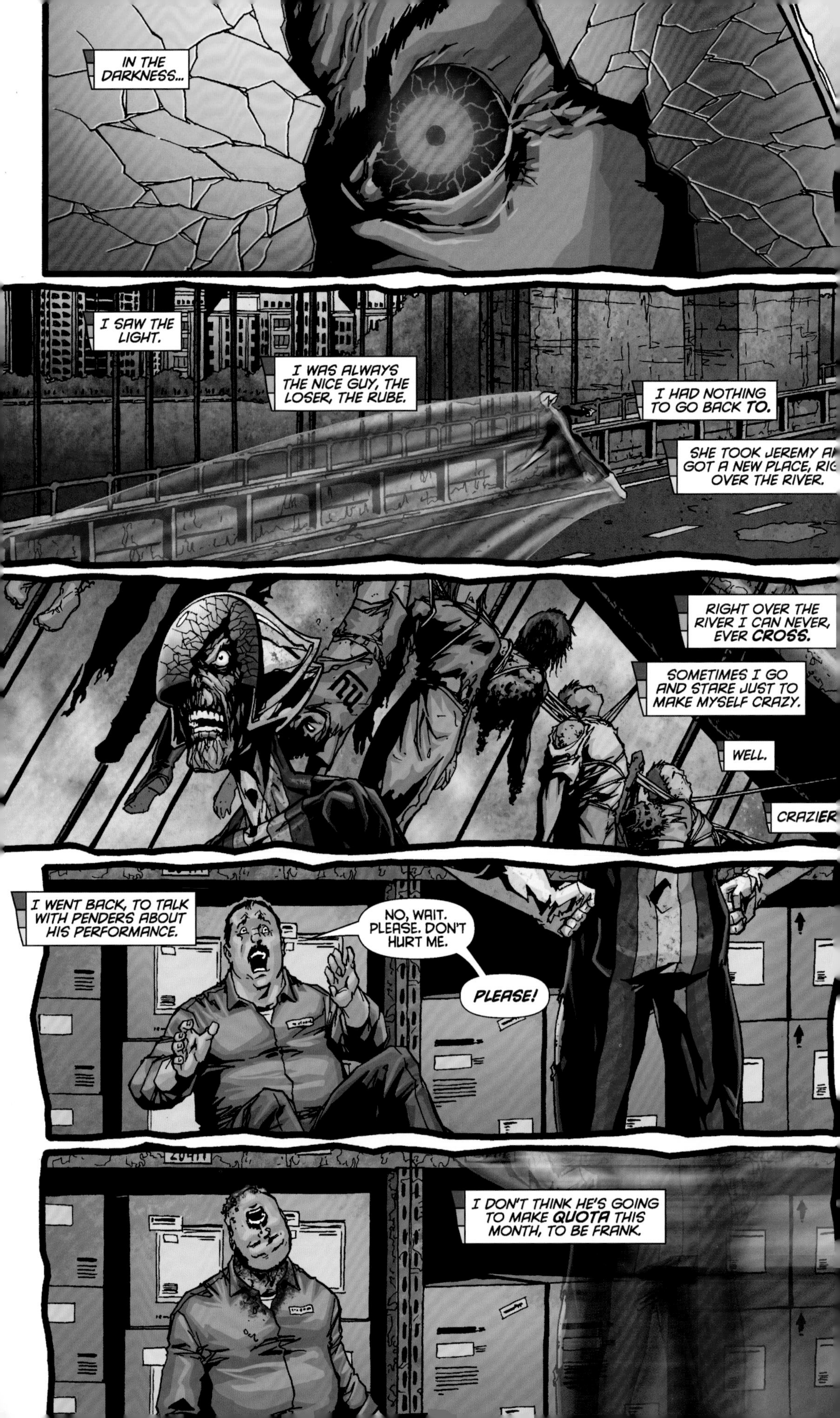

IN THE DARKNESS...
I SAW THE LIGHT.
I WAS ALWAYS THE NICE GUY, THE LOSER, THE RUBE.
I HAD NOTHING TO GO BACK TO.
SHE TOOK JEREMY A
GOT A NEW PLACE, RIG
OVER THE RIVER.
RIGHT OVER THE RIVER I CAN NEVER, EVER CROSS.
SOMETIMES I GO AND STARE JUST TO MAKE MYSELF CRAZY.
WELL.
CRAZIER
I WENT BACK, TO TALK WITH PENDERS ABOUT HIS PERFORMANCE.
NO, WAIT. PLEASE. DON'T HURT ME.
PLEASE!
I DON'T THINK HE'S GOING TO MAKE QUOTA THIS MONTH, TO BE FRANK.

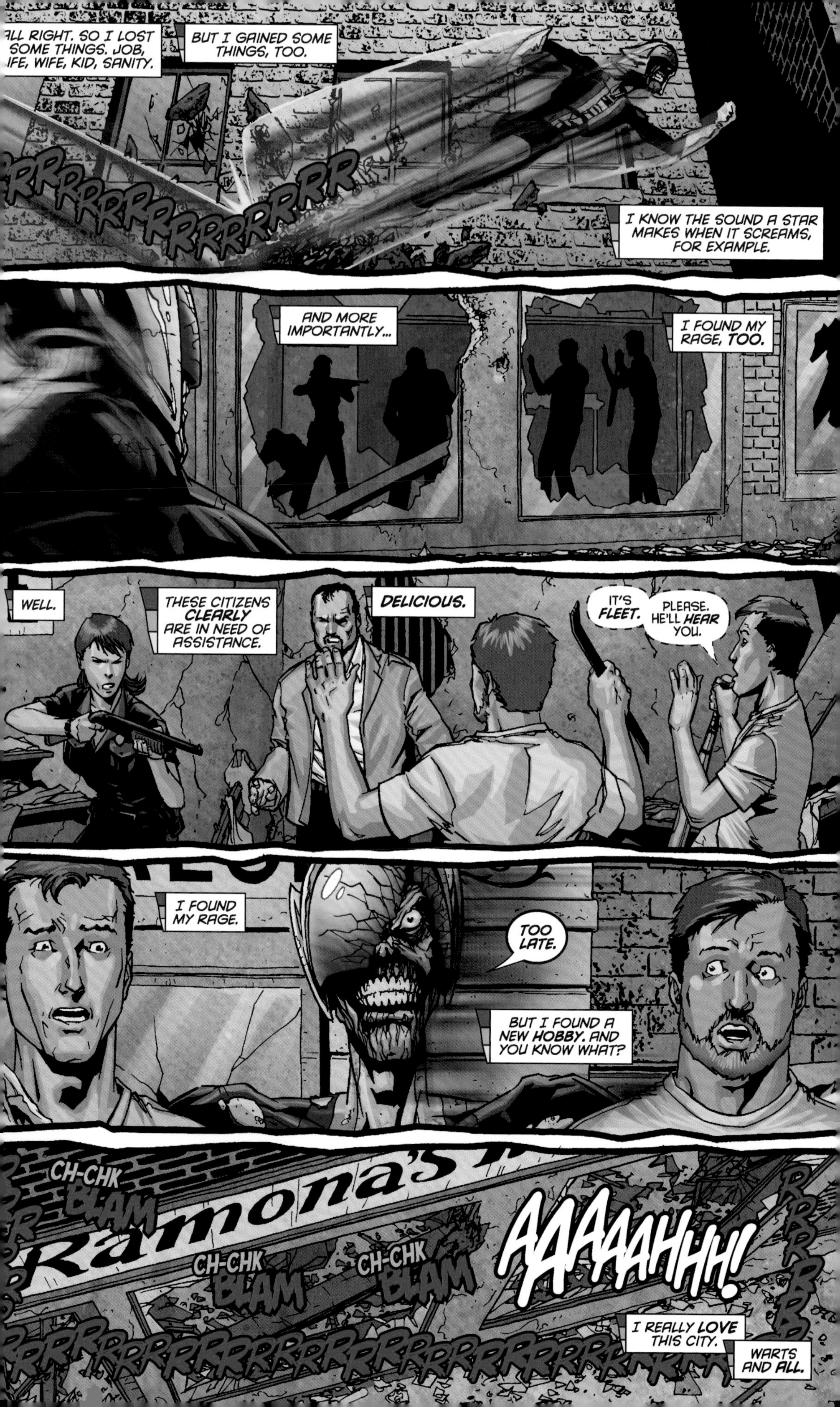

ALL RIGHT. SO I LOST SOME THINGS. JOB, LIFE, WIFE, KID, SANITY.
BUT I GAINED SOME THINGS, TOO.
RRRRRRRRRRRRRRRR
I KNOW THE SOUND A STAR MAKES WHEN IT SCREAMS, FOR EXAMPLE.
AND MORE IMPORTANTLY...
I FOUND MY RAGE, TOO.
WELL.
THESE CITIZENS CLEARLY ARE IN NEED OF ASSISTANCE.
DELICIOUS.
IT'S FLEET.
PLEASE. HE'LL HEAR YOU.
I FOUND MY RAGE.
TOO LATE.
BUT I FOUND A NEW HOBBY. AND YOU KNOW WHAT?
Ramona's
CH-CHK BLAM
CH-CHK BLAM
CH-CHK BLAM
AAAAAHHH!
RRRRRRRRRRRRRRRRRRRRRRRRRRRR
I REALLY LOVE THIS CITY.
WARTS AND ALL.

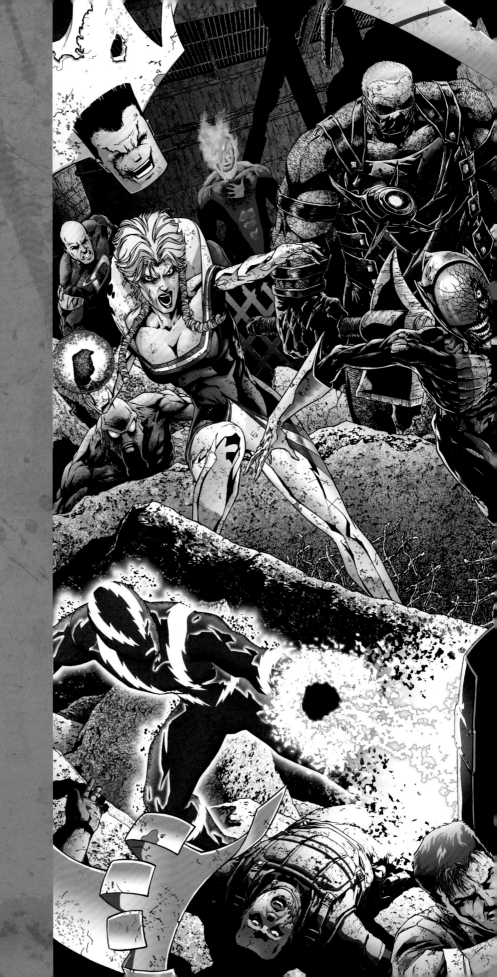

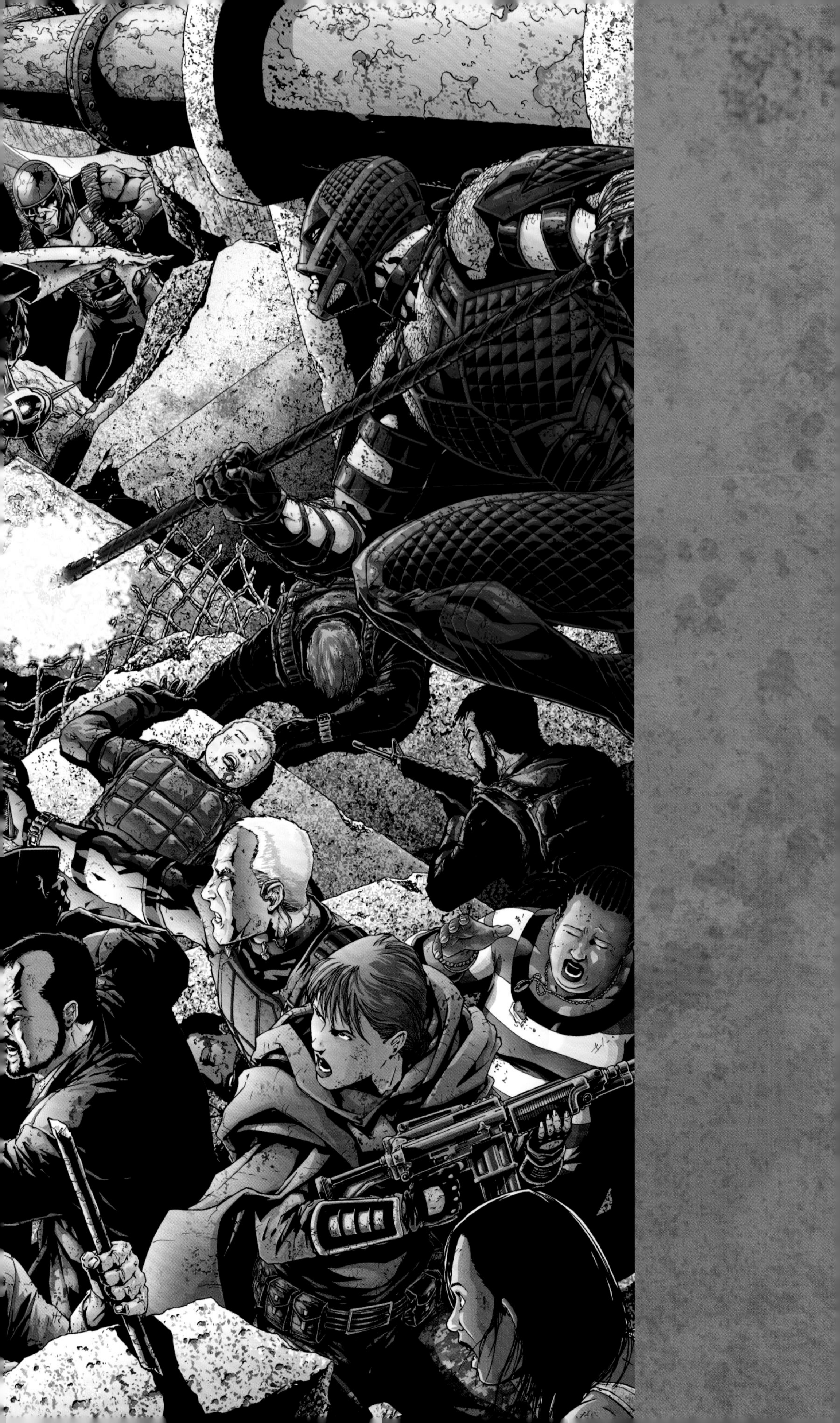

HIDDEN WOODS SHOPPING ARCADE
MEGALOPOLIS, USA

LETTERS FROM A MALL

by Gail Simone

Chaz,

I miss you. I miss your smile. I miss your arms around me.

I'm sorry I let you open that door.

It's only been a day and I still can't think straight. I know there are things I should be doing, I know it's not safe to stay here in the mall forever, but then I think of you and my knees go weak. It's only fitting that the very last expression on your face was a smile.

I always envied you that, Chaz. Your hope, your optimism. I don't remember ever feeling those things with the intensity that you expressed them, over nothing—a good cup of coffee or a half a rainbow after a shit 'Polis rain.

I wish I had been more honest with you. The last time we made love, I should have been honest with you.

My head is pounding. I keep thinking of odd thoughts from my childhood, and I feel these waves of shame for things I couldn't possibly have changed. I can never protect anyone, Chaz. That's the terrible truth, and you dying five feet away from me just reminded me of that sad fact.

I keep thinking of this thing my Nana used to tell me during target practice . . . I've heard it so much it feels like a piece of NRA bullshit. "Guns don't kill people. People kill people."

I know, right? It's almost a joke. Except it's true, Chaz. It's true.

A person makes the choice to hurt someone, to burn someone, to tear someone up. A person holds the gun, loads it, aims it, and pulls the trigger.

Chaz, we are the weapons that are never unloaded.

Guns don't kill people, people kill people.

Guns don't kill people, people kill people.

Guns don't kill people, heroes kill people.

Was there ever a time when that wasn't true?

I'm sorry, I think I am a bit in shock. I've been staying in the security office, watching the monitors. The security office is still connected to backup generators, at least for a while. The news reports are spotty and incomplete. Whatever happened to our city seems to be localized. At first people were saying it was terrorists . . . but the satellite photos show some blurry images downtown that—

I don't want to write about that.

I know I am ranting. I feel like I have a head wound from the inside.

Tomorrow, I am going to get a shovel from Karver's Sporting Goods and bury you, somehow. I don't care if THEY see me. I don't care what they do.

Nothing makes sense and nothing matters and I don't know if I want to wake up ever again. When that bastard came down out of the sky at you, all I wanted was a gun to blow his goddamn brains out. Now, when I am here, alone in the dark . . . maybe it's just as well that I don't have a firearm close at hand. I can't decide.

I love you, Chaz.

Mina

Dear Nana,

I never really thanked you, when you were alive, for all the things you did for me. I know it was hard for you and Papa Jasper to care for a granddaughter so full of pain and cussedness, when you were well into what should have been your retirement. And I know I mystified you, as I often mystified myself.

You were never the type of grandmother who spoiled her grandkids, not with affection, anyway. You were the type who made biscuits and fresh ice cream, who packed lunches every school day, who fretted over me when I was ill, and who had no patience whatsoever for anyone who looked at me unkind.

I think I'll take that over the drooly kisses and meaningless hugs the other girls got, Nana.

And I thank you for the advice you gave me that put enough steel in my spine to never become like, well, like my mamma. You told me never to be "no one's trash," and I think I have done a pretty okay job on that count so far.

I found a good man, and some asshole came and took him from me. I sometimes wonder why everything I care about is so hated by the Lord.

Yesterday, I let a group of strangers into the mall. They came looking for supplies, they say, but I think there's more to it. I think they were born to be consumers and this stupid, cheap-ass mall somehow represents safety and comfort to them. This shitty, overblown strip mall is their homeland.

They were led here by a middle management type named Wilkins . . . Says he has a family in the suburbs that he has to get back to, but that he felt "obligated" to help get these stragglers someplace safe, before heading out. It seems that like a lot of "good men," it's very important to him to let everyone know what a huge sacrifice he is making just to be a decent person.

I never trust anyone who wants to lead people. There's always a spider in that porridge.

There's a teenaged girl, maybe fifteen, pretty as a picture, named Sazi, whose family was killed. Wilkins keeps looking at her, when no one's looking. I started to, I don't know, assert dominance a little, or some such horseshit. This mall IS my job, or was.

But it was clear they were having none of it. Little brown mall cop isn't going to tell a bunch of white people what to do in their place of worship. They were very polite and thankful. But they didn't hear me at all, not a word. I think for some of these damn idiots, living in a mall isn't the nightmare it is for me, a farm girl. More like a wet dream for them, really.

Fuck 'em. I have all the stuff I need and I don't have the energy to teach them what the new world is going to be about.

Remember when you taught me to shoot, Nana? Remember how you asked me, "Can you pull the trigger, Mina? When you are looking down the barrel and two eyes are looking back, can you pull the trigger?"

That question has been on my mind ever since. I think about the thing that burned my heart out, first as a child, and just two days ago in this mall.

Yes, Nana. I could pull the trigger.

Until there are no bullets left in the world.

Miss you always and hope Papa Jasper is there beside you in Heaven,

Mina

Dearest Mamma,

I have been thinking about you a lot since the thing happened.

I keep wondering, if this all goes badly (a distinct possibility), will I see you again in some better world?

When you died, at the service, the pastor sat me down and told me with absolute conviction that you were looking down on me always. I still half believed in Santa—how could I not believe him?

I know he meant it as a kindness, but I was in terror that you were watching me and felt shame and disappointment all the time. And even worse, I had this idea that you felt like you had been a bad mother, for not leaving when Dad got bad.

You did the best you could, Mamma, and your last action was to protect me. You did the best you could. Don't you know your daughter loves you?

In my whole life, I have never been able to protect anything or anybody. And you, knowing the end was near, used your last breath not to plead for your life, but to send me away, upstairs.

I don't know what I am going to do with my life if I get out of here. I have a terrible decision to make and I can't THINK in this shitty place.

The strangers, they have settled in a little bit. Wilkins, whom I have taken to calling the GOOD MAN, did a very shitty thing, and I think he is already thinking of something worse. He has taken over the furniture store. He says that's his "home away from home," now. So he has all the comfortable beds in the entire mall, and he's got a couple of guys acting sorta like bodyguards already.

He had the kids gather up the food from the food court that could be salvaged. He said it's for safekeeping, nothing to worry about. But next is rationing, I'm sure of it. And I have to ask myself if I care enough about any of these assholes to make this my problem.

The GOOD MAN is something worse than an asshole, I think. And he has Daddy's smile.

I am still bunking in the security office. Wilkins winked at me today, and it made me feel like shit on a snowshoe.

I'm locking the doors now.

Love you, my beautiful mother.

Dad,

Go fuck yourself.

You burned my mother, and now Hell is burning you.

Good.

Stay warm,

Mina

LETTERS FROM A MALL

CHAZ,
   Things went a little tribal last night.
   I told you I am in the security booth, right? Monitors and cameras everywhere. It's a mall. Most of the job is keeping grabby hands from five-finger discounts.
   Well, I checked in on the camera at the furniture store.
   And the GOOD MAN was tearing Sazi's clothes off.
   It was dark. I tried to tell myself I wasn't seeing it.
   But I was. Family man, sacrificing leader . . . about to rape a child.
   I thought about it. I know you would have run down to help without even thinking. But there are THREE guys in that store, Chaz.
   And I might be willing, but I didn't have a trigger to pull.
   I was glad the cameras didn't have sound. I couldn't take hearing Sazi cry.
   I didn't think long. I took my baton and I used the bulk delivery tunnels. Those guys never thought about it long enough to realize I had those keys.
   He wanted privacy, so he was at the back of the store. His "security" was up front.
   And then I really did hear her tears for real.
   Guns don't kill people, but I certainly could have at that moment.
   He was squeezing her, trying to take the fight out of her. I thought of my mother for some reason and I just lashed out, hard, on his wrist. I heard something snap.
   He turned to me, mouth open . . . He was going to say something, but I know it would have been some variation of "But I'm a GOOD MAN," so instead of waiting, I broke his other wrist solid. I heard the bones crack like glass under a hammer.
   He started to howl, and I hit him just once more. I'm not going to say where. But he shut up pretty quickly.
   Sazi was afraid to come with me, until the "security" started coming to the back of the store. We made it into the access tunnel and locked it behind us.
   I felt this horrible mix of elation and shame. I threw up, but I've gotten used to that lately and so we just ran on until we got to the security room. It took a while to get Sazi to sleep, and I've just been waiting, waiting for the move I know is coming.
   It won't be hard for him. He's an important man, and I'm nothing. I'm trash in a mini-mum-wage uniform for life.
   He'll convince even the ones who know he's lying that this is my fault, that I am a hazard to their security. And broken wrists or no, he will come up to this office and they will break the door down and then I may end up envying the way my mother went out.
   But we are the weapons that are never unloaded, Chaz.
   And I'm going to crack a few good men's skulls before that happens.
   Love,
   Mina

LETTERS FROM A MALL

Chaz,

Sazi left. She got up while I dozed and decided she was safer out on the streets with the caped killers than in here with the good, good citizens of Megalopolis.

Once again, I can't protect anything. I'm sorry, Sazi.

We also had another contact with the killers in capes. There was a cop, a lady cop, in the parking lot. We don't know if she came to help or to find shelter, but we did, GOOD MEN and myself alike, all cheer as if civilization had returned in a black-and-white squad car.

Wilkins, with his wrists set, made a silent "hush" gesture to me . . . His way of telling me to keep my mouth shut about any "indiscretions" that may have happened.

Fuck you, Wilkins, I'm telling everyone, I thought.

But it wasn't to be. The winged one—someone called him Cupid, I guess?

He came down and lifted the police car and threw it, ripped the lady cop out and cracked her neck, laughing the whole time . . . Not like a mad scientist on a cartoon, Chaz . . . More like someone who'd just been told a hilarious joke.

She was dead before he dropped her. His eyes went black and red, night and fire, and then he was gone. Thirty-plus years this woman lived . . . for nothing, for no reason, in the end. Because she died broken in the parking lot of the Rite Aid on the city outskirts.

No one said anything. We all just went back to neutral corners. My monitors were full of people crying to themselves, and for the first time, I actually felt sorry for them.

Mina

My dear baby boy,

I say "boy," although I have no way to know for sure. And I am afraid to name you, in case you are never to be.

I am sorry that your mother isn't rich and safe. I am sorry she lives, for now, on a cot in a security office.

Your father wanted you, very badly. He was a kind man, a strong man. I was afraid. I was afraid I'd be a terrible mother.

I didn't tell him about you. I didn't know how. And I was still having doubts.

But I was going to tell him. I don't know what the right thing to do here is. This is a terrible life for a child . . . but you are all that remains of the only man I ever loved.

I don't know what the right thing is. But I know what I'm going to do.

Before dawn, I am going to go out there to the parking lot and take that policewoman's uniform. There are still going to be people who are afraid of the police, and I can use that. I will take her guns, too, if I can.

And then I am going to head north. I will stop for no one. I will make no friends, I will join no groups. I will meet no more GOOD MEN.

I'm going to get out. I am going to take you somewhere safe.

And I'm going to give birth to you, my beautiful child.

Your mamma,

Mina